FREDERICK II
A MEDIEVAL EMPEROR

DAVID ABULAFIA

FREDERICK II
A MEDIEVAL EMPEROR

ALLEN LANE
THE PENGUIN PRESS

for Anna

===

ma eo no'l celeraggio,
com'altamente Amor m'ha meritato,
che m'ha dato a servire
a la fiore di tutta caunoscenza
e di valenza . . .

ALLEN LANE THE PENGUIN PRESS

Published by the Penguin Group
27 Wrights Lane, London W8 5TZ, England
Viking Penguin Inc, 40 West 23rd Street, New York, New York 10010, USA
Penguin Books Australia Ltd, Ringwood, Victoria, Australia
Penguin Books Canada Ltd, 2801 John Street, Markham, Ontario, Canada L3R 1B4
Penguin Books (NZ) Ltd, 182–190 Wairau Road, Auckland 10, New Zealand

Penguin Books Ltd, Registered Offices: Harmondsworth, Middlesex, England

First published 1988

Printed in Great Britain by
Richard Clay Ltd, Bungay, Suffolk

Typeset in 12/13½ pt Lasercomp Bembo

British Library Cataloguing in Publication Data

Abulafia, David
    Frederick II: a medieval emperor.
    1. Frederick, *II, King of Prussia*
    2. Prussia (Germany)——Kings and rulers——
    Biography
    I. Title
    943′.053′0924   DD404

ISBN 0–7139–9004–X
LCCN 88–60417

CONTENTS

═══

LIST OF ILLUSTRATIONS

═══

LIST OF MAPS

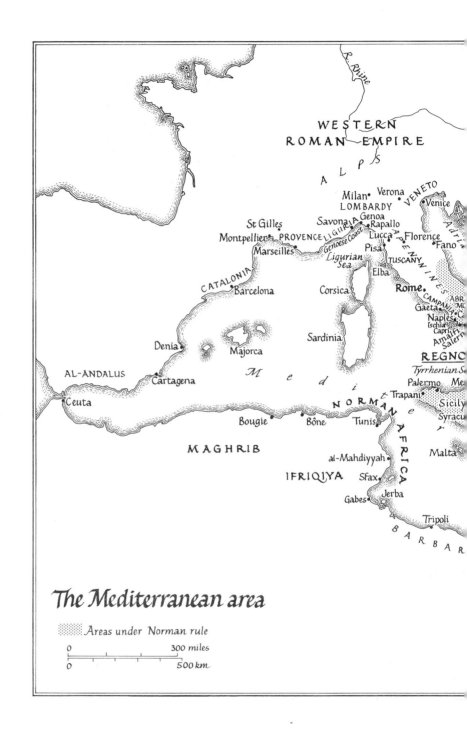

WESTERN
ROMAN EMPIRE
A L P S

A L P S

Milan• Verona
LOMBARDY   VENETO
Savona•A Genoa   •Venice
St Gilles   •Rapallo
Montpellier• PROVENCE LIGUR• Lucca• Florence
•Marseilles   Genoese Coast Pisa•   •Fano
                    Ligurian   TUSCANY
                    Sea   Elba• APENNINES
CATALONIA   Corsica•   Rome•
        •Barcelona   ABR
                                 CAMPANIA MC
                    Sardinia   Gaeta• Naples• C
Denia•   Ischia• Capri•
    •   Majorca   Amalfi•Salern
AL-ANDALUS   M e d i   REGNO
        •Cartagena   Tyrrhenian S.
•Ceuta   Palermo• Me
                        N O R M A   •Trapani Sicily
        Bougie•   Bône• Tunis•   Syracu
MAGHRIB   A F R I C A   Malta•
            al-Mahdiyyah•
IFRIQIYA   Sfax•
        Gabes• Jerba
                    Tripoli•
                    B A R B A R

The Mediterranean area

Areas under Norman rule

0 _____ 300 miles
0 _____ 500 km

HUNGARY

CROATIA

R. Danube

Black Sea

SERBIA

LMATIA

Ragusa (Dubrovnik)
(1170s−1190s)

Durazzo (1185)

Bari

Via Egnatia

Thessalonika
(1185)

Constantinople

APULIA

Otranto

'ROMANIA'

BASILICATA

Corfu
(1147)

G   Thebes

Aegean
Sea

Antioch

Athens

Port St Symeon

Ionian
Isles

Corinth

(1147, 1185)

S
Y
R
I
A

Damascus

Acre

Crete

n   e   a   n   S   e   a

Jerusalem

KINGDOM
OF
JERUSALEM

Damietta

Alexandria

Cairo

EGYPT

R. Nile

The Kingdom of Sicily

The Papal States in the thirteenth century

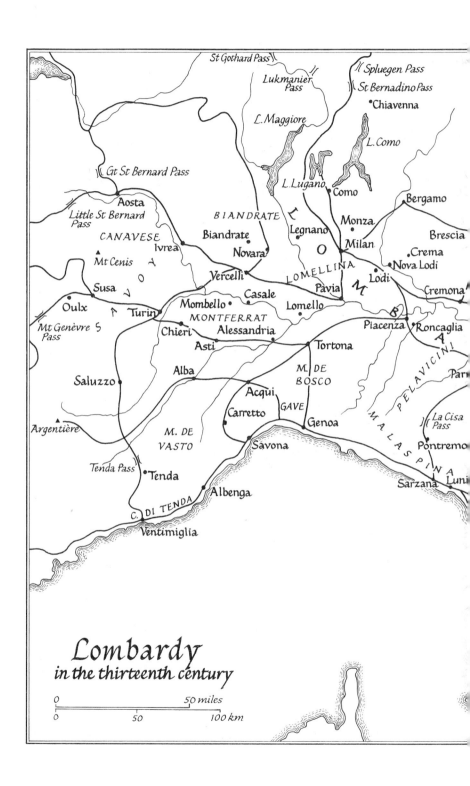

St Gothard Pass

Lukmanier Pass

Spluegen Pass

St Bernadino Pass

Chiavenna

L. Maggiore

L. Como

Gt St Bernard Pass

L. Lugano

Como

Bergamo

Aosta

Little St Bernard Pass

BIANDRATE

Monza

Milan

Brescia

CANAVESE

Biandrate

Legnano

Crema

Mt Cenis

Ivrea

Novara

Nova Lodi

Susa

Vercelli

LOMELLINA

Lodi

Cremona

Oulx

Turin

Casale

Pàvia

Mombello

Lomello

Mt Genèvre Pass

Chieri

MONTFERRAT

Alessandria

Piacenza

Roncaglia

Asti

Tortona

Saluzzo

Alba

M. DE BOSCO

Acqui

GAVE

Par

Argentière

Carretto

Genoa

La Cisa Pass

M. DE VASTO

Savona

Pontremo

Tenda Pass

Tenda

Sarzana

Luni

C. DI TENDA

Albenga

Ventimiglia

Lombardy
in the thirteenth century

0   50 miles

0   50   100 km

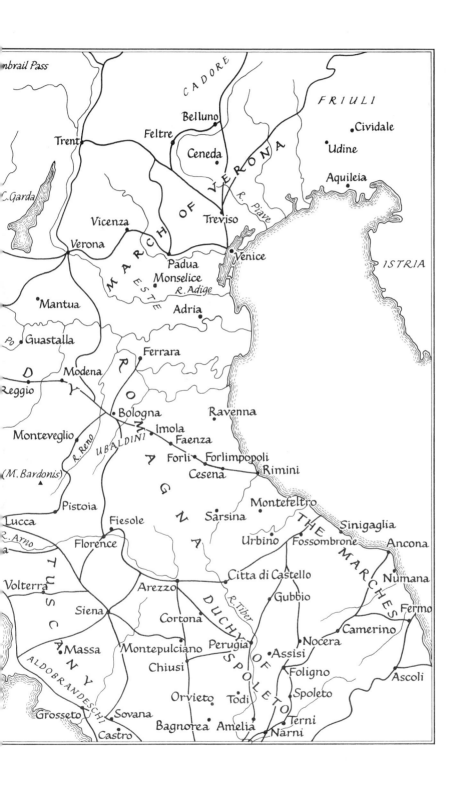

North Sea

RÜGEN

Eider • Kiel
WAGRIA
HOLSTEIN
HOLSTORMARN
R. Elbe
Lübeck
Ratzeburg
MECKLENBURG
POMERANIA

Hamburg

Bremen
BRANDENBURG

R. Warta
Posen

LAUSITZ

R. Oder

Brunswick
Magdeburg
Liegnitz

Hildesheim
Goslar
Harzburg

S A X O N Y
R. Weser
R. Unstrut
HARZ
Merseburg
MEISSEN
R. Mulde
VOGTLAND
R. Elbe

Paderborn

THURINGIA
Eisenach
Erfurt
R. Werra

R. Rhine

Bouvines
Liège
Aachen
Cologne

Koblenz
FRANCONIA
Fulda
Eger
EGERLAND
BOHEMIA
MORAVIA

Frankfurt
Gelnhausen

R. Meuse

Trier
Mainz
Worms
Wurzburg
Bamberg
Nuremberg
R. Mosel

Annweiler
Speyer
Heidelberg
PALATINATE
Regensburg
R. Danube
AUSTRIA

Trifels
Hirsau
Hohenstaufen
R. Neckar

Hagenau
ALSACE
R. Rhine
SWABIA
R. Danube
Augsburg
R. Wertach
BAVARIA
R. Inn
Vienna
R. Fischa
R. Leitha

Basel
Constance
R. Lech
Salzburg
R. Enns
STYRIA
R. Mur

Besançon
Innsbruck
Reichenhall
R. Drau

Meran
Brenner Pass
CARINTHIA
Villach

St Gothard Pass
Lukmanier Pass
Chiavenna
Bozen
Cividale

BURGUNDY
St Bernard Pass
L. Como
Trent
Treviso
Aquileia
Grado
CROATIA

R. Saône
Como
Cortenuova
Brescia
Verona
Venice

Legnano
L. Garda
Mantua

Milan
Cremona

R. Po
Pavia
Parma
R. Po
Ferrara

Alessandria
Piacenza
LOMBARDY
Modena
ROMAGNA

Tortona
Canossa
Ravenna

Genoa
Bologna

R. Rhône
TUSCANY
Florence
Ancona

Arles
Pisa
R. Arno

PAPAL

Perugia
Assisi
Spoleto

Grosseto
R. Tiber
STATES

Viterbo
CAMPAGNA
KINGDOM

Sutri
Rome
Tusculum
S. Germano
Civitate
Monte Cassino
Lucera
Barletta
T. DI LAVORO
OF
C. del Monte
Gaeta
Capua
Benevento
APULIA
Naples
Brindisi
Salerno
Taranto
Amalfi

SICILY
CALABRIA

Germany
in the thirteenth century

‖‖‖ *Frontier of the Empire*

░░░ *Areas of greatest concentration of*
Salian and Staufen estates

⋯⋯ *Area of the Countess Matilda's estates*

0   100   200 miles
0   100   200   300 km

PREFACE

I

Frederick II is one of a small band of medieval rulers who possesses modern admirers. His wide cultural tastes, his apparent tolerance of Jews and Muslims, his defiance of the popes have earned him an exceptional reputation. He is portrayed as a genius, thinking the thoughts of later generations, seeking to create a new, secular, world order. Even if none of this were true, the fact that he has been seen in this light would entitle him to the close attention of historians and readers of history books. As a matter of fact, this book contends that rather little of his reputation is soundly based. His involvement in a series of struggles with the popes attracted to him legends about his behaviour, or magnified aspects of his behaviour out of proportion to reality. He was an ideal target for gossips. Few other medieval rulers corresponded with the sages of Judaism and Islam; no other Holy Roman Emperor wore his crown in the Church of the Holy Sepulchre in Jerusalem; no contemporary could match in efficiency and tightness of control the bureaucratic machine of Frederick's Sicilian realm. And it is basically true that after his death the Holy Roman Empire experienced a long recession from which it hardly emerged until Charles V imposed his rule on Germany as well as Spain in the early sixteenth century. A common problem for both emperors was that of managing a double inheritance, German and Mediterranean; and in many respects Frederick II accomplished the task with less difficulty than his stolid Habsburg successor.

Thus the reign of Frederick II marks a major stage in the

transformation of Europe from a community of Latin Christians under the headship of two competing universal powers, pope and emperor, to a Europe of nation-states, in which the Roman Emperor counted for much less. In some respects Frederick's other major territory, the smaller but better-controlled kingdom of Sicily (often called the *regno*, the kingdom), is the place to begin any study of the emergence of the nation-state; its inhabitants were far from being a 'nation' in any sense of the term, but the centralized methods of government adopted in Sicily were as important in the development of the nation-state as were the gradually evolving notions of ethnic, cultural or linguistic unity that Sicily acquired more slowly than most other European kingdoms. Frederick ruled both a universal empire and a territorial monarchy, and he ruled them in very different ways, with no intention (contrary to frequent assumption) of integrating them into a monolithic Roman autocracy stretching from the borders of Denmark through Italy to Sicily.

A monarch whose rule extended over lands that now form all or part of the two Germanies, the Netherlands, Austria, Poland, Czechoslovakia, France (southern Burgundy and Provence), Italy, Malta, Cyprus, Israel and Lebanon, who launched the Teutonic knights on the conquest of what later became the Baltic States, who even won influence on the coasts of Tunisia, demands from his biographer a range of expertise beyond that which I can offer. My own research interests, in the Sicilian kingdom, in the crusades and the Latin East, in the society and politics of the north Italian cities, do not qualify me to pass judgement on his activities in Germany, nor on the cultural life of his court. Yet I have not hesitated to come to some surprising conclusions about the latter topic. As for Germany, my only claim is that I have integrated what is known about Frederick's policies there into a wider picture of his aims in Italy and the Latin East. Given the relative lack of attention to Frederick's last fifteen or so years, I have concentrated much of my own original research on the period from about 1235 to 1250, plus a certain amount of research on Frederick's childhood and on his crusade. In particular, I have studied in detail the papal registers preserved in the Secret Archive of the Vatican and the unique register of Frederick II's documents, from 1239–40; in each case I have returned to what remains of the manuscripts, rather than relying on incomplete or faulty editions.

But I do not claim to have discovered a large amount of new factual information about Frederick: most of the sources, except the register of 1239–40, have been gutted time and again by learned Germans in search of their most enigmatic emperor. For this reason I have made the difficult decision to sacrifice notes in favour of a longer text; I know well that Ernst Kantorowicz was condemned for acting the same way when in 1927 he published a biography of Frederick, but it has to be said that my interpretation of the reign stands at a far remove from his own. The *Ergänzungsband*, or supplement, to Kantorowicz's book, and the notes in the *Jahrbücher* of the German empire will, in any case, provide a permanent place of reference to scholars who wish to follow up those points in my text where no source is cited.

For the intention of this book is to provide an overall inter-pretation of his reign, not to quibble over the details of (for instance) what happened at the battle of Cortenuova. On these issues there are solid factual guides, such as Winkelmann's lab-orious and anaesthetic studies of the early part of the reign, or van Cleve's massive biography, where the interpretation is simply wrong on large and small points, but where the course of events is explained soberly and clearly. For the basic outline of Fred-erick's life is not in doubt, except among those historians who, altogether regrettably, make a parade of fine but inconsequential scholarship. I would insist that enough is now known about the events of Frederick's life to make a re-assessment of his aims possible; what is strange is that I have found it possible to come to very different conclusions to, say, van Cleve or Haskins while very often using the evidence they have presented in defence of their argument. Thus some of what I say consists of a de-construction of van Cleve or Kantorowicz, rather than an attempt to return entirely to all the sources and compile from scratch an entirely new account of his life. For, when it is a matter of the facts only, that is not necessary. What is needed is a view of the emperor's intentions and achievements.

This means placing Frederick in a wider context than has so far been tried. To isolate him from his Norman background is to enlarge him out of scale; I have therefore thought it essential to include a lengthy opening chapter offering my view of the Norman creation of the kingdom of Sicily, making constant reference to problems the Normans experienced in common with Frederick II. Roger II, Frederick's grandfather, dominates not just the first chapter; his shadow is cast throughout the book. In any case, there are no existing surveys of the Norman kingdom of Sicily dealing thematically with the topics I try to describe in this chapter. Equally, I have outlined the German background to Frederick II, looking in the second chapter at Frederick Barbarossa and his son Henry VI, the father of Frederick II; here not merely the political problems of Germany but also the reasons for German involvement in Lombardy, Tuscany and the crusading movement have to be discussed, if sense is to be made of Frederick II's career. And, moving to the end of the book, I felt it essential to trace the fortunes of the Hohenstaufen beyond Frederick's death in 1250, which marks an almost insignificant moment in a struggle that had gained full momentum by then: his disappearance did not lead the pope to call off his hounds, and the struggle between Frederick's house and the papacy really culminated in the events of 1282 known as the Sicilian Vespers. It was the whole dynasty, as the popes and their allies said outright, that had to be annihilated. Such a perspective makes it clear that Frederick II did not die defeated by the papacy; the position in 1250 was at best (from the papal viewpoint) a stalemate. To finish suddenly in 1250 is to ignore the paramount obsessions of the protagonists: a concern with the survival or extinction of a dynasty, a concern that all medieval rulers, all secular lords, shared. And the problem of dynastic survival mattered all the more to a German emperor, for his princes fought to retain their power to elect their ruler just as the ruler sought to establish a principle of hereditary succession. Another theme in the final chapter is the later reputation of Frederick II, whose name as late as 1500 still conjured dreams of a new era of mankind.

Frederick's adversaries deserve a good deal of space, too. I have not set out to write a denunciation of the medieval popes. But (like Frederick) I remain deeply suspicious of religious leaders who bend the truth to serve what they believe to be a higher end. The thirteenth-century papacy did become obsessed with the Hohenstaufen threat; I am unconvinced that such a threat really existed. So too in Lombardy and in the Latin East assumptions were made by Frederick's foes that were at least on occasion based on a misreading of the emperor's intentions. Since Frederick was both fallible and inconsistent, it is no matter for surprise that his enemies believed reports about his behaviour that, taken selectively, appeared to present him as a destroyer of communal liberties or of the wealth and power of the Roman Church.

But, in essence, Frederick saw himself as the prince of peace, the upholder of *justitia*, that is to say, the principle of moral righteousness that should underlie all good government; and even beyond that he had a single-minded ambition that gave shape to his policies: the preservation of his dynasty and of its lands.

II

It is a pleasure to thank Sir John Plumb for his initial invitation to write this book; Peter Carson of Penguin Books has shown great patience with revised deadlines; the late R. C. ('Otto') Smail was a constant source of encouragement and of good sense and I much regret that he was never able to read any of the manuscript; Christopher Brooke has read the entire text and has provided me with copious and very welcome comments; John Gillingham and Jonathan Riley-Smith have shown much kind interest at seminars in England, as has James M. Powell in the United States. Michael Clanchy first urged me to write what could have been – maybe for the better – a much shorter book on Frederick. Sir Steven Runciman's magnificent account of the Sicilian Vespers, and Viscount Norwich's lively histories of Norman Sicily, were among the first books to draw me to the island's history; and this book may perhaps claim to fill the gap between those works. Philip Grierson has been a particular source of help with Frederick's magnificent coinage. Some ideas were tried out at one of the delightful (for the speaker, at least) Antiquary lectures in honour of Denys Hay at the University of Edinburgh, and at a seminar of the Institute for Advanced Study of the Hebrew University of Jerusalem organized by Benjamin Kedar and presided over by Joshua Prawer. I particularly wish to thank David Jacoby for extending an invitation to spend several months at the Department of History of the Hebrew University of Jerusalem, and thereby allowing me plenty of time to think about how I might approach the theme of this book, as well as providing a chance to visit the crusader sites in Israel known to Frederick II. On these visits, Sylvia Schein was a particularly able *cicerone*. Space prevents individual mention of all the historians, at each Israeli university, who showed limitless hospitality. From Jerusalem I moved on to Rome, and there had the benefit of residence in the British School at Rome, thanks in part to a grant from the Faculty of Archaeology, History and Letters of the School and in part to a grant from the British Academy. Luciana Valentini was, as ever, endlessly helpful in the library of the British School. But my main aim was to spend each day in the Secret Archive of the Vatican reading Innocent IV's documents, and here Mgr Charles Burns was a model of consideration and good company. On an earlier visit to Italy I was able to consult the photographs of the destroyed register of Frederick II of 1239–40, owing to the kind help of Professoressa Jole Mazzoleni of the Archivio di Stato di Napoli. Graham Loud, Jeremy Johns, Norman Housley, Larry Epstein and Henri Bresc have generously shared with me their scholarly interest in Sicily and southern Italy. Georgina Morley and Judith Flanders at Penguin Books have given every help in seeing this book through the press.

I first heard of Frederick II, as far as I can remember, as a pupil at St Paul's School, and my guide to his reign was Colin Davies, now of Charterhouse, followed later by Hugh Mead and Peter Thomson. Without their early inspiration and encouragement, I much doubt whether there would be this book. To the Master and Fellows of Gonville and Caius College, Cambridge I should like to express fulsome thanks for the stimulating ambience and the outstanding research facilities that the college provides. Mrs Edna Pilmer typed much of the text in college, and the provision by the college of a magnificent word-processor enabled me to work further on the text.

Anna Sapir Abulafia has accompanied me on my journeys to Italy, the Middle East and elsewhere (not least to Frederick's birthplace at Jesi); her own skills as a medieval historian saved time in the archives of Naples; she has been the first to read and comment upon what I have written. To her the book is dedicated with my love.

D.S.H.A.

Gonville and Caius College, Cambridge
26 December 1986: 792nd anniversary of the birth of Frederick II of Hohenstaufen.

PART ONE

The Emperor Charles V in the coronation regalia earlier worn by Frederick II

CHAPTER ONE

THE NORMAN INHERITANCE

I

When in the thirteenth century the Holy Roman Emperor appeared arrayed in crown and vestments, on the great festivals of the Church, he wore tunic and dalmatic of Sicilian silk, red shoes and stockings, also of Sicilian silk, and red gloves studded with pearls. His mantle was deep red in colour, embroidered in gold with the figure of a lion pouncing on a camel (repeated symmetrically); and around the edge was an inscription in Arabic, declaring that this mantle had been made in 1133–4 for the most glorious King Roger, in his city of Palermo. And the crowns too were objects of unrivalled splendour: the imperial crown, worn in Germany and northern Italy, or in Rome, and handed down from the Saxon emperors of the late tenth century, was a circlet adorned with enamel plates and mounted with an intricate arch, above a small cloth mitre; but the crown worn in Sicily and southern Italy was of a type made fashionable by the Byzantine emperors, entirely closed, whether of embroidered cloth or of precious metal, with long jewelled pendants – half an orb, to symbolize the temporal dominion of the ruler.

These textiles and crowns are not simply items of beauty and splendour. They are a visible expression of a monarchy that drew on Greek, Latin and even Arab ideas of rulership to elevate the king to a position far above his subjects. It was a monarchy whose ultimate model lay in the universal Christian Roman empire of Constantine and Justinian. Yet the fullest expression of these ideas of rulership obtained not in a territory that regarded itself as an integral part of a universal empire, but in a territorial

kingdom, a newly created monarchy whose very survival was
threatened by the German and Byzantine emperors: the kingdom
of Sicily. Even when, in 1194, this kingdom was conquered by
the German emperor, it remained a separate entity, not united
with the empire, but a personal and special possession of the
emperor *qua* king of Sicily. The question of the relative status of
empire and Sicilian kingdom was to plague the politics of the
thirteenth century; and the most vigorous exponent of the idea
of the special identity of the Sicilian kingdom was Frederick II.

Those coronation vestments represented part of the confusion.
It seems Frederick wore them as emperor, yet they were the
ancient coronation robes of the kings of Sicily. They were made
in Sicily, by the silk-workers installed in the royal palaces; by
workers who were Arabs, or Greek Jews kidnapped by his grandfather Roger II of Sicily. The red silk, perhaps the same colour as
the Byzantine 'purple' long coveted in the west, spoke for the
Roman descent of the power wielded by the ruler: these were
the colours worn by Byzantine emperors, by popes and those
who claimed universal or absolute authority. The tunic, dalmatic
and mitre spoke for the view that the consecrated king was *rex et
sacerdos*, king and priest, elevated by his unction into a status
above that of the common man, mediating (like a priest) between
God and man, reflecting the majesty of God on earth. A famous
mosaic in Palermo shows the first Sicilian king, Roger II, being
crowned by Christ; the identity of features between the king and
Christ is no coincidence, for the king is seen to be Christ's deputy
on earth.

But the crowned heads of Latin Europe had rivals in their
claim to act as God's deputy. The papacy possessed a special
relationship with those very kings of Sicily who asserted the
direct descent of royal power from Christ. The Norman kings of
Sicily were papal vassals, holding their royal authority (in papal
eyes) from the pope, though they received some compensation
in the form of a much-disputed grant from the papacy of the
right to manage the affairs of the Sicilian Church without close
reference to Rome. And the Holy Roman Emperors had long
been embroiled in conflict with the papacy over papal claims to
universal authority, involving also the right to admonish, correct
and even depose sinful rulers; the clash between Pope Gregory

VII and King Henry IV of Germany, at the end of the eleventh century, was still vividly remembered in the thirteenth. In the early thirteenth century the contradictions between different claims to authority resulted in the most violent of all the clashes between secular and spiritual power: the reign of Frederick II, king of Sicily and Holy Roman Emperor, saw the intensification of an already bitter conflict, and extended the struggle downwards from the courts of Europe to the town halls of Lombardy and Tuscany.

II

Sicily was the home of these ideas of monarchy. Sicily was Frederick II's most cherished kingdom. Sicily was a major object of strife between pope and emperor. Sicily was wealthy (or had been wealthy) and had command of the trade routes across the Mediterranean. All these factors were intertwined. Yet there were several 'Sicilies'. There was the mainland, Apulia, Campania and Calabria, plus the marcherlands of Abruzzi and Molise which bordered on the papal states; as against Sicily proper, with Malta and the central Mediterranean islands. These separate parts, mainland and island, were to earn the name 'Two Sicilies' in the late Middle Ages. In another sense two Sicilies existed: the Sicily mentioned already, a monarchy with highly developed absolutist ideas, with an elaborate bureaucracy, a reasonably well-filled treasury, a mixed cultural heritage reflected by the presence of Greeks, Jews, Arabs at court. Here was a Sicily that could pay its way in grandiose wars of conquest, in Africa, Greece or the Levant, even in Spain; here was a Sicily whose monarch understood his duty as divine representative on earth, and defended that duty, by protecting his subjects from the onslaughts of the kingdom's rapacious enemies. This was, in some measure, the Sicily of Roger II, created in the first half of the twelfth century on the basis of one man's indomitable will. In the first half of the thirteenth century, could this ideal kingdom still win its battles? Could it still find the resources to do so?

Against this, the other Sicily: a kingdom wracked by the

rebelliousness of subject peoples, above all the Muslims of western Sicily; a kingdom bled dry by relentless financial exactions, in order to pay for wars against the ruler's foes in Rome or northern Italy, who only occasionally posed a threat to Sicily's own inhabitants; a kingdom whose reputation for wealth, whether or not still deserved, attracted adventurers in search of a crown; a kingdom whose bureaucracy served the interests of the crown far better than that of the crown's subjects, who were irked by fiscal demands, interference in rights of inheritance, levies of military service.

At the heart of many of the thirteenth-century problems lay this assumption that Sicily and southern Italy were wealthy lands. In the twelfth century the revenue from Palermo alone is said to have equalled that received by the king of England from his entire kingdom: a point all the more remarkable in that England too was, in the twelfth century, a very wealthy kingdom, rich in silver. Just as England drew its wealth from wool, Sicily drew its wealth from grain and raw materials, not least cotton and skins. Sicilian wheat was predominantly a hard wheat, well-suited for storage, and it had been exported since antiquity. Sicily, North Africa and Egypt were the bread-baskets of the classical world; in the twelfth and thirteenth centuries North Africa had lost many of its wheat-lands to nomadic predators or to erosion, and Tunisia in consequence became Sicily's best market. This was a fact of which Frederick II was aware, and of which he took advantage. Sicily itself was the main source of grain, cultivated on hillsides in the west and south-east of the island; the population of Sicily seems to have been rather low during the twelfth and thirteenth centuries, but the labour force was subject to strict corvées, and production for the market was abundant. The more so, indeed, since yields were astonishingly high by thirteenth-century standards: ten grains or more for every one sown, the sources assure us; and famines were rare before the late thirteenth century.

But the towns in southern Italy and Sicily were different in one very important respect from those of the north. In the north, the towns were masters of the countryside round about, the *contado*, whose lords had settled in or made pacts with the cities, or occasionally had been conquered by the cities; a northern

Norman copper *trifollaris* minted at Palermo, in imitation of classical models

Gold *tari* of Amalfi with Arabic and Latin inscriptions, from the first years of Frederick II's reign in Sicily (before 1209)

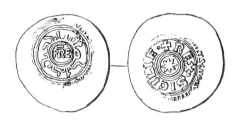

Denarius of Frederick II from Sicily or southern Italy, 1225. $\frac{1}{6}$ silver, $\frac{5}{6}$ base metals

Augustalis of Frederick II, 1231–66. $20\frac{1}{2}$ carats gold. This coin continued to be minted under Frederick's son, King Manfred

Reale of Charles I of Anjou, 1266, succeeding the *augustalis* of the Hohenstaufen, minted at Barletta. $20\frac{1}{2}$ carats gold

The coinage of Norman, Hohenstaufen and Angevin Sicily

town really was master of its food supplies, at least until it outgrew its *contado*. (This happened to Genoa, Florence and other large towns; Venice had no local *contado* to speak of.) In southern Italy, the heavy hand of Norman rule intervened: the towns did not control the locality in similar degree, the administration of supplies rested more with the royal bureaucracy than with the townsmen. This lack of mastery over the countryside perhaps explains the more passive nature of the merchant class in the south Italian towns: solely the merchants of Amalfi and Messina possessed a notable reputation on the international trade-routes; the Genoese, Pisans and Venetians became by far the most dynamic elements in the international trade of southern Italy and Sicily, achieving important advances well before 1200. As early as 1156 the Genoese were given privileged access by the king of Sicily to cotton, skins and wheat supplies, on which they were to pay low taxes.

Low taxes on the prime resource of the kingdom, an item in demand throughout the Mediterranean: wheat. For the twelfth and thirteenth centuries saw a major expansion of population throughout Europe and much of the Mediterranean world: meaning, an expansion of demand for food. So much the better if that food was the storable, versatile wheat grown in Sicily. Thus it became the prime ingredient of ship's biscuit; it provided the raw material for pasta, now appearing on northern Italian plates; usable too for couscous in North Africa (*cuscusu* is also eaten in Sicily, especially with fish at Trapani); it was eaten as far afield as Egypt, when the Nile failed to rise, and in the Latin kingdom of Jerusalem. Whoever controlled production could draw much benefit from sales and taxes on sales. In the thirteenth century, Frederick II worked hard to improve standards of production. His anxious letters about a plague of caterpillars in the wheat-fields of Sicily were not simply a quest for information by a dedicated natural scientist (though he was that as well). Exactly what proportion of wheat grown was exported is very unclear; what is very clear is that the crown was a, or the, major beneficiary from sales of wheat abroad.

The kings of Sicily were, in fact, the most powerful landlords in their kingdom. In the twelfth century, much of Sicily seems to have been royal demesne land, that is to say, land not granted out to feudatories, but controlled directly by the central government. Little of the island of Sicily was in the hands of Norman barons; one family, the Aleramici, had been granted estates in eastern Sicily, though it was of north-west Italian origin, and closely related to the kings (Adelaide of this house was mother to King Roger II). Otherwise, the great lords were ecclesiastical: the abbey of San Salvatore, the great Basilian Greek monastery at Messina; then, in 1182, the abbey of Monreale, a Latin foundation, which was granted the lands still largely inhabited by the Muslims, forming a great native reservation, *Bantustan*, in western Sicily. On the mainland, the position was rather different: overall, the king controlled as royal demesne about 30 per cent of continental southern Italy, but much of this land was surely mountainous and unproductive. There, at least, great landlords, such as the Conversano family in Apulia, still controlled great grain estates. Yet the concentration of economic power in the hands of the king and his close relatives, in Sicily at least, was unusual by the standards of Latin Europe.

The Sicilian kingdom in its heyday produced other desirable items than grain: mulberries and raw silk in Calabria and Sicily; even processed silk, though of lesser quality than the silks of the east. Around 1060 mulberry cultivation was widespread and it is possible that raw silk was being exported to the Byzantine empire. And it has been seen that the kings of Sicily maintained in their treasury a group of specialized silk-workers, at least some of whom were servile captives brought from a raid on Thebes, in Greece, in 1147. In the eleventh and twelfth centuries, silk was conveyed as far as Egypt and the Yemen, as the letters of the Cairo Jewish merchants testify. Very abundant are the finds of what is identified as Sicilian silk in the tombs of north European princes and bishops of the twelfth century; alas, it is not always certain which silks are Spanish, Byzantine, Egyptian, Syrian or Sicilian – the designs, right down to the Arabic inscriptions, are much the same; the ancestry, in Coptic or Persian textiles, again the same. But Sicily was well-placed to satisfy demand all over the Mediterranean; and its links to western Europe, via Genoa, Pisa, Venice and the Provençal towns, ensured that demand for its luxury goods remained fairly buoyant. Favours to the foreign merchants encouraged them to draw more and more heavily on the kingdom for supplies, and even, in the long term, gave them economic mastery over southern Italy and Sicily, at the expense of the native merchants of Amalfi and elsewhere.

Yet it would be wrong to assume that the Sicilian kings failed to encourage local industry, that they were content merely to draw their revenues from grain sales and cotton sales. Frederick II encouraged indigo planting, and there were sugar estates too; in the late twelfth century a vigorous ceramics industry grew around Gela. This care for diversification was not new to the Normans or Hohenstaufen. In the Muslim period, plenty of new products came to be grown in Sicily, which was famous for its fertility – a land with a relative abundance of water (compared to North Africa), where almost anything seemed to grow. The Spaniard ibn Jubayr, who visited Sicily in 1184–5, may be excused for his patriotism.

The prosperity of the island surpasses description. It is enough to say that it is the daughter of Spain in the extent of its cultivation, in the luxuriance of its harvests, and in its well-being, having an abundance of wild produce, and fruits of every kind and species.

And he says of Termini, the town mid-way between Cefalù and Palermo:

It enjoys an extreme fertility and abundance of victuals; indeed the whole island in this regard is one of the most remarkable in God's creation.

Everywhere were markets, gardens (in and around the towns), orange groves, land 'such as we had never seen before for goodness, fertility and amplitude'. Land even better, as he finally admits, than the *ganbaniyah*, *campania* or countryside, of Cordoba itself. Prices were low too, he says. Yet there is little doubt that, as a result of persecution of the Muslim peasantry, some of the old agricultural skills common to Islamic civilization were being lost in Sicily by 1200: hence, indeed, the anxiety of Frederick II to reintroduce such oriental specialities as indigo, sugar and henna. Meanwhile the proportion of land given over to wheat production was tending to increase, especially in western Sicily, offering its surplus to Palermo, Naples, Tunis, Genoa and elsewhere.

What matters is not whether this Sicily of plenty actually existed. For this was the image the island (and, to a lesser degree, southern Italy) presented to its would-be conquerors. To them it is necessary to turn.

III

The term 'Norman' Sicily has conjured up an image of a kingdom analogous to the Norman state in England and France, conquered and held by a powerful aristocracy of Norse descent. As far as Sicily is concerned, the label 'Norman' is really of use only as a dynastic label, with which to describe its ruling family, the Hautevilles, who established the Sicilian monarchy with the help of Norman, Italian and other knights. It has been seen that these knights did not win great estates in Sicily proper, though they prospered in southern Italy where there were more Norman settlers, but also many Latin Christians of native origin. The Normans intermarried with the south Italian aristocracy and, personal names apart, lost most of their links with the duchy of Normandy. Memories of the Norman connection remained alive, but more in the minds of Anglo-Norman chroniclers anxious to project a vigorous image of the *stirps* or race from which William I or Henry I of England came, than among the Italianized Normans of Apulia, Calabria or Sicily.

In the late tenth century Norman fighters began to earn a reputation across Europe as fierce and tough mercenaries. Since 911 a Norman duchy with Norse inhabitants had existed in northern France, and (once again) these inhabitants rapidly lost contact with their Scandinavian origins. Indeed, it is likely that only a minority of the Norman counts and knights was descended in the male line from Viking settlers. Inheritance customs in Normandy are often said to have left younger sons disadvantaged; it was eldest sons who inherited estates, and younger brothers were expected to make their fortune elsewhere. Romantic historians see in this a continuation of the Viking spirit; perhaps they are even right. So by about 1000 there were Normans moving south to the Muslim-Christian frontier in Spain, to the

Byzantine empire and to its foes, offering their services in return for booty and, not least, fame. They had no scruples about fighting one another, if they found themselves on opposing sides, nor against fighting their Scandinavian remote cousins, who, as 'Varangians', had taken service in the Byzantine army. Nor, indeed, were they all younger sons: some of the leaders of the Norman takeover in southern Italy were eldest sons; the lord of Cullei in the early twelfth century left home to found a short-lived Norman principality in Spain, at Tarragona. At the same time they were often devout. By the end of the tenth century Norman pilgrims were appearing in southern Italy, at the shrine of the Archangel Michael on Monte Gargano, the spur that sticks out of the Apulian coast. St Michael was an important cult figure, a warrior saint who attracted much attention in Normandy itself: witness the abbey of Mont-Saint-Michel on the Norman–Breton frontier. According to one version, the Norman involvement in southern Italy began in 1013 at the shrine of St Michael on Monte Gargano, when a Latin rebel against Byzantine authority in southern Italy, Meles, invited the Normans to serve him as mercenaries. But there is another version that brings Norman mercenaries to southern Italy fourteen years earlier, in 999, at Salerno, on the other side of the peninsula. It was certainly the Monte S. Angelo group of Normans that had the greater influence on events. They were able to intrude themselves in a battle zone where the established Byzantine government faced vigorous challenges from the local Lombard nobility, nominally subjects of the Greek emperor, but for long, at Capua, Benevento, Naples, Amalfi and elsewhere, effectively masters of their own fate; the Lombards of the coastline of Apulia were alone in experiencing direct control by a Byzantine *doux* or governor, and their leaders were anxious to acquire the autonomy already gained by the other Lombard princes of south-western Italy. Norman mercenaries were a tool for the creation not of a Norman but of a Lombard state in Apulia.

The Norman mercenaries returned in 1016 in greater numbers, properly equipped for war. By 1030 one of them had acquired his own estate, at Aversa, in the hinterland behind Naples. What had begun as an offer of service in return for booty became a series of attempts at the winning of control. The mercenaries took over the rebellion, and ran it for their own ends. They acquired wives among the Lombard rebels. They continued, none the less, to change sides when opportunism dictated. This was not an 'invasion', nor a 'conquest'; it was a takeover, a series of petty *coups d'état*, engineered by self-seeking Norman warriors who had no vision of a future Norman kingdom, no sense of contributing to the glory of the *gens Normannorum*. So, not surprisingly, a number of Norman states emerged, on the ruins of Byzantine, Lombard and civic governments. One state, that founded at Aversa, gained control by marriage, war and diplomacy of the principality of Capua, south of Rome; this dynasty lasted for a hundred years, independent of, and in rivalry with, a second group of Normans, who by the 1130s gained control of Capua and finally displaced them. This second group, the descendants of Tancred of Hauteville, founded the Sicilian monarchy and launched the most ambitious of all the Norman wars, against the Byzantines in the western Balkans and against North African emirs in Tunisia. Yet even in the 1120s few could really have predicted that the dispersed Norman territories would be welded together into a single monarchy.

The descendants of Tancred of Hauteville took on a much more difficult task than did the house of Capua. Whereas the Norman princes of Capua exploited Lombard disunity to seize an existing princely throne, and continued to operate the Lombard bureaucracy and military machine once in power, the Hautevilles sought to destroy the Italian power-base of the greatest Christian state of the eleventh century, the Byzantine empire. They also contended with petty princelings in Naples, Salerno, Amalfi and with rival Muslim emirs in Arab Sicily. The power of Byzantines and Muslims was cracked by the brothers Robert, nicknamed the Guiscard, or Wily, and Roger. They fought on several fronts: Bari, the last Byzantine base in Italy, fell in 1071; but Palermo, capital of the most intractable emirate, fell in 1072. Their successes in southern Italy brought them into the politics of Rome and the Holy Roman Empire too: both the pope and the German emperor had to decide whether the extinction of Byzantine power in southern Italy would be to their real advantage. By the 1070s, the popes saw in the Normans a powerful potential ally, able to protect Rome from the intrusion of

German or other foreign armies; and the German emperors, despite a brief acquiescence to Norman claims to rule Apulia as imperial dukes, saw in the Normans usurpers of the sovereignty of the western Roman empire in Italy. That this part of Italy had received few visits by German emperors since the coronation of the first Saxon emperor, Otto the Great, in 962 did not mean German claims were dormant. The western Roman emperor, as successor to the Caesars and to Charlemagne, as king of Italy too, asserted that southern Italy was very much his concern. The Byzantine emperor, likewise, regarded southern Italy as a historic part of his own true Roman empire. The Normans to some extent exploited this rivalry; though at times the threat of joint Greek–German action emerged (for instance in the 1080s), they found a third claimant to supreme authority in southern Italy and Sicily: the pope. In the late eleventh century, the papacy was emphasizing its claims to overlordship over all Christian society, as spiritual overseer of secular rulers; the papacy also seized the opportunity to reactivate its historic claims to lands and property in Sicily, Sardinia and other areas once containing extensive papal estates. ('Once' means in the sixth century, or at least before the rise of Islam.) The eleventh-century popes thus welcomed the appearance of a Hauteville duchy in southern Italy, held by Robert Guiscard as vassal of St Peter. Guiscard, for his part, proved an embarrassingly stout defender of the papacy and of Rome: when in 1085 Pope Gregory VII seemed to be at the mercy of the German imperial armies, and of a rival anti-pope, Guiscard spirited him away from Rome and flushed out the enemy by the time-honoured technique of destroying their stronghold – that is, Rome itself, which was set on fire.

Guiscard's attention concentrated, however, on the struggle first to expel the Byzantine government from Apulia, and then to ensure the Byzantines did not return. Several of the Apulian cities remained restive; archbishops of Bari retained links, not entirely surreptitiously, with Constantinople, and the danger of pro-Byzantine risings did not end before the mid-twelfth century. Nor was this because the Apulian townsmen were predominantly Greek in language, culture or religion; they were more often than not Latins, who had been carefully cultivated by the Byzantines in an effort to ensure their firm loyalty. Byzantine successes in this direction were so great that even Guiscard could not shatter the emotional and political ties to Constantinople. *Ergo*, a new policy: to set foot on the Balkan coasts, to invade the Byzantine heartlands. If Guiscard and his band of Normans could conquer a Byzantine province in Italy in twenty years or so, could they not penetrate the soft underbelly of the empire and reach Constantinople? It is difficult to be sure what Guiscard's intentions were, but on two occasions he launched invasions of the Balkans by way of Dyrrachium (Durazzo, on the coast of modern Albania). He had in tow a claimant to the throne of Constantinople, but it is likely he saw himself as future emperor. And his son Bohemond, the true inheritor of Guiscard's outlook and policy, accompanied him into the Balkans and gained experience of campaigning in a region that was to obsess him later in life, when he joined the First Crusade and marched via the Balkans and Constantinople to conquer Antioch in Syria. What is important here is not so much the ambition of Guiscard to rule from Constantinople, as the combination of envy and admiration for Byzantium shown by the Normans of southern Italy. Guiscard, as successor to the Byzantine *doux* or duke in Apulia, wore the costume of a Byzantine governor and tried to maintain a splendid court (at any rate, he spent heavily on silks and other articles required at court). Robert Guiscard thus plays a role in the transmission of Byzantine ideas of government to the later Norman rulers; in addition, as has been seen, he was largely responsible for the close tie between the Norman rulers and the papacy.

The third group of Norman rulers after those in Capua and Apulia was that in Calabria and Sicily. In the 1060s Robert Guiscard's brother Roger conquered the toe of Italy, with Guiscard's help and blessing (amid occasional quarrels). This area had for two centuries been the front line between Byzantine Italy and the Islamic world, the victim of repeated Arab raids, depopulated and demoralized. Calabria began to recover around the time of the Norman conquest – perhaps a little earlier; the Normans must not be given all the credit here – its mulberry groves were apparently replanted, new settlements were founded, especially around vibrant Greek monasteries, from the early eleventh century onwards. Calabria in the eleventh century, even more than earlier, was a Greek region; and its Norman conquerors continued to operate a Byzantine administration, controlled by Greek families. Some of these families, such as the Maleinoi, were to play a major role in the introduction of Byzantine administrative methods into Sicily proper.

The security of Calabria depended, as the previous centuries painfully revealed, on the neutralization or recovery for Christendom of Muslim Sicily. This was Roger I's great project. Did he see it as a holy war against the infidel? Most of his charters do speak in glowing terms about his role as a warrior of Christ; but most of his charters that survive are actually forgeries of later date. Contemporary chroniclers do sometimes suggest that Roger saw himself as a conqueror with a Christian mission. Adulation of Norman Sicily has been taken to extremes by modern historians, so that the Hautevilles are presented instead as models of tolerance and even as free-thinkers in an age of fanatics; this is a gross distortion of their outlook, and it has helped generate an image of Frederick II too as a man of three cultures and uncertain religion. In fact, Roger I had a list of priorities, and toleration for his non-Christian subjects was more a tool of government than an end in itself. The Christianization of Sicily could not be achieved overnight: over half the population was Muslim; there were many Jews; the Christians were all or mostly of the Greek rite. What was important was to bring this island under Latin Christian rule, to push back the political frontier of Islam, to win control of the central Mediterranean. The conquest of Sicily forms part of a forward movement, in which not just Normans but Pisans, Genoese, Catalans were extremely active; the objectives included the freeing of Sardinia and the coasts of western Europe from Saracen raids, the 'liberation' of Majorca and the coast of Spain, the winning of the west Mediterranean. Roger I's achievements, it should be noted, include the building of a fleet with which to hold the Saracens of Africa at bay, as well as manoeuvres on land.

And in the long term, yes: the preaching of the Word in Sicily. In 1098 the pope, Urban II, founder of the First Crusade, met Roger II and bestowed upon him a status equivalent to that of apostolic legate. Roger was to be free to appoint bishops, to collect Church revenues, to judge ecclesiastical problems within

Sicily; to all intents, he possessed within Sicily much of the authority of the pope himself. This grant has astonished historians. Just at the moment when the papacy was asserting its rights of supremacy throughout western Europe, here, in Sicily, on the doorstep of the Patrimony of St Peter, a Norman adventurer finds himself elevated to quasi-papal status! Yet the explanation is simple: Urban II could see that Sicily, lacking any firm ecclesiastical institutions after centuries of Muslim rule, needed to be assigned diocesan boundaries, needed to be brought out of the Greek obedience into the Latin, needed too a vigorous programme of missionary work among the Muslims. These tasks were tasks for its military conqueror, who could set up centres of regional government, determine the best way of dealing with the Muslim majority, plan new settlements inhabited by Latins or at least by Christians. Under Roger I areas such as the Lipari islands were made the focus of Christian settlement; and his wife Adelaide brought with her from northern Italy a wave of 'Lombard' settlers who colonized the east of Sicily. In other words, Roger's task as apostolic legate was to increase the number of Christians in Sicily. At the same time, Roger's secular standing was not (in theory) high. He was count of Sicily and Calabria, a vassal of the duke of Apulia, who was himself a papal vassal. Urban II was happy to grant legatine authority to Roger of Sicily because the pope regarded Sicily as a territory dependent on the holy see. Yet, by granting that authority, he also provided the rulers of Sicily with a range of theoretical arguments that enabled them to set aside any attempt by the pope to interfere in Sicily's affairs. Yes, ultimately the pope was their overlord; but so too did the ruler of Sicily exercise in Sicily the authority of the pope. This tradition of control of the Sicilian Church would become a serious problem in relations between the Hohenstaufen and the thirteenth-century papacy.

The citizens of Rome complained in the mid-twelfth century to the German king, Conrad III, that Roger I's son, Roger II, wore papal attire – the mitre, tunic and dalmatic, as well as the red sandals; and it has sometimes been argued that the Sicilian rulers thereby sought to emphasize their apostolic legateship. As has been seen, it is not easy to know whether these vestments were really Byzantine or papal in inspiration. What is clear is

that the Norman rulers seized every opportunity to emphasize
their legatine status: in the cathedral at Cefalù, built by Roger II,
the ruler's throne was placed on the north side at the entrance to
the choir, with the bishop's throne opposite. Norman practice
was to have the bishop on the north side, but here the ruler
exercised authority over the Church, so the prime position was
the proper one for him. These cases reveal something else that is
important: Roger II assumed he had inherited his father's
legatine authority; the popes tried to argue that the grant had
only been for Roger's lifetime. And Roger II tried to extend the
authority to Apulia and Capua, too, demanding rights of appointment to sees there also. This controversy remained alive a
hundred years later, under Frederick II, with dramatic consequences.

When Robert Guiscard died in 1085, vainly attacking the
Ionian isles, Sicily was all but conquered: Noto fell in 1090. 'Fell'
is perhaps a big word here: the conquest was achieved as much
by treaty as by arms; Muslim towns under threat were encouraged to sue for peace, on favourable terms. Ibn-ath-
Thumnah, emir of Catania, obtained guarantees for the Muslims
of eastern Sicily in the 1060s; in western Sicily, large areas were
little touched by the conquerors, so long as they paid their taxes
and lived in peace. Hence, indeed, the great *Bantustan* south of
Palermo, dominated by the Muslim dynasty of ibn Hammud,
virtual palatine lords of western Sicily. In Girgenti (Agrigento)
the bishop did not dare to reside: a fleeting visit to one of the
former Greek temples at Agrigento, later a mosque, now a
cathedral, was enough to establish his rights, and the bishop
visited the town fearful for his security. In Palermo and other
large centres, mosques were converted into churches: such is said
to be the physical origin of the enchanting church of San Giovanni degli Eremiti in Palermo; a cathedral was erected on the
site of the great Friday mosque, utilizing stones carved with
Arabic inscriptions. Yet Muslim religious life did not cease to
function. Ibn Jubayr, the Granadan traveller, assures us that
Trapani was full of mosques. No doubt, rather as in Constantinople after its fall to the Turks, the best buildings of one
religion were expropriated for the use of another; but Muslims
and Jews continued to meet openly for prayer. The Christiani-

zation of Sicily, projected by Roger I, was a slow process. There are signs Roger II hankered for it around 1150, and that his own successors pressed harder and harder for it; but the extinction of the Muslim communities was only achieved under Frederick II, in a manner which itself caused concern to the papacy. As for the Jews, they survived, speaking Arabic and engaged in modest crafts and in the silk industry, up to the end of the fifteenth century, when they were caught up in the wake of the expulsion of the Jews from Spain.

The period of Roger I, who died in 1101, has left few documents or monuments. The ruler was heavily involved in the work of 'pacification', by force or diplomacy. He still ruled largely from Calabria, operating an administrative base at Mileto. For Sicily was still the frontier.

IV

Guiscard and his brother held their lands together by force of personality. The latter died leaving two young children, and a determined wife who kept government working. On the mainland, the position was less auspicious. Guiscard left his lands in 1085 to his younger son Roger 'Borsa' rather than to the headstrong Bohemond, who was older and more experienced. Bohemond was not content with the pretty title 'Prince of Taranto', and the call to crusade, or rather to conquests in Syria, was one that roused him at once, in 1095. As for the Lombard-Norman nobility, it saw in the death of Robert a chance to shake off central control, to consolidate the estates won during the Norman 'conquest' of southern Italy. Rebellion, fragmentation, in some areas collapse: southern Italy at the beginning of the twelfth century seemed as divided as it had been a century before, when the Normans first arrived and took advantage of its rivalries to hoist themselves into the saddle. Major towns such as Amalfi rose in rebellion. Had the Byzantines not been so distracted by the First Crusade and the antics of Bohemond in the Balkans and Antioch, the Greek emperor might have been able to invade again and re-establish his authority in Apulia. But one Norman

territory remained firm (relatively, at least): Sicily plus Calabria.
In 1105, Roger I's younger son, Roger II, succeeded to the
county, and he gradually revealed an astuteness worthy of his
uncle and father. Thus he offered his cousins in Apulia support,
but asked in return for a relaxation of the already loose control
exercised by the duke of Apulia over Sicily. After its conquest in
1072 Robert Guiscard had retained half of Palermo for himself;
this was traded away in return for Sicilian armed help during the
early twelfth century. By the 1120s all Sicily was under the
control of its count. The rebellions in Apulia thus served the
interests of the Sicilian count, at least indirectly. The count of
Sicily could be thankful that on his island there were no over-
mighty vassals able to contest his authority. Roger II, indeed,
began to look beyond his island's shores. In 1090 his father had
occupied Malta and freed Christian slaves or captives there; there
are signs that Roger I saw North Africa as a military objective.
As early as 1116, Roger II launched his first, premature, assault
on the Tunisian coast, utilizing the large, effective Sicilian fleet
founded by his father. Roger II did not see Sicily as the limit of
his power; he was drawn also towards Africa, by Muslim raids
on the coast of Sicily, and by appeals from beleaguered emirs in
need of a protector, any protector, even a 'polytheist' Christian
count of Sicily, against their local rivals.

Eastwards, too, he began to see promising opportunities. His
mother Adelaide spent a brief, inglorious period as queen of
Jerusalem, having gone east to join in marriage the bigamous
Baldwin I. This gave Roger II a claim, of sorts, to the throne of
Jerusalem: it had been agreed that he would inherit Jerusalem if
Baldwin and Adelaide had no heir. But Adelaide was sent back
in ignominy when the king remembered he had already married
before (a vast dowry in gold was retained). Roger's claim to
Jerusalem was voiced at the Sicilian court; but nowhere else did
anyone listen. According to William of Tyre, the twelfth-century
historian of the Latin kingdom of Jerusalem, Roger was so
insulted by the treatment accorded his mother in the Holy Land
that he and his successors would give no substantial aid to the
crusader states. This is probably exaggeration, but Roger's dealings with the kingdom of Jerusalem do seem to have left a sour
taste, and he looked to Egypt rather than to the crusader states

for friends. Roger did (like Frederick II) correspond directly with the rulers of Egypt in Cairo, and even seems to have won their praise: if only you were not a Christian but a Muslim, they said, you would be the wisest king in the world! Arabic prose is given to flattery, but the Egyptians could not but be impressed by Roger's interest in philosophy and the sciences, and his patronage of Muslim scholars. At any rate, Roger secured a commercial agreement with Egypt. Another crusader state interested Roger II: Antioch, where his cousin Bohemond had ruled. Here too he had a claim to succeed, though the nobility of Antioch (many of whom were Normans) set it aside; Roger worked hard on those with whom he had any contact, such as the patriarch of Antioch, who visited Roger and was flattered with sweet words: you are also the successor to St Peter (he was told), holding a see founded by the apostle before he even reached Rome; you are the equal of the bishop of Rome. But flattery could not secure Antioch.

These extraordinary ambitions, so far from Sicily, reveal a great deal. Roger was prepared to play with other patriarchs than the pope; on other occasions he seems to have thought of approaching the patriarch of Constantinople too, for he was embarrassed at the fact of papal overlordship over his territories and saw in the aid of other patriarchs, even an Orthodox one, a chance to shake it loose. Roger also saw in the crusader states another group of territories poised between the Byzantine and Muslim worlds, pointing in this case at Byzantine Cilicia, Seljuq Turkey and Fatimid Egypt. He may have learned from Bohemond the idea of using both Italy and Antioch as springboards for assaults on Byzantine territory. But, most of all, these contacts show that, even in the 1120s, Roger aspired to a crown. Jerusalem could provide a crown, but the county of Sicily, a dependency of Apulia and ultimately of Rome, could not. Finally, there does seem to exist an idea of a Latin Mediterranean empire, founded on the ruins of the ancient Roman empire, encompassing Sicily, parts of Africa and the Levant – even parts of Spain, where Roger II and the count of Catalonia were planning a campaign south to Muslim Valencia, in 1127–8: a great maritime empire, held together by the Sicilian navy and financed, in part at least, by the revenues of Sicily.

Just as Roger's Spanish plans began to crystallize, new opportunities arose on the mainland of southern Italy; and he
suddenly withdrew his fleet from preparations against Valencia
and turned towards a Christian city instead: Salerno. In 1127
Roger Borsa's son William, duke of Apulia, died; his duchy was
in tatters, and he was childless. Roger II yet again had a claim to
succeed, though he also had plenty of rivals. He invaded at once
southern Italy, and took the region by surprise. By 1129 even the
Norman prince of Capua, whose dynasty had never depended
on the Hautevilles, acknowledged his overlordship. It was such a
dramatic victory that Roger did not give enough thought to the
consolidation of his position. He was to face a long series of
rebellions and even invasion (from Byzantium) before his authority was grudgingly accepted as permanent. But, riding on the
crest of the wave in 1129, he seemed at last to have united
southern Italy and Sicily – to have achieved unity also among his
old and new vassals. In 1129 a great *parliamentum*, or gathering of
his barons, met at Melfi, in the south Italian hinterland, and
proclaimed a land-peace; strife among vassals was to cease, central
justice was to prevail, roads and merchants were to be protected.
This itself was the prelude to much greater events. In 1130 his
barons begged him to take a crown. No doubt the future king
immodestly suggested the idea to them; but, in any case, he did
not rely solely on their judgement. Anacletus II, one of two
claimants to the papacy, and in 1130 the stronger claimant, sent
an emissary to Palermo, where on Christmas Day 1130 Roger
was crowned 'king of Sicily and Italy', constituted king by his
overlord the pope. This appeal to the constitutive power of an
assembly of nobles, but also to the constituting power of the
vicar of Christ, is yet another example of Roger's willingness to
draw on a wide variety of contrasting ideas in order to achieve
his objectives.

The creation of a new kingdom was not, in the Middle Ages, a
casual act. Brand new kingdoms, such as Sicily, Cyprus or
Armenia, were constituted by popes or emperors in the twelfth
century. (The Latin kingdom of Jerusalem was exceptional in
not being so created by a higher authority.) So the question
arose, when a new kingdom was created, whether the western
emperor approved the pope's creation, or vice versa. It will be

seen that the problem of how Cyprus had become a kingdom much exercised Frederick II's policy, when he visited Cyprus on his crusade. In the 1130s, the German emperors violently opposed the creation of a Sicilian kingdom, for they regarded southern Italy as part of their own *regnum Italicum*. Roger's choice of title, 'king of Sicily and Italy', did not help, since it implied Roger's authority extended over all or part of the *regnum Italicum*. In fact, the title reflects a problem of a different sort: Roger ruled a miscellany of lands, some Latin (the Abruzzi), some partly or largely Greek (Apulia, Calabria), even largely Muslim (western Sicily). There was no single, simple title he could use; by 1139 he adopted instead, under papal pressure, the revised title of 'king of Sicily, of the duchy of Apulia and the principality of Capua' – an odd title, for how could one be king of a duchy? But it satisfied papal requirements, because the new title made plain the continued, separate existence of the south Italian Norman states, even if under one ruler and one government; and these states were historically vassal states of the papacy.

A miscellany of lands, and a miscellany of ideas about the nature of this monarchy: the kings of Sicily drew inspiration from contrasted sources, from the Byzantine emperors and their deputies in erstwhile Byzantine Italy; from the papacy, or rather from the power and status of the apostolic legate; from western feudal practice, expressed in the *parliamenta* which approved and encouraged Roger's acts, as law-maker and would-be king. No doubt something too was acquired from the Muslims; on the coins issued in the African towns conquered by Roger, the king is described as protector of the Islamic faithful (even though not himself one of the faithful), in exactly the language his predecessors had used. Was it simply an eclectic bundle of ideas of monarchy, based on a highly workable principle, that the king must project himself to his Greek subjects as a Byzantine *basileus*, to his Muslim ones as an emir, to his Latin ones as a feudal monarch? Some scholars have not even argued for this, but have emphasized one facet out of proportion to the others. Ménager stresses the western features: the use of 'papal attire' (though, as has been seen, the term is vague, even in the twelfth-century sources), the use of liturgical acclamations, or *laudes*, of north European origin – derived from Rouen in Normandy, apparently.

ently. The *parliamenta* serve his case too. He rejects the view that
the Norman monarchy made a great show of being 'Byzantine';
when he has to deal with mosaics portraying the king in Byzantine dress, and in one case modelled on Byzantine metropolitan
iconography, Ménager argues that this is not evidence for anything; the mosaicists of Sicily were immigrants from the heartlands of the Byzantium, so how else could they portray a ruler?
These arguments of Ménager are useful, insofar as they describe
one view of the king, probably current on the south Italian
mainland in the twelfth century – in the 'new territories', of
Latin population, won by Roger from 1127 onwards. But in fact
in that part of the kingdom, Roger had native traditions upon
which to draw: the Lombard princes of Capua and Benevento in
the tenth and eleventh centuries had been anointed into office
and wore vestments modelled on those of the Byzantine emperors
or the popes or both; the archbishops of Benevento wore a tiara,
though eventually the papacy suppressed the practice. The point
is that in southern Italy by the tenth century the idea of the
princeps as an autonomous, sovereign ruler, representing in its
totality the authority of his ultimate overlord in Constantinople,
was well-entrenched. The Lombard princes in southern Italy
were the only secular rulers other than kings and emperors to be
anointed into office: an act of consecration of great moment,
sacralizing their power and elevating them above the status of
common man. Such traditions were seized upon, modified and
re-utilized by the Normans – by Guiscard, the two Rogers.

But Roger II added a great deal, too. Walter Ullmann demonstrated that Ménager's position does not explain everything.
There was a common theme: Roger did not simply accumulate
random ideas of monarchy, nor did the feudal practices Ménager
has stressed come to the fore. The Norman kingdom was a
territorial state, its ruler was 'emperor in his own kingdom', that
is, an entirely autonomous ruler, in whose hands lay the right to
exercise to the full control over his subjects' affairs, secular and
religious. This is not to say that Roger saw his kingdom as a
nation-state: it was so diverse in population and religion that this
was inconceivable; and he did not assume, any more than Guiscard had assumed, that its boundaries should stop on the coasts
of Italy and Sicily, if he could push his armies into Africa or the

Balkans. *'Omnes possessiones regni mei mee sunt'* – all the possessions in the kingdom are mine, the king warned a group of bishops. This attitude was recognized by contemporaries, and described in a word, as 'tyranny'; some, such as John of Salisbury, used the term in a technical sense, to describe Roger's assumption of total control, though others, such as St Bernard, realized its potential as a term of abuse. The source of inspiration for these ideas was not Roger himself. It was the code of Roman law. Texts, though corrupted or out of date, seem to have circulated in southern Italy, based on Justinian's law-code; it seems certain that the Norman rulers were able to draw on a considerable body of material, now lost, but in the early twelfth century largely unknown north of the kingdom's frontiers. Roger II was several decades ahead of the German emperors in making use of Roman law codes, and it can be argued that he grasped their principles more quickly and firmly than did the emperors:

no one should dispute about the judgement, plans and undertakings of the king. For to dispute about his decisions, deeds, constitutions, plans and whether he whom the king has chosen is worthy is comparable to sacrilege.

The king stood above the law: this was pure Justinian, cited by Roger, with the substitution of the term *rex* for *princeps*. In other words, it was a law which was intended exactly to apply to Roger's kingdom. The idea of the crime of *maiestas*, or treason, was developed on Roman lines, and was extended to heretics as well, for by questioning the parameters of religion they questioned implicitly the divine election of the ruler.

Thus the Sicilian monarchy was not entirely a novelty. The ideas that inspired Roger were late-Roman legal ideas, transmitted through Byzantine Italy, but applied to a new set of conditions: a territorial monarchy whose ruler saw himself as detached from the higher jurisdiction of western or eastern emperor, even of pope. Old legislation was seen to confirm the rights and powers of a new institution, the Sicilian monarchy; what was revolutionary was the transformation of the idea of monarchy from the universalism of the late-Roman codes into the regional autonomy of the Sicilian kingdom.

Roger even sought to argue that his kingdom was not so new

after all: there had been 'tyrants' in Syracuse and elsewhere fifteen hundred years before. This was all very well, but it added fuel to the criticisms of those who saw in Roger a tyrant pure and simple. None the less, Roger did issue coins of bronze which were copied from ancient models, apparently to convey the message that the Sicilian kingdom had been revived and not created *ex nihilo*.

Roger's II's attitude to his monarchy has nowhere been so misunderstood as in his dealings with the Byzantine emperors. Much of his reign was taken up with open or threatened conflict with Byzantium; but in 1141 and 1143 he sent embassies to the emperors John and Manuel Komnenos, demanding recognition of his status as *basileus*. This is just the moment when his minister George of Antioch commissioned the mosaic of the king being crowned by Christ, and when his relations with the pope were once again difficult over the apostolic legateship. What did Roger mean? The term *basileus* gave rise to problems. Westerners knew that it was the core title of a long list of titles held by the Byzantine emperor (the Byzantines, for their part, knew that the divinely bestowed authority of the emperor surpassed ordinary human description). In ancient Greek, *basileus* was the word for 'king'. Western rulers who wished to irritate the Byzantines would send letters to Constantinople addressed to the 'king of the Greeks'; but the Byzantines saw their ruler as 'emperor of the Romans', that is, universal emperor, appointed by God, successor to Constantine. Roger's idea of a territorial monarchy, separated out of the universal Christian community, was not easy for Byzantium to accept; there was a tendency in Byzantium to preach an elaborate fiction, and to treat the kingdoms of the west as petty provinces 'allowed' to function under a system of self-government (though southern Italy and Sicily were a different case – they had been 'stolen' from Byzantium by the Normans). What Roger wanted from Constantinople was recognition of the new reality; when he asked to be treated as a *basileus* he was not cheekily asking to be reckoned as the emperor's equal, or as the western emperor (in lieu of the German ruler), but as a territorial monarch possessing the plenitude of monarchic authority, described in Justinian's law-codes. Nevertheless, the Byzantines regarded even this as the height of impudence; the Sicilian ambassador was imprisoned, and relations became even worse than before.

A sidelight on these events is perhaps cast by a book written at Roger's court by a Byzantine scholar just at this time: Neilos Doxopatrios' *History of the Five Patriarchates*. This book rebukes the Normans for seizing the lands of the Roman emperor – an extraordinary statement in a work dedicated to a Norman king – but it also argues that Sicily and southern Italy belong to the patriarchate of Constantinople, and are not under the ecclesiastical authority of the bishop of Rome. Roger may have seized on this idea, already exploited in his dealings with the Church, to approach the Byzantine emperor and to offer to re-enter the Orthodox fold. It would be, at the very least, a deft way to put pressure on the pope when he was making difficulties over the apostolic legateship.

At the heart of these activities, diplomatic, even cultural, was the principle of autonomy. Roger was aware of the Roman heritage of these ideas, and it was to the Rome of Constantine, or at least to the Roman empire of Justinian, that he turned for inspiration: to the best available model for Christian Roman monarchy. It is no coincidence, therefore, that he and his successors used tombs of porphyry, purple marble, just like the Roman emperors of the past, and like many of the popes. Indeed, in Byzantium use of porphyry had been abandoned, apparently because supplies were not plentiful. This was another example of the Sicilian monarchy going back to Constantinian models, and it drew inspiration here from the papacy. From the end of the eleventh century onwards, the papacy had commissioned mosaics in a new, 'pure' style, closer to that of Ravenna or the early Christian basilicas than to current Byzantine models – a change all the more remarkable, in that the workmen were themselves Byzantine. Such mosaics also existed in the kingdom of Sicily, especially at Salerno; in Palermo itself, however, the king followed current Byzantine norms, which could be used to express his exalted ideas of monarchy. But the point is not one of style. In Rome and Sicily, two closely intertwined areas, there was a return to ideas of Constantinian monarchy, made visible in art and based on the reading of Roman law texts among other sources. It will be seen what effect the reading of these texts had on papal attitudes to monarchy, particularly under Frederick II. A common source: but very different types of monarchy, papal, Sicilian and western imperial.

V

In 1129, at the Melfi assembly, Roger II had presented himself as an omni-competent ruler, whose concerns included his vassals' vassals, foreigners such as pilgrims and merchants – all those who resided in or visited his territories. In 1129, in other words, the ruler already functioned as an all-seeing monarch, and what was lacking was the consecration of his special status through coronation and anointing. Royal authority gave greater unity to Roger's legislation and administration; but even before 1130 the Norman territories were being governed with greater precision, and greater success, than other west European states: the disruptions in Apulia after 1085 had not dismantled a system of government borrowed from that of the Byzantine province of Italia; in Calabria and Sicily, a highly centralized administration was built on Arab and Byzantine foundations. Roger II was not the architect, really: his father, uncle, but above all the Greeks of southern Italy, played a crucial role. From the mid-eleventh century right through to Frederick II's reign there was constant reshaping of a system that, in basic structure, long pre-existed the Normans.

What was new, however, was the attempt to place control of the ruler's subjects in the hands of one person: the king himself. This may not appear odd; but the principle of feudal jurisdiction was that the king reserved to himself judgement mainly of matters concerning his status, lands and needs, and left his greater vassals free to judge their own feudatories. In England in the twelfth century this principle was severely eroded. In Sicily it was even more stoutly resisted by the crown. The king reserved the right to control inheritance to fiefs, thereby retaining a sanction over inheritance by vassals he considered unsuitable, because they were too young or too hostile. He naturally reserved the right to judge capital crimes, among which the most serious were offences against his person and his officers. Yet he did not abolish entirely the palatine jurisdiction of some great landholders in southern Italy – the abbots of Montecassino, for instance, or the counts of Conversano. Increasingly, however, Roger demanded military service in return for recognition of such special rights, even from monasteries. The point was that it was in the king's hands to permit or to cancel these rights; even the exercise of palatine jurisdiction was only made possible by the king's will, and could (theoretically at least) be withdrawn at royal whim. And there too the power of life and death was removed from the count or abbot to the king's courts.

There was, of course, a problem of access to justice. In the more remote parts of southern Italy, where the king never or rarely set foot, deputies needed to be appointed. Here, Roger II simply elaborated the Byzantine judicial and military structure, handed down by Guiscard and the dukes of Apulia. Under Roger II a system of justiciars developed, officials with individual circuits, who were to bring justice from the royal court into the heart of southern Italy. Many of the justiciars in the twelfth century were local barons of standing; Count Boamund in south-eastern Italy was given a circuit in lands adjacent to his own extensive estates. The use of great landowners did not continue into the thirteenth century, when Frederick II reshaped this system; even under Roger II one can perhaps see signs that the crown wanted to ensure the justiciar did not operate in the area where he himself held most of his estates. Although the justiciars had seats in the main towns of their circuit (Terra d'Otranto circuit had seats at Brindisi, Lecce, Otranto, Taranto), the justiciar was expected to travel into the country for on-the-spot investigations. This was exactly the task that Byzantine governors were performing in the tenth and early eleventh centuries. Clearly there were two sides to this activity. The king, by the sheer exercise of his judicial power, signified to his subjects the reality of his authority, his ability to operate government even when personally absent. The judges were the reflection of his authority; they spoke with the king's voice. But in the second place justice meant money. The profits of justice – fines, confiscations, payments by plaintiffs for services rendered – also contributed to the well-stocked Norman treasury. A busy bureaucracy, watching and controlling inheritance rights, judging land disputes, with the machinery to issue privileges and to secure unquestionable judgements, paid for itself.

The crown looked after other interests of its own in the provinces. The king created chamberlains (*camerarii*) to oversee his own rights over royal demesne land, forests, the privileges of foreign merchants and so forth. These chamberlains were themselves backed up by a group of bailiffs (*baiuli*), who were spread through the localities. Some south Italian families made good in government service: the Tassilgardo family in Apulia, owners of urban property, but not great barons, provided several generations of chamberlains and other officials in south-eastern Italy. The use of knights and well-off townsmen in government service, of men who owed their status largely or entirely to the king's favour, can already be seen in the twelfth century; and in the thirteenth century Frederick II was to take this principle very much further. Not surprisingly, the monarchy's dependence on bureaucrats of relatively modest birth was also a source of tension. The Norman–Lombard aristocrats looked down on Maio of Bari, chief minister after Roger II's death: a mere Apulian oil merchant, they said, though he was probably a member of the local patriciate in Bari. Both Normans and Hohenstaufen were aware that ill-feeling against the *novi homines* could erupt into violence. Maio himself was assassinated by his enemies.

Southern Italy posed special problems: it was still dominated regionally by great barons, and the royal legislation on inheritance and the exercise of justice could not, in itself, crack their power. Roger and his successors could only win the great nobles to their side by showing that justice worked well, that it was reasonably impartial, that its end was good Christian government in the interests of the king's subjects. From 1129 onwards, Roger II achieved remarkable success in making this point. But in Sicily proper he was under milder restraint. Here was the power base of the Hautevilles – land largely in the ruler's own hands, or in the hands of knights who owed service and loyalty to the ruler directly. Here too was the place of residence of the king: Palermo was the Norman capital, in a real sense (when other medieval kingdoms had generally not concentrated government in one place). William I ('the Bad'), Roger's successor, spent most of his reign in Palermo, and most of his time in Palermo in the pleasure-gardens and harems of his palace, or so his enemies alleged. The presence of the ruler in Sicily thus made it possible to develop a rather different system of administration there, built on Arab as well as Byzantine foundations. The *diwan at-tahqiq al-mamur*, or *mega sekreton* or *duana de secretis*, one department under three names, functioning in three languages, looked after island affairs, though not (or not very much) those of the mainland. Its interests were revenue from the king's estates, many of which were on the island anyhow, and control of the island chamberlains and bailiffs. Land registers were compiled, often compared by historians to the Domesday Book of Norman England, but based on older Greek and Arabic records from Byzantine Calabria and Muslim Sicily. These registers do not themselves survive, but there are extracts from them in land grants, listing even the names of Muslim serfs who worked the soil. A scholarly debate has raged, from Japan to Italy and England, over the exact competence of the *duana de secretis*, and its relationship to a second *duana*, the *duana* of the barons, which appears in the late twelfth century, and seems mainly concerned with the south Italian mainland. Reshaping of the *duana de secretis* by Frederick II into the Sicilian *secrezia* only complicates the problem further. Basically, a separation between Sicily (plus Calabria) and the rest of southern Italy seems to have been maintained by the Normans, and this surely reflects the different nature of royal influence and the different extent of royal landowning, between island and mainland. Those scholars who have tried to see in Norman Sicily a 'model state' have ambitiously assumed that the king's writ was as effective in the countryside of north-western Sicily as on the frontiers of the Abruzzi. But the kingdom was not so homogeneous in the twelfth century; only under Frederick II do signs emerge of homogeneity in government. The 'model state' was, in the twelfth century, Sicily and the toe of Italy; these were the areas where royal authority was more or less untrammelled, but even so there were exceptions – the Muslim *bantustan*, the Lombard estates of eastern Sicily, the restive city of Messina, the lands of some of the Greek monasteries.

A second assumption is that methods of government did not change greatly, that government in Sicily represents the application of reason in order to achieve maximum efficiency. But medieval government was not like that. Expedients, experiments, sudden changes were the order of the day. After Roger's death, the king took less prominent a role in day-to-day government, and his chief minister, the so-called emir of emirs, moved to the fore: this was Maio, later murdered. Once he was done away with, the barons of southern Italy demanded that his office be abolished. So it was; but a chancellor soon emerged, with similar powers.

A third assumption is that Sicilian government was sensitive to the needs of all the king's subjects, Greek, Latin, Jewish, Muslim. Documents were issued in Greek, Latin and Arabic; a famous miniature shows the *duana de secretis* at work in 1189, with scribes of three origins: a tonsured Latin, a bearded Greek, a turbaned Muslim. Multi-lingual administration was itself, however, an expedient; the king, as has been observed, did not look on all his subjects with equal favour, but he knew that, if his administration were to function, it must address all his subjects to equal effect. In the highest echelons of government, tolerance was not the norm. Muslim administrators, at least of high rank, were expected to convert to Christianity; Philip of Mahdia did so, but when it was discovered that he was a backslider he was burnt at the stake as a heretic. This was in 1154, Roger's last year; his condemnation of Philip is occasionally explained away as the aberration of a sick king, facing divine judgement. It was nothing of the sort. Philip, a baptized Christian, was guilty of *maiestas*, treason, by maintaining Muslim practices. Later kings, such as William II, seem, it is true, to have turned a blind eye to such behaviour at court; but ibn Jubayr describes a prominent courtier who told him:

> You can boldly display your faith in Islam, and are successful in your enterprises, and thrive, by God's will, in your commerce. But we must conceal our faith, and, fearful of our lives, must adhere to the worship of God and the discharge of our religious duties in secret.

Some Muslim divines argued in the twelfth century that the faithful had a religious obligation to leave Sicily; it was wrong for Muslims to be under Christian rule. Judging from the rapid decline of the Muslim population in Sicily in this period, their strictures were not unheeded. Yet as late as the early thirteenth century there were administrators of Muslim origin at Frederick II's court, most notably Uberto Fallamonaca.

As the Muslim population declined, so declined the Arabic output of the *duana*. There are few surviving documents in Arabic from the thirteenth century. Equally, the Latin output increased: originally, under King Roger II, in Palermo, there was only one scribe at a time producing Latin charters for his majesty, and he doubled as a royal chaplain. Most documents were in Greek: that was the language of administration *par excellence*, a language the Norman rulers (and possibly Frederick II) understood, alongside a smattering of Arabic. Roger II seems to have enjoyed Greek sermons and to have used Greek in public; he attached his sign, or even signature, to documents in Greek. By the late twelfth century, Greek documents too seem to be in decline, relative to Latin ones; and this reflects the gradual Latinization of Sicily in population, religion and language. There remained powerful Greeks at court, especially the Emir Eugenius, member of a great bureaucratic family, but even they found conditions increasingly difficult. They were resented as Greeks, and they were swamped by Latin courtiers; Eugenius in any case was fluent in Latin and had Latin friends aplenty. The shift to the Latins reflects two developments. One was the arrival of a stream of northern career-seekers and adventurers, who achieved very high office in Roger's kingdom, and became yet more prominent in the late twelfth century. Stephen de la Perche, a Frenchman, was chancellor under William II; Richard Palmer was bishop of Syracuse under the same king, and was one of several courtiers who arrived from England. This group did not have great sympathy for the interests of the non-Latins at court, Greeks or Arabs. A second change was the increased assertiveness of the Norman–Lombard barons. From the time of their rebellion against Maio of Bari, their resentment at over-government became very plain; they expected, too, to wield more influence at court, as the king's natural advisers. In part this was good: an earlier generation of barons had flirted with Byzantium and Germany, trusting in the destruction of the Sicilian monarchy and their liberation from its shackles. From the 1150s onwards, the baronage acquiesced in the existence of the monarchy, but in return demanded a greater say in the direction of affairs. They tended to dislike the parvenu

Frenchmen and Englishmen, and they opposed the king's reliance on Muslim and Greek servants. The non-Latins, who owed their position entirely to royal grace and were in all respects the king's men, represented vividly the reality of royal autocracy, the distance between the king's policy-making and the rights and interests of the baronage. Nor was this fantasy. Roger II had clearly calculated that, with half Sicily Muslim, he must use and appear to respect his Muslim subjects, not just to win their favour but to make plain to his Christian subjects that he possessed a vast well of loyalty, entirely his own.

The great rapprochement with the barons really occurs under William II (1167–89). Maybe the appearance of a separate *duana baronum* for the mainland is part of this process, an attempt to free the mainland barons from the surveillance of Palermo. One of its early acts was, in 1187, to abolish taxes charged on the movement of goods through royal demesne lands in southern Italy. Here too we may see an attempt to cosset the mainland barons. William II, 'the Good', was also an active legislator, and the combination of a king well-disposed to the baronage and a ruler who sought to maintain the impartial, higher law espoused by Roger II won him acclaim. The times of the good King William were cited, within a few decades of his death, as the golden age of Norman government, as the ideal to which later rulers avowed they wished to return – Frederick II, Charles of Anjou, Peter of Aragon. Even Boccaccio could not escape William's attractive reputation, and devoted two stories in his *Decameron* to adventures at the court of King William. It is unimportant, really, whether the reputation was entirely well deserved. William II's rule was followed by a period of calamity: a contest for the crown, German invasion, factionalism, Frederick II's long minority. It was seen as the lull before the storm. William was, too, the only Norman king to show passionate concern for the fate of the Holy Land, under dire threat from Saladin in the 1180s. He launched his fleet against Alexandria in 1174, Thessalonika and Durazzo in 1185, even Majorca in 1181. These actions too, though largely inconclusive, won him fame. By founding the abbey of Monreale, and endowing it with the Muslim *bantustan*, he aimed also to win favour in the court of heaven; the abbey was dedicated to the Virgin Mary. Yet behind all these impressive acts, there are signs of a weakening in royal control: the concessions to the barons did, though only to a limited degree, erode the power of the monarchy. The barons were not actually restive in the 1170s and 1180s, but they became more and more concerned to wield influence over the government of the whole kingdom. When, therefore, after William's death they were faced with rival claimants to the Sicilian throne, they extracted from the king they elected, Tancred of Lecce, concession after concession; even cities such as Naples were granted extensive freedoms, in return for a promise to resist Tancred's rival, Henry of Hohenstaufen, who stood poised to invade and seize the crown. And in the process the financial and political strength of the crown was much reduced. Norman autocracy proved surprisingly fragile.

VI

Roger II, then, built on his father's Byzantine–Arab government of Sicily to create a formidably powerful monarchy. His successors, William the Bad and William the Good, proved less sensitive to Roger's principles, partly because changes in population made it impossible for the king to juggle Latins, Greeks and Muslims. By the 1180s Latinization was proceeding fast in Sicily.

The 'Lombard' community of eastern Sicily continued to grow during the early twelfth century, winning special privileges (even exemption on occasion from service in the royal fleet), in the hope that the Lombards would cultivate the thinly populated fields and help build the prosperity of the crown. In the 1160s the Lombards made more elbow-room for themselves; their leader, Roger Sclavus, a relative of the king, launched a series of pogroms against the Saracens, who mostly fled westwards to their safe-places between Palermo, Girgenti and Trapani. The steady stream of settlers from the north, largely it seems from the area around Genoa and Savona, can still be observed under Frederick II, when new privileges were issued exempting immigrants from tax payments for up to ten years. Frederick, in fact, brought Jews from Tunisia as well as Christians from northern Italy to his island; but the main trend was towards Latinization, at the expense of the Muslims and to lesser degree of the Greeks.

Other medieval kings were worried about the lack of settlers – in Spain, the kingdom of Jerusalem, and the Baltic frontier (with the last of which Frederick was also concerned). These regions to some extent competed against one another; Sicily drew settlers who stopped there *en route* for the Holy Land, and were charmed by the opportunities the island offered. But, as has been indicated, royal policy also comes into the picture: the Normans and Hohenstaufen worked hard to ensure that settlers did come; in other words, they saw several advantages, political and fiscal, in the presence of the Latins in Sicily. Roger II even went so far, at the end of his life, as to permit Cluniac and Cistercian monks to found houses on the island; the Cistercians were famed for their work clearing forests, operating great sheep granges. Frederick was much less enthusiastic about donations of (and to) monastic orders, or so the papacy proclaimed.

Another way the monarchy exercised control over economic activities, with fiscal benefits in view, was by the assumption of central controls, or regalian rights, over the production and sale of certain commodities: the term 'regalian right' does not quite signify 'monopoly', but some historians have assumed this to be so. Here come together several important themes: the exercise of Norman absolutism, requiring by decree that some products of the soil and of the sea are reserved to the crown; and the pursuit of money, in the form of profit from the sale of these goods. Under Frederick II, the system of controls became much more carefully regulated, but the emperor built (as ever) on Norman foundations; it is instructive to compare the loosely operated regalian rights of the twelfth-century kings with the tight controls, genuinely monopolistic, of the thirteenth century. Under Frederick, for instance, saltpans were brought under royal control, but under the Normans, and even as late as 1226, the ruler was prepared to recognize private ownership of saltpans; the Norman monarchy controlled not the production but, as far as can be seen, the movement of salt, demanding a tax on its transportation. But the crown did own, in Calabria and elsewhere, extensive, profitable saltpans, and these formed the core of the state salt system built up by Frederick II in 1231 and after. Now, salt was a natural product, in the sense that it could not be made to 'grow' like wheat; it could not be harvested in the same way as the product of man's toil. It was, as a natural good bestowed by divine blessing, the prerogative of God's representative on earth, the king, who was custodian of the public good. The idea of minerals, sea-produce, treasure trove, as public good, for which the ruler was custodian, was derived straight from the Roman law-codes; it was also highly convenient to a monarchy that believed in making money. So we have a coming together of two themes that underlie the Sicilian monarchy: fiscalism and the idea of the ruler as inheritor to the Roman *princeps*, possessed of all his authority.

Thus iron too became a regalian right, and the manufacture both of steel and of pitch. By 1300 it was assumed by south Italian lawyers that the Norman kings had operated either a monopoly or at least an elaborate system of taxation of these products. The practical motives were clear, no less than the higher principles: these were war materials, not in massive supply, much in demand throughout Europe and the Islamic world. Access to the royal forests, to cut wood (for ship-building or house construction) was also limited. Here one cannot be sure whether the crown was acting as feudal seigneur, reserving the forests to its own use, as William the Conqueror did in the case of the New Forest, or whether principles of Roman public law were once again being enunciated. No doubt Roger I saw the question more in the former light; but Roger II, and even more Frederick II, were keen to stress the public law angle, the theme of royal absolutism. The list of articles controlled by the crown runs on: tunny fish, the great sea-beast whose very capture was a great physical feat, which teemed in Sicilian waters; treasure trove, of course. By 1231 the crown was anxious to include a whole list of rare or prized fish, such as sturgeon and lampreys, under the heading of regalian rights. How lucky the monks of S. Giovanni degli Eremiti in Palermo were, to be granted twenty-one barrels of tunny fish a year by Roger II! Fish of course also meant salt, in the Middle Ages; cured fish was more important than fresh, in many areas. Royal interest in salt production was thus not unconnected with interest in the fisheries. And, spreading the picture wider, salted meats and cheeses were among the prime exports of Sicily, especially to continental Europe where pork products were eaten; so the salt proved its worth yet again, as a preservative for high-quality foodstuffs.

The Norman monarchy thus prepared the ground for Frederick II's assumption of tight controls over the economic life of his subjects. This is not to say that a coherently perceived objective existed in the twelfth century, of assumption of such control. The Norman kings exercised their rights over the natural resources in a patchy, often inconsistent way; they were prepared to make substantial concessions, irrespective of higher principle. Thus, in dealing with mainland barons or abbeys, they saw it was futile to insist on the full exercise of what in theory were their rights. When William II endowed the abbey of Monreale in Sicily, he withdrew from the crown's control a vast area, rich in the natural resources his predecessors had traditionally reserved to themselves. At the same time, it was an area of Muslim population, where he quite possibly found tax-collection difficult; it would henceforth be Monreale's problem to rake in the proceeds. In other words, there existed a gap between the theoretical rights of the crown and their exercise. It has been seen that, in 1187, the king abolished certain taxes levied on the movement of goods across royal lands in southern Italy. Yet this was not simply an act of grace; the crown had long been aware that the taxes it was entitled to collect were not arriving in the treasury. It was not that they failed to be collected, but those who collected them were corrupt tax pirates, who kept all or most for themselves. Royal control was impressive by western European standards, on a par with that of (say) the caliphs in Cairo, but it would be wrong to assume it was total or irresistible. This too was a difficulty Frederick II decided to resolve.

VII

==

At this stage it is worth asking where the money so efficiently raised actually went. It seems that the Norman kings of Sicily did

not face the financial crises that on occasion forced the contemporary kings of England into the clutches of their barons.
The south Italian magnates had no such hold over their monarch,
however tyrannical they thought his financial exactions to be;
only King Tancred, tightly cornered in the early 1190s, was
forced to submit to demands for concessions. Royal expenditure,
as well as accumulation of funds, was substantial. Romuald of
Salerno, chronicler of the Norman court, characterized Roger II
as a moneymaker and also a miser; yet the latter description
seems far-fetched. The most obvious use of his wealth was in
war, though, as fought by Roger, war could bring some profits
at least: booty, tribute, taxes on conquered lands in Africa. The
Normans maintained a combined army, formed of mercenaries
but also of knights and townsmen owing military or naval service. A register of military service from the mainland, the so-
called 'Catalogue of the Barons', gives an idea of the resources
upon which Roger II and William I could draw; but some
important military activities, such as ship-building and the maintenance of garrisons, may only have been partly sustained by
feudal service. Another military expense was bribery, in order to
stave off attack – good Byzantine tactics, these. The Norman
kings pumped money into the north Italian towns to encourage
their resistance to the German emperor, Frederick Barbarossa
(Frederick II's other grandfather). The rationale is clear: the
German emperor planned also to invade southern Italy and Sicily,
and it was sound strategy to tie him down in Lombardy instead.
Alongside bribery, there was magnificent public display. When
Roger II's mother Adelaide was sent east to become queen of
Jerusalem, it seemed to observers that her ships were weighed
down by wheat, wine, oil, salted meats, arms, horses and, not
least, an infinite amount of money. War and diplomacy could be
funded from the king's revenue, and by a levy of military service;
there is no clear evidence that the Norman rulers needed to raise
loans to cover their war costs, nor indeed that they waged war in
the hope of securing wealthy lands which would pay for their
future campaigns. For that was what the German emperors may
have had in mind, at least in the late twelfth century, when they
aimed to capture Sicily; Sicily itself was the land of promise, to
rule which was to stand in a shower of gold. This stands in stark

contrast to the situation in the thirteenth century. Frederick II borrowed from the bankers of Rome and northern Italy to pay for his wars; the Norman kingdom could no longer provide sufficient funds for its ruler's needs. Under the Normans and also under Frederick, the kingdom continued to mint gold coins, and – apart from brief and barely perceptible fluctuations under Frederick – the coins remained of a constant purity, 66.7 per cent gold. This implies that the treasury was not forced to take gold out of circulation in the twelfth century; in the early thirteenth there are signs of a new policy, but it was short-lived only.

Money was spent on entertainment too: on extensive patronage of learning, on the upkeep of well-staffed palaces and pleasure-gardens, on heavy consumption of luxury goods at court. Comfort and spectacle were considered worthy objects of expenditure. A monarchy so conscious of its stature, so insistent on recognition of its rights, not surprisingly maintained a lavish court, and tried to draw towards it some of the leading intellectuals of the time. But this was not all for show: Roger II, William I and II, were themselves interested in the sciences, were multi-lingual, and they found a worthy intellectual successor in Frederick II, despite the tight budget that in his day constrained expenditure on palaces and mosaics.

The flavour of cultural life at court is often characterized as an eclectic mix of Arabic, Greek and Latin learning, in the hands of Jewish, Christian and Muslim scholars. This very characterization has much in common with the idealistic view of the Norman monarchy as a praiseworthy mixture of administrative talents. Indeed, the personnel of administration and of cultural activity overlapped greatly. Therefore, not surprisingly, we see the same shift from cultural activities in which the Muslims were well-represented, under Roger II, to a more Latinate culture (with strong Greek elements) under William II. In the thirteenth century there was still contact with Muslim scholarship, but the intermediaries were much more often Jews than Arabs; the Jews apart, Frederick's court had a more decidedly Christian (if free-thinking Christian) character. To begin with Roger II: in the early twelfth century Muslim poets gravitated around his court, singing his praises, partly in the hope of rewards, partly in admiration at his wisdom. Many of these poets divided their time between Sicily and Africa; some were Sicilian or Maltese, but not all. The rather cringing verse they wrote was presumably understood by the king, though it is hard to be sure his Arabic was very fluent. Under Roger, the Sicilian court formed part of a wider network of central Mediterranean courts, otherwise Islamic. Some of these poets, such as ibn Hamdis, achieved a lasting reputation.

Roger's primary interest lay, however, in science. Here again we see both foreigners and natives at work, on projects directly encouraged by the king. A tri-lingual inscription now set in the wall of the royal palace in Palermo, near the entrance to the royal chapel, commemorates the building of a water-clock by a Muslim subject of Roger, from Malta. But the dominating figure was not a native: al-Idrisi, scion of a north African princely family, a political refugee really, was given the king's patronage. His project was to describe the produce and natural resources of each region of the world, and to make a great silver map of the world. The silver map was destroyed during a sacking of the palace in 1161, but his first work of geography, the *Kitab Rujar*, or *Book of King Roger*, still survives. It was based on a mixture of recent travellers' tales, of existing Arabic geography books, of personal knowledge, and it is therefore very uneven; it is very detailed in its treatment of Sicily and North Africa, but the further north it goes, the vaguer it becomes, and when it reaches China and India fantasy prevails. Its oddities on the Far East are no surprise, but its lack of serious treatment of northern Europe is strange, when it is remembered that many at court were of north European origin or descent. Basically, it seems that Arabic writers had less regard for the eye-witness accounts of Latins, and no regard for the existing works of Latin geography. Idrisi's work suggests that the Norman court did not see very profound intellectual intercourse between Christian and Muslim. To exist side by side is not to observe and instruct one another. For van Cleve, Idrisi provided Frederick II with a model: Frederick's own methods in natural science were, he suggests, borrowed from Idrisi's book; and Frederick's relationship with his astrologer and scientist Michael Scot was very similar to Roger's with Idrisi. This is another example of the way broad similarities are used to create an exaggerated image of a homogeneous Norman-

Hohenstaufen court, impregnated with the ideal of non-denominational scientific brotherhood.

Idrisi worked also for William I, but the role of Muslim scholars at court became less significant in the late twelfth century. The pressure to convert exerted by the monarchy led to a demoralization of the Muslims, witnessed by the traveller ibn Jubayr, and that seems in turn to have led to a decline in Muslim scholarship in Sicily. Foreign scholars did not wish to come to the Norman court from Muslim lands; Sicilian Muslims of intellectual bent went to Africa to find their heritage, and tended not to return. Sicily withdrew from the cultural world of Islam, though gradually; ibn Zafar's *Book of Comforts*, of the late twelfth century, reveals that the traditions did remain alive. But it has to be remembered that the flowering of Islamic culture in Sicily was very much the achievement of the early Norman rulers; little evidence exists for vibrant court culture in the eleventh century, when the Muslim emirs held sway. Just as Calabria was re-Hellenized at about the same time as Roger I's conquest, so Sicily, or rather intellectual life in Sicily, was rejuvenated with new Islamic impulses under Roger II. Hence in part the praises of al-Hafiz and other Egyptian caliphs. This remarkable, but very brief, efflorescence did, however, leave a legacy: though there were few or no Muslim scholars in Frederick II's entourage, Arabic books, in the original or in translation, and Jewish scholars acquainted with them, kept the Sicilian ruler's interest alive; he corresponded with Arabic scholars, as will be seen; yet this was a very different type of cultural relationship to that of Roger II's day, when Muslims were prominent at court. Paradoxically, though, Roger's entourage seems to have been less successful in mixing Arabic and Christian learning, so that Latin, Greek and Arab civilization existed side by side without great community of interest; Frederick did seek to apply the acquired knowledge of the east to western traditions of scholarship, particularly in the natural sciences.

The Sicilian court is usually seen as one of the major centres of translation work, alongside Toledo in Castile. In one sense this is true: Latin scholars at court acquired manuscripts from Constantinople, seizing the chance of diplomatic missions or the exchange of gifts to obtain Ptolemy's *Almagest*, the *Meno* and *Phaedo* of Plato, the Sibylline oracles. Henry Aristippus, courtier to William I, was especially active in translation from Greek into Latin; later, Eugenius the emir, himself a Greek, continued the tradition. What is striking is that the Sicilians were translating straight from the Greek, generally, whereas the schools of translators in Toledo went through several versions: typically, a Christian would put into Latin a romance translation by a Jew of an Arabic text, translated long ago from Syriac, itself translated from Greek. In the process, the original text lost its fine edge, to put it mildly. But Toledo had more impact: its court lasted longer, texts existed in greater abundance, and not just the texts were to be found but commentaries by Arabs and Jews, that eased their assimilation into western culture. By contrast, Palermo offered little more than the text *tout court*, not terribly accurately translated by Greek-speaking courtiers. Moreover, it might be asked whether the activities of translators by their nature reveal quite that multi-cultural exchange that is often assumed to have existed. Works were being selected from the Greek philosophical canon for transmission to Latin audiences; that is to say, they were being taken out of the Greek cultural milieu in which they had been found, and directed towards a new audience that did not care so much what circumstances had produced them; the audience sought to utilize these sources' ideas and methods in the context of western philosophy. This is not to deny that some western scholars, notably Adelard of Bath, saw in Sicily a source of challenging new materials on philosophy, the natural sciences and so on, but the point is that they did not see in Sicily a point of contact with Byzantine culture, or even Arabic. What they prized was access, whether via Sicily or Spain, to the learning of ancient Greece and Rome. There were scholars from the Byzantine world at court, none the less; the most scintillating period seems once again to be the reign of Roger II. His encouragement to Doxopatrios or Doxapater has been mentioned already, and Doxopatrios' work, though written a dozen years before Idrisi's, fits into a pattern: patronage of works on geography, in the widest senses – physical, human, even ecclesiastical. More direct was the flattery bestowed by the homilist and preacher Theophanes Kerameios, on whose behalf great claims have been made – even that he designed the Cappella Palatina in Palermo, working out an iconographical scheme based on Byzantine models, but intended to flatter the Sicilian monarch. Certainly he was unsparing in his bestowal of praise on Roger, and he is known to have preached in Greek before the king. In 1140 he was accorded the honour of delivering the Palm Sunday sermon; this was an occasion medieval monarchs (Sicilian ones not least) seized upon, to stress their role as Christ's representative on earth. Roger rode into church on a white donkey, Christ-like, to be told how his God-given triumphs would be remembered across the world for all time.

Later in the twelfth century, the Greek scholars become less numerous. Eugenius wrote very passable verse in Greek, and he was a dab hand at Latin prose too; it was he who translated the Sibylline oracles from Greek into Latin. He has even been accorded the honour of having written one of the greatest Latin works of the Norman kingdom, the history of the reigns of William I and II, attributed to a certain Hugo Falcandus. Actually, the name 'Falcandus' seems to have been a fantasy of the sixteenth-century printer who published the work; there are no firm grounds for believing 'Falcandus' and Eugenius to be one person. What is important is that Eugenius and 'Falcandus' shared a political outlook: hostility to Maio, to the outsiders. In other words, Eugenius really belonged to a mixed Latin and Greek cultural milieu; but by his time it was the Latins who were clearly preponderant. 'Falcandus', for his part, wrote a stylish Tacitean prose which reveals close attention to classical models.

VIII

The other obvious area of patronage was building and the fine arts. Most of the cathedrals and mosaic series surviving from the twelfth century were hardly added to under Frederick II: the loggia and some additional mosaics at Cefalù come to mind. The great Norman buildings provide, rather, a physical setting for his youth in Palermo; several, such as the Palatine Chapel, the church of St Mary of the Admiral, or the abbey at Monreale, spoke a language of royal aggrandizement and absolutism that seems to have influenced Frederick II. Here was the king receiving his crown directly from Christ, without papal intermediary: a scene portrayed at St Mary's and also, less grandiloquently, at Monreale; here was the king portrayed as the new David, possessor of the earthly Jerusalem, shown in the mosaics of the Palatine Chapel. Mosaic was, as Otto Demus has said, 'the imperial art *par excellence*', the only art form that could do justice to the exalted idea of monarchy in Sicily. It was a Byzantine speciality, however, and it was to Constantinople that the Normans had to turn for mosaicists. A native school of mosaicists may have developed by the late twelfth century, but it has to be admitted that under Frederick II mosaic art lost its prominence, either because Constantinople was no longer able to supply high-grade artists (it had been in Latin hands since 1204, and its cultural life suffered), or because the native Sicilian school of mosaicists did not maintain momentum, or because Frederick was not prepared to pay the high price that mosaicists had to demand for their meticulous work.

The palaces and churches of Norman Sicily are usually seen as a further example of Sicilian *convivencia* between Greek, Latin and Muslim. The Palatine Chapel has a painted wooden ceiling of Arab workmanship, Byzantine mosaics, a Latin ground-plan and Romanesque sculptural features. But do they cohere? The existence side by side of several cultures did not, as has been seen, make for the emergence of the single mixed culture some scholars have posited. The mosaics sought to present the royal court as the new Jerusalem, ruled by the new David. But the Arab wooden ceiling of the Palatine Chapel not merely had no Christian reference – that is hardly surprising – but it stands detached from the rest of the building stylistically, strangely out of place; and the reign of Frederick also saw rather little Islamic influence on the arts of Sicily and southern Italy. The one exception – ceramics – does not really count as court art.

The Norman kings, sensitive or not to these stylistic differences, built magnificent palaces in their capital city. Southern Palermo was almost ringed by parks and lakes created for the ruler's pleasure. Kiosks and summer-houses, adorned with mosaics and fountains, were erected in a style basically copied, the mosaics apart, from North Africa. These palaces and parks also expressed, indirectly, a view of the monarchy and of the kingdom: set in well-watered gardens, the palaces spoke for the legendary fertility of the island of Sicily; while the king's harem, his Saracen bodyguard, his Arab chef, encouraged Muslim visitors such as ibn Jubayr to see in the Norman kings magnificent emirs, even though Christian, barbarian by origin but not by behaviour. Here too, in the pleasure parks, the kings indulged their taste for the magnificent and marvellous, without losing sight of their interest in the natural sciences: when in 1194 the German emperor Henry seized Palermo, his prizes included a giraffe and camels, animals that excited great wonder from Rome northwards to Germany. The Norman kings of England also maintained a menagerie, but the Sicilian menagerie was almost certainly more spectacular; diplomatic contacts with Africa, Egypt and the Levant ensured a supply of weird and wonderful beasts. Even in Guiscard's Apulia, the elephant became a sculptor's favourite. A raid on the palaces in 1161, by enraged Palermitans, led to the escape of many wild animals; but the zoo was evidently restocked. Frederick II maintained the zoo, and even took his animals on his north Italian campaigns, a habit which only contributed to the view that he was some sort of sorcerer, surrounded by an élite corps of monsters. In reality he and his predecessors delighted in rare animals as evidence for the endless wonders of the natural world: for had not Adam been given dominion 'over the fish of the sea, and over the fowl of the air, and over every living thing that moveth upon the earth'? The rulers of man were also God's trustees for the rest of Creation; a royal menagerie symbolized this position of trust.

The Norman monarchy did not earn unstinted praise for its scientific interests, its contacts with Islamic learning, its magnificent style of living. In the twelfth as in the thirteenth century it was easy for critics to seize precisely on these themes, and on the exalted idea of royal authority, to portray the ruler as a bandit king, no better than the Saracens over whom he ruled. The pope even considered launching a crusade against Roger II. These criticisms were to be revived under Frederick II, even more persistently.

IX

The intention here is to show from what roots Frederick II derived his concept of, and style of, monarchy, his cultural outlook; too many historians of his reign have started with his birth, seeing him as the messiah-king whose very arrival in the world heralded a New Order: thus the view of Ernst Kantorowicz. No account of his Norman pedigree would be complete without a look at Norman 'foreign policy', at relations with the Byzantine and German emperors and popes, as well as African rulers. A full account, giving due proportion to each area of Sicilian concern, is not needed here: among the great rivals of the Normans, the Byzantine emperors disappeared dramatically from European politics in 1204, with the capture of Constantinople by the Fourth Crusade; and relations between Sicily and Germany obviously had a very different flavour after 1194, when the western emperor conquered the Sicilian kingdom. The question whether southern Italy should or could be returned to the control of the Roman emperor (of west or east) was not, therefore, an important issue after the twelfth century; the new question, under Frederick II, was whether the ruler of southern Italy should or could be the same person as the western Roman emperor. In other words, the question was very nearly reversed: not the reunification of southern Italy with the Roman empire, but its separation from the Roman empire.

At the heart of this debate, the pope. For here too was a claimant to overlordship, recognized as suzerain by Guiscard, Roger II, William I and II, a close ally of Tancred. It has been seen that the papacy decided Norman military aid was the best defender of the liberties of St Peter, in the late eleventh century. In the twelfth century, there were serious complications: the schism of 1130, in which Roger of Sicily supported Anacletus II; the need to negotiate terms with Anacletus' rival Innocent II, ultimate victor in the contest for papal power. Yet Roger with great agility secured what he saw to be his rights, not least papal recognition of the newly conferred royal title. He established, too, a technique that later kings of Sicily were to imitate: when in conflict with the pope, seek to lay hands on his person. This proved very easy. Innocent II made the mistake of encouraging, and joining, German armies of invasion in southern Italy; he was captured and forced to come to terms. William I, in 1156, secured recognition of his rights from the petulant Hadrian IV, by capturing him too, at Benevento. Benevento was a papal enclave, deep within Sicilian territory, and its defence against Norman 'tyranny' was a cause dear to the heart of the early twelfth-century popes. Unfortunately, they cared so deeply about the town that they even went there; hence the ease with which William secured the pope's person. He secured too recognition of the continued existence of the Sicilian monarchy and of the apostolic legation. In return, the pope was promised payment of the *census*, the tribute of the king of Sicily to his overlord; later rulers, in particular Frederick II, resented the obligation to pay tribute, and this is hardly surprising, given the concept of divinely bestowed monarchy which was current in Sicily. More valuable, perhaps, was Sicilian defence of the papacy in the late twelfth century. The policy established by Guiscard matured by the 1160s into a close alliance, aimed at the protection of Italy against the claims to authority of the German emperor Frederick Barbarossa. William I and II stoutly defended Pope Alexander III during his eighteen years of struggle against Frederick I; the Sicilians played an important part in the peace conference at Venice, in 1177, when pope, emperor, Lombard cities and Sicilian king ended their long conflict and came to terms. Both Rome and Palermo were the objective of Barbarossa's great Italian campaign of 1164; fortunately for the Sicilians, the German army was decimated by disease at the gates of Rome. The threat of German domination of Rome and central Italy was also a threat to southern Italy: an intended one, since not until 1177 did Frederick Barbarossa accord recognition to the Sicilian kingdom established nearly half a century before; until then Sicily was treated as a pariah state. Equally, the planned German invasion of southern Italy was seen by the papacy as a mortal threat to the city of Rome, a potential denial of papal freedom of action. Although Barbarossa never achieved his objectives in Rome and the south, his son Henry did (in very different circumstances) win Sicily by arms. Not surprisingly, Pope Celestine III vigorously supported his rivals in Sicily, Tancred and his young son William III. Celestine saw how serious a danger to his authority was posed by the personal union of empire and Sicilian state. In other words, he foresaw precisely the problems that were to arise under Frederick II.

The German emperors did not adopt a consistent policy towards the Norman kingdom. Before 1177, they regarded its rulers as usurpers of their own sovereign rights; after 1177, they were prepared to enter a marriage alliance with its dynasty. In the first phase, Norman Sicily seems almost an obsession: Lothar II launched two invasions, in concert with Innocent II, in 1135 and 1137; nominally the motive was to defend Innocent's interests against Roger II and against his rival, Pope Anacletus II; but in fact Lothar realized he had no power base back home in Germany, and saw in southern Italy a source of wealth, prestige and military resources. His successor Conrad III was prepared to divide southern Italy with his allies the Byzantines, but there was a reversion to higher principle under Frederick I, from the 1150s onwards: this was part of the *regnum Italicum*, and the legitimate possession of the Roman emperor; there was no notion of dividing the region with Byzantium, for the claims of the Greek emperor to authority in southern Italy were now considered null. Precisely because the German emperor posed so direct a threat to the Sicilian kingdom's very existence, the Norman kings worked hard on all possible fronts to embarrass and tie down the emperor; their financial aid to the Lombard cities, rebels against imperial authority, was particularly effective. Actually, Sicilian, Byzantine and Venetian money helped bring Frederick literally to his knees before Pope Alexander: not entirely predictably, because those three powers had very different ideas about the future of Italy; and Venice, though basically opposed to Barbarossa, was also prepared on occasion to fight on his side against Byzantium, to achieve local objectives.

On his knees before Alexander III, in Venice in 1177, Frederick inaugurated a new policy towards Sicily. In 1183, he proposed a marriage alliance, consecrated in 1184 with the wedding of his son Henry to Roger II's posthumous daughter Constance (her very name redolent of Roger's Constantinian view of monarchy). For Sicily too this was a diplomatic turnabout.

William II of Sicily had been hoping in the 1160s and 1170s for a marriage alliance between himself and the daughter of the Greek emperor, Manuel Komnenos. But, actually left waiting at the quayside for a bride who never arrived, William lost faith in Byzantine promises. Incidentally, it is likely that Manuel promised to make William his heir in Constantinople; deprived of the right to succession by these means, William attempted another method, and launched a savage attack on Byzantium in 1185; Thessalonika and Durazzo fell to him, but not for long. It is no coincidence that his great assault on Byzantium follows soon upon his final agreement with the Germans. Sicily was henceforth Barbarossa's ally, a change of diplomatic stance unthinkable twenty years earlier.

It is often supposed that the marriage of Henry and Constance was the master-stroke of Barbarossa's later years. William II was childless; Constance would succeed if he died; in other words, Henry of Hohenstaufen would rule Sicily in right of his wife. After many complications, that is what happened. But in 1183 William was young, and there was no reason to suppose he would die childless. His wife, Joanna of England, actually did give birth after William's death, having remarried Raymond VI, Count of Toulouse and foe of the Albigensian crusaders. By contrast, Constance was the princess likely to remain barren; she was forty years old when she provided Henry with an heir, the future Frederick II, after several years of childlessness. William did not, therefore, see the union of crowns as a serious target; his purpose was to consolidate an alliance, not a union.

Norman relations with Constantinople can be dealt with more quickly. The Byzantines certainly resented Roger II's pretensions, and those of his heirs, but they also showed themselves able to accept the *de facto* existence of the new state, should that acceptance serve their western strategy. Thus in 1158 Manuel Komnenos made peace with William I, who had only recently been battering his empire; but the opportunities for a decisive attempt to re-establish Byzantine influence at Rome and in central Italy were growing, and the Greek emperor did not want to be distracted by Norman Sicilian issues. The great mistake was over the marriage alliance between William II and the Byzantines. William seems to have maintained his anti-Greek grudge until his invasion of 1185, after which the Sicilian kingdom remembered that for a brief period it had held sway over the western Balkans. This was a legacy that was passed to Henry of Hohenstaufen and his family, and can be argued to have contributed to the conquest of Constantinople by the Fourth Crusade. Frederick II, for his part, cultivated good relations with the Byzantine princes who survived the Fourth Crusade, living on the fringes of the shattered Greek empire and excluded from Frankish Constantinople. The lack of a *basileus* in Constantinople able to make the universalist claims voiced by the twelfth-century Byzantine emperors, made it easier for Frederick II to project himself as the one true Roman emperor, and successor to Constantine.

A final 'foreign policy' concern of the Normans was different in character. Popes, Germans, Byzantines asserted rights to suzerainty over the south of Italy. And the Saracens occasionally reminded the Islamic world that Sicily had until recently been part of the *dar-al-Islam*, and that its inhabitants included very many Muslims. But (a few murmurings from Saladin's court and the Almohads of Morocco excepted) the great Islamic empires posed little threat to Sicily. The continuing problem was that of relations with the petty emirs who ruled Tunisia and Tripolitania up to the mid-twelfth century. At war with one another, they were prone to demanding Sicilian military aid against their rivals, irrespective of the fact that the Sicilians were under Christian rule. Roger II, campaigning in North Africa originally on behalf of suppliant Africa emirs, built for himself a petty African empire, including such towns as al-Mahdia, terminus of the gold caravans, and Tripoli. Only Tunis managed to resist his attempt to gain control of the entire coast opposite Sicily; and even Tunis possibly paid him tribute. The Norman Italian chronicler Romuald of Salerno says:

Because he had a proud heart and a great will to rule, because he was not simply content with Sicily and Apulia, he prepared a vast fleet, which he sent to Africa with very many troops, and took and held Africa.

Roger even seems to have encouraged Christian settlements in Africa, though there is no great reason to suppose he saw his African wars as a crusade in defence of Christendom; many of his troops must have been Muslim themselves. In the 1150s, this African empire fell to pieces; a new Islamic power, the fundamentalist Almohads, swept westwards from the Atlas Mountains and seized the last Norman possessions in 1160. Yet the Almohads too found their fanaticism on the wane. By the 1180s the king of Sicily was on reasonable terms with the Almohad sultan in Tunis. The provision of Sicilian grain to Africa probably never ceased, nor the extraction from Africa of Saharan gold dust to manufacture the gold coinage of the Norman kingdom. What is important is that the Sicilian kings, even in the thirteenth century, continued to take a close interest in north African affairs.

There were several reasons for this. The profitability of trade with Tunisia was surely one, in a monarchy which drew much of its wealth from taxes on trade. The Sicilian kings seem to have continued to hope they could establish their rule over part of the African coast, also. This was not just a matter of prestige, though many at court had seen the loss of Africa in 1160 as a terrible blow to the dynasty's pride. Control of Mahdia, Tunis or Jerba meant control of the seas between Sicily and Africa, through which merchant shipping and navies passed: a major source of revenue, and of political control. Genoese, Pisans, Catalans, not to mention occasional Muslim ships, would be more securely at the mercy of Sicilian tax officials and sea police. This could provide the monarchy with diplomatic leverage as well as financial advantage. Then there was the hope of drawing tribute from Africa, if direct rule could not be achieved: and here Frederick II showed some success, building on Norman precedents at Tunis. Finally, and perhaps most importantly, there was the problem of Muslim piracy and of Muslim raids on the southern coasts of Sicily. Muslim slavers saw in Sicily a bottomless pit full of the commodity they required, human beings. Some Muslim raiders gave support, in manpower or arms, to Saracen rebels in western Sicily; under Frederick II this became an acute problem, though it was not at all new. And of course Muslim interference with Sicilian or Christian shipping off the coast of Sicily threatened the profitability of trade routes from which the monarchy drew great benefit. Some of the more ambitious anti-Muslim campaigns of William II may have been directed against pirates: the attack on Majorca in 1181, for instance.

X

Africa is symbolic of an important dimension to the Sicilian monarchy. Yes, the Normans saw its conquest, even its re-Christianization, as a high objective, worthy of the Constantinian monarchy they aspired to create. Indeed, the German emperor objected that the African wars of Roger II trod on his rights — Africa, though lost, was part of the *imperium Romanum,* no less than Italy and Sicily. Yet Africa symbolizes too the practical side of Norman monarchy. Fiscal and political interests were not entirely dependent on the principles of Roman absolutism cultivated in Palermo. Raising money, protecting shipping, preventing aid to the Saracens of Sicily were straightforward practical objectives. Equally, the recognition of papal suzerainty was a practical act, securing a valuable ally and peace on the northern frontier; and questions of principle, here very embarrassing, had to be ignored. So too high-sounding statements of general law, of Roman derivation, were used more to project an exalted image of the monarchy than to provide exact means of government. The local laws of Lombards, Normans, Greeks, Jews and Arabs continued to function and to be respected.

Norman absolutism thus had a very practical side. The king had clear ideas about the extent of his authority, and a clear awareness how far these claims could be pressed. Restive mainland barons, turbulent island Arabs, threatened royal power and had to be held in check by compromises. The expertise with which Roger II, and to a lesser extent his successors, steered their course, and managed to bring a degree of unity to the Norman territories, is very impressive. A degree of unity only: unity was expressed in the king's person, in his inner circle at court; but as has been seen the administrative system, also the cultural life of the court, were less expressive of unity than is generally supposed. Absolutism helped hold back forces that threatened to tear the kingdom apart, not least the continuing desire for autonomy or independence of barons, townsmen and Arabs. In the event of a disputed succession, or of invasion, the test of loyalty would be applied. In the 1190s, when Henry of Hohenstaufen did invade southern

Italy, the opportunity to break the autocracy seemed to present itself. Only under Frederick II was the autocracy re-imposed, after three decades of strife.

Frederick II inherited much more from his Norman ancestors than the crown on his head and his red hair. The attitude to monarchy, the structure of administration were carried through the apparent anarchy of his youth to form the basis for a re-constructed Norman autocracy in the 1220s and after. The Constantinian monarchy underwent one particularly important transformation, however. It ceased to be merely a territorial monarchy, an attempt, in contemporary eyes not very happy, to reconcile Roman autocracy and even universalism with the fact of rule over a limited area, a new kingdom. Frederick, as emperor, took Norman ideas of monarchy on to the world stage; the element missing in the Roman absolutism of Roger II, the universal strand, was now present and was vigorously used.

It is significant, indeed, that when Frederick was born in Jesi he was given the name 'Constantine'; and, even though this name was dropped at baptism, he was admitted to Christian society under the name Roger as well as Frederick. Here, perhaps, we can see his mother's influence. Nor was it lost upon him in later life.

CHAPTER TWO

THE GERMAN INHERITANCE: FREDERICK BARBAROSSA AND HENRY VI

I

The career of Frederick II's other grandfather, Barbarossa, also left a complex legacy: a monarchy seeking its origins in the Roman empire of antiquity, trying (and largely failing) to assert its authority in Italy, faced by dissensions in Germany; a monarchy, too, which developed a more profound interest in the crusading movement than did the Sicilian kings. Each of these aspects of Frederick I's career, and of the career of his son Henry, greatly influenced the behaviour and outlook of Frederick II. Behind these difficulties lay the problem of relations between pope and emperor. In principle, the pope desired an emperor who would function as the 'temporal sword', exercising justice by good government and (if appropriate) by the exercise of corrective force against sinners. Pope and emperor were natural allies; did not the emperor receive his crown from the hands of the pope? The dream of cooperation, enunciated again and again in the twelfth and thirteenth centuries, gained piquancy from reality: the refusal of the western emperor to acknowledge that his authority was derived from the pope, that he was in some sense the pope's agent. Frederick Barbarossa's first brush with the papacy occurred over precisely this issue: in 1157, Hadrian IV casually mentioned in a letter to Frederick that the empire was a *beneficium*, bestowed by the pope. This term *beneficium* was one of calculated ambiguity. Did it mean 'benefit' in an abstract sense, referring to the act of coronation, but implying no subordination of emperor to pope? Frederick was sure Hadrian meant to intrude another meaning: *beneficium* in a feudal sense, a property granted out by the pope to his vassal. And he replied sharply that he held his crowns from God alone, once he had been constituted ruler by the election of the German princes; indeed, the pope did not understand his Petrine commission if he thought otherwise.

But it was not simply a matter of rebutting papal claims. The constitutive authority of the German princes, mentioned here, was itself an embarrassment. On the death of a German monarch, there was no assurance that his male heir would succeed; but a strong ruler could hope to assure the ascendancy of his dynasty. The first German emperors, the Saxon dynasty in the tenth century, had managed to consolidate their power so successfully that by the end of the century the great German dukes accepted a minor as their king. But minorities, while they paid tribute to the dynastic success of earlier monarchs, also spelt the disintegration of royal power. The great princes were aware there was no powerful king able to challenge their attempts to accumulate land. In the eleventh century, the monarchy (after a period of efflorescence in mid-century) was dangerously weakened first by the minority of Henry IV and then by his bitter conflict with the papacy. Pope Gregory VII, anxious to assert papal supremacy in the face of the most powerful European ruler, tried to break Henry's power by encouraging the election of an anti-king, a new focus for the loyalty of the princes. Actually, Henry managed to ride out the storm, but in the process royal authority was seriously eroded. As a result, the German kings of the early twelfth century found their power challenged by that of mighty subjects in Bavaria, Swabia and Saxony. Noble families, such as the dukes of Zähringen, were able to consolidate their power, building castles and winning to their side a group of dependent vassals, the so-called *ministeriales*, men often of modest origins who rose rapidly in their service. The towns emerged too as a powerful force, such as Cologne, under princely patronage.

It can be seen that the German monarchy was entirely different in character to the Sicilian. In Germany, an itinerant monarchy, with a relatively undeveloped administration, faced powerful princes whose obedience at times was only formal; in Sicily, a powerful bureaucracy based in a capital city controlled, generally effectively, the mainland barons. Nor, indeed, was the German monarchy based on any sense of German nationhood (here it is quite similar to Sicily, in fact). In the tenth century, a group of eastern Frankish nobles had separated themselves from the much weakened authority of Charlemagne's descendants in Paris, to constitute a second *regnum Francorum*, comprising also Saxons and (eventually) Bavarians, Swabians, Thuringians and even Lombards; the king's subjects were mainly speakers of Germanic languages, but many spoke forms of French and, in time, Slav languages or Italian. Literary affectation introduced the term 'Teutonic' to describe this mix of peoples and languages; and there was an awareness even in the tenth century that these people were descendants of the barbarian nations that had invaded and settled nearly every corner of the ancient Roman empire.

Indeed, it was argued that the empire had been transferred from the Romans to less effete nations such as the Lombards of Italy, Burgundians of Provence and Saxons of Germany. This statement became a standard defence of German claims to hold the Roman imperial title, especially in the face of criticism from those other successors to Constantine and Justinian who lived in Constantinople. In the tenth and eleventh centuries (with a brief exception around 1000) the German rulers made use of the imperial title not to claim their Roman heritage, but for other ends. Otto I, conqueror of the Lombard kingdom of northern Italy, the so-called *regnum Italicum*, came south to Rome to defend the papacy against faction struggles in the holy city: he walked in the footsteps of Charlemagne, who in 800 had received an imperial crown in Rome for services rendered. Otto, ruler of the east Franks and now of *Italia*, greatest prince in Europe, received from the pope in 962 the imperial crown also. The significance is twofold. Otto's claim to rule northern Italy was recognized by the pope; rival claims from Burgundians and Lombards were thereby rebutted. Second, Otto now had a broad title, *imperator*, which could be used to paper over the confusion of peoples and territories that made up his assorted empire. When the German princes elected him ruler, there existed a possible counter-claim from the Carolingians in France; it was still very unclear what sort of kingdom he had come to rule. The bestowal of the

imperial crown consolidated and sanctified this collection of
territories into a single Roman *imperium*. But the title was still
treated as a sign of honour rather than as a clear indication
that the power and status of the Caesars had come to rest on a
German head. Propagandists did extol the universal authority
of the emperor, but – especially in the face of Byzantine disapproval – there was little practical application of these ideas,
nor opportunity for it. Even the *regnum Italicum* was rarely
visited, and by the 1020s consisted of little more than a fiscal
administration based at Pavia. Then, in an uprising, the fiscal
records went up in flames; and it became more and more difficult for the German ruler to enforce his rights in northern
Italy.

Those rights were themselves partly determined by the itinerant character of this monarchy. The royal army was to be fed
and supplied when it arrived in the towns of the *regnum Italicum*;
historically, too, the monarchy drew revenue from taxes on river-
traffic, on mints, on the issue of charters and appointment of
imperial notaries; the king endowed new towns with charters of
privilege and (though this brought him into serious conflict with
the papacy) assumed the right to intervene in the election of
bishops and other Church officials. These theoretical rights were,
indeed, still more undermined by the conflict between Henry IV
and Gregory VII. The bishops had functioned as governors of
the towns in the eleventh century, and were often drawn from
the local nobility. Papal attempts to resume direct control over
appointments thus posed a threat not merely to royal rights, but
also to the urban aristocracies. The late eleventh century saw a
series of internal conflicts in the north Italian towns, varying
very much in character: popular uprisings in Milan and Parma,
tension between bishop and nobility in Pisa, but very often a
smooth transfer of power from the bishop's court to committees
of noble families. In other words, the same people often ruled,
but from the Palace of the Commune rather than that of
the bishop; and the bishops, drawn more and more from outside the town, correspondingly lost influence in day-to-day
politics. Of course, it is important to remember that the
'communes' of northern Italy had very diverse origins, even
though, by the mid-twelfth century, they affectedly used very

similar, Roman, language to describe their institutions: 'consul' for their chief officials, '*cives*' for their enfranchised inhabitants.

German emperors-to-be traditionally made an expedition into Italy early in their reign, to receive the 'iron crown of the Lombards' at Monza or Milan, and to march south to Rome to be crowned emperor there. It was the duty of the Lombard towns to provide aid and sustenance to the German king on this *iter Italicum*, but it was also understood that the purpose of the visit was largely ceremonial: the king would show himself, receive homage, take his crowns and go. Serious intervention in Italian politics was reserved for later emergencies: Lothar II's defence of Innocent II's interests in the 1130s, for instance. In other words, Italy, especially Lombardy, saw itself as immune from large-scale intervention by the German kings: an immunity won through the rapid decay of the institutions of the *regnum Italicum*, and by the gaining of autonomy of the newly formed communes in the late eleventh and early twelfth centuries. Attached as they were to their 'Roman' identity, as communities modelled on the ancient Roman republic, the Italian city-states had no room for German imperial claims to authority. They did indeed recognize that the emperor was their suzerain, and derived valuable benefit from his readiness to license their notaries, to confirm their privileges, even (rarely) to settle their disputes. But they expected him to remain at arm's length. The Genoese insisted, for instance, that they owed 'only loyalty (*fidelitas*), and could not be summonsed for any other purpose': thus they addressed Barbarossa, who wanted troops, ships, money. For Barbarossa, this was nonsense: what was *fidelitas* if it had no material expression?

II
==

Frederick Barbarossa, second German king of the Swabian dynasty of Hohenstaufen, was elected ruler in 1152. He had already made a name in the Second Crusade, where he seems to have learnt his dislike for Byzantine pretensions to universal authority, a dislike he translated into policy in the 1160s. Competition with Byzantium, with the 'other' Roman emperor, was one source of his idea of imperial power. Even before his coronation as emperor in Rome, he presented himself in his letters to Constantinople not as King of the Romans, the technical title of the emperor-elect, but as true Emperor of the Romans, addressing the mere Emperor of the Greeks. A second source of his ideas about empire was his conflict with Hadrian IV in 1157, over the use of the term *beneficium* to describe his office. Immediately after this quarrel, we find language being used to refer to the empire which is unstinting in its claims: his is the *sacratissimum imperium*, the most holy empire – a term chosen to match the standard description of the Roman church as the *sancta Romana ecclesia*. Under Frederick I, the German empire is transformed from a mere empire of the German nation, Roman in name, into the Holy Roman Empire of the German nation. Eventually, to enhance still further the ruler's standing, Frederick obtained from an anti-pope the canonization of the founder of the revived Roman empire, Charlemagne. This symbolized the rebirth of the empire yet again under his rule.

Such claims had their sources not merely in rivalry with Byzantium or the papacy. There were texts, too, on which the ruler could draw. Here, slightly later in time, we see a striking similarity with the Norman kingdom of Sicily: the appeal to Roman law, the rediscovery of Justinian. The late-eleventh-century popes stimulated the search for Roman law-codes, as part of the wider search for justification of papal claims to authority. Unfortunately, Justinian had nothing to say about the temporal power of the papacy, but a great deal to say about that of the emperor. Probably it would be true to say that the German court was more selective and less conscious of the underlying principles of Roman law than the Sicilian court was. Roman law for Frederick I was a source of rights, enshrined by antiquity, a clear statement of imperial supremacy. But there was no attempt to enact general law on the scale of the Sicilian Assizes; application of Roman law texts was piecemeal, intended to guarantee the ruler's revenue, the service of his Italian vassals and – for here a wider theoretical question does emerge – to underline the autonomy of the Roman emperor in his dealings with the pope. But the principle expounded here was one deduced from Justinian; there was less attention to the specific ideas of late Roman princely authority, so studiously investigated in Sicily and southern Italy. Not surprisingly, Frederick did deduce that imperial authority extended far beyond the kingdoms of Italy, Germany and Burgundy, whose crowns he wore. Roger and William of Sicily were usurpers of his authority in Italy; there was nothing very new in the view that southern Italy was an integral part of the *regnum Italicum*. But the rulers of France and England were also, or should be, his deputies, provincial *reguli*; a letter of Henry II of England (though of disputed meaning) seems to accept that Barbarossa was in some sense a superior ruler, and it is likely that the enforced homage of Richard I of England to Frederick's son Henry after the Third Crusade also reflects the principle that the emperor, as universal monarch, had the right to command lesser kings. (The sending out of crowns to Cyprus and Armenia, again under Henry VI, also fits this universalist view.) In theory, Frederick stood as emperor in relation to the Christian monarchs rather in the same position as he stood as king of Germany in relation to the German princes, possessing an over-arching authority even where practical expression was lacking.

Frederick Barbarossa realized too that the law texts at his disposal painted a very different picture of his rights in the *regnum Italicum* to that accepted by his predecessors. Innocently enough mingling genuine Roman texts with German imperial decrees of the tenth and eleventh centuries, Barbarossa concluded that he could legitimately demand from the Italian communes not merely provisions for his armies, but a wide range of taxes and services, the so-called *regalia*, that is, royal rights. It is noticeable that Frederick I did not try to distinguish ancient and Ottonian legislation. He saw the Ottos as successors to the Caesars, linking them in his own decrees to Julius, Augustus, Tiberius. The argument that the empire had been transferred out of the hands of the Romans lost its importance; Frederick was not, by blood, a Roman, but he was the lineal successor to the Roman emperors, by divine grace. It was proper that he should demand what he believed (slightly confusedly) to be those emperors' rights over the Lombard cities. So, at Roncaglia in 1158, camped in the plains of Lombardy, he issued a series of decrees demanding restoration of his rights in Lombardy. This was not just a matter of principle, though. He was aware that the potential revenue from Lombardy was enormous. It has been objected that much of this revenue could only be raised when he was on the spot: *fodrum* and *gistum*, the hospitality rendered to court and army, most notably. And his Italian wars never gave him much chance to return across the Alps laden with Italian silver. But that does not mean he failed to see in northern Italy a great opportunity for enrichment. More than that: he knew that the German monarchs had long been at a disadvantage in their dealings with the great princes because they possessed only limited resources inside Germany. The Saxon dukes, for instance, could and did challenge royal power from within Germany, based in a powerful principality, active in the conquest of new Slav lands to the east. If the monarchy could consolidate its own territorial strength, even outside Germany, it might become less easy to challenge it inside Germany. The plans for the conquest of Sicily and southern Italy are a good example of this mixture of principle with practical aims: yes, Sicily was a pirate kingdom, created in imperial lands, quite illicitly, and thus ripe for seizure; but it was also a potential source of money, manpower and prestige. We shall see whether these aspirations were ever realized when Frederick I's descendants did indeed rule both Sicily and Germany.

The challenge to Italy was rapidly appreciated in Lombardy. Were the emperor to activate what at Roncaglia he proclaimed his rights to be, there would be an end to communal autonomy, at least in certain respects. Frederick believed it was his right to appoint the supreme officials in the towns. Later events show that he was prepared to interpret this right in a mild way: to confirm in office those whom the citizens chose (and no doubt he received a fat fee for so doing). But there was also an extreme interpretation, applied to the more recalcitrant cities: the imposition of German commandants to run the towns, a policy pursued, for instance, at San Miniato in Tuscany.

More complicated was Frederick's view of his duty to the Lombard cities. He did not see his role simply as that of a suzerain demanding literal application of his rights. He offered something in return, and was confounded by the lack of gratitude for his efforts. In 1153, at a Diet in Constance in Germany, he sat to hear the pleas of his subjects. There came before him two dispossessed citizens of Lodi, near Milan, to complain at the Milanese conquest of their town. For the communal liberties the Lombard towns aspired to win for themselves were not respected by their mightier neighbours. The absence of imperial intervention in northern Italy in the 1140s had left the bigger towns, the bully-boy towns, free to grab their neighbours' lands and even nearby cities. Milan was by far the most powerful city of western Lombardy, and it seized its chance to consolidate its hold over a large area between the Italian lakes and the foothills of the Apennines. Barbarossa saw his Italian mission also as the pacification of Lombardy, the suppression of Milanese petty imperialism; to achieve this was to exercise to the highest degree his function as supreme judge. It was therefore understood that the Lombards must accept his right to deliver judgement, and that to defy this right was to court the wrath of the emperor. In thinking this way, Frederick I was laying the foundations for his grandson's view of the Lombard problem. Acceptance of imperial rights was seen as the way to peace; yet insistence on those rights, under both Fredericks, paved the route to war.

Alongside this, there was an inability to understand what the communes were, and therefore why their 'liberties' should be fully respected. Frederick I's uncle, Otto of Freising, left a chronicle of the emperor's reign which states explicitly that Frederick could not appreciate the principles of corporative government and equality among the citizen body that lay behind the communes. In part, it is true, these principles were enunciated but not very seriously practised, in the Lombard cities: the real power remained in the hands of the urban aristocracy, in league with influential rural magnates who had thrown in their lot with the commune, and, generally, with the most successful members of the rising merchant class. Formally, however, the citizen body elected its consuls, and citizenship was certainly prized by those who possessed it, not necessarily all the long-term residents in the city. To an outsider, the town did appear exceptional, outside the feudal order, but within its walls an old feudal aristocracy still exercised great influence, and controlled large squads of retainers. Indeed, in the twelfth century the city government itself had often not succeeded in imposing its will on the whole town;

enclaves of private jurisdiction survived, though the commune worked hard to bring their owners into the corporate government. Tensions between the ruling clique and rival families, who resented either their exclusion from government or, indeed, their forced inclusion into the commune, greatly destabilized the north Italian cities: the history of twelfth-century Genoa is a succession of assassinations, street-fights and disputed elections. This turbulence within the cities also struck the Hohenstaufen emperors as a sign of acute disorder, that only the emperor, as supreme judge, could correct; and it generated appeals to the imperial court by plaintiffs who saw imperial intervention as the only way to gain restoration of their claimed rights. Here lie the origins of the groups known as the 'Ghibellines', pro-Hohenstaufen factions in the cities, visible already (without that name) in the twelfth century.

Barbarossa's threat to the Lombard cities was, then, primarily directed against those who bullied their neighbours. To prove he meant business, he marched against Milan, and sacked the city; when it persisted in opposing his policy, by helping to arm his other Lombard enemies, he returned and razed the greatest city in Lombardy to the ground. Precisely because his reaction to Milanese opposition was so severe, Barbarossa succeeded in uniting the Lombard towns against him, even those like Cremona that were traditionally friendly to the emperor. The threat to communal liberties became more serious than the threat offered in the past by Milanese expansionism. And the Cremonese even provided aid to their old enemies when the Lombards, defying Frederick yet again, rebuilt the walls of Milan. Perhaps Frederick counted on the past history of divisions among the Lombard cities: it was inconceivable to him, no doubt, that they should unite against him, friend and foe alike. Yet this is just what happened, with the formation of the first Lombard League. Here were the destroyed city of Milan, Cremona, Mantua, Brescia – the last two like the first ancient rivals – united in a single cause; and many other towns, including a group in north-eastern Lombardy, followed suit. In 1167 a single league came into being, bringing together the western Lombard group of towns and the eastern. Earlier historians, optimists for Italian unity, saw in the league the first stirrings of national feeling, generated by the insensate demands of a German, a foreigner. The Lombard League was not quite that: yet it had some very important characteristics. It was not a 'federal government', and it did not interfere in the internal affairs of member cities; it was governed by rectors from those cities, and its main purpose was to organize military defence against Barbarossa. It benefited from the donations of Venice, Sicily and Byzantium, but despite the warm approaches of the Byzantines it did not place itself under the authority of the other Roman emperor, of Constantinople. For the function of the league was to act in place of the emperor, in matters where the emperor's judgement or decision would normally be essential. Thus the League licensed notaries, because the cities could not ask the emperor to do so; the league had a seal, a version of the imperial one, even adorned with the imperial eagle; the league also tried to prevent the outbreak of serious quarrels between towns, especially where they threatened the military organization of the league as a whole. All these were functions taken over from the western emperor. So too was the right to found new cities: the league established Alessandria, a watching-point in the hills of western Lombardy, much to Barbarossa's fury, not least since it was named after the papal foe of Barbarossa, Alexander III. When negotiations between Barbarossa and the Lombards were under way in the late 1170s, one sticking-point was the continued existence of Alessandria: an affront to imperial authority by its very existence and name. (Finally it was agreed to rename it Caesarea. But its citizens soon changed the name back; Alessandria it remains.)

Yet the league did look to a higher authority, not, it seems, as overlord, but as patron or protector: Pope Alexander III. He was a key figure in negotiations with Constantinople and Sicily. Lombard towns and papacy saw a common interest: they both opposed Frederick's exalted pretensions to universal Roman imperial authority. But their motives otherwise had little in common. Alexander's quarrel concerned Frederick's recognition of his rival Victor IV as pope, after a disputed election in which Frederick did not really have a hand. The Lombard quarrel concerned the *regalia*, or rather the emperor's attempt to make his rule over the *regnum Italicum* a reality. It is true that German armies campaigned in some areas of Italy that were traditionally regarded as part of the Patrimony of St Peter, such as the march of Ancona, Romagna and the duchy of Spoleto; here the towns were smaller, poorer, less able to defend themselves, and the communal movement in some cities had not gained much ground. But the Lombard struggle was the main problem. Attempts to crack the nut by besieging Rome in 1164, or even conquering Sicily and controlling Italy from the south proved over-ambitious.

Another important feature of the Lombard League is, quite simply, its unity. The first Lombard League provided a model for later leagues, especially against Frederick II. It was easy for later rebels to appeal to this heroic moment in the cities' struggle for recognition of their liberties. Then, they had pulled together: never again. Cremona did not return to the Lombard fold. Even the first Lombard League had its strains, as when Venice decided to join Frederick's attack on the rival maritime port of Ancona in 1173, despite its otherwise stalwart support for the resistance against the emperor. Indeed, Frederick worked hard to exploit these strains, by trying to win Cremona back to his side and by showing other towns, such as Mantua and the central Italian cities, that his demand for recognition of his regalian rights need not mean substantial limitation on their freedom of internal government. He was prepared to bargain a fair amount away, if communes accepted that the *regalia* were his as of right; then he would regrant them to the communes, obtaining in return promises of military service. This way he raised some troops for his Roman and Sicilian war of 1164. In the 1170s he pushed hard for agreements of this type with the towns of north-eastern Italy. The aim was to wear down the Lombard League; to neutralize towns on whom, in the heady days of 1167, the Lombards had hoped to rely; to isolate Milan and its friends. It was this diplomatic activity that enabled Barbarossa to survive defeat at Legnano in 1176, and to come to the conference table with his head reasonably high. In 1177 he even tried to interfere in factional rivalries in Venice, to ensure that a pro-imperial party would hold sway in the city at the time of his peace conference with Alexander III and the Sicilians. Even at the last moment, he kept trying.

Between the Peace of Venice in 1177 and the marriage of

Henry to Constance of Sicily in 1184, he gave away many of his rights. It is wrong to see in the Peace of Venice a victory for Barbarossa; it was the failure, not the apogee, of his statecraft, but he was reconciled to the Church, and he had a new, surprising and enthusiastic ally in William II of Sicily, now free from German threat. He had to recognize that the Lombard towns could collect their own tolls and taxes, regalian rights or not; officially, he now graciously conferred on them the right to do so in perpetuity, so that honour was salved. As for control of consular elections, this consisted of little more than occasional oaths of homage by consuls visiting his court; control of elections was vested in the bishops, where they still held power, or in German commandants, but this was only possible in the less politically mature regions of Tuscany and Umbria. Here, indeed, Barbarossa did secure a victory, though it was largely unconnected with the Peace of Venice: the cession to him, by the will of the Saxon duke Welf VI, of the 'Matildine lands' in Tuscany and the Apennines, a legacy that worried the papacy. The popes saw themselves as protectors of the Tuscan estates, mindful of their own good relations with the Countess Matilda after whom, in the late eleventh century, the lands were named. German garrisons had not in the past won the emperor much loyalty from Italian townsmen, and Frederick's striking success in winning acceptance in Tuscany and Umbria can surely be attributed to the much lighter touch of imperial administration after 1177. Even Milan eventually won recognition of its right to recover the regalian taxes. A brief period of relative peace followed the negotiations between emperor and Lombards; even his ambitions in central Italy, among the Tuscan towns, seem not to have caused enormous concern in the Lombard cities. The Lombards had, in essence, won what they wanted, and were not disposed to give comfort to the pope or the central Italian foes of Barbarossa. This attitude, town-centred, oblivious of events much further afield, will be seen to recur during the conflict between Frederick II and the papacy.

III

In Germany, too, Frederick's policy acquired a different flavour. Here he was concerned at the power of his Welf rival the Saxon duke, Henry the Lion, who had built a vast territorial state on the eastern frontier, and who felt able to defy imperial demands for service or loyalty. Henry's failure to provide a large detachment of troops to Frederick on the eve of the battle of Legnano seems to have confirmed the emperor's resolve to destroy Henry. In addition Henry was engaged in an attempt to abstract the lands of the bishop of Halberstadt, a territorial dispute which suggested to Frederick that he could find friends in Germany anxious to curb the power of the Welfs. The assault on Henry began soon after the Peace of Venice, with a summons to Henry to explain himself at the Diet of Gelnhausen. The Lion ignored the summons, and was dispossessed of the Saxon duchy, though it must be emphasized that the power of his dynasty was by no means broken: the emperor could not seize Henry's ancestral family lands, only those he held as duke of Saxony, and in consequence the young Frederick II was to find a formidable rival in Henry's son Otto IV. Frederick I also tried to break up large territorial units, and to instal in key regions princes who were, or who he hoped would become, loyal followers: Henry Jasomirgott in Austria, for instance. The emperor took advantage of the spread of feudal ideas to bond the German nobles to himself, by acts of homage and grants of land. The embarrassments of his Italian policy did not undermine his status in Germany; indeed, the Italian wars seem indirectly to have stimulated his German policy into new life. He could not hope to draw from Italy a particularly large income; any dreams he may have had of serious state-building south of the Alps had to be abandoned (Tuscany excepted). In Burgundy, too, where he held a crown separate from that of Germany, he worked hard to resuscitate the power and authority of the ruler. He brought together his Provençal and Burgundian vassals at Arles, when he was solemnly crowned in the cathedral of St Trophime. It would be hard to argue that the Arelate brought him massive returns; this was showing the flag, little more.

IV

====

Barbarossa appears here as a would-be Roman emperor in the tradition of the Caesars, who thinks none the less in the cruder language of twelfth-century politics. The high rational principles of Roman Constantinian autocracy are not for him: that is the world of the Sicilian tyrant, or *tyrannus*, a word his courtiers freely used of the Normans. And we can go beyond even the pragmatic, obstinate, rather inflexible Barbarossa to find another dimension, expressed in the works of his uncle Otto of Freising. He is also the Emperor of the Last Days, the eschatological figure chosen by God to inaugurate the final sequence of events in human history: the battle with the Antichrist, the Last Judgement in the Valley of Jehosaphat, by the walls of holy Jerusalem. It is difficult to know how seriously to take the paeans of praise to Frederick expressed in this language. It is a theme that did not die with Barbarossa. Frederick II too was credited with a similar eschatological function. When he also failed to deliver all mankind, there was Frederick, Aragonese king of Sicily (in the fourteenth century), or the dreary Emperor Frederick III of Germany (in the fifteenth century), each of whom attracted further millenarian enthusiasm. It is a theme closely tied to Barbarossa's last act, the crusade, and even if the eschatology left his grandson cold, the crusade was one of Frederick II's central concerns.

The Second Crusade had taught Frederick I a distaste for the Byzantines. It was also a failure; its ultimate objective, to recover Edessa, was far from achieved. During Barbarossa's long reign the Muslim threat to the crusader states in the east grew very much more severe. The unification of Egypt to the rest of the central Islamic lands, under Saladin, was seen in the Latin East as a potentially fatal blow. It was realized that the kingdom of Jerusalem owed its survival as much to the divisions of the Islamic world – Shia, Sunni and other rivalries – as to hard work by crusaders and settlers. Constant appeals to the west, to Sicily, France, England, Germany, met with limited response. Money and men were promised; promises were not enough. In 1187, at the battle of Hattin, the armies of the Latin kingdom were virtually annihilated, the relic of the 'true cross' was carried off by the heathen. Soon after, the Holy City fell; all the Holy Land except Tyre was conquered. It was the greatest emergency the Latin East had ever faced, and the response in the west was rapid: a crusade was announced as soon as news of the disasters came, and the great kings pledged their assistance. Tradition bestowed on the French leadership of the crusade, though many early French crusaders had been subjects not of the French crown but of the German. In this emergency, however, Frederick Barbarossa's insistence on participation was very welcome. It was not unheard of for a German king to go on crusade to the east: Conrad III had done so, to little effect, though the papacy had been keener for him to stay behind, where he could not conspire with Byzantium. But in 1187, there was the chance for the temporal sword of the Roman emperor to be wielded in defence of Christendom. It was just how the popes saw the emperor's function, as *gladius Christi*, 'sword of Christ'. The greatest prince of the west, at last at peace with the pope, could now turn from the destructive wars of Lombardy to warfare in a worthy cause.

Those campaigns in Lombardy, costing so much, had distracted the flower of German and Italian knighthood from the just war to be fought in the east. As for the eschatological element, it had certainly been preached in the emperor's presence: go to Jerusalem, hang up your shield on an olive tree, inaugurate the final era of peace. Perhaps Saladin seemed to make a good Antichrist, though when western princes came to know him better, their outlook changed rather favourably. It was also a chance for Barbarossa to visit the other Roman emperor in Constantinople and to show his flag in Hungary, a borderland between Germany and Byzantium whose kings switched their loyalty faster than even the Greeks and the Germans usually realized. Almost in Syria, Barbarossa drowned by accident in a stream in southern Anatolia. The German crusade continued in part, severely demoralized, carrying the emperor's pickled body along. But great hopes had been drowned too. The Hohenstaufen did not lose their enthusiasm for the crusade, however: the new emperor Henry set to work to launch a new crusade; his own son Frederick II was to be entangled with crusading too. The principle remained alive that the German emperor, most powerful ruler in Europe, athlete of Christ, should lead the campaign to deliver the holy places of Christendom from the infidel. No higher duty could be imagined.

And, slowly but separately, in folk-legend, the tale of the sleeping emperor begins to take form: an emperor whose watery end has been replaced by a long sleep, in a German mountain-cave, on the Kyffhäuser, sitting there with his beard growing through the table, awaiting the moment for his redemptive return. As the legend develops, there is acute confusion between grandfather and grandson. But the legend fits Barbarossa better, an emperor who did seem to be preparing for the end of time.

V

Frederick's successor, Henry VI, determined to complete his father's work. Barraclough remarks: 'few reigns have given rise to such diverse judgments as that of Henry VI.' It was during his brief reign that Sicily fell under the rule of a German emperor, and his plans for a crusade, as well as his demands for tribute from the Byzantine empire, reveal that he possessed to the full his father's belief in the claim to universal authority of the Holy Roman emperor. It has been mentioned that he even demanded recognition of this authority from the captive Richard I of England, who had made the mistake of returning home from the Holy Land by way of German lands. What is important is that his claim to Sicily was not at all based on the same principles. England, even Byzantium, were made to acknowledge their subordination to the western Roman emperor, but Sicily became his special possession, ruled directly by him. He was heir to its throne, in right of his wife Constance, and he did not seek to reintegrate Sicily into the empire or the *regnum Italicum*. Here we see a contrast between his plans and Barbarossa's. In the 1160s, the armed conquest of the bandit kingdom was a firm imperial objective. The kingdom itself must be eliminated, though we can be sure that Barbarossa intended to dismantle little of its wealth-giving bureaucracy. Sicily would return to mother empire. Henry intended to maintain the separation of Sicily from the empire; he ruled in Palermo as successor to his wife's Norman ancestors. Rule over Sicily was not, in future, to be disposed of by the German princes, when they elected the King of the Romans on behalf not merely of German interests but Italian and Burgundian. Sicily was to be the private possession of the Hohenstaufen dynasty, a power base over which the German nobles had no claim whatsoever.

The principle could not be put into effect at once. Shortly before Barbarossa's sudden death, William II of Sicily died childless, in 1189. The south Italian magnates, fearful of rule by a foreign prince, elected a bastard member of the Hauteville dynasty to be their king: Tancred, Count of Lecce. The act of election posed constitutional difficulties; but Roger II had also, in 1130, been begged to take a crown, so it was not entirely a novelty. Tancred realized that his acceptance of the crown would draw southwards Henry's armies, but he perhaps calculated on much longer delays than occurred: the Third Crusade was still under way; Barbarossa was still (though not for long) alive; Germany posed problems to its ruler, especially since Henry the Lion had returned from exile in England to resume his Saxon state-building. But when Henry VI found himself king of the Romans the position changed rapidly. There would, of course, be the traditional *iter Italicum*, to receive the iron crown of Lombardy and the imperial crown in Rome. Thereafter, Henry could seize the opportunity to march further south, and recover his and his wife's rights in Sicily and southern Italy. A first invasion, in 1191, did not succeed, partly because the German army was smitten by disease at Naples. But Henry made a yet more determined effort in 1194; the south Italian magnates sur-rendered, and he marched through to Palermo. By then, anyway, Tancred was dead, and his young son William III was an easy victim for the Hohenstaufen: he was blinded and carried off north to Germany, to end his short life in prison. It is interesting to find that – notwithstanding the rather different principles behind Henry's claim to Sicily – Henry resuscitated his father's invasion plans of the 1160s; the very wording of the emperor's treaties with the Genoese and Pisans, upon whom he relied for naval aid, was identical. The Italian maritime republics were, as before, promised trading-stations, lands, entire cities (such as Syracuse); but Henry, once he had conquered Sicily, realized he was powerful enough to send them home with empty hands; though they were indispensable in achieving the conquest, they failed to realize how very dispensable they would become thereafter.

It was as king of Sicily, of the duchy of Apulia and of the principality of Capua that Henry ruled Sicily. There were few changes in the structure of government. Indeed, many of the handsome privileges, granting urban liberties to Naples and elsewhere, with which Tancred had purchased support, could now be revoked. Norman absolutism had been relaxed by Tancred; it was reimposed by Henry. The appearance of a revived silver coinage, modelled on the coinages of northern Italy, may be one of the few significant innovations under Henry: perhaps he hoped to appropriate the existing gold coinage entirely to himself, an idea tried later by Frederick II. And there was a brief moment of triumph when great treasures of gold and silk, not to mention the slave-girls of the harem, and the menagerie, were transported northwards across the Alps: here was the Roman *triumphator* displaying his spoils and thereby warning dissidents against resistance. Certainly, the wealth of Sicily was a lure: he saw southern Italy and Sicily as a base from which he could launch, with new resources of manpower and money, the crusade for the recovery of Jerusalem, that was now long overdue. (A small expedition was indeed launched at the end of his life.) From Sicily, too, he could terrorize the eastern Roman empire; he announced to the Byzantines that he wanted back the extensive lands conquered by William II in his ambitious invasion of the Balkans of 1185, or at least he wanted compensation for their surrender into Byzantine hands. The threat, coming from a Sicilian king who was also Roman emperor, was taken seriously: he received handsome tribute (less than he hoped, though), which was to be used to maintain crusades in the great war for Jerusalem. Henry seems to have inherited the foreign office traditions both of Sicily and of Germany, utilizing Sicilian claims against Byzantium, but also insisting on the universal authority of the western Roman emperor. The dreams of a Constantinian Mediterranean empire under Roger II seemed now nearer fulfilment; and even continental Europe seemed in danger of being sucked into

Henry's schemes, with claims over England and even maybe France being voiced. It has been seen that Cyprus and Armenia received crowns from Henry, and his bestowal of a crown on Cyprus was to add complications to Frederick II's crusading policy; Cyprus was henceforth a vassal kingdom of the empire.

There were important obstacles. Henry the Lion caused grave difficulties in northern Germany, and in 1192 and 1193 the region seemed ready to break out in rebellion. But ex-Duke Henry died in 1195, and the danger to the emperor was for the moment reduced. More important still was the opposition of the papacy. The claims to Sicily worried the papacy, for Hohenstaufen rule both north and south of the Patrimony of St Peter would severely limit the pope's freedom of political action. Not just that: the unresolved disagreement about papal and imperial claims to overlordship in the Matildine lands, in Umbria and in the march of Ancona, threatened to become a major issue. Pope Celestine III therefore supported Tancred during that king's lifetime, and, after Henry's defeat of Tancred's party, he tried hard to oppose imperial pretensions in central Italy. Henry tried to bargain: posing as the great crusader, he asked Celestine to accept imperial claims in central Italy, but to accept also as a permanent gift the revenues of the churches of the Holy Roman Empire. In other words, he asked the pope to set aside the longstanding claim to exercise temporal dominion in the area between Rome and the Adriatic, in return for an assured and very handsome income. It was tempting; but the offer had many flaws. It was likely to make the pope dependent on the goodwill of the emperors: a future foe could cut off these precious funds. More significantly still, there was an important principle behind the temporal rule by the papacy of central Italy; it was a demonstration that the papacy possessed temporal as well as spiritual cares, exercising rule entirely freely, without subordination to the emperor or any secular ruler. The emperor, on the other hand, wielded only the temporal sword, not the spiritual as well: so the papal propagandists had long demonstrated. Powerful arguments against imperial pretensions had been built precisely on this belief. It will be seen, too, that the years around 1200 saw a rapid stride forward in the consolidation of papal control over central Italy, blocking the reactivation of Henry VI's policies there.

The papacy realized that its freedom of movement could only be recovered by edging Henry out of central Italy, southern Italy or both. Maybe already the papacy presented the demand that Frederick II was to receive again and again: the emperor must choose whether he wishes to be a German or a Sicilian king; he cannot wear both crowns. Henry, never lacking in decisive acts, entrusted to his deputy Markward von Anweiler the march of Ancona and the roads linking north-eastern Italy to the Sicilian *regno*. The message was plain: the emperor intended his negotiations with Celestine to succeed his way, and had no time for papal prevarication. Indeed, he spent much of his energy trying to win the support of the German princes to a plan that flew in the face of papal policy: the election as king of Germany of his baby son Frederick, heir already to Sicily. He was determined to transform the elective powers of the German princes into a safeguard for a very different principle of succession, the hereditary principle. In France and other kingdoms it was common for princes in line to succeed to take their crown before their father died, and to rule as co-king. Henry's objective in Germany was thus the survival of his dynasty, by similar means; he was continuing the policy of the defence of his family interests that had characterized the reign of Barbarossa, and that was to dominate the reign of Frederick II.

The measures were only partially successful. The German princes promised to elect Frederick, in 1196, but Henry had hoped also to involve Celestine in the election. If he could persuade the pope to baptise and crown Frederick, Henry would strike a further blow against the German princes. The right to crown the king of Germany was vested in the archbishop of Cologne, a powerful elector, and Henry hoped to take it out of his hands. Thereby the elective powers of the princes would be seriously undermined: no sanction would be left to them, if an emperor decided to by-pass their decision and demand the anointing of his chosen heir by the pope.

Henry's wilfulness, his unstinting demands, only concentrated opposition against him. Pope, German princes, above all Sicilian barons, began to agitate in 1197; Lombardy too became restive, and the Lombard League was re-established, by eleven cities. Here it is, as usual, hard to be sure whether a great question of principle, such as defence of papal interests, motivated the north Italians. Henry had made some controversial judgements in Lombardy, such as the transfer of the city of Crema to the overlordship of the imperial ally Cremona; he permitted Pavia rights over river-routes claimed also by the Milanese. Not surprisingly, Milan became the focus of opposition to Henry, as it had been to Barbarossa; and smaller cities, threatened by Milan, such as Como, Lodi and Bergamo were encouraged, directly by Henry, to unite against Milan. The struggle was not, however, very obviously one about regalian rights or the extension of imperial power by Henry. The Lombards were basically concerned about the frontiers of the city-states and about claims to overlordship by Milan, Cremona and other boss-cities over the smaller towns. As for imperial overlordship, it was exercised relatively lightly; the Peace of Constance functioned reasonably effectively as guarantor of the cities' rights of self-government, and Henry was even ready to bestow new favours on towns such as Piacenza that insisted on their loyalty to him. Here, indeed, is a case of what could go wrong: Piacenza was granted rights of jurisdiction over Borgo San Donnino (now known as Fidenza), but Henry seems to have been unaware, or not to have cared, that Parma down the road also claimed such rights. This was the sort of issue that really inflamed Lombard tempers in the 1190s. Nor, as will be seen, did the outlook change greatly even under Frederick II. Just as the struggle with Barbarossa was partly concerned with the right to levy taxes and elect a city government, that with Henry VI and Frederick II was much concerned with internal affairs: local rights over territory, over taxes on roads and rivers, the lordship of one town over another; and behind all this, the need to secure supplies of food and raw materials, in the face of bitter competition. So much for issues of principle.

VI

In 1197 Sicily erupted. Henry's stern rule stimulated opposition; even Empress Constance was out of sympathy with his uncompromising methods. The taste of relaxed rule under Tancred had re-awakened hopes among the Norman–Lombard barons of lighter rather than stricter government. The arrival of a German emperor as king had perhaps been seen as a chance to win yet more concessions: here was a ruler who must be absent for long periods, whose personal supervision of the bureaucracy would be at best fitful, who did not even understand two of the languages of administration. Especially restive were the Saracens of western Sicily. The Muslims, in serious population decline already, were now largely under the lordship of the archbishop of Monreale. Pressure to convert, pressure of taxation, long-boiling resentment at Christian rule exploded. The Saracen rebellion flickered on for much of Frederick II's reign, though it was seriously broken by 1223. The rebellion of the barons was suppressed more rapidly and more effectively. One, who was said to have aspired to the throne, was punished by Henry in symbolic fashion: a red-hot iron crown was hammered into his head. The merciless brutality of Henry towards the 'traitors' has parallels in the behaviour of Roger II, and subsequently of Frederick II; but his reign of terror in Sicily was unrivalled in intensity. He knew that a serious challenge to his power in Sicily would incapacitate him just when he needed also to impose his will in central Italy, in Lombardy and in Germany. The traitors in Sicily thus threatened not merely his tenure of the Sicilian throne, but the fulfilment of all his policies.

After the revolt was over, his mind returned to the crusade. He had promises of support from the great German nobles; here was a chance to show his mettle and win the loyalty, through effective military leadership, of his most influential subjects in Germany and Italy – even, perhaps, to cow the pope. Disease struck Henry down suddenly in summer, 1197, and he died in September. The conquest of Sicily had been only the start of his plans; and even that had been threatened in the last year of his life, by the uprisings. Some of his ambitions remained alive in the plans of his family: his brother Philip of Swabia who, quite apart from an attempt to gain the German crown, was involved in the Fourth Crusade and entertained ambitions, through his Byzantine wife, to influence in Constantinople; his wife Constance who remained in Sicily, surrounded by Norman and native bureaucrats, including Tancredian loyalists who had opposed

Henry himself, and kept the Norman tradition of government on its feet; Markward von Anweiler, in control of central Italy, but aspiring to control of southern Italy too. These figures were to dominate Frederick II's reign long after they had died; for the rivalries they generated did not die with them.

Two central questions: would the Norman state survive? Would it retain its links to Germany? The key figure was a child of two, Frederick Roger, king of Sicily.

PART TWO

CHAPTER THREE

===

THE CHILD KING,
1194–1220

I

===

The circumstances of Frederick II's birth have much to do with Henry VI's conquest of Sicily. Empress Constance, already heavy with child, was travelling down the eastern flank of Italy to meet Henry in Sicily when she was forced to stop, since birth was impending, at the town of Jesi in the march of Ancona. Now an attractive walled city full of sixteenth-century palazzi, Jesi at the end of the twelfth century was one of the key communes in the disputed central Italian territories. Papal and imperial claims conflicted here; just as Ancona, down the road by the sea, was generally favourable to the papacy, Jesi tended to support imperial interests. The more so once Frederick was a man: this was (he was later to say) his special city; its very name seemed to recall that of Jesus; it was the new Bethlehem. Indeed, Frederick drew the analogy even closer. He was born on 26 December 1194, not merely the day after Christmas but the day after his father was crowned king of Sicily and southern Italy in Palermo. Thus from the moment of birth he was heir to the crowned king of Sicily, born to the purple, and heir also to the Roman Empire (if Henry could get his way). The original choice of the name Constantine for the child emphasized both his imperial birth and his Norman heritage, since after all his mother was herself Constance. She was now about forty years old; her very success in bearing a child was wondered at, and later writers embroidered legends, portraying the empress as an old hag, taken from the seclusion of a monastery; these legends reflect not merely the search for the marvellous and irregular in Frederick's ancestry, but also the uneasy reaction of the Sicilian loyalists to the birth of a successor both to the hated German king and to the last Norman princess. And meanwhile, Henry's success as conqueror seemed doubly assured: he had not merely a crown but an heir.

But there were opinions very favourable to Henry, too, in southern Italy. The flattery of the native historian of Henry's victory, Peter of Eboli, was itself of classical derivation: the Augustus, Henry, has fathered an heir who will be even more *felix* than Henry himself: 'this child in every way will be blessed.' The inspiration to Peter of Eboli, who wrote in verse, was the flatterer of an earlier imperial dynasty to which Henry's line had now succeeded on the Roman throne: Augustus Caesar himself, as portrayed by Virgil. Here too we see a coming-together of messianic themes and enthusiasm for the Hohenstaufen. Virgil's Fourth Eclogue was generally interpreted as a prophecy of the birth of Jesus, but it was reshaped in Peter's verse to refer to the child at Jesi. Further north, the poetry of the Continuator of Godfrey of Viterbo made a similar point, stressing that the child was heir to *imperium, regnum, monarchatum*: empire, kingdom, monarchy. What the Continuator is saying here is that the personal union of empire and Sicilian kingdom must endure. And Henry himself pressed this argument when he asked the pope to baptize and crown his son, despite Celestine's obvious opposition to the continued union of empire and Sicily. Here was the future Caesar, who would inherit an empire far vaster than that of Barbarossa (if Henry's plans succeeded). Here was the son of Constance daughter of Roger, who, as has been seen, projected a self-consciously Constantinian ideal of monarchy. And the final choice of the baptismal names, Frederick Roger, instead of Constantine, underlined the point about the dual heritage of the future Caesar yet another way.

Henry's sudden death from illness in 1197, at Messina, set all this in doubt. Frederick had not yet been presented to the German princes, not even baptized. His candidacy to succeed his father was hardly promising: the German princes would seize the chance of a minority to erode royal power; but in any case, there were much older and weightier candidates. The first was Henry's brother Philip of Swabia. He had been charged in 1197 with the task of winning the agreement of the German princes to the coronation of the baby Frederick as king of Germany, and arrived in Germany as Henry's representative, before the emperor died. His own career looked promising in early 1197. One of the prizes that fell into his lap on Henry's conquest of Sicily was the young widow of Tancred's elder son Roger III, who had been crowned king but had predeceased his father. She was a Byzantine princess, Irene, and the court poets, not least the talented Walther von der Vogelweide, adored her. Philip had also been placed in charge of the Matildine estates in northern Italy, so he stood at the heart of the disagreement between pope and emperor over territorial rights in Italy. He seems to have been no less popular than his wife, and in the early days after Henry's death he faithfully pursued his brother's aims, trying still, despite the disaster, to win German loyalty to Frederick. Even a group of German crusaders in the Holy Land was impressed by news of events, and swore their oath of loyalty to the child, at Beirut.

The second group of candidates represented the resurgence of an old threat. Henry the Lion was dead, but his Welf sons still had ambitions. They were encouraged by powerful German princes, not least the anglophile archbishop of Cologne, still adamant that Hohenstaufen attempts to create a hereditary monarchy must be resisted. Henry's attempt to involve the pope rather than the archbishop in Frederick's coronation as king of Germany still irked the archbishop. And it was precisely Adolf of Cologne's reluctance to accept Frederick that pressed the German princes towards another solution, hardly more favourable to the Welf cause: the election of Philip himself as king of the Romans, in March 1198. But several princes, including the archbishop, were absent, and they riposted with the election three months later of a Welf prince, Otto of Brunswick, younger son of Henry the Lion. Otto had important supporters outside Germany too: an English delegation was present at his election, for Richard Coeur-de-Lion was determined to derive some benefit from his ignominious submission to Henry VI as overlord. He claimed a stake in the election as of right, now that he was a liegeman of the emperor. The English distaste for the Hohenstaufen was accentuated by the existence of the friendly links between Cologne and England; Cologne was one of England's prime trading partners in the late twelfth century and after. Philip of

Swabia was deeply conscious of the Welf threat; indeed, he justified his acceptance of the German crown on the grounds that otherwise Frederick would still have been passed by; there was no hope for the young prince's claim, and there was an acute danger that a choice would be made 'from those who have long been enemies of our family and with whom we could have neither peace nor tranquillity'. So, looking back over the last eight years, he wrote to Pope Innocent in 1206, in order to justify his exalted title.

And in Frederick's other kingdom, problems grew with Henry's death. The rebellion of 1197 had been suppressed; Sicily was quiet. But when Constance found herself free to rule on her own, she adopted a very different set of policies to her husband. She surrounded herself with a group of native advisers, and worked hard to exclude Markward von Anweiler from a position of power. This was difficult in the extreme; Markward had a strong power base on the Italian mainland, and managed to consolidate his hold over parts of southern Italy. He also possessed what he claimed to be the real testament of Henry VI (which was supposedly in his favour), and insisted that he was a loyal follower of Henry and Philip of Hohenstaufen. Finally, Constance ordered Markward's departure from the *regno*, but this was wishful thinking: his lands in central Italy abutted on the *regno* itself, and lay close to his own fief in the kingdom, Molise, which he had received from Henry VI. Constance has been portrayed as the betrayer of Henry's principles: she made warm approaches to the pope, and accepted without qualm the overlordship of the holy see; she abandoned the legatine authority, long but unsuccessfully under demand from Rome; she even, it has been pointed out, omitted reference to the German crown when, in May 1198, her small son was finally anointed king of Sicily. The early documents issued in the little king's name do not mention the title 'king of the Romans', and thus abandon the claim Philip of Swabia had originally gone north to activate. It is possible she took into account, and accepted, the fact that it was Philip, not her son, whom the German princes were prepared to take as their king, as successor to what was still in the princes' eyes an elective monarchy. But it is also plain that she was being remarkably compliant towards the papacy. The new pope, Innocent III, hoped like his predecessors for a separation of Sicily from the empire; what he also gained was a much closer bond with Sicily than the papacy had ever experienced, even in the heyday of Norman papal cooperation. And that was what Constance particularly wanted. She saw the defence of the monarchy's interests inside Sicily as her first objective; she realized that Markward and the other German captains stood in the way of this objective; and she saw no advantage for Frederick in the prosecution of a claim to Germany that would seriously damage relations with the papacy and distract her court from more urgent cares at home. Germany and the Germans (including the little-lamented Henry) had caused enough problems. Her prime effort had to be the restoration of royal authority in Sicily, and in this her brief reign foreshadowed that of Frederick II; but her attempts were foiled by death, not by her earthly enemies.

So, in her will, she entrusted the young king as ward to his suzerain, the pope. She died in late November 1198, having reigned on her own for only a year and a half. Her aim was to restore the Norman monarchy, and she did not believe sub-mission to the papal curia gravely damaged its rights; but her willingness to abandon the apostolic legateship was an aban-donment also of one of the central principles of monarchic auton-omy, as developed by her own father Roger II. Perhaps this surrender indicates the depth of her respect for the Church and for papal policy, which sought, rightly in her view, the separation of Sicily from the empire. But there was also a highly practical side. She was a determined, able woman, but she needed to make her kingdom inviolable. Her negotiations with the papal curia promised to achieve that. She died aged nearly forty-four; and her care to find a protector for her little son was not misplaced. Innocent, as overlord of a minor, Frederick, hardly needed to be appointed his guardian; it was his feudal duty, as suzerain of the king of Sicily, to protect his ward once Frederick's parents were both dead. By actually appointing him as Frederick's guardian in her will, Constance reminded the world of the inviolability of her son's inheritance. Sicily was ruled by a minor, but protected by a pope. It was a policy that made considerable sense, given the emergency.

II

The new pope, elected in 1198, was a relatively youthful lawyer of good Roman family, Lotario de'Segni, Innocent III. Few medieval popes were so insistent on the rights of the Vicar of Christ, and few so consistent in their attempts to apply these rights. It was natural for Innocent to regard seriously the vassal status of the king of Sicily, to demand payment of the Sicilian *census* or tribute and to make plain that the apostolic legateship was in his gift, both to bestow and to remove. The pope stood between God and man, as mediator between man and God; as possessor of spiritual authority, which was inherently superior to temporal, he was also superior to kings and princes. His was the power to correct sinners and to demand of rulers the exercise of justice. By the application of the ideas of the canon lawyers of the late twelfth century to the realities of papal power, he greatly enlarged the scope and meaning of papal authority. Even in 1198, soon after his accession, he spoke firmly of his rights: God, he said,

instituted two great dignities, a greater one to preside over souls as if over day, and a lesser one to preside over bodies as if over night. These are the pontifical authority and the royal power. Now just as the moon derives its light from the sun and is indeed lower than it in quantity and quality, in position and power, so too the royal authority derives the splendour of its dignity from the pontifical authority.

His words to the archbishop of Ravenna, the same year, that ecclesiastical liberty is best defended when the Roman Church has full power in the temporal as well as the spiritual sphere, fit well the arrangements made with Constance of Sicily, and echo also the current interpretations of the Donation of Constantine. Temporal power was exercised in other ways, too. Innocent pursued single-mindedly the aim of recovering control over the Patrimony of St Peter. He is often seen as a major architect of the papal states. And one of the obstacles in his way was Markward von Anweiler, imperial representative in the march of Ancona.

The clash between Markward and Innocent in 1199, in which

Frederick was a mere plaything of the two parties, concerned much more than the Patrimony of St Peter. For Innocent, Markward represented a multiple threat. He had reasonably cordial links with Philip of Swabia, and Innocent assumed, probably wrongly, that Philip aimed not merely at the German crown but the Sicilian. In any case, the pope believed he possessed the right to judge the suitability of the rival candidates for the imperial throne: who, after all, in the end crowned an emperor, if not the pope? Unimpressed by Philip's early reluctance to accept the crown of Germany, Innocent remained worried at the danger of a revived Henrician empire, encompassing Germany, Lombardy, central Italy and Sicily. The answer gradually became clear: support Otto the Welf, who was supposed (wrongly, as it proved) to offer the best guarantee of the continued separation of empire and Sicily. Markward's links to the Hohenstaufen thus made him the prime local target of Innocent's wrath. A second serious problem was caused by Markward's insistence that he was legitimate regent of Sicily, following the death of both Frederick's parents. This claim is not stated in the surviving partial text of Henry's testament, but of course Markward maintained he possessed the full text; he was remarkably reluctant to submit it for inspection. Van Cleve is surely right to see in the so-called testament a preliminary draft by Henry VI: an 'eventual plan'. In 1200 papal troops captured Markward's baggage, testament and all, and parts of it are inserted in the chronicle known as the *Gesta Innocentii Tertii*; but, not surprisingly, it is the clauses most favourable to the papal interest that survive, stating that the holy see is indeed overlord of Sicily, and that the kingdom's government would revert to the papacy if the Hohenstaufen line were to die out. Markward's claim was perhaps based more on verbal promises, and still more on the facts of the day: he actually did control much of central Italy and the Molise, and believed he could make his demands into reality by armed force.

The problem of Markward was accentuated by attitudes in Palermo. For Constance's concessions to the papacy did not win much approval in the Council of Familiars that had assumed the reins of power, and now found itself responsible to the pope. The central figure was Walter of Palear, a worldly south Italian prelate who held the office of chancellor. He brushed aside the claims of a papal legate who came to Palermo to present his master's views, though he seems to have continued to pay lip-service to Innocent's claims. He was not particularly well-disposed towards Philip of Swabia, and to that extent he occupied common ground with the pope. Walter was a survivor, mobile in his policies, who was to serve Frederick II for some years; and the art of survival involved keeping his links both to Innocent and to Markward open. It was a delicate balancing-act; by late 1199 it seemed to be in danger of toppling. An important plank was the ability to buy support by making grants of land and rights to waverers. In 1199 Innocent complained that 'much of the royal demesne has been granted by you to various persons'. As guardian of Frederick's interest, the pope was well aware that Walter was eroding the traditional power base of the crown. Among territories lost at this period may have been Malta, whose count, Guglielmo Grasso, was a well-known Genoese privateer; he also cooperated with Markward at a crucial moment in the would-be regent's plans.

In October 1199 Markward searched out Grasso, who was at home in Genoa, and persuaded him to supply ships for an armed landing in Sicily. The seizure of the capital was the aim; it was the only way Markward could hope to impose his authority as regent. Some suspected him of ambitions to claim the crown itself. As for Walter of Palear, he could not decide which way to turn. Markward landed in Trapani, on the western tip of Sicily, and began to work his way eastward; he realized that the restive Muslim population of western Sicily was worth courting, but here he exposed himself yet more openly to papal wrath. He had taken Innocent partly by surprise, because past invasions of the *regno* had been launched from the east instead, through southern Italy and across the straits of Messina. It was a bold act to enter Sicily by the back door. Innocent responded with a thundering letter addressed to the Sicilian people, on 24 November 1199: Markward, he said, has conspired 'not merely against the Sicilian kingdom, but against the Christian people'; he was 'another Saladin', both an oppressor of Christians and an ally of the Saracens, 'a worse infidel than the infidel'. Innocent spoke of the danger that Sicily would once again fall into the hands of the Muslims; quite apart from the horror of that possibility, there was the effect it would have on the Holy Land. Sicily was the place from which 'it will be easiest to aid the Holy Land', and one could forget entirely the idea of recovering Jerusalem if Markward persisted in his plans. But the pope had an answer: all who resisted Markward were to receive the same privileges (remission of sins and other crusader rights) as if they were campaigning in the Holy Land. In other words, a war for the recovery of Sicily was being declared, which was to be treated as a crusade, since its ultimate objective was the defeat of the infidel and the defence of the supply-lines between western Europe and the Latin East. This letter was the culmination of a propaganda campaign waged by the papacy throughout 1199; even before the arrival of Markward in Trapani, the pope looked with deep concern at his activities in southern Italy, for instance his invasion of the 'lands of St Benedict' around Montecassino. The first signs that the pope intended to classify the war against Markward as a crusade can in fact be found in a letter to Capua, of spring 1199, threatening to offer crusader privileges to 'all who subdue the violence of Markward and his followers'; the autumn letter was an attempt to turn the threats into action. Moreover, the pope was on the lookout for a champion. Innocent found one in a surprising quarter: the husband of King Tancred's daughter, a French knight named Walter of Brienne. His family was to remain embroiled in south Italian affairs throughout Frederick II's reign. Walter had already taken crusader vows; he was intending to fight in the Latin East, but Innocent either dispensed him of these vows, or persuaded him that they could be fulfilled on the soil of southern Italy. The pope dangled before him the rights to the county of Lecce, held by Tancred before he became king of Sicily in 1190, on condition that he acknowledge Frederick as rightful king and renounce any residual claim through his father-in-law Tancred. Here was the nub of the pope's problem: a succession of Sicilian kings had been striving to aid, even to over-awe, the pope during the twelfth century; that was the basis on which papal–royal relations had been built. Now, with Innocent as formal guardian to a child king, a new reality had emerged. The papacy did not possess the military might to defend its vassal. To that extent, Innocent was an inappropriate, even incompetent, protector of his ward's just rights.

Hence the crusade, hence the search for a French champion, who would act on the papal and Sicilian behalf. The crusade against Markward was never, as far as is known, seriously preached, and there is no real evidence that the papal armies that resisted Markward saw themselves as crusader armies, with all the special privileges a crusade bestowed. One participant in this 'crusade' was the young and knightly son of a merchant of Assisi; his father, who traded with France, had given him the name Francesco, and, as Francis of Assisi, he was on his return home to renounce the life of war and lucre in which he had been raised.

What is important is not how widely Innocent broadcast his idea of a crusade against Markward – only the two letters survive promising crusade privileges to Sicilian and south Italian opponents of Markward – so much as the evidence the letter provides for Innocent's thinking. Innocent saw the corrective power of the papacy as a power that could be unleashed through licensed acts of violence. He had no doubt that the crusading instrument was the appropriate corrective method. Yet he still took care to speak the traditional language of crusading: this was a campaign which was intended to benefit the Holy Land; it was a war against the Saracen infidel and their false Christian ally Markward. Later in his career, Innocent showed much more ambitious use of the crusading weapon: the war against the Albigensian heretics in southern France, from 1209, was preached as a crusade, though even on his accession he was threatening similar punishment to like-minded heretics in northern Italy and Bosnia. The extension of the crusade outside the Holy Land was not new; wars in Spain against the Moors and in eastern Europe against the Slav and Baltic pagans were generally regarded as crusades too. Innocent's mention of the Saracens of Sicily in this context is also an attempt to link his crusade against Markward to crusades of that type. But what is new and very significant is the use of the crusade to defend the interests of the Church in Italy and Sicily. In the 1130s threats of a holy war had been made against Roger II by Pope Innocent II, but they came to nothing. Even during the wars between Frederick Barbarossa and Alexander III, the pope had never preached a crusade, although he had excommunicated the emperor. Kennan remarks that the tone of Innocent's denunciation of Markward is 'almost apocalyptic in its vision of Markward's evil. It is far closer in mood to the terrible imprecations directed at Frederick II.' And, as will be seen, it was Frederick II who was to be the butt of political crusades and of the licensed violence of the papacy.

Since on his entry [to the island] he made an alliance with certain Saracens, he called on their help against the king and the Christians; and so as to stimulate their spirits more keenly to the slaughter of our side and to increase their thirst, he has spattered their jaws already with Christian blood and exposed captured Christian women to the violence of their desire. Even if there are some whom the cause of the boy king does not move, is there anyone not moved by the cause of the king of kings, not touched by the injuries to the crucified one? Who would not rise up against him who rises against all and joins the enemies of the Cross, so that he might empty the faith of the Cross and, having become a worse infidel than the infidels, struggles to conquer the faithful?

Yet it is probably an exaggeration to see the war against Markward as the 'first political crusade', waged within Europe against the lay *Christian* enemies of the Church. This is Kennan's view, but it is plain from the characterization of Markward as an 'infidel' that the papacy was still anxious to class this war within the accepted categories of crusading, as a struggle against the foes of Christendom, Muslims, pagans and their collaborators. It was a war against an infidel, against a renegade Christian. It was only in the 1230s and 1240s, in the conflict between Frederick II and the papacy, that the idea of the 'political crusade', waged by Christian against recalcitrant Christian, would really be created. The campaign against Markward was merely a false start.

Crusaders or not, the papal forces landed in Sicily and defeated Markward in battle at Monreale, outside Palermo. But they could not so easily break his power. Chancellor Walter vacillated. He did not want Walter of Brienne in Sicily; the present papal army was not, in fact, under Walter's command, for the *condottiere* had to return to Champagne in order to enlist troops. Walter must have been aware that, now the Muslims had been stirred up, there was every chance of a long-drawn conflict; Innocent too realized the depth of the danger, for he wrote a cooing letter to the Saracens themselves, assuring them that Markward would abandon them before long; he himself posed as their best defender!

Walter of Palear soon saw that, despite the setback at Monreale, Markward was deepening his power base on the island; the only solution was to come to terms. He agreed to divide the government of the kingdom, in what seems at first sight the very opposite way to what might be expected. Markward, long powerful on the mainland, would rule only in Sicily; and on the mainland Walter of Palear and his Council of Familiars were to hold sway. Palermo was not to be handed to Markward for the time being; but Walter of Palear himself left for the mainland. Young Frederick was put under the protection of Walter's brother, the count of Manopello. Here lay a fatal mistake. Markward's unbridled ambition tempted him to seize the king. Hence, indeed, the rumours that Markward intended to kill Frederick and place himself on the throne instead. Not just the king's person was Markward's target: the seals of government, and the power to act in the king's name, were irresistible too.

In autumn 1201, Markward pounced. Palermo opened its gates after a short siege; Frederick's protector, the count of Manopello, was away in Messina, and made no effort to interfere, perhaps even by prior agreement with Markward. On the morning of All Saints' Day the well-fortified royal palace was breached, with the complicity of the traitorous castellan. There is a detailed report of the events that followed, in a letter by the archbishop of Capua, Rainald, to the pope; it is the first sight of Frederick's character and much – perhaps too much – has been built on it by historians playing at psychology. Once Markward was let into the palace, we are told, Frederick went to hide with his tutor in the depths of the building. But the castellan knew where Frederick had gone; a second time he betrayed his king. When Markward came forward to seize him, Frederick strongly resisted. He leaped on Markward in fury, and then, seeing that he would achieve nothing, he threw off his robes, rent his clothes and tore his flesh. The upstart German had presumed to tread upon his royal dignity; it was inconceivable that he should not defend his kingly status, even as a boy of five and a half. The archbishop of Capua was exceedingly impressed. He compared Frederick to Mount Sinai, which at the time of the giving of the Law had stood inviolate, even to animals. If only Frederick's life could be assured, Rainald implied, this was someone who would become a mighty figure.

But it was the king's living person, not a corpse, that Markward wanted and needed. The physical possession of Frederick was an unequivocal challenge to Pope Innocent: the real guardian was not the absentee one in Rome, but the German soldier in Palermo. Perhaps, too, Markward was stimulated to seize the king's person by news from the mainland. Four days after he entered Palermo, but before he had laid hands on Frederick, the armies of Markward's confederate Dipold of Acerra, and of Walter of Palear, met in battle the smaller force of Walter of Brienne, back at last from Champagne (22 October 1201); and Walter of Brienne, perhaps to papal surprise, proved to be the victor. Thus Walter's dream of recovering Lecce became a reality; so too did papal rule over much of southern Italy. Walter was given care of the administration of Apulia and Campania, except that he received his instructions directly from the pope rather than the disgraced Council of Familiars. A new order seemed painfully to be emerging in half at least of the kingdom of Sicily, although Walter of Brienne seemed happier to consolidate his rule in Apulia and was disinclined to lead the promised papal army into Sicily to deliver the king.

Equally, Markward himself was not the whole problem. He died unexpectedly in late 1202, near Messina (which until then had held out against him, once again glorying in its separatist tradition). But this did not mean the collapse of Markward's party; other German warlords claimed power, though increasingly they found themselves in rivalry with one another. William 'Capparone' was, at first, the most successful: Palermo itself, and Frederick, were in his grasp, and he does not seem to have asked for permission before calling himself *Defender of the King and Great Captain of the Kingdom*. Another German, Conrad von Urslingen, was granted authority by Philip of Swabia, whose own title to dispose of Sicily was, to say the least, questionable. What is apparent is that Innocent III gained least advantage: the guardianship of Frederick became less and less effective, and physical possession of the young king proved the real source of power in Sicily. The pope could do no more than agree to the assumption of control by William 'Capparone', and it was some comfort that Innocent thereby won acknowledgement of his suzerainty in turn from Sicily's new ruler. In that sense, William was a distinct improvement on Markward. Moreover, the death of Walter of Brienne, at the hands of the German Dipold of Acerra, removed Innocent's main support on the south Italian mainland, and the recovery of influence over Sicily, however restricted, was a modest compensation. Poor Walter was killed in June 1205 by the simplest of surprises. Encamped outside a German-held fortress, he failed to place a guard on his pavilion; Dipold himself, with some companions, came by night, cut the guy ropes and precipitated the whole tent upon Walter, whom they then cut to pieces.

It has been argued that the fault in Innocent's policy lay precisely in his support for this adventurer. Walter's lack of enthusiasm for a Sicilian campaign is seen to prove how little advantage he brought the pope. Innocent would be better off, therefore, with William 'Capparone', with the mainland Germans, with Walter of Palear who about this time came to terms with the pope (though not because of the Brienne murder alone). The trouble with this argument is that it assumes Innocent realized, before 1205, that he could only exercise indirect control over the kingdom of Sicily; it assumes too that he wished to remain guardian of Frederick solely in order to secure permanent recognition of papal suzerainty over the *regno*. Alas, Innocent possessed more ambitious objectives. Characteristically, he found it difficult to comprehend the existence of war-lords in Sicily who rejected his power to command, not merely as overlord but as vicar of Christ. The arrival of Walter of Brienne, self-interested though he was, suggested an ideal means by which Sicily could be tamed. But equally, Walter of Brienne's death was the stimulus to a reassessment in the papal curia of policy towards Sicily. It rapidly came to be seen that, since no champion was to hand, a compromise with the southern war-lords was necessary.

III

During these years major concessions of rights were granted to territorial lords and foreign merchants in Sicily and southern Italy. It has been seen that the royal demesne began to diminish soon after Constance's death. A further betrayal of royal interests is revealed in the hearty expression of gratitude for aid rendered to Markward von Anweiler by the Genoese. Markward bestowed total tax exemption on Genoese merchants trading in the kingdom: a tremendous source of benefit to them, but a serious loss of revenue to the crown. The Norman system of government was not, it must be stressed, dismantled; but factionalism in the kingdom encouraged those in power to use royal assets as a means to gain military and political support. The documents issued by the royal chancery did not undergo major changes of form; the main difference was, rather, the more restricted income received by the crown, and the more restricted influence of the bureaucracy on the remoter provinces, where German warlords held sway. Respect for royal rights was limited even among those who formally owed their title to the crown: a certain Alamanno da Costa, Genoese pirate and conqueror of Syracuse, claimed to be count of Syracuse, 'by the grace of God, the king and the commune of Genoa', although it was hard to understand what say the Genoese had in the appointment of the counts of a foreign kingdom. The re-establishment of royal power in the 1220s would thus be conditional on the king's subjugation of the German barons and of other non-Sicilian groups, not least the Genoese. The events of 1198 onwards are precisely reflected in the fierce legislation of 1220 onwards. But the native barons seem to have been no less active in fostering their territorial interests. Innocent III, in a letter of 1207, blamed the Sicilian magnates for their hardening of heart: the kingdom's misfortunes had not, as he had hoped, made them more conscious of their duty to act justly, but had proved an irresistible temptation to disorder.

Until 1208, Innocent carried little weight in the kingdom. A series of *coups d'état* in Palermo, in which power was seized from William 'Capparone' by Dipold of Acerra, and from Dipold by Walter of Palear, reflect the cunning of the contenders for power, not the influence of the papacy. Actually, Innocent had been obliged to treat with all three would-be rulers of Sicily, and his one success was to win custody of Frederick himself. A papal legate, working with Walter of Palear, gained charge of the young king. But even Walter's attempts to displace Dipold met with only partial success. He arrested the German war-lord, but Dipold, ever willing to display his prowess, escaped from custody and managed to reach the south Italian mainland. There he re-emerged as an unashamed opponent of the pope: a position all the more threatening because he and his allies were able to wage war almost under the pope's nose, on the northern borders between the kingdom of Sicily and the papal states. It was only the stalwart resistance to the German threat of some native barons that enabled papal influence in the *regno* to survive. The abbot of Montecassino himself led the loyalists against German strongholds in the border country dividing Sicilian from papal lands, and delivered a double blow on Innocent's behalf: papal authority in the Roman campagna as well as in the *regno* was suddenly enhanced.

So much so, indeed, that the pope was able to enter the kingdom, in June 1208, at last turning into reality the powers of lordship he possessed there. Of course, he could not yet penetrate to Sicily, where Frederick remained. But at a council held at San Germano, not more than a few miles inside the Sicilian frontier, but in that very zone where the Germans had recently held sway, Innocent began the slow work of reconstruction. Leading members of the south Italian nobility were charged with the administration of justice; they were reminded that their duty lay towards the young king; an expedition to Sicily, for the restoration of order there too, was announced. Basically, Innocent was trying to restore the bare framework of the Norman judicial system. He did not wish to exercise direct control, and disputes among the barons were to be settled by the justiciars and master captains for whose appointment he arranged. The task was simple to describe, less simple to put into effect: yes, there existed a rich tradition of royal legislation against the over-mighty subject, about land disputes, not to mention the tradition of accountability by royal officials to the king. But the king was a minor and his mainland officials were his great barons. The temptation to feather their own nests was soon visible. Frederick in the 1220s and 1230s tried to limit the role of the magnates in government, and created in lieu a body of professional bureaucrats, not all of grand origins. This attitude has its roots in the betrayal of trust that occurred among the south Italian barons during his youth.

Sicilian affairs could not be detached from those of the empire, so long as Philip of Swabia claimed rights over Frederick, in rivalry with Innocent. Philip's capacity to interfere was, in fact, considerable. He long maintained links with Dipold of Acerra. More than that, he sent Liupold, bishop of Worms, into Italy with an army. He hoped to restore German rule in central Italy, where the papacy had been making steady advances since Henry VI's death; and he saw the bishop as a valuable agent in his contacts with the German warlords of southern Italy. It must be stressed that Philip was not proposing to dispossess Frederick: far from it, he wished to make use of Frederick's crown in order to extend his own influence south of the Alps, and maintain pressure on the papacy. Innocent's support for Otto of Brunswick rankled; and the presence at the head of Philip's army of a bishop, willing to fight papal forces, symbolized the support of part of the German Church too for Philip against Otto and the pope. Though Bishop Liupold was defeated, badly, by the papal army, his expedition proved surprisingly effective. In late 1206 Innocent admitted that his support for Otto was proving too dangerous: central Italy was threatened as a result. Moreover, Philip seemed to have plans for a marriage alliance between Frederick and the ducal house in Brabant, as a means to the consolidation of Hohenstaufen influence in the Low Countries. Philip's diplomacy, balancing vigorous threats to papal policy against Innocent's recognition of Otto, proved triumphant. Philip and Innocent came to terms. At the same time, Philip managed to win more German nobles to his side. By 1208 his authority seemed much stronger.

So strong, indeed, that a discontented suitor for the hand of Philip's daughter, Otto of Wittelsbach, was roused to fury by his rejection, in which he saw the disappointment of all his own ambitions. He struck Philip dead; and to Otto of Brunswick, Philip's rival, it seemed that the victory in the contest for Germany's crown had been won at a stroke. But this was not to destroy the Hohenstaufen claim to Germany's throne. Frederick of Sicily emerged into the limelight, not because he or Innocent or the Sicilian barons for a moment wished to press his claims, but because Philip left behind a solid core of anti-Welf nobles in Germany, in need of a king.

IV

A second major change that occurred in 1208 was the coming of age of Frederick. He was fourteen at the end of the year; Innocent relinquished his guardianship, but of course his suzerain authority persisted. Innocent also provided for the future, by arranging the marriage of the young king to a woman several years older, Constance of Aragon, widow already of the Hungarian ruler; for Innocent, the matter was all the more urgent, because of the danger that Philip would find a German bride for Sicily. Aragon was not yet a particularly mighty kingdom, but its ruler was a papal vassal and members of its royal family held valuable lands in Provence from the Holy Roman Emperor. And Aragon made even more sense, since it was becoming famous as a source of high-quality troops, foot-soldiers, light cavalry and much else. Innocent had promised troops to Frederick already: at the San Germano conference he had talked of two hundred knights who would bring peace to the island of Sicily. When Constance of Aragon arrived in Palermo in summer 1209, she was accompanied by no less than five hundred of the flower of Catalan and Provençal knighthood. This was the first, and least successful, of a series of Aragonese expeditions to Sicily: in 1282, on behalf of another Constance, descendant of Frederick, the Aragonese would conquer Sicily itself. In 1209 battle was not even joined; disease struck and the survivors, demoralized, returned home to Aragon. Yet one figure of importance stayed: Constance herself, who provided much counsel to the young king and, despite an age gap of maybe ten years, drew very close to him. At her death, in 1222, Frederick, in an apparent outburst of emotion, placed his own crown in her antique marble sarcophagus in Palermo cathedral. We may surmise that not just in name Constance of Aragon provided a substitute for the mother who had died when he was very small.

Another view suggests that Frederick was already mature beyond his years: the words are virtually a quotation from a letter of Innocent III sent to Spain in an attempt to win the approval of the Aragonese to the marriage proposal; the age gap was here being dismissed as unimportant. For Kantorowicz the letter of Innocent rings true: there are references to Frederick's resentment at being treated as a minor at the age of thirteen; being king should mean freedom from guardians and regents. But it was an unsophisticated maturity, rooted in impatience and in memories of past insults (the early episode with Markward not least). In 1207 Frederick was thought rather unrefined: for Kantorowicz this was the result of irregular education; systematic training had simply never taken place. And so Kantorowicz takes us on a journey of the imagination through the souks of Palermo, where the boy king wandered, uncontrolled but often hungry, 'through the narrow streets and markets and gardens of the semi-African capital', past synagogues, mosques and churches. Dismissing the tutors whose names can be identified, not least Guglielmo Francesco, Kantorowicz appeals to the existence of an unknown 'Chiron', no doubt a philosopher-imam. And the result: an education quite unlike that of any other royal child. What he knew about nature, which was considerable, he knew from youthful wanderings as much as from readings of Aristotle; observation was his principle, and he learned it before he was fourteen.

The university of life, then; but other evidence points to careful enough tuition. A letter describing him dates from the months when he assumed power in his own right: highly literate, for he was a great reader of 'histories' – no doubt legends of Alexander more than monastic chronicles; a very accomplished rider, who also understood the value of bloodstock; a good fighter, with both the sword and the bow. He showed enormous industry and energy, exercising both body and mind relentlessly. Later observers rudely remarked how little money would be paid for such a physique in the slave-markets of Africa, but in his adolescence he seems to have been sturdy enough; only of moderate height, admittedly, something that detracted a little from his kingly presence, for medieval kings were occasionally distinctive for their height; but strong. Not perhaps very handsome, but bearing a spirited expression; like the young David, red-haired and perhaps rather florid of face. Later his eyesight seems to have deteriorated: probably plain myopia, but this did not discourage him from his enthusiasm for hunting with birds, where keen sight might be expected to matter. Some did find him handsome, but it is possible these sources are speaking in more general terms of his physical build, of his bearing and of the impression he conveyed when adorned with his royal robes. By the middle of his life he may have acquired Greek and at least a smattering of Arabic, but in his youth Latin and Italian were probably his main languages. At what stage he learned German it is hard to say. Van Cleve's view that he did receive an adequate education seems to fit the evidence better than the delightful, romantic alternative.

The assumption of authority was not greeted with acclaim in the kingdom. 1209 saw the first outbreak of disorder on the island of Sicily, among barons who had obtained parts of the royal demesne during the minority, and who were extremely reluctant to hand back their illicit gains. Frederick imposed his will by appearing at the head of a squad of troops, and by sheer coercion of the ringleaders, once they were in his hands. At the moment, his policy was to recover what had been lost rather than to punish those who insulted his royal authority. It is, however, likely that he understood already the basic principles of Norman rulership: that any attempt to diminish the royal possessions was an act of rebellion, and that resistance to the crown was resistance to God. How and when he learned these ideas in detailed form is not known; there is no reason to suppose his tutors or guardians were subtle enough to hide from him the difference between the Norman practice of monarchy and their own rather corrupt methods of government. A sign that Frederick was already thinking in his Norman predecessors' way is provided by a clash between king and pope over the correct procedure for electing a new archbishop of Palermo. Frederick presumed he had the right to confirm the election, on the basis of the legatine authority granted to Roger I. Unfortunately, Constance his mother had already bargained this authority away, as has been seen; and there was an ordinary papal legate in Sicily now, sent by the papal curia. Pope Innocent's complaint to Frederick is of especial interest because it mentions the bad counsel the king was receiving from his advisers. Innocent at least assumed that there existed a group of royalists around Frederick, or perhaps, to save embarrassment, he politely attributed the king's errors to his advisers. One adviser was Walter of Palear, that great survivor. The demesne Walter now worked to recover had, ironically, once been granted out by him to others, around 1200. Somewhat surprisingly, he remained a leading figure at court until the Fifth Crusade, when blunders he committed led him to fear the king's wrath; he then fled to Venice, a city beyond Frederick's jurisdiction.

V

Innocent was, however, more worried by the problems of the German than the Sicilian crown. The death of Philip of Swabia seemed to him to solve one difficulty: Otto was now the only German prince wearing what he claimed was the crown of Germany. The continuing irritant was the existence within Germany of factions strongly opposed to Otto. On the other hand, some non-German rulers, not least the English king, John, would be pleased to see their ally more securely on the throne. The accession of Otto as undisputed ruler, therefore, would necessitate compromises. One form these compromises took was an act of blood-letting; the murderer of Philip of Swabia was hounded across country, and dismembered on the banks of the Danube. Such was the fate that faced those who insulted the power of the greatest clans in Germany. The act of vengeance could thus be countenanced with approval even among the Welfs. And the second form compromise took was a marriage between Otto IV (as he now was) and Philip's first daughter. Here the pope had a hand, because the betrothed were related to one another within the prohibited degrees, and could not marry without papal dispensation. But Innocent III, throughout his career, was quick to exercise his power to bind and to loose when political advantage, and in this case peace too, might be expected to result. Another advantage Innocent was quick to seek was a series of promises concerning future relations between the German king and the papacy; the elections of prelates were no longer to be the subject of royal interference, and appeals in ecclesiastical matters could be made henceforth to the papal curia. Abuses such as the appropriation of the revenue of vacant sees were to end. There is much here in common with the issues that divided John of England (or indeed his father Henry II) and the papacy, and the demands must be seen as an integral part of Innocent's programme for all Europe: royal power over the Church was to be tamed, and the liberty of the Church was constantly to be protected. For that act of protection was itself the mark of a good monarch. We can see too why Frederick II received short shrift from Innocent over his own attempt to provide to a major see in Sicily. What was new here, however, was the pope's success in bringing to heel not a vassal monarch, such as the Sicilian king, but the future emperor; a new era in relations between papacy and empire was assumed to have dawned. Innocent, protagonist of peace, had decisively demonstrated the wisdom and effectiveness of his policies.

And a second issue was also about to be settled between Otto and Innocent, or so it seemed. Actually, Otto had been insisting on the point since he entered German politics in 1201, but only now did it seem possible to act as promised. The question was that posed by Henry VI, of the title to the lands in central Italy, including Tuscany, Umbria, Romagna and the marches, to which Henry had unashamedly laid claim: lands over which, in addition, Innocent had been asserting his authority during the ten years of his pontificate. So Innocent expected of Otto confirmation of existing papal policy in central Italy, and the conferment of areas still under the control of pro-Hohenstaufen or other factions. Here, perhaps, Innocent wandered into the most dangerous minefield of all. The rivalries within the Italian towns, including those of northern Tuscany, remained bitter, but factions increasingly identified their cause with the defence of a higher principle. Otto was one such principle, or protector; the Hohenstaufen were a rival protector. This identification with an outside protector was made with little attention to the real wishes of Otto or the Hohenstaufen. But it was from the German factions – Welf and Staufen or Waiblingen – that were derived the Italian faction labels Guelfo and Ghibellino, terms that were to dominate Italian politics for a century and a half.

In 1209 Otto came to Italy to be crowned emperor. It was then that the pope discovered the emptiness of the fulsome promises extracted with such ease from the candidate emperor. What should have been suspicious about Otto was precisely his carefree approach to the papal demands. Yes, yes, yes in fact meant no, no, no. And there he was in Tuscany, soon after his coronation, planning to assume control over vast regions of Italy. He did violence to his oath concerning the central Italian lands by issuing privileges to towns in the march of Ancona and Umbria, as if those regions were under his rule. No less worrying, perhaps, was the fact that the towns accepted such grants. Papal rule in the Matildine lands or in the duchy of Spoleto was a more immediate threat to city liberties than was Otto the Welf, far away in Germany; Otto performed well in 1209, as protector of the Italian communes that sought to defend their liberties. Too many historians have imposed a rigid structure on the Guelf–Ghibelline disputes. Towns simply wanted freedom from outside interference, defence against land-grabbing neighbours. Otto seemed willing to provide this: an emperor with a difference.

But Otto's ambitions were not confined to ceremonial grants in central Italy. Sinister acts there were, too. He discovered something of consequence, that the kingdom of Sicily was not a fief of the papacy, but an integral part of the Roman empire. This was not, of course, a new idea. Barbarossa had marched south under a similar assumption. It is, nevertheless, odd to see the argument at work now, because Henry VI's claim to Sicily had explicitly accepted the separate existence of the Sicilian state. Of course, Otto's 'discovery' that Sicily was rightfully his had many motives. The desire to establish a power base in the wealthiest agricultural region of Italy; the desire to unseat Frederick, nephew of his recent rival and son of the dynamic Henry VI; the determination to defy papal demands, which had gone too far, and detracted seriously from imperial dignity; even the encouragement of the maritime republic of Pisa, whose merchants had never received from Henry the commercial and territorial concessions promised to them in return for aid in conquering Sicily: all these were important motives, but there was also an *éminence grise* at work. Dipold of Acerra met Otto at Pisa, argued (it must be assumed) that Otto had rights over all southern Italy, and was confirmed in office as master captain of Apulia and Terra di Lavoro, in the Sicilian kingdom. As well be hanged for a sheep as a lamb: he was made duke of Spoleto as well, thereby expressing Otto's claim to rule the papal patrimony too. By the start of 1210, the papal curia was on red alert. The dispossession of Frederick seemed imminent.

In November 1210 all that the papacy had most feared from the Hohenstaufen came to pass at the hands of the Welfs. As Otto entered the Sicilian kingdom, he was formally excommunicated by the pope. If the papacy could find any comfort in events, it must be that Henry VI had been beyond the range of papal weaponry: his claim to Sicily was unfortunate, but arguable in law, by reason of his marriage to Constance. Otto's claim was a total negation of Innocent's authority. Moreover, he had surprisingly little difficulty in enforcing that claim. The Apulian towns, ever anxious for promising concessions, accepted Otto as their lord, and so did the toe of Italy. By mid-1211 his authority extended over much of southern Italy. It seems that the disturbances of 1209 had their legacy in continued unrest throughout Frederick's kingdom. Indeed, even the Saracens of Sicily established contact with Otto; their tendency to support Frederick's foes was becoming firm. Frederick held on to Palermo and a few other parts of Sicily proper, but he realized that he might have to leave Sicily entirely, and return to fight another day. At Castellamare near Palermo a ship stood ready to ferry the king to Africa. Frederick also attempted to appease Otto; he protested that he did not wish to claim his father's German inheritance, and he was prepared to make a fat donation to the Welf funds. Otto, well aware of the vast benefits that would accrue from the conquest of Sicily, was contemptuous. All was set for the crossing to Sicily: Otto's Pisan allies were on their way with naval aid; victory seemed assured.

Such good fortune for the Welfs in the deep south was not matched in northern Italy or Germany. At the heart of the resistance to Otto lay not the powerless Frederick, nor even Innocent III, but Philip Augustus, king of France. Here international power politics saved pope and Sicilian king. Philip of France was anxious to create a Franco-Swabian axis against the Welf-English alliance; at stake was his ability to resist English claims to French lands (he had seized Normandy already, in 1204, from John 'Lackland'); there was also the knotty problem of Flanders, borderland between France and the empire, whose counts and bishops had manoeuvred themselves into a position of considerable independence. Philip had already warned Innocent against trusting Otto IV, rightly enough. Yet it was not simply for Frederick's sake that Philip Augustus, backed by the scared pope, whipped up resistance in Germany to Welf expansionism. Not that this was difficult: the assassination of Philip of Swabia had produced only a temporary reconciliation, and Otto's actions against the Hohenstaufen king of Sicily aroused the ire of Philip's past supporters. The consequence of this outlook was the argument that Frederick himself must be elected king of Germany: he was surely the rightful heir, dispossessed by the Welfs. In 1211 news reached Frederick that he was being offered Germany's throne. At the same time, the north Italian towns and nobles began to work together against Otto. The threat to them was clear. Welf domination of the Italian peninsula, working northwards from central and southern Italy, would (they feared) mean the suppression of the civic liberties for which they had fought against Barbarossa. But the north Italian towns were not as united in opposition as they had been in the 1160s and 1170s. Cremona opposed Otto, Milan welcomed him. In general, the pro-imperial towns of the reign of Henry VI resisted the Welf, while the cities that had worked hardest against the Hohenstaufen favoured him. But there were bitter internal rivalries too, which determined the outlook of the city governments. In Tuscany, Florence was torn between the pro-Swabian Uberti and their Guelf rivals; these are the years, according to the chronicler Villani, when bitter feuds broke out, graced by the names Guelf and Ghibelline. But family rivalries and economic competition were the real source of tension now and during the long-lasting struggles of the two great 'parties' of Italian politics.

The outbreak of revolt in Germany and in parts of Lombardy was well timed. Otto realized that he could not seize Sicily while his power in the north was under such direct challenge. Perhaps he erred here: had he captured Frederick and established a power base in Palermo his authority might not have evaporated so fast. It is possible he believed he could rapidly suppress the revolts in the north. Delusion was easy to come by. Moving steadily northwards, he held court at Lodi before crossing the Alps, and it seemed that all Lombardy was there to pay him homage. But many key towns were in fact not represented, at least by their real government. It is also true that Otto's propaganda machine was proved effective: the view of Frederick presented was of a king who was merely the pope's tool; and the pope's interference in German elections was pointedly criticized even by those, such as the poet Walter von der Vogelweide, who had in the past spoken bitterly of Welf ambitions. Walter's readiness to side with Otto in 1212 reflects the shifting, bewildered outlook of the German princely courts. On the one hand they wanted a king who would put to an end petty wars, bring justice and defend Germany against papal wiles; on the other hand they could see that Otto's policies were directed at objectives far beyond Germany or even Lombardy, threatening long conflicts with the papacy in Italy and with a Hohenstaufen king in Sicily for whom many retained vestigial sympathy.

Frederick himself had just become a father. His son Henry was named after a great Hohenstaufen emperor. Soon after the birth news came of Frederick's election as German king by princes opposed to Otto. Frederick was called to the north by his subjects. Moreover, the pope had agreed to the proposal: he had little choice, though he sought to dictate terms; Henry was to be crowned king of Sicily at once – not for fear Frederick might never return from Germany, but in order to maintain the separation of Sicily from Germany. The precaution made all the more sense since the Sicilian kingdom was still recovering from Otto's assault; there were plenty of south Italian barons who wanted Otto back, and it was an act of courage, indeed foolhardiness, for Frederick to leave Sicily just now. Many courtiers advised against his departure. The views of his late mother were still being propounded: Germany was a foreign kingdom, with whose affairs Sicily had little common interest, except as target for over-zealous emperors' armies.

Frederick had, in any case, to pay the papacy for its favours. The promises of Constance concerning the relationship between Sicily and the holy see were renewed. Innocent seized the chance to make public his approval of Frederick. This, like Constance's Sicilian agreement, might seem to diminish Frederick's authority. Innocent was making plain the pope's power to choose and to depose emperors; Otto he had crowned, but Otto he now set aside. Frederick came to Rome, to be acclaimed (but not yet crowned) as Roman emperor by the *populus Romanus*, at papal instigation. Later Frederick made the best he could out of these circumstances: his propagandists argued that 'not the pope, nor the German princes, but the Roman people, yes, glorious Rome herself, had sent him forth, as a mother sends out her son, to scale the highest heights of empire': preposterous verbiage. But in fact he delivered his oath of homage to the pope for the kingdom of Sicily, renewed his promises to respect papal authority and received money from the pope to help with his war expenses. The emotional climate was none the less charged. He was young, he had rather little funds and no great army behind him; but he had professions of loyalty (for what they were worth) from sundry German and Italian princes. Innocent was desperately anxious he should succeed; but in Sicily and in Germany there were plenty of pessimists and mockers.

The Pisans had supported Otto; indeed, their fleet stood in Frederick's way off the south Italian coast. He eluded them (and, to be fair, much of Pisa's history was spent in alliance with the Hohenstaufen emperors, not against them). But the opposition of Pisa was, by 1212, the surest way for him to win the support of Genoa. The rivalries of the cities had broken out anew in Sicily itself, in Frederick's childhood, when Pisa and Genoa battled for control of Syracuse. The Genoese won. Among the victors, there was Henry 'the Fisherman', count of Malta, would-be lord of Crete, and Genoese privateer of the widest repute. He was with Frederick in Genoa, where they arrived on 1 May. The city was banking on Frederick's success: literally, for the commune offered £2,400 in expenses. In return the commune was to win confirmation of its trading rights in Sicily, themselves exceptionally generous. Markward von Anweiler had exempted the Genoese from all customs dues. Frederick did not have the time to argue; he saved his irritation for another day. He also promised the Genoese government 575 pounds of gold, which more than repaid his debt of £2,400. Perhaps this was in compensation for Henry VI's failure to fulfil the generous terms of the treaty with Genoa agreed upon before the German conquest of Sicily. Two and a half months were spent in Genoa, and it has been argued that Frederick was unable to move north while the Italian roads and Alpine passes were unsafe. Yet his stay in Genoa brought advantage, too. The citizens of those towns which opposed Otto in Lombardy had a chance to make close contact with their candidate for the empire. The Pavians came to offer a contribution to his travelling expenses. The Cremonesi were traditionally pro-Swabian and were, of course, delighted by his presence. Lombardy as a whole was not won over; the Milanese remained especially obdurate. Their aim was to capture Frederick; and their attempts, as will be seen, only enhanced that king's wondrous reputation.

Frederick's route towards Germany was not, could not be, a straight line. He must jump from one pro-Swabian town to another, and zigzag through the Alps, avoiding Otto's allies. The first major test of Frederick's determination, and even of his physical condition, occurred after he had passed through Asti and Pavia, on the way to Cremona. By the banks of the River Lambro a Milanese platoon watched for Frederick, and the boatmen of Piacenza scoured the Lombard rivers in search of a barge which might carry the king. It was the Milanese who caught up with Frederick and his escort of Pavian knights, just as they reached the Lambro. On the other side of the river waited an escort provided by loyal Cremona for Frederick. When the Milanese struck, Frederick and the Pavians were relaxing near the river, no doubt luxuriating in relief at having eluded the enemy before reaching the Lambro. Taken by surprise, many Pavians were slaughtered or seized. Frederick jumped on an unsaddled horse and guided it across the water to the Cremonese side. The Milanese annalist tried to make a brave face of Frederick's near-escape from his city's clutches, 'Roger Frederick,' he said, 'bathed his bottom in the Lambro.' But he was safe.

The next stage, taking him via Mantua to Verona, was not so dangerous. The serious difficulty lay ahead. He must cross the Alps avoiding Bavarian territory, for the duke of Bavaria was a supporter of Otto IV. North of Verona, the lords of Merano, in the Alto Adige or south Tyrol, were also opposed to him. Thus the obvious route through the valleys was closed. His route took him instead through the Engadine towards the lands of a friendly prelate, the bishop of Chur. He had reached Germany. And he had reached his allies. From one Swiss abbey to another the news of his arrival passed; troops were supplied. Now he had about three hundred cavalry, largely supplied by churchmen. It seemed that Innocent's activity on his behalf had been rewarded.

Yet there was one decisive act facing Frederick. Otto IV was closing in on him, moving towards the city of Constance. There Frederick must try to install himself and win a following. If Constance would not support him, it was hard to see how his expedition into Germany could succeed. But time was short. Otto's cooks were already at Constance; a great reception was being prepared. The emperor was the other side of Lake Constance; he could be in the city within hours. Frederick suddenly reached the city, out of nowhere; he demanded admission. The local bishop was well aware that a momentous choice rested with him. He demurred. But Frederick put to good use his papal connections. Every minute counted. The papal legate, the archbishop of Bari, spoke: was not Otto excommunicate? Was it not wrong therefore to welcome him and defy Innocent's wishes? The bishop of Constance remained unhappy. But he opened the gates: the young king entered, summoned the citizens to defend his crown (by fortifying the bridge along which Otto was due to ride). Within three hours Frederick had won the town's allegiance. Guillelmus Armoricus, writing in France, reported that if Frederick had delayed a mere three hours Germany could never have been his.

There is something more than mere surprise here. Frederick's coup was achieved precisely because his power seemed frail, his name a shadow of past glories. Then, all of a sudden, there he was, miraculously, in person, invoking divine aid. Modern historians might attribute his success to luck, whatever they mean by that. Certainly, his arrival at Constance was a matter of urgency; he could not, of course, tell what the result might be. The conviction that this was the necessary course of action, that he was being guided by God towards fulfilment not merely of his rights, but towards the inauguration of a new era, grew in Frederick. Of course, the success at Constance did not open all Germany's gates. But there was greater and greater confidence in the ranks of the German nobles. Frederick knew that he could win yet more solid support by confirming the political and fiscal

rights of the princes and towns in Germany. He did not try to
interfere in his followers' liberties; he knew he could only win
their support as defender of those liberties. So Basel and Stras-
bourg came over to him, and he began a progression Rhinewards,
heading towards the north of Germany. Here lay the greater
towns, seats of the bishop electors, and here too lay some of
Otto's closest allies. Frederick, his forces now much enlarged,
was not disposed to avoid Otto's own armies. Indeed, he pushed
Otto northwards, and the Welf retreat seemed to be turning into
a rout. The period of time involved here was amazingly short.
Frederick reached Germany in mid-September; Otto had already
been forced northwards to friendly Cologne by early October.
Cologne, of course, symbolized the English connection, through
its trade; and Otto, ally of the English crown, pondered more
and more the possibility of English aid. For the English king was
anxious to strike a decisive blow against the French crown, and
Frederick's links with Philip of France were well known. John of
England hoped to restore his fortunes in Normandy, and there was
a good chance Otto could draw him into a common campaign.

VI

Frederick was not deluded by his initial success. Yes, the German
populace had greeted him with extraordinary joy and devotion.
In Alsace he was acclaimed with fervour. Here was David set
against Goliath. Here was the pure, innocent child, or *puer
Apuliae*, 'child of Apulia', come to seek his inheritance; his very
existence symbolized the return to justice. The disinherited
orphan, subject of the clauses of Magna Carta in England, was
in this case not a petty vassal whose rights had been expropriated
by a tyrant king (as in England under John), but a genuine king
in his own right, expropriated by the grasping Welf. It was an
easy theme on which to play. Frederick did not mind the epithet
'child'. But he was far from immature in his dealings either with
the German princes or with Philip of France. Here too dramatic
events seemed to enlarge reality: the need for a defensive alliance
against Otto led Frederick to meet Philip's son Louis at Vau-

couleurs. During the journey an attempt was made to assassinate Frederick. Rumour reached Frederick that he was to be murdered in his sleep, so he changed bed, and made a servant sleep in the royal bed instead. The servant was indeed struck down in the night. Even if, as is very possible, this story is an exaggeration or invention, it is evidence that tales of Frederick's miraculous escapes and achievements were being reported world-wide: the author of this story lived in the kingdom of Jerusalem. At Vaucouleurs Frederick received what he required: a promise of joint action against mutual enemies; a considerable amount of money (20,000 marks), not so much for war expenses as to bribe and reward the German princes – war expenses in an indirect form, though, because the princes had the power to command the large armies Frederick could not, on his own, hope to raise.

Formally elected king on 5 December at Frankfurt, Frederick was crowned king of the Romans four days later at Mainz. But it was not with the imperial robes, which were in Otto's hands (whether the 'imperial robes' were the old Norman–Sicilian ones taken by Henry VI, or a German set, it is hard to say); more importantly, the great imperial crown of Otto the Great was with Otto IV, and must if possible be retrieved before coronation in Rome as an emperor. This first coronation was a prelude to Frederick's active war against Otto. The complexion of the struggle changed now; he began to gather his forces around his bases at Hagenau in Alsace, and in the castles of Swabia. The threat from Otto was less urgent, but it had by no means vanished. Not to suppose, however, that the struggle had or would become what Kantorowicz called the famous duel between 'extreme types of the two races', the boorish Welf against the Latinate Frederick. In fact, its climax was reached in a battle fought not between Frederick and Otto but between Philip Augustus and Otto, at Bouvines, just on the German frontier, in 1214. The English forces of King John had already been put to flight, at the hands of Louis son of Philip. Then the Welfs were crushed too. The victory at Bouvines restored French influence in Flanders and consolidated Philip's hold on the lands conquered already from the English. For Germany too, Bouvines was a source of stability. Otto's power crumbled. The duchy of Brabant, which had provided soldiers to Otto, now found itself forced to submit to Frederick. Symbolic, as recent historians have noted, was Philip Augustus' capture of a golden eagle from the baggage of Otto IV. This he passed to Frederick, thereby according the clearest recognition of the new king's status.

But it would be wrong to exaggerate the impact of Bouvines, too. There were areas that resisted Frederick still. Aachen, with the tomb of Charlemagne, ancient seat of the western Roman empire, was one problem; Cologne was another (Otto had gone to ground there), and of course Welf Saxony continued to prefer its home-grown emperor. When Aachen fell with no real struggle in the summer of 1215, Frederick gained the chance to demonstrate publicly the meaning of his kingly authority. On 24 July he entered Aachen; on 25 July he was crowned there. This second coronation was rendered necessary by the tradition that it was here, with the appropriate robes, that the king of the Romans was anointed and crowned; his earlier coronation at Mainz had juridically been acceptable, but it did not visibly establish Frederick in the continuous line of western Roman emperors. One of his symbolic acts was to re-inter the body of Charlemagne himself in a great reliquary of silver and gold, labouring himself alongside the workmen who were installing the new shrine in Aachen cathedral. For here was the figure to whom the western emperors had constantly turned: Otto I, in renewing the empire; Otto III in proclaiming its Roman character; Frederick Barbarossa, in having Charlemagne declared a saint. This link to the heroes of earlier times was reiterated when Frederick issued privileges to the city of Aachen, confirming rights granted originally (so it was said) by Charlemagne.

The avowed intention of becoming the new Charlemagne was announced most clearly at the coronation ceremony itself. For Charlemagne had not merely been, so it was thought, the defender of the papacy and the restorer of imperial dignity in more senses than one. He was also believed to have been an early crusader, hammer of pagans in eastern Europe (including the then-pagan Saxons, ancestors of the Welf dukes!), in Spain, as the Roland legends stated, and in the Holy Land itself. The view of Charlemagne as a model emperor and model crusader deeply influenced Frederick in Aachen; so too the memory of an earlier Frederick, his grandfather, who had died on crusade; so too perhaps the crusading plans of Henry VI, who had seen the strategic value of Apulia and Sicily for the reconquest of the Holy Land. The chronicles profess surprise at the events of the coronation, but in this context surprise seems superfluous. Frederick was determined to show himself as the new Charlemagne. So, after mass was ended, Frederick took the cross and vows, in the manner of a crusader, exhorted his followers to do likewise, and spent the following day, a Sunday, in the cathedral from dawn to dusk, listening to crusade sermons. Both princes and men of lesser standing followed Frederick's lead. What seems plain is that Innocent III was rather less pleased when he heard of these events. The plan had perhaps germinated in Frederick's breast, and the availability of crusade preachers that day is no coincidence. Yet the preachers were not there to address the emperor-elect. Their task was to raise an army for the crusade being planned against Damietta, in the mouth of the Nile: the so-called Fifth Crusade. A later pope remarked that Frederick had acted on his own will, and that he had not sought papal advice; it is quite likely that few in his entourage knew his plans; it is even possible that the idea occurred to him in the intense religious and emotional atmosphere of his coronation service. He had fought for, and recovered, his own inheritance; must he not also fight for Christ's?

And the fact that he was even there in Aachen was itself proof to him of God's blessing. He saw, according to a letter written several years later, a chance 'to repay God for the many gifts bestowed on us'. What substitute could a crusading vow be, he went on to say, for the act of sacrifice on the cross? To struggle for the defence of the Holy Land was the best way, though inadequate in itself, in which he could express his gratitude to God, and at the same time serve God in concrete fashion. The very act of taking the cross, it must be emphasized, had tremendous symbolic importance: the cross of the crusader represented the cross of redemption, raised at Golgotha outside Jerusalem, found again by Constantine's mother near the future Church of the Holy Sepulchre, seized by Saladin, along with Jerusalem itself, in 1187, and, like Jerusalem, in urgent need of recovery. A king who could, with rather little effort, bring most of Germany so rapidly under his command, was duty bound to place at God's disposal the arms, skills, resources he had gathered together.

Yet the taking of the cross is usually seen also as an example of subtle statesmanship. There is a tendency to look for subtle meaning in all Frederick's acts, and this one may be the result of impetuosity or a long-brewed but private passion, rather than of cold calculation. Had he mentioned the scheme to Innocent III when they met in Rome? No doubt it was one among many plans discussed, in a general way: it was a subject on all lips just then. But Innocent was certainly more at ease with the image of the *puer Apuliae*, made king with his encouragement, bound too by concessions concerning Church and secular government in Sicily and Germany. Precisely this image, with which Frederick had been taunted since 1212, seemed shattered by the king's assumption of the cross; and Frederick was probably aware of this. To Philip Augustus' role in crusading would be added that of an even mightier ruler, the emperor-elect. France had long dominated the recruitment of crusaders, despite past Hohenstaufen participation. But the ideal of a crusading emperor, projected also in contemporary oracles and 'prophecies', had not died with Frederick Barbarossa. More significantly, the assumption of the cross without papal approval implied that the leadership of the crusade lay at least as much with the secular arm, in the shape of the emperor, as with the spiritual. Although in canon law it was indeed the pope who proclaimed, and ordered the preaching of, the crusade, there was a well-established tendency for secular rulers, not least Conrad III, to press their own candidature as crusaders even when the papacy counselled them not to participate. Frederick was not, as will be seen, a great respecter of papal control over the crusading movement. Indeed, his assumption of the cross generated such bitter conflict between pope and emperor in the late 1220s that he clearly came to regret his youthful enthusiasm. On the one hand the papacy resented his manner of crusading; on the other hand, the papacy would never let him forget his oath.

VII

Frederick's oath reveals his high optimism. Germany had been won, and pacified, almost at a stroke. This was to underestimate the problems of government in Germany, and a long-standing question has been whether Frederick wished to, or was able to, impose his authority on his new kingdom. The contrast between his meticulous involvement in a programme of government for Sicily and his apparent lack of interest in German affairs has led historians to describe his rule over Germany as an 'abdication'. For Barraclough, he 'deliberately sacrificed' the chance to create a centralized German government, working on the foundations laid by Frederick Barbarossa and his team of *ministeriales*. The early success of Frederick's rule in Alsace, based at Hagenau, is argued to prove that the framework of government survived, ready to be elaborated and exploited. Revenues from the German cities could, by the 1240s, have provided the crown with a solid financial base within Germany. Yet as early as 1213, in the 'Golden Bull of Eger', the new king recognized the exemptions, judicial and fiscal, of the German ecclesiastics; at the same time, he confirmed the rights of the secular princes who had offered him support. In other words, the price paid for his crown was little less than the full authority of that crown. More than that, concessions to the bishops themselves brought under ecclesiastical control some of the richest cities of Germany, at a time of economic expansion and of agitation within the towns for untrammelled city governments on the model of the Italian city-states. Where cities were not under the political control of the bishops, Frederick tended to grant them very favourable concessions; these were the so-called 'imperial cities', whose rights to collect taxes, elect governments and exercise justice were recognized, though not all at once, by the new king. So when it came to episcopal cities, Frederick was content to let the bishops rule; when it came to imperial cities, he was content to let the citizens rule; as for imposition of his own rule, it was neither achieved nor intended. Although he sometimes maintained a watching brief over appointments to high office within the towns, the tone of his policy was exceptionally liberal. Even in Alsace, where his authority seemed so extensive by 1215, he extended the rights of the cities; bestowing, for instance, municipal charters on new towns, such as Colmar. But by 1219 he had brought towns of central Germany, even cities as far east as Nuremberg, under his beneficent patronage.

The apparent contrast between an intended liberality, towards non-episcopal towns such as Nuremberg, and a restrictive conservatism, towards would-be communes in areas under ecclesiastical control, has given rise to much puzzlement. For van Cleve, the liberal approach represents the real Frederick; he simply realized that he could not, in his dealings with the bishops, prejudice the crown's standing by the recognition of town liberties to which the ecclesiastical princes were opposed. The *Confederatio cum principibus ecclesiasticis* of 1220, a decree in which Frederick established virtually unlimited powers of government on the bishops' estates, seems to be the culmination of this policy towards the bishops; Frederick dispensed with his right to levy any new taxes on ecclesiastical lands, to interfere in the succession to fiefs contrary to the bishops' wishes, to build towns or fortresses on episcopal estates. The creation of the territorial principalities, above all those of the Church, seemed to be Frederick's object, either through acceptance of reality, through gratitude to those who had served him, or through impatience to move from Germany to grander matters: his imperial coronation in Rome, his crusade and (not least) the restoration of royal authority in Sicily. At this stage in his life, Frederick seems not to have been terribly interested in the finer details of German politics. Later his son (Henry VII) would begrudge him this attitude. The fact is that his mind was on imperial objectives, in the wider sense: the leadership of Christendom against the infidel, the establishment of the authority of the Caesars across the Christian world, in Lombardy and Sicily too; the creation of a sound *modus vivendi* with the papacy.

Traditionally, Germany had been dominated by the great princes; in a sense that was what Germany was – a large, inchoate kingdom in which the princes held power, and in which one of the greater princes possessed, not for his family but for his lifetime, the crown of the Roman empire. As universal ruler the emperor delegated authority to princes: to the *reguli* or petty kings of England, Castile and elsewhere, and, within the core territories of Germany, to the bishops, dukes and other great lords. The theory of delegation left the emperor as overseer of German affairs, but not as a busybody king in the English or Sicilian mould. Nor would it be right to assume that Frederick's policies in Germany were a sell-out to the papacy, that he was still the pope's king. The German bishops did not possess so consistent a record of loyalty to the papacy; indeed, Frederick seems to have believed that his generosity would bond the bishops more closely to himself, rather than to Rome. However, their increased freedom of action only made them the more choosy. They now saw themselves once again as arbiters of the great issues that faced Germany and the empire: relations between Frederick and the papacy; even (by the 1240s) the continued recognition of Frederick as king.

Yet it is also clear that Frederick intended to make the empire the real focus of his policy. Sicily remained a source of worry – he had left the kingdom before real order had been imposed; there were still German war-lords on the loose; the Genoese were abusing their rights; but he was still prepared to accept papal demands for a separation of Sicily from the empire, during 1216. His aim, he said, was to aid both the Church and the Sicilian kingdom; he would therefore abandon Sicily to his son Henry, already crowned in early infancy, and he would place the government of Sicily in the hands of a papally appointed guardian. This declaration to Innocent III is all the more surprising, for several reasons. Frederick's own experiences as a child had shown how little effect papal rule over Sicily and southern Italy might have. Second, there are signs that Frederick was also hoping Henry would be crowned as his heir in Germany. To some extent, the concessions to the German princes were intended to secure their support for recognition of Henry as co-king. Yet it would be wrong to see here a Machiavellian exercise of deceit. In 1216, the outlook was promising, but the skies were not yet clear. Otto IV lived on. The proffered aid of the German princes needed to be tested again, in the final destruction of the Welfs. The presence of an alternative monarch on German soil, even if he had been run to ground in Saxony, was a source of concern.

Of course, then, Frederick worked to ensure the recognition of a Hohenstaufen succession. His own crusade plans, or involvement in northern Italy and Sicily, might take him away from Germany for years. He must find a means to retain German loyalties. Prince Henry was one among the means. On the other hand, he did not abandon his father's principles. He insisted to Innocent that the *regno* was not united with the empire; they were separate entities, and it was therefore proper that they should not even be held in personal union. Only the second part of this statement exceeds Henry VI's policy. But the statement as a whole was also a clear denunciation of the act whereby Otto IV had sought to quell pope and Hohenstaufen at once: Otto's invasion of Sicily, on the grounds that it was actually part of the empire. Frederick's success in Germany left Innocent with the Welf problem in re-verse: Otto had threatened to conquer Sicily from a power base in Germany; now Frederick had conquered, or gained mastery over, Germany, moving north from Sicily. Innocent could only con-template such an event if he had assurance that the union of crowns was only temporary. It made sense for Frederick's only son (so far) to inherit Sicily, where hereditary succession under papal suzerainty seemed better established; the future of Germany would depend on Frederick's fertility, on papal influence in Ger-many and, not least, on the German princes, ecclesiastical and lay.

An example of the way Frederick successfully bought support is provided by his relationship with the king of Denmark, Val-demar. In 1214 Frederick ceded the rights of the German monarchy over the borderlands of Schleswig, or Slesvig, which were in any case under Danish occupation. This was another example of the recognition of reality. But it proved to have more subtle aspects too: the support of the Danes enabled Fred-erick to put pressure on the power base of the Welfs in northern Germany. Around Bremen and the estuaries of northern Germany the struggle between Welfs and Hohenstaufen (plus Danes) intensified from 1216 onwards. What was important was not so much a final blow against Otto, but success in pinning him down to a restricted area in the north, where he could not interfere with Frederick's successes further south: the assumption of Hohenstaufen control in the north of Switzerland, on the Zähringen estates, and the building of Hohenstaufen influence in the Low Countries and Lorraine. To some extent, the questions here were local dynastic ones, and, whereas a few years before rival claimants might have appealed for, and won, Welf or Hohenstaufen aid, the capacity of Otto to intervene had now been decisively limited. Germany was not, then, peaceful, but the great contest for the throne was now only confined to the north-east. Nor was Otto so firm in his own resolve. In May 1218, mortally ill, he instructed his elder brother, Henry, to keep the symbols of imperial power, including the holy lance and the crown of Otto the Great, but to pass them twenty weeks after his death to the elected choice of the German princes. If the German princes elected no successor, but accepted Frederick of Hohenstaufen, so be it. Henry of Brunswick proved dilatory: the imperial emblems were thought to have a special importance, for their possession sanctified and brought prestige to the ruler. But by summer of 1217 Frederick had obtained their surrender. Soldier of the cross, future deliverer of Jerusalem, he now possessed the lance which (it was said) had pierced the side of Christ at the crucifixion; while the imperial crown of the Ottonian emperors, adorned with enamels recalling David and Solomon, worn by his father and grandfather, now rested in Frederick's hands. But not yet on his head.

Now there were two great objectives: one, the crowning in Rome, with the newly won crown itself. The second, the crusade. Both closely involved the pope; and Innocent III was no longer pope. His successor, Honorius III, was generally a conciliatory figure, clear about papal rights, but reasonably satisfied that he and Frederick could work closely together for the good of Christendom. He seems to have been less sure about Frederick's desire to lead a crusade, though any reluctance stemmed from highly practical motives: Frederick was clearly tied up in Germany, unable to organize a massive expedition at once; and the future of the Latin states in the east was a matter of extreme urgency. Frederick II could not play the part of Frederick I, the crusading emperor who had made his peace with his subjects and with the papacy. Frederick II's tasks were inside Europe, not beyond it. What he could provide was material aid. The Fifth Crusade had made a good start, even without Frederick's leadership; it had captured its first objective, Damietta, but there had followed dissent among the crusaders about the way to follow this victory through. By December 1218, Frederick himself was so anxious about the crusade's future that he informed the princes that he intended to leave Germany for the east some time next year. A diet was called at Magdeburg, for March 1219, to appoint a regent during his absence.

It was simply impossible to balance the desperate needs of the Latin East against the constant distractions of Germany. No Magdeburg meeting was held, though Frederick maintained close contact with the princes for another end: the election of Henry his son as German king. It is too easy to see this as an attempt to set the crusade on one side because at long last the political climate seemed right for the election. But the election, given the dangers of the expedition to the East, made sense: the new German king might never return from Egypt or Syria, and, as has been seen, there was a strong desire, going back generations, to ensure a Hohenstaufen succession. Frederick was, indeed, so keen to encourage the crusade that he invited the pope to excommunicate those who did not fulfil their crusade vows; a deadline of 24 June 1219 was suggested. Unfortunately, Frederick himself was in danger of falling foul of this provision; even in 1220 he was still not ready for the expedition, and Honorius III reminded him what the consequences of a breach of his vow could be. Later popes were to remember this discussion with glee. Yet it is clear that Frederick's failure to depart was not the result of evaporation of his early enthusiasm. The German king was all the more anxious to win recognition of Henry as his heir. Until that was achieved, the crusade seemed to him far too risky, at least for Germany. He managed only in 1220, when bombarded with papal demands for action, to wring from his German magnates general recognition of Henry. By now, the position in Damietta was desperate. The city, though still in crusader hands, was threatened by the armies of the sultan of Egypt, al-Kamil, and it was unclear how long it could hold out. The crusaders had rejected an extraordinarily generous offer from al-Kamil, under which the sultan would trade Damietta for Jerusalem itself and for the rest of the Latin kingdom as it had been before Saladin's victory in 1187. They had been so confident of the force of their arms when they won Damietta; but now it seemed all would be lost.

Frederick's answer was twofold. He must hurry on with his work in Germany, in order to secure the unqualified aid of the German princes during his absence. Only after ensuring that the country was immune from the danger of a Welf revival or civil war could Frederick leave for the East. Second, he must send what aid he could to the East, now, in 1220. It has already been seen that the *Confederatio* of 1220, also known as the 'Privilege in Favour of the Ecclesiastical Princes', was an attempt to ensure German peace, by guaranteeing the loyalty of the bishops – the very element that might, at a time of disputed election or rebellion, have the greatest power to influence loyalties in Germany, not just through the prince-electors but through the *scriptoria* and propaganda machinery of abbeys and sees. The essence of the privilege was the acceptance by Frederick of the principle that he had no real right of interference in the administration of, and succession to, ecclesiastical estates in Germany. Church courts, the seizure or even temporary management of property during vacancies, rights of control over sub-vassals, the operation of mints and the levy of commercial taxes: these were long-standing areas of disagreement. The ecclesiastical princes gained all the rights of jurisdiction and fiscal control for which they had hoped. For many, this was simply to see confirmed, in an imperial edict, individual privileges granted during the Welf–Hohenstaufen struggle, or rights obtained by long usage during decades of near anarchy. Too much should not, therefore, be made of Frederick's concessions. The ecclesiastical principalities were a reality; he could do very little to restrict their liberties, unless he wished to sacrifice their political support. Nor would it be right to see in his concessions an attempt to placate the papacy, irate at the delays in crusading, or to ensure that – if trouble brewed between pope and king – the bishops would side with him against Honorius. Frederick had convinced himself that Church control of key towns and regions in Germany was a permanent and acceptable feature of German government; he believed too, in 1220, that the defence of Church rights within Germany was precisely what his imperial office (soon formally to be acquired) demanded of him. Again and again his letters to Rome, or his privileges to the bishops, speak of his desire 'to look after the interests of the Roman Church', 'to preserve and enforce rights on behalf of the Church'. A new era had dawned, of cooperation between pope and emperor-elect, between king of Germany and German bishops.

It was not Frederick's powerlessness that was in his mind when he issued his *Confederatio* privilege; though powerless he may seem. It was his role as prince of peace, reconciling Church and secular government, as temporal sword acting on behalf of the spiritual, as protector of the Church alongside his spiritual father the pope. And as crusading emperor, too, winning a long-needed victory for Christendom. But such objectives were easier to proclaim than to fulfil. As for the crusade, Frederick's supply of aid was limited and tardy. It cannot have been easy to organize a fleet; the privateer Henry Count of Malta travelled north to Germany in 1218, by way of his home-city of Genoa, and it appears that the pirate and Frederick discussed the crusade at some length. Henry already had experience of the east Mediterranean shores. The Genoese annalist, predictably, stresses Frederick's willingness to confirm his city's privileges for trade in Sicily, and makes it appear that Henry's task was concerned with the propagation of Genoese trade. Unlikely: Henry emerged from Germany as 'Admiral of the Marine Fleet' of Sicily, and in 1221 went to Damietta with Walter of Palear. But this was after excessive delays – Damietta fell moments before their ships loomed into view.

Frederick's commitment to the crusade, expressed in the appointment of Henry as his admiral, is not in doubt. But his ability to achieve great victories in the East would depend on much more than his own enthusiasm. In 1215 it had seemed that a mass crusade could be unleashed under his patronage, not unlike the great twelfth-century crusades (including Barbarossa's). Only in 1212, the Children's Crusade, an apocalyptically inspired expedition of the poor, the 'innocent' and the young, had revealed the strength of popular devotion to the name Jerusalem. By 1220 Frederick was faced with an issue of different character. The great movement for the liberation of Jerusalem, encompassing all of Europe's knighthood and countless other enthusiasts for the holy war, had not taken off. A carefully planned crusade with defined military objectives, the Fifth Crusade, had become bogged down, literally, in the Nile delta. This contrast between the ideals of 1215 and the realities of 1220 holds valid not merely for the crusade itself, but for Frederick. The idealistic *puer Apuliae* who had excited such devotion in 1215 was now the unchallenged ruler of most of Germany, but issues concerning the nature of his authority, his relationship to his subjects, his role as arbiter in disputes between the nobles, were only gradually coming into focus. By 1220 Frederick had become profoundly conscious of the differences between his actual power within Germany and his potential power within a restructured Sicilian absolutist state.

CHAPTER FOUR

##

ROMAN EMPEROR, DEFENDER OF THE CHURCH, 1220–27

I

The expedition to Rome, to receive the imperial crown, was blocked by only one major problem: the continuing opposition of several Lombard cities, not least Milan, which had been strong supporters of Otto IV since 1212 or before. Milan was placed under the imperial ban in 1213; that is to say, its citizens were liable to confiscation of their goods, and its government was treated as a rebel one with whom Frederick was not prepared directly to negotiate. On the other hand Frederick was well aware that his imperial expedition was in jeopardy so long as a group of pro-Welf cities agitated in Italy. Two events made Frederick's journey easier. The death of Otto IV meant that the Lombard opposition had no real focus for its resistance to Frederick; no longer could the Milanese and their friends pose as the defenders of the rights of the true emperor, Otto the Welf, against the pope's protégé. Second, the papacy achieved some success as mediator between Frederick and the Lombard opposition. This was a slow process; and, precisely because a solution was reached in stages, the Lombards became reconciled to the new reality. A series of papal legates first ensured the support of the traditionally pro-Hohenstaufen towns of which Cremona was the most powerful, and then turned attention to the Milan-centred bloc of cities. The papal legates naturally saw the achievement of peace as the main end: if the Lombard towns could end their petty wars, exchange prisoners and agree to settle their disputes without recourse to arms, the prime objective had surely been achieved. In December 1218 it was already clear that the Lombard opposition was prepared to accept papal guidance: Milan and Cremona made peace. But Frederick's outlook was different. For him the question of Lombardy was not simply one of a truce among the towns. Order could only be achieved by the act of recognition of his higher authority, for he was the source of order, as emperor-elect. He expected the Lombards to acknowledge him as rightful king of the Romans. In doing this, the Lombards did not exercise any constitutive authority; they merely recognized the reality of his election and coronation in Germany. In other words, it was the difference between a mere cease-fire and an act of submission. But even the Milanese came round to Frederick. In 1219 and 1220 they were suspicious of his intentions, but they could not identify any very controversial demands, fiscal or political, that he was making upon them.

A continuing source of opposition lay further south, in the former Matildine lands of Tuscany. In Florence an ugly murder supposedly took place around 1215, reopening the rift between Guelfs and Ghibellines: the Buondelmonte murder, if a historical event, really concerned the rivalry for political influence of the great aristocratic clans, one of which, that of the Uberti, railed at the insult offered by a young knight who had accepted and then rejected an offer of marriage into the Uberti clientèle. Local issues may have been at stake, but from then onwards Florence became a battleground of pro-Hohenstaufen and pro-Welf factions. Neither faction cared much for the rights of the papacy; the main aim was to assert the autonomy of the city-state from outside interference of any sort, and Frederick was accorded little recognition in Tuscany. But it would be wrong to suppose this mattered very much. Of the Tuscan towns in the early thirteenth century, only Pisa and Lucca possessed political and economic influence to rival the power of the Italian towns further north; Siena was a growing commercial and financial centre; Florence was only at the very beginning of a phase of startling economic growth that reached its peak decades after Frederick II's death in 1250. What mattered to Frederick was the attitude of the Lombards, whose towns were bigger, richer, more numerous; and whose towns already possessed an unfortunate tradition of successful resistance to imperial authority.

Frederick's anxiety not to irritate the north Italians during his coronation journey had several motives. He did not want to stir up Lombardy when his main objective was Rome, and the main function of the expedition was the winning of wide prestige through the assumption of the imperial crown. Would-be Holy Roman Emperors generally wore (figurative) velvet gloves when they travelled south for coronation; and Frederick, impatient to organize his crusade, was no exception. Second, he was keen to revisit, and bring back to order, the kingdom of Sicily, from which he had been absent for eight years. He was thus conciliatory both to the pope and to the towns. He accepted papal representations about the future status of the Matildine lands, but agreed only to a temporary solution: the papacy was to manage the central Italian estates until a final agreement could be reached. As Frederick marched south across the Alps in 1220, his conciliatory attitude, to pope and to cities, assured him a smooth road. Here, indeed, was a striking contrast to the events of 1212, when the road north had been blocked by his enemies. But in 1220 he avoided recriminations.

Naturally, he was anxious also to show his resolve: he was not a papal puppet, and the existence of polite public disagreement with Honorius III was a good way to display his energy and independence. At Bologna he had to face a series of complaints from the pope's emissaries: why have you allowed young Henry to be elected king of the Romans against the pope's will? Do not forget your promise to separate the German and Sicilian crowns! Why have you not yet organized your much-awaited crusade? Some historians, bestowed with hindsight, have seen here the first outbreak of a quarrel that was to wrack the empire throughout the 1220s. Yet it has to be said that Frederick's policy concerning the two crowns was still very fluid. He had not re-established his authority in Sicily; he could not be sure of his return from the crusade; he had not made up his mind – perhaps he never did so – what was the standing of Sicily in relation to the Roman empire: was it an integral part? Was his simply a personal union of crowns? Nor had he, in 1220, resolved to use his rule over Germany and southern Italy to squeeze the papacy, the Lombard cities, the Tuscan towns, so hard that they would submit to his will. These were open, undetermined, even indeterminate questions; and we should not look for a Hohenstaufen master-plan in 1220. It is precisely Frederick's inconsistencies in his dealings with Honorius III that reveal his uncertainty about the nature and extent of imperial authority in Italy. Among these inconsistencies: yes, he did accord the title of duke of Spoleto to Rainald, son of one of the German war-lords, and yet Spoleto was part of the Patrimony of St Peter. But, as Frederick pointed out, in imperial practice it was quite common to hold a title without extensive lands in the region referred to (Henry, count of Malta kept the title even when he lost the island, for instance). Another problem: he had invited the Sicilian magnates to the imperial coronation, and expected them to renew their fealty to him in Rome. Here emerges a crucial difficulty. On the one hand he wanted to seize a chance to bind to him a group of his subjects notorious for their unruliness: when better than the moment he appeared before the world arrayed in all his glory, as successor to Constantine and Charlemagne? On the other hand, the universalist claims of the Holy Roman Emperors made it seem obvious that, even if Sicily were a *corpus separatum*, it was still a 'separate body' under the ultimate authority of God's vice-regent on earth, the Roman emperor. Needless to say, this view also conflicted with papal insistence that the Sicilian kingdom was a vassal state of St Peter. The conflict between Sicilian auton-omy and vassal status had not been resolved during the twelfth century, except temporarily on Constance's death-bed; it could hardly be resolved at a stroke in 1220, when a new factor, the elevation of the Sicilian ruler to the German and imperial thrones, also intruded itself.

That Frederick's mind was turning more and more to Sicily is revealed by an incident that occurred when he had reached the territory of Bologna. Ambassadors arrived from Genoa, the city that had benefited most from the chaos after Henry VI's death. First there had been the installation of a line of Genoese counts on Malta and Gozo, which were part of the royal demesne in Sicily. Then there had been the massive concession of tax exemption by Markward von Anweiler in 1200. There had been the seizure of Syracuse from a rival pirate force of Pisans, by Henry of Malta and his friend Alamanno da Costa, 'count of Syracuse'. There had also been the confirmation of Sicilian trading privileges by

Frederick II, when he reached Genoa in 1212, on his way to Germany. By 1220, however, his gratitude seemed to be gone: the hospitality of 1212 could not be traded upon for ever by Genoa. Frederick told the Genoese ambassadors that he could only confirm their privileges in the empire, that is, in Germany and Lombardy. Sicilian matters would be left on one side until he was in Sicily; that, he insisted, was the proper place to look into their Sicilian trade privileges. The Genoese rightly saw this as a blatant threat to their extraordinary status in Sicilian trade, and their support for Frederick cooled dramatically. But the incident is interesting for another reason, too. Whereas Frederick had mingled affairs of Sicily and of empire in his invitation to the southern magnates to come to the Roman coronation, he continued to separate affairs of Sicily and of empire in his dealings with the Genoese. If Frederick saw Sicily merely as a subsidiary crown within his empire, it is very odd that he should refuse to recognize Genoese rights in Sicily on the grounds he cited. Of course, he was playing for time too: he wanted to keep the question of Genoese rights open until he was able, by direct action on the soil of Sicily, to discipline the Genoese and other lords of misrule.

There is thus no reason to doubt the sincerity of Frederick's protestations to the pope that he intended to maintain a separation between Sicily and the empire. But what the papacy envisaged was a total divorce of the crowns; what Frederick envisaged was a personal union, in which his universal authority as Roman emperor would provide a loose blanket of authority over Sicily. There were still uncertainties here, because the constitutional standing of the *regno* was a matter of such ancient dispute. Trying, however, to appease papal fears, Frederick announced a further set of promises, as soon as he had reached Rome in November 1220. From his camp on Monte Mario, on the outskirts of the imperial city, looking down on the Constantinian basilica of St Peter and on the great works of his own predecessors, the Caesars, Frederick assured Honorius that the crown of Sicily would never be united with that of the empire; that he recognized for all time the dependence of Sicily not on the empire but on the see of Rome; that he would maintain an entirely separate bureaucracy in Sicily, which would have no imperial brief, and vice versa;

that the kingdom of Sicily had been obtained by his father in right of the Norman princess Constance, and that it had not been conquered as part of the Roman empire. Once again, these promises echo the fears the papacy had felt when Otto IV had revived twelfth-century German claims that Sicily was no more than a wayward fragment of the Italian lands of the Roman empire. But what is clear from Frederick's promises is that he wished to maintain the personal union of empire and Sicily, that he was unrepentant at the naming of Henry as heir to both Germany and Sicily, that he saw in a broader sense his imperial authority as a universal corrective agency, comprehending all secular kingdoms irrespective of the legal niceties that in Sicily and elsewhere tied their rulers to the pope. As Roman emperor his authority was general, just as the pope's authority to correct sinners was not restricted solely to those princes, such as the kings of Aragon or of England, who held their crown from the pope. A letter of February 1221 in which Frederick rejoices in his newly won imperial power, portrays the emperor as the chosen of God, whose duty it is to serve God in heart, mind and with all possible strength. This is the language of universalism, expressed by a ruler who accepts no qualifications of his authority.

The imperial coronation took place in St Peter's on 22 November 1220. The city of Rome was more peaceful that day than it usually was for this occasion: in Rome at least faction struggles between Guelfs and Ghibellines were not visible. The day proceeded smoothly from the moment Frederick left Monte Mario to enter the city; he did not linger there, out of respect for papal rights within Rome – a paradox indeed, that the seat of empire was also the city where the emperor's presence was least encouraged. In St Peter's all the controversial symbolism of an imperial coronation was played through: the promise to protect the Church, the offer of tribute to the Church, the act of confession to the Cardinal-Bishop of Ostia, with normal consecrated oil, on his arms and on his shoulders. Some have seen in the absence of use of chrism, and in the omission of unction on the head, a papal attempt to diminish the importance of the imperial coronation (not new in 1220: this form of coronation ceremony had been practised since the eleventh century). On the other hand, the constitutive act in a coronation, the anointing of the ruler, had already been carried out in Germany; Frederick was already raised higher than ordinary man by his coronation as king of the Romans; too much may have been made by historians of the significance of the more modest form of unction practised in Rome. For when he reached Rome he was already a king, and the purpose of the ceremony was to elevate him from the status of territorial *rex* to universal emperor. The ordinary niceties of unction did not apply here. What mattered was the stage in the ceremonies when the new emperor was displayed before the people: mitred and crowned, with Otto I's ancient diadem, carrying sceptre, orb and sword, symbols of his right to rule, his universal authority, and his corrective power in temporal matters. At the end of the ceremony, there was the controversial act when the emperor held the pope's stirrup to allow the pontiff to mount his horse, and then led the mounted horse a few paces. This, as Barbarossa had in the past realized, could be taken to symbolize the junior standing of emperor as against pope; to recall Innocent III's words, the natural seniority of the spiritual power against the temporal. But the main aim of any emperor-elect was to have himself crowned emperor as soon as possible by the leading spiritual figure in the world, and the subtleties of the ceremony, though not lost on the emperors, were easily disregarded amid the winning of prestige as successor to the Caesars.

Frederick seized the chance of the coronation to affirm again his crusading vows. By 1220 the papacy was fully reconciled to his earlier wish to go on crusade, for the continuing difficulties of the armies at Damietta made Frederick's departure all the more urgent. It is thus clear that – whatever Innocent III's doubts at Frederick's crusading plans – the papal curia now keenly wished the crusade to go ahead; and it saw the crusade as Frederick's first major act as emperor. He was to leave for the east by August 1221, and meanwhile he was to send help to the beleaguered armies. Frederick's willingness to cooperate with the papacy is indicated by his other actions, too. He issued a decree, the *Constitutio in Basilica Beati Petri*, in celebration of his imperial coronation, which guaranteed to the full the liberties of the Church: ecclesiastics were to be freed from the jurisdiction of secular courts, and they were to be free from secular taxation too. Measures were to be taken against heretics, above all confiscation of their property and expulsion from the lands where they lived. The *Constitutio* adds little new to the promises made already to the papacy; its importance lies in the fact that it was issued at the coronation, as the first act of the new emperor; and its unmistakable message was concord between papacy and empire. Frederick's peccadilloes in encouraging his son's election in Germany, or in inviting Sicilians to his coronation in Rome, must be set against the clear signs of willingness to work alongside the Roman Church, in defence of ecclesiastical liberties, of peace and of the Holy Land. Not to deny, however, that there were secular dimensions too to the decrees, whose common characteristic was protection of the defenceless against seizure or usurpation: the pilgrim and traveller, at the mercy of both bandits and tax-inspectors; the merchant not least, whose rights over salvage after shipwreck were re-affirmed; the peasant, whose ability to defend his right to land was weakest, not least in thirteenth-century Italy, where major changes in the nature of land-holding and succession rights were gaining ground. Here, then, was the clearest expression of Frederick's programme, offering peace and security to all subjects, while honouring the Church.

II

And so southwards to Sicily. Here Frederick seems to have been confident of his ability to restore order. Once again in his career, the act of coronation had projected an image, true or false, of a ruler without equal, a determined monarch with a mission to restore order. In 1220 the very proclamation of peace would be enough to obtain peace, with rather little material backing. Some pressure had already been placed on the German war-lords of southern Italy by loyal officials of the Sicilian crown, between 1212 and 1220, but Frederick now proposed to destroy entirely the illicit power of those who had seized lands and rights during his minority. He had barely entered the kingdom of Sicily, when, at Capua, he issued a series of decrees intended to restore royal power rapidly and effectively (December 1220). The 'Assizes of Capua' are a combination of Norman legislation and a sort of practical conservatism: by going back to the system of government in the late twelfth century, and by sweeping aside the abuses of the last twenty-two years, Frederick sought to re-establish the Sicilian monarchy in the spirit that it had been exercised by Roger II and William II. The wording of the Capua assizes is often based upon that of the Norman assizes. Justification for his decrees was sought, too, in the statements of principle enunciated by earlier kings of Sicily: the crown was henceforth to control succession to fiefs, and marriages by the barons must be licensed by the king. Subinfeudation, the granting out of land by a baron to a vassal, was henceforth to be permitted only with royal approval. Just as the royal estates must not be diminished, so must not the baronial. But it was on the royal estates that Frederick knew the problems were greatest: much land, he complained in the assizes, had been unjustly seized by those who took advantage of his childhood; and the royal seals had been misused, not least by Markward von Anweiler, who had claimed the right to act on behalf of Henry VI and Constance. The king-emperor therefore insisted that privileges granted since the death of William the Good in 1189 should be surrendered for scrutiny; legitimate privileges would, of course, be confirmed (justice, not vengeance, was the order of the day); but barons who failed to submit their charters for examination by the set dates would simply lose whatever rights they claimed, automatically. This was hardly an act of tyranny. Western rulers since the twelfth century had seen the confirmation of privileges as a very handy way to achieve a number of objectives. First, the re-issue of charters cost the beneficiary a fee; the crown would make much money from its policy. Second, here was a chance for loyalists to identify themselves and for the opposition to declare itself: those who defied the king now could be singled out for punishment, if necessary by military means. Third, much land could and would be brought back to the crown (amid occasional displays of generosity by the king, calculated to win friends); thus the crown's fiscal position, and its resources in knights owing military service, would be enhanced at a stroke. Among other rulers who

insisted on the confirmation of privileges had been Richard I
of England and Roger II of Sicily. Henry II of England had,
from 1154, pursued a similar policy of demanding also the cession of 'adulterine castles', built without licence during the
years of disorder preceding his accession. Here, as in England,
royal policy proved very effective: the sheer presence of the
king-emperor on south Italian soil generated a political earth-
quake; castles were surrendered, often without real struggle.
The mere declaration of law was frequently enough to achieve
results, in those heady days after the assizes of Capua; and, if
not, it was sufficient to parade the royal army under the
battlements. Southern Italy bowed before its ruler, either
exhausted by years of misrule or cowed by his successes and
prestige.

The assizes of Capua expressed concern, too, for the old
Norman system of government, which still creaked on in
Palermo. There was nothing fundamentally new in Frederick's
insistence that the crown was the fount of justice, and that the
king would approve the appointment of judicial officials, other
than whom none might function, and to whom all respect was
due, as extensions of the king's own person. Another much-
vaunted principle of Norman government, revived by Frederick,
was the suppression of urban autonomy. The Campanian and
Apulian towns had received generous privileges since Tancred's
day, and, although they did not possess the independence of the
Lombard cities, they elected their own consuls or governments.
Frederick, acting in the spirit both of Roger II and of Frederick I,
announced that appointments were to be made henceforth by
the crown; the towns were thus re-integrated into the royal
system of justice and taxation. The fiscal motive may have been
very pressing here: Frederick took pains to forbid the continuation of new tax systems, developed in the towns since
William II's death; probably what he had in mind was levies for
the benefit of the city government or for that of private individuals. For the moment he would not even sanction the use of
new ports and roads; these too needed to be brought under the
authority of the royal customs officers, and the right to build and
maintain these facilities was seen in Sicily, as very often elsewhere,
as a royal prerogative. For roads and ports were part of the *bona*

publica, open facilities, access to or along which should depend
on royal protection and sanction. Thus under the Normans the
roads of Apulia had been famous for their safety and utility. It
was this combination of order and fiscal advantage that dominated Frederick's assizes.

If we want to see these provisions seriously put into operation,
then Frederick's policy towards the Genoese offers clear evidence
of his methods. The Capua assizes put an end to Genoese claims
to special status; the Genoese were clearly among those who had
taken full advantage of the minority to enhance their rights in
Sicily, with Markward's collusion; they had freely operated their
own tax system, producing no revenue for the crown and simply
providing for the running costs of their colonies in the *regno*.
As for Syracuse, it had been used as a base in Genoa's war for the
conquest of Crete: a war in which Sicilian interests counted not
at all. During 1220 and 1221, the erosion of Genoese status
proceeded apace. Alamanno da Costa was kicked out, as were
other Genoese leaders, and property was expropriated, including warehouses and, quite possibly, country estates. Frederick's
attitude to Genoa was surely conditioned entirely by the feeling
that the Genoese had exploited his youth quite ruthlessly. He
did not take political considerations into account; he was so
confident of his ascendancy that he was not greatly worried at
the prospect of losing an influential ally in northern Italy.
Besides, as many Mediterranean rulers were aware, the best
way to dispense with the demands of the Genoese was simply
to shower favour on their inveterate rivals, the Pisans, or their
newer foes, the Venetians, who had recently won Crete from
Genoese control. Equally, there was no need to bestow on Pisa
or Venice privileges as generous as those the Genoese had
plucked from Markward; Pisa had supported Otto the Welf,
and was glad to win any favours from Frederick; nor is it
clear that he permitted the Pisans special trading rights in Sicily
itself, though he did permit free trade in northern Italy and
Germany where in any case the towns were free to ignore
Frederick's command, since they and not he controlled the levy
of taxes.

From Capua, Frederick zigzagged across southern Italy, visiting parts of the kingdom he knew hardly or not at all. No doubt

his love of Apulia, the low-lying south-east of Italy, dates from this period. But his target was Sicily, and in Spring 1221 he reached Messina. Here too he issued a series of important assizes. Here too the spirit of legislation was partly that of the Norman monarchy he was seeking to restore, firmly rooted in the law-codes of the late Roman empire. Yet in fact the canon-law origin of his Messina decrees is their central feature: at first glance, their content, as reported by Frederick's chronicler Riccardo di San Germano, seems trivial. There are laws against gambling and against jesting. Gambling encouraged blasphemy, and, while gambling itself was not forbidden, it must be con-ducted in a seemly fashion. Such blasphemy could earn the loss of one's tongue or worse. Two other laws concerned Jews and prostitutes. Both were to wear distinctive (though different) clothes, and male Jews must grow their beards; prostitutes must live outside the city walls, though they could visit towns and on one day each week they could be admitted to the public baths. There was indeed a connection between Frederick's policy to-wards Jews and towards prostitutes. Both were groups of out-siders who threatened, in his view (or rather that of his late Roman and canonist sources), to 'contaminate' the Christian society in which they lived. They must therefore be made visible, and restrictions on their free contact with the rest of society would help to preserve the moral health of that society. This legislation raises other questions, too. Frederick's tolerance to-wards the Jews, praised by many historians, seems called into doubt. He was, of course, reiterating ecclesiastical legislation, published at the Fourth Lateran Council of 1215; it is hard to say whether the Jews were really obliged to wear the murky gar-ments the laws described; and religious Jews were probably already distinctive in Sicily by their hairstyles, clothes and use of Arabic in daily speech. In the thirteenth-century Mediterranean, Christian and Islamic, the wearing of distinctive costume was not always seen as a disability, except among the very rich and in-fluential, who could anyway buy their freedom from the law. But why legislate against Jews when Sicily possessed (at least before 1200) a much larger community of Muslims? In fact, Frederick was about to develop a singularly harsh policy for his Muslim subjects too. More important was the idea that had

germinated in Frederick's entourage of the kingdom of Sicily as
a Christian state, whose non-Christian subjects, or those who
acted in a non-Christian manner (like the prostitutes) were the
outcasts of society; they could never fully participate in the state,
and were believed to be a danger to its moral fabric. So they
must be marked. Another connection between Jews and prostitutes was a concern that sinful sexual liaisons should be controlled: Christian must not marry or have sexual intercourse
with Jew; prostitutes, while a by-product of human lust, were
also a source of fornication and sin. In fact, the emperor's policy
towards the Jews, from one kingdom to another and one decade
to another, was not very consistent. In Germany they were 'serfs
of the royal chamber', technically under the ruler's protection; in
Sicily, by 1231, elaborate legislation was issued to protect, up to
a point, moneylending by Jews. And at the same time Frederick
made use of Jewish men of science at court. Once again, it would
be wrong to look too hard for signs of consistency, still less of
toleration in a modern sense. Roman law, everyday practice and
the needs of science diverged rather than converged.

As for the Muslims: they too were a matter for concern, once
Frederick landed in Sicily. Their revolt against the crown really
began in the years around Frederick's birth, and had continued
ever since. The original sources of tension included the disbanding
of their semi-autonomous region in western Sicily, which was
largely handed to the abbey of Monreale by William the Good,
as well as the steady pressure on Muslims to convert to Christianity. Already in the twelfth century there was a stream of Muslim
converts, though many, strangely enough, became Greek Orthodox rather than Latins. By the early thirteenth century, Islam
was confined mainly to the west of Sicily, to the Monreale estates
and the area between Girgenti and the coast: here Muslim guerrillas waged a running battle against the ecclesiastical authorities
and the central administration. They even minted their own
coins, the clearest possible defiance of the commands of the
Norman assizes. The archbishops of Monreale were rightly concerned at the depredation of their estates. Moreover, the Muslims
had involved themselves in wider political issues: they had
supported Markward von Anweiler, so that they too could be
classed among the malevolent exploiters of Frederick's youth;

they had links with North African emirs, who supplied arms, funds and even manpower. They were irredentist, and their methods appalled Frederick. By 1219 Girgenti had become a refuge and focus of resistance for the Saracens: Christian churches were reduced to ruins, and on one occasion the bishop himself fell into the hands of the Muslim rebels. Under these circumstances Frederick could not pursue his Capuan policy: it was not enough to legislate, to appear in his glory, to intimidate by a display of his majesty. Naturally, he confirmed the rights of the cathedral of Monreale over the western Sicilian estates, but this action could not in itself restore order. He must lead an army against the infidel. It is interesting that he did not request the pope to declare his war a crusade for the defence of Christendom. For he saw the Saracen revolt as an act of treason against the crown no less than as a threat to Christianity in Sicily. Nor, indeed, had the papacy succeeded in its own limited efforts to quell the Muslims, in the days of Markward von Anweiler.

There were two measures that had to be taken. One, to seize the Saracen strongholds within Sicily. The other, to prevent further aid coming from Africa. In 1222 Frederick launched an assault upon Iato, where the leader of the revolt, Benaveth, or ibn Abbad, was holed up. Isolated, ibn Abbad surrendered after an eight-week siege. He was taken to Frederick's pavilion, a prisoner. There he fell on his face, begging the emperor's pardon. But Frederick, furious at the Saracen's past treason, dug his spur into the side of the prostrate rebel and tore his body open. Ibn Abbad survived; but within a week he was hanged at Palermo, alongside two merchants of Marseilles, shady characters who had aided the Muslims, and who may even have been responsible for the sale as slaves of the young participants in the Children's Crusade, a decade earlier. The destruction of the Muslim leadership was an important achievement. There had long existed an alternative, Muslim, dynasty in western Sicily, the ibn Hammuds, whose leadership of the Saracen community had been respected by the early Norman kings. By 1222 the continued survival of a focus of Muslim opposition could not be tolerated. Moreover, the outrages committed by the Saracens were a matter of genuine concern: they were thirteenth-century irredentists, political cause and all.

And, like more recent guerrilas, North Africa supplied them with hearty encouragement. In 1223 Frederick II sent ships against Jerba, the island off the coast of Tunisia that had long supplied much of this aid. It was a notorious nest of pirates, and in the 1130s Roger II had seized the place, to protect the south of Sicily from lightning raids and to guarantee the security of shipping in the central Mediterranean. It was a fertile spot, and its large and ancient Jewish community seems to have been skilled in agriculture, especially the cultivation of indigo, dates and semi-luxury foodstuffs. Frederick II's capture of Jerba was eventually followed by an invitation to these and other North African Jews to settle in Sicily, and to introduce their skills there. Many did so. But Frederick did not, at this stage, push his African frontier further: perhaps control of Jerba was enough to intimidate the Tunisian emirs into cooperation, or at least neutrality.

As for the Saracens within Sicily, their resistance had not entirely ended even with the brutal killing of their leader. Frederick spent several more years distracted from other tasks (not least the crusade to the east) by his war against the Muslims. As the Saracen strongholds fell, so the war acquired more and more of a guerrilla character. Perhaps there is little truth in the idea that the Mafia has its origin in the Muslim guerrilla resistance to central authority. But at least the general characteristics of the Muslim resistance have much in common with the banditry of Giuliano and his peers in the 1940s. Frederick began to realize that the problem lay in the wide diffusion of Muslims across the western Sicilian hills; they lived in areas often difficult of access, and were impossible to control all at once. Hence his brainwave: to pick them all up, to put them all in one place, as far as possible from the land of their irredentist dreams. The deportation of Sicily's last Muslims began, their destination, the region of Lucera in Apulia, an old Byzantine settlement in low-lying countryside. Frederick decided in the end to require his Muslim subjects actually to live inside Lucera, which became a Muslim town. With the arrival of the Saracens, the bishop of Lucera found himself forced to flee the town. Lucera was to be a special Muslim enclave, and the future loyalty of its inhabitants was assured by their isolation from the Islamic world. Probably somewhere between fifteen and twenty thousand Saracens were deported from Sicily, though not all at once; even if only two-thirds or so reached Lucera, it was still a sizeable city by thirteenth-century standards, once the Muslims had arrived. Some Saracens did escape deportation, for there was a further Muslim rebellion in Sicily in the 1240s; many of the participants may have been relapsed converts to Christianity rather than open Muslims, plus a few die-hard guerrillas in the hills.

Frederick did not interfere with the practice of Islam at Lucera, though he demanded payment of the poll-tax levied, in more peaceful days, on the Muslims of Sicily. The poll-tax was, of course, a Muslim institution, normally levied in Islamic lands on Christians and Jews; Frederick levied it, in Norman fashion, on Jews and Muslims. The exercise of Muslim law was permitted, again in the Norman (and indeed Byzantine) tradition of southern Italy; not far from Lucera there were, or had been, Slav settlements that also functioned according to their own customs. But was Lucera an example of 'rare enlightenment', to cite van Cleve's extraordinary statement? There is no doubt that Frederick came to like the place. Later, papal taunts at Lucera's very existence endeared the Saracen colony still more to Frederick. In the 1230s a fine palace was built there, and excavations have revealed the luxurious life of its occupants in the thirteenth century. Whether it was Frederick II or one of his successors who delighted in Chinese celadon ware and other Eastern ceramics it is impossible to say. But it must be assumed that the palace at Lucera was recognizably oriental in style, with its harem, its Muslim sentries and Eastern exotica amid the décor. For Frederick, of course, this was no real departure: the palaces at Palermo in which he had spent his childhood were also modelled on North African examples. What was new at Lucera was the ruler's willingness to accept that the Saracens would stay Muslim; whereas, as has been seen, William the Good discouraged open exhibition of Islam at court, Frederick was unworried by the devotions of his Saracen servants. In the first place, he knew that they had fought hard for their faith; a hundred and fifty years of Christian rule had not converted them. They were five or ten per cent of a very much larger Muslim population that had been converted or slaughtered, or had left, often voluntarily, for Africa: a hard fighting core, whose military skills he could exploit. In the second place, they were his: serfs of the chamber in the same way as the Jews. They owed no other allegiance, and were at his beck and call. While the Jews, skilled craftsmen and farmers, were encouraged to work in industry and specialist agriculture, the Muslims were also used as soldiers, personal servants, concubines; some attempt was made around 1240 to provide them with oxen so they could resume cultivation of the soil in Apulia. A Saracen bodyguard travelled with Frederick, even to Jerusalem on his crusade! But Saracen bodyguards had protected his Norman predecessors too. The Saracens possessed military skills, as light cavalry and archers, that could not easily be rivalled from other sources. Thus Frederick bonded to himself the most troublesome of his subjects, by a policy extremely tough in the short term – the misery of deportation – but almost generous in the long term. This does not mean he was especially tolerant towards Muslims. He used them for practical purposes. If Muslims rose high in government service, it was as converts to Christianity; Uberto Fallamonaca is said to have been of Muslim ancestry, and became one of Frederick's closest advisers. As in Norman Sicily, real positions of power were closed to the Saracens, and they survived at the royal pleasure, as royal property. Within Sicily, a few Muslims continued to hold out, but to all intents the history of Islam in Sicily ends with the deportations of 1223 onwards.

III

Frederick's preoccupation with the Muslims of Sicily made it difficult for him to give attention to the Muslims of the East. Henry of Malta's crusade flotilla of 1221 had failed to save Damietta, which fell on 7 September of that year. In Europe blame was heaped on those perhaps least guilty of the Fifth Crusade's endless errors: on Frederick, whose promises that he would lead the armies eastwards had not been fulfilled; on Honorius III, who had rather little control over events in Damietta, but was anxious to shift such blame as there was on to other shoulders. The course of action was obvious to the papal curia:

Frederick had a chance to free himself of accusations of indifference to the crusade, by at last taking up arms against the Muslims in the Levant. The papacy was helped in this policy by the propaganda poems of the troubadour Peirol; he wrote: 'Emperor, Damietta awaits you, and night and day the White Tower weeps for your eagle which a vulture has cast down therefrom.' The antithesis between the imperial eagle, signifying Christian legitimacy, and the Muslim vulture, signifying Muslim usurpation, is well expressed. The emperor, Peirol said, should be ashamed that the sultan and not he had won honour from the crusade. But it cannot be concluded that Frederick had become lukewarm to the whole enterprise. In March 1223 he met the pope at Ferentino, at a conference to plan the expedition; and in new ways Frederick bound himself to the venture. He reiterated his crusade vow, this time setting 1225 as the date of departure; he began to build a fleet in southern Italy, and made it plain that passage to the East would be gratis for those who wished to join him – the terrible financial difficulties of the Fourth Crusade, whose participants were unable to pay Venice their fare, were to be avoided. The fleet was large: fifty transport ships to carry crusaders and their horses, plus a hundred galleys (he had already sent forty to Damietta): the Sicilian navy, under Henry of Malta, was on the mend, and Henry VI's dream of using it for a crusade was about to be realized. The pope did his best, too: a new wave of crusade preachers was sent across Europe, and the king of Jerusalem himself, John of Brienne, visited the royal courts in search of aid. This John was a member of the same French family on which Innocent III had tried to rely for action against Markward; he was king in right of his late wife Sybilla, heiress to the Latin kingdom. An almost constant succession of female births had deprived the Latin East of native male leadership for forty years; and, although distinguished western princes had been recruited as husbands for the queens of Jerusalem and had become thereby titular kings of Jerusalem, it would be hard to say that John of Brienne was in the same league as some of his predecessors. His assumption of a crown brought little benefit to the kingdom of Jerusalem, still under severe threat from the Muslims despite a partial recovery after the death of Saladin. He had played a major role in the Fifth Crusade, and had a hand therefore in the appalling political and military mistakes that led to the collapse of the expedition. His and the papal legate Pelagius' are, perhaps, the shoulders on which the blame for the Damietta disaster should be heaped, not Frederick's or the pope's. He and Pelagius had not seen eye to eye: they disagreed violently about who should rule Damietta, and John even minted his own coins there, to indicate his sovereignty.

His redeeming feature, in the planning of a new crusade, was his daughter, Isabella, or Yolande. In 1223 Frederick II was already a widower; Constance had died, to his deep sorrow, in 1221. Here, then, was a queen of Jerusalem awaiting a husband who could defend her inheritance. Unfortunately the question of her father's status, as king in right of her mother, was not looked at closely; the effect, in any case, of Isabella's marriage would be that a *second* king by right of marriage to the heiress of Jerusalem would come into being. And who better than the would-be crusader and leader of the Christian world, Frederick of Hohenstaufen? At Ferentino it was decided: Isabella would come from the East, Frederick would gain the title king of Jerusalem; Jerusalem would at last have the protector it needed – not a tin-pot ruler from Champagne, like John of Brienne, but the greatest ruler in the west. This was an ambitious plan; its consequences, as has already been hinted, were not thought through very carefully. Honorius aspired to a situation where Sicily and Germany would be separate kingdoms, where Frederick would wear the imperial crown but would not concern himself, at least closely, with the affairs of the constituent kingdoms of his world empire. It is unlikely the pope thought that Frederick could be encouraged to live and fight in the East; but it is more likely that he hoped Frederick would provide a male heir to the Latin kingdom, who would, in due course, refound the dynasty of Jerusalem, once again as a separate kingdom. This certainly fitted best with the idea the Latins of the East had of their kingdom. It was not a part of the Roman empire, nor was it a vassal state of the papacy; there were links of affection to France, but in essence it was a kingdom whose overlord was God. As emperor, Frederick exercised no authority there; as head of a crusade, he would command considerable influence, but not explicit political power; but as king in right of his wife he would possess the capacity to organize, defend and save the beleaguered kingdom.

Even 1225 seemed hardly practicable as the date for a crusade. For one thing, the response to crusade preaching was rather poor. 'Few or none' were roused by John of Brienne's appeals, discouraged by the recent fiasco on the Nile. All the more reason, therefore, for the pope to place his trust in Frederick. By the early thirteenth century the idea of a mass crusade, swept forward on a surge of popular enthusiasm, was giving ground to a different, more sober view: a carefully planned expedition, with chosen targets, appointed leaders and close liaison between papal curia and crusading army was what was needed. (It had been tried, of course, on the Fifth Crusade.) Frederick II's crusade, backed by the material resources of southern Italy, was to be this sort of war; and, rather than random recruits, organized companies were needed, as well as funds, drawn from Frederick's dominions – from Germany, so far very lukewarm, from northern Italy. The absence of German magnates at the meetings when the crusade was planned, especially at Ferentino, was therefore a cause for concern. Honorius accepted that the organization of a crusade of this type was not an overnight task. The delays, though regrettable, were highly excusable. The obvious distractions in Frederick's way were also taken into account. So it was accepted that departure in 1225 was not feasible; during a new conference at San Germano, 15 August 1227 was set as the date for departure, and numbers (2,000 cavalry) and funds (625 pounds of Sicilian gold) were specified. If Frederick delayed, he must understand that he was liable to excommunication. At this stage, the threat of excommunication was no more than an effort on the pope's part to obtain an absolute guarantee of Frederick's departure. As has been seen, it was a threat already employed in the past, to goad recalcitrant crusaders on their way. Since Frederick was still resolved to lead a crusade, there is a no reason to see in this threat an assault by Honorius on Frederick's prestige or power. Everything that had to be agreed had been agreed: the crusade, once an army could be put together, marriage to Isabella, financial aid to Jerusalem. There is simply no reason to see in the San Germano promise a 'reckless gamble with the imperial office', in which the emperor challenged the universal primacy of the holy see. The keynote of his crusading policy at this stage, as of his attitude to papal authority as a whole, was a willingness to work side by side with the pope, on agreed and urgent objectives; the recovery of the city of Jerusalem and defence of the Holy Land did indeed constitute a very urgent objective. That Frederick was occasionally irritated by papal demands for quicker action in fulfilling his crusading vow, or that he was obstinate in his desire to keep the German and Sicilian crowns together, should not be taken to indicate a deep divergence between papal and imperial policy. There was general agreement over the major objectives, but not always, at this stage, about the best way to achieve those objectives, or about the order of priorities as between Germany, Italy, Sicily and the Latin East.

Nor did San Germano mean that Frederick had seized control of the crusade in the wake of papal failure (through the legate Pelagius) at Damietta. It has been argued that Frederick brought the crusade under imperial command; to that extent, San Germano would be an imperial coup. Here, hindsight has deluded historians. When Frederick *did* go east, in 1228, he did so in defiance of papal imprecations; he made the crusade into an imperial expedition, because by then he had lost papal favour and backing. But what was new about the crusade was not its imperial tang, so much as its royal flavour: here was a king of Jerusalem (admittedly by marriage) defending and expanding his inheritance. Frederick had done so well in defence of his Sicilian and German inheritance, that contemporaries might easily assume he could work the magic touch in the East too. So the marriage was celebrated: first by proxy in Acre, followed soon by Isabella's consecration as queen in Tyre; then, after Isabella arrived, borne on Henry of Malta's ships, it was celebrated again in Brindisi, in the presence of the nobility of Jerusalem and of King John. The presence of the leading magnates of Jerusalem was an opportunity for Frederick to demand from them an oath of homage as king. The problem was that John of Brienne was there too at court, and he was deeply offended by Frederick's unhesitating assumption of the crown of Jerusalem. Frederick expected to be acknowledged as effective ruler of Jerusalem, and expected John now to stand aside; Frederick's rights as husband to the living heiress must be preferred over John's as widower of the deceased queen. In a way, the problem was not, or not yet, a serious one: Frederick was not on the soil of the Holy Land, and rule was exercised there through a *bailli*, or regent. But Frederick might wish to appoint his own *bailli*; he might make new demands of the Jerusalem baronage, and become involved in the bitter faction fights that already divided the nobility of the Latin East. John of Brienne was well aware that Frederick's haste in claiming full exercise of sovereign rights would not endear Frederick to the independent-minded groups of barons and lawyers out East, at least those who insisted that royal prerogatives were in any case very restricted. John of Brienne hurried to the papal court to complain at Frederick's behaviour. The emperor was beginning to receive the bad press that characterized much of his reign; even his marriage to Isabella was being construed as a greedy attempt to add another crown to those of the empire and of Sicily. The wonder-child of Apulia had been forgotten.

And Isabella too, or rather rumours about her treatment, entered into the complaints. She was still only about fifteen in 1225, and so the situation was very different to that of the marriage to Constance. Now a mature king was wedded to a young queen, not a mature queen to a young king. It may be true that Frederick neglected her, at least occasionally, for his harem girls, though it is also true that he travelled a good deal in her company. As van Cleve has noted, the hostile tales come from pro-Brienne circles; and many come from the remote Latin East, where accuracy about Frederick's bedtime cannot have been very high. But they, or at least John of Brienne's complaints, disturbed the pope greatly. He rebuked Frederick for his haste in taking the title of Jerusalem, and Honorius then omitted to use the title king of Jerusalem in his letters to Frederick. Honorius' attitude confirms the argument that the pope wanted two things from the marriage: an effective crusade, and an effective heir to Jerusalem. But Frederick himself was not to be that heir; his son by Isabella was to fulfil the role (a son, Conrad, was born in 1228). Thus from 1225 onwards the papacy was increasingly at a loss to understand Frederick's motives or actions. As far as the crusade was concerned, it was suspected that Frederick would not, after all, pay close attention to papal advice.

As for Frederick, it has to be assumed that the title to Jerusalem had special significance in his eyes. He was the first Roman emperor to bear that title; he was still enchanted by the echoes of Charlemagne (as perceived in contemporary legend) and of the revival of Roman rule throughout the Mediterranean. Islam was the great challenge to the Christian Roman empire, and it was quite proper to attack it at its heart (as seen from the west), in Syria and Egypt. But Frederick's youthful enthusiasm had largely evaporated. The practical difficulties involved in imposing his rule over Germany and Sicily could not be ignored. The crusade he had wished for in 1215, the crusade of the youthful hero-emperor, had now become a burdensome question of timing, logistics, money and even recrimination.

IV

An indication how serious the emperor was in his crusading plans is provided by his decision to call an imperial Diet together at Cremona over Easter 1226, to discuss the expedition to the East. The Diet of Cremona marks a critical moment in Frederick's career, for it was followed by an interminable Lombard rebellion; and it gave rise to considerable misunderstanding, both in 1226 and among modern historians. When he summoned the Diet, addressing the German princes as well as the Italian towns, Frederick made plain three aims: the prosecution of the crusade, the suppression of heresy in his domains, and recognition of his imperial rights. It has therefore been assumed that Cremona was planned as the resuscitation of Barbarossa's policy, so disastrously enunciated at Roncaglia in 1158: the recovery of the fiscal rights of the emperor and of administrative control over the free communes. In fact these issues had been regulated by the Peace of Venice of 1177 and the Treaty of Constance of 1183, and – despite the almost total relaxation of German control over the communes since Henry VI's death – there are no real signs that Frederick II wished at this stage to deny the Lombards their hard-won liberties. On the other hand, he was still disturbed at the attitude of several Lombard towns, not least Milan, which had so grudgingly accepted him in lieu of Otto of Brunswick. But even Milan was a divided city: in 1221 there was street-fighting between the old patricians and newer factions based on wider middle-class support; and the new elements, the 'popolo', appealed for aid to the pro-imperial cities traditionally hostile to Milan, especially Cremona. Another city whose opposition to Frederick had been very bitter in 1212, Piacenza, was also split between warring factions, though by 1226 the anti-imperial groups had the upper hand. In choosing Cremona as meeting-place for his Diet, Frederick was taking care to avoid the cities whose loyalty was divided or suspect; equally, in choosing Cremona he aroused the suspicion that he was about to inaugurate an ambitious policy for the restoration of imperial control in northern Italy. At the Diet, the German princes would be accompanied by armies from the north, ceremonial as much as anything, but a visible threat to the cities; in any case, the north Italians preferred not to be reminded so forcefully that the *regnum Italicum* was a mere appendage of the German monarchy.

Some Lombards, too, resented the promise to suppress heresy. The Cathar heresy, recent victim in southern France of the Albigensian crusade, had attracted many followers in northern and central Italy (Florence was especially infected); Cathar refugees from southern France had come to Italy, spreading even more virulent forms of Catharism, in which it was taught that two principles, the good God and the evil, coexisted in more or less eternal rivalry, one ruling the world of the spirit, the other that of the flesh. Although, later on, the north Italian heretics tended to side with the Hohenstaufen, their sole defence against the papacy and its inquisition, in these years it was clear how bitter an opponent of heresy Frederick was: he saw heresy as a denial of royal authority, since heretics questioned the accepted relationship between God and man, in which he, as divinely appointed monarch, was the pivotal figure.

But the central fear was that urban liberties were to be dis-mantled. It was apparent from Frederick's legislation at Capua in 1220 that he was no respecter of such liberties in southern Italy: Naples and the other cities had been stripped of freedoms in any case much more limited than those of the Lombards. Of course, the panicky Lombards might also have looked at Germany, where urban liberties were being extended on the imperial estates, even though the cities had fared less well in episcopal territories.

The mistake was to assume that Frederick's policy could be deduced from a handful of actions – the Capua assizes, the use of Cremona as his base. Cremona, in fact, was rewarded with handsome privileges, praising the city's past and future role as defender of imperial interests in Lombardy. Even Frederick's recognition of Cremona's rights did not satisfy the opposition. Of course he would favour Cremona, which had always toadied to the emperor; of course he would use Cremona as a lever to undermine the power of Milan and its allies. Thus the thinking of the Milanese leaders. As for Frederick, he was worried by the danger that conflict among the north Italian towns might break out anew. He found it hard to reconcile the declared love for liberty of the Milanese with the internal disorder of the city; he found it hard to reconcile claims to autonomy with Milanese attempts to establish a land-empire in Lombardy, embracing Lodi, Como and towns even further afield. The towns themselves had frequently recognized how serious was internal disorder, by calling in non-native lawyers as governors (*podestà*) for a year, to act impartially, above faction. Under the terms of the Peace of Constance these *podestà* were supposed to be approved by the imperial court. Frederick's perplexity at Lombard politics did not constitute radical hostility to the idea of the autonomous commune. But he hoped that his presence would tame the more troublesome cities: he was ready to act as arbiter, as indeed his imperial duty demanded, and he was anxious to protect the smaller cities which were being bullied by Milan and its friends (not that Cremona was any more innocent of bullying).

Frederick's proclamation of the Diet was discussed by representatives from Milan, Brescia, Mantua, Padua, Treviso and Bologna at a meeting in Mantua in March 1226. Rather than wait to hear Frederick's policy declared at Cremona, they acted at once to refound the Lombard League, convinced that the decrees of Barbarossa were on top of the new emperor's baggage. The cities promised to hold together firmly in resistance to the emperor, for twenty-five years or more, until the threat to their liberties had been eliminated. What is impressive is that the meeting in Mantua brought together spokesmen of cities scattered over a wide geographic area, and included one or two participants, especially Mantua, who had not always been hostile to the Hohenstaufen in the past. The refoundation of the league gave a fillip to spirits in Lombardy. Smaller towns joined too, including several that had suffered in the past from depredations by their neighbours: Lodi, Vercelli, Faenza were there as well as the staunchly anti-imperial city of Alessandria, founded in open defiance of Barbarossa, and the newly emergent city of Turin. The marquis of Montferrat was the most important of the great landowners who also joined.

But the meeting at Cremona was threatened even before the league grew to its new size. The Milanese and their allies blocked the Alpine passes, and even those German princes who had crossed the mountains, including Frederick's son Henry, were forced back at Trent, on the road down to Verona. Verona, not surprisingly, was involved too in the Lombard insurrection. Cremona itself sent troops to the Alpine passes, but could do little to help the German princes. The princes' own military resources, contrary to Lombard fears, were rather limited; and, humiliated, they made their way back to Germany. Thus the Cremona Diet had to be held amid great political unrest; rather few of those summoned were even present, and among them were some deputations whose future loyalty could not be assumed, such as the Genoese. Como was represented, as befitted a town very near Milan and long coveted by Milan. Pisa, now in receipt of Hohenstaufen favours, was there to protest its loyalty after its embarrassing friendship towards Otto the Welf; Parma, Modena and Reggio Emilia, a line of towns between Piacenza and Bologna, were unhappy about the revival of the Lombard League by inveterate foes. Asti and Lucca had cooperated with Frederick I or Frederick II in the past. The head of the house of Este, which in future was to play a major part in the Lombard wars, was there too. There were a few German princes who had evaded the Lombard blockade. Nor, indeed, did the Diet concern itself with the demolition of Lombard liberties. Frederick believed he had asked no more of the communes than was legitimately available under the terms of the Treaty of Constance in 1183; but the rebels were convinced that the self-same treaty gave them the right to resist the emperor if he exceeded his powers.

Yet he had not done so. He had no intention of doing so. The Lombard rebels had thought ahead too far and too fast. There are no reasons for supposing the main aim of the Diet of Cremona was not discussion of the crusade. Naturally, the new emperor also wished to show himself to his Lombard subjects. But the purpose of the emperor was in this respect ceremonial rather than constitutional. There were to be delegates from Sicily as well as Germany and Lombardy, so that all his subjects would be symbolically united under one rule. But the real subject-matter was the crusade. The Lombards themselves could not cite exact evidence of the emperor's supposedly hostile policy towards the cities; they simply averred that he intended to undermine their liberties, but without details. They were wrong; they had over-reacted. A few references in imperial letters to the 'rights of the empire' or the restoration of the empire do not constitute evidence for a revival of Barbarossa's policy, even though Frederick II may still have considered urban liberties as exaggerated, and have seen in Milan a troublemaker whose power must be broken. Naturally, the refusal of Milan to participate in the Diet was already seen as a denial of Frederick's authority as rightful successor to the *regnum Italicum*, while Milan's role in the formation of a new Lombard League was regarded in imperial circles as an act of treason and the rebels were outlawed – placed under the imperial 'ban'. The submission of Milan and her allies to the imperial crown became – but at Lombard prompting, really – a central theme in Frederick II's policy. Moreover, it critically enlarged the range of the emperor's concerns, beyond Germany, Sicily and Jerusalem to the north of Italy, an area whose affairs Frederick had until then done his best to ignore. The entry of Lombardy into the emperor's anxieties had considerable effects, too, on his relations with the papacy, because the holy see feared that the assumption of imperial control in northern and southern Italy at the same time would threaten its own territorial interests in central Italy and the Romagna.

Thus the papacy was keen to put an end to the Lombard rebellion. Even more importantly, the rebellion threatened to delay the crusade still further. Frederick pressed this case when he met the cardinal of Porto, who had travelled to Lombardy to discuss the crusade and other problems. The papacy was thus drawn into the Lombard rebellion, but by no means in opposition to Frederick. The emperor, notwithstanding his traditional role as mediator in the disputes of the Lombard towns, wisely ceded the role of mediator to the papacy. Imperial mediation had never worked well in the twelfth century; and, besides, Frederick and the pope had a common objective, the crusade. What is striking in 1226 is the trust between emperor and pope. For, although Frederick was aware that the rebellion was a stiff blow to his prestige, he was not looking for vengeance against the Lombards. As an earnest of his desire for peace, he did not lift up arms against them. For one thing, his German reinforcements had not been large, and most of them had been forced back in the south Tyrol. For another, Frederick was well aware that a Lombard uprising could tie him down in one part of his empire when so much work still needed to be done in his other territories, and above all in his new kingdom of Jerusalem. The signs are all the clearer, therefore, that Frederick never seriously intended in 1226 to impose the fiscal and political demands made originally by his grandfather; it would have been the greatest folly to do so; all his energies were concentrated on the rapid pacification of Lombardy, even by papal agency.

Papal mediation was overwhelmingly concerned, once again, with the crusade. The cardinal of Porto had long taken a special interest in recruitment for the crusade in Germany; he hoped to draw from Lombardy yet more crusaders. So it was agreed between the pope's legates and the Lombards that no obstacle would be placed in the way of Frederick's crusade; it was even agreed initially that Henry son of Frederick would be allowed through Trent with over a thousand cavalry, to come to Cremona for discussion of the crusade. But in compensation the Lombards demanded that their league be allowed to exist, and that an imperial ban should not be placed upon it. At Frederick's court a group of loyal bishops made public the imperial view: Frederick had no intention of bringing harm to the cities, but he did not intend to diminish the rights of earlier emperors. This surely means that he wished as far as possible to abide by the terms of the Treaty of Constance, as he understood them. But claims and counter-claims rebounded. Henry returned to Germany, having never been allowed down the Adige valley. The papacy did its best to encourage Milan to come to terms. The papacy threatened the Lombard towns with the interdict,

spiritual equivalent of the imperial ban. Frederick gave his fullest
encouragement to the papal legates throughout several difficult
months of negotiation between Lombard rebels and the imperial
court. He reminded Honorius III, in a letter of August 1226, that
'the honour of the Roman Church, as well as our own honour
and that of our empire' had been challenged by the Lombards.
Another reason for mediation was, simply, that the Lombards
refused to have any dealings with the emperor; the oath re-
founding their league stated this explicitly. Thus the only means
to settle the issue, other than war, was mediation by a mutually
acceptable party. In the early stages at least, it is evident that the
legates sympathized very strongly with Frederick's frustration.

How far Frederick was prepared to go to achieve a settlement
is apparent from the terms of the agreement reached between the
league and the emperor, in December and early January, 1226.
The central principle was that the emperor, despite the alleged
offences of the Lombard rebels, would pardon them and revoke
his ban. Property and prisoners were to be restored, in appropriate
cases. The issues made plain when the Cremona Diet was
summoned were to be followed through: the Lombards must
supply four hundred cavalry for two years, for the crusade – so
reduced was enthusiasm for the crusade that forced levies were
needed as well as volunteers. And the cities must prosecute and
expel heretics. Even here, the existing statutes of the cities (presumably, in respect of the property of exiles, and so on) were not
to be contravened. In all, a very mild package. Frederick accepted
it because, despite the lack of penalties for the Lombard League,
it should leave him free to depart on crusade at the planned time.
It was probably not easy for him to accept that Milan and its
friends should be forgiven for an open act of treason against his
authority.

The burden on the Lombards was so light that it surprised
him, and Pope Honorius, when the league procrastinated. Its
rectors protested that their copy of the terms had fallen into the
water and could barely be read. Honorius certainly believed that
this excuse was impossibly feeble. Either the Lombards must
agree to this settlement, and help the crusade, or he would use all
his power and that of the emperor, to chastise them. The threat
of excommunication, accompanied by a renewal of the imperial

ban, was clear. So too were Honorius' priorities. The Lombard procrastination, not to mention their rebellion, was damaging the Church, the interests of the emperor and those of Christ. Honorius' denunciation of the Lombards thus leaves no doubt that cooperation between pope and emperor remained an important principle of his policy. The contrast with the first Lombard League, abetted by Pope Alexander III, could not be clearer. Indeed, the lack of a papal protector for the second league was a cause of concern to its rectors. They had already held a meeting with John of Brienne in late spring, 1226, at Faenza, and must have seen him as a potential war-leader against his son-in-law Frederick.

Honorius' letter shattered the confidence of the Lombards. Finally, in late March of 1227, they accepted the terms, four months late. Their rebellion had lasted about a year, and it had brought them no tangible benefits. It might be added that they did not supply the knights promised to the crusade, even though Frederick generously insisted that he would bear the costs of transport to the east. They saw the agreement of 1227 more as a truce than as a recipe for long-term peace. In a sense they were right: the agreement was so heavily concerned with the crusade that it left little room for other problems, such as might arise after the crusade. It represented a mere return to the position in the early 1220s. It did not shake the power and influence of Milan; and the Milanese, out of favour at the imperial court, must have wondered what policy Frederick might adopt once he had performed his crusading vows. Equally, the attitude of the papal legates alarmed the Lombards. They did very little actually to aid the league, and the threats from Honorius were clearly meant seriously. The death of Honorius, in mid-March, shortly before the Lombards agreed to terms, only renewed Lombard uncertainty about future prospects. His successor, the cardinal bishop of Ostia (former patron of St Francis), who took the name Gregory IX, had been associated with Honorius' policies. In March 1227 there was little reason to suppose the era of papal–imperial cooperation to be at an end.

Honorius III had sought during his pontificate to show that a policy of conciliation and cooperation, not least with the new emperor, was the road to peace within Europe. It was also, he felt, the best guarantee of a crusade; and, as with so many medieval popes, concern for the Holy Land was his highest priority. He adopted a milder tone than Innocent III before him or Gregory IX and Innocent IV after him; he believed the best of Frederick, though he was always prepared to rebuke him over issues where he was sure Frederick was exceeding his rights – the election of Henry in Germany, or Frederick's occasional interference in the papal patrimony (often using the controversial duke of Spoleto, Rainald von Urslingen). Perhaps it was Honorius III who, by taking Frederick at face value, saw Frederick and his aims more clearly than the other popes with whom Frederick had dealings. Honorius revealed that there was indeed common ground between pope and emperor, and accepted that differences of outlook, though almost certain to occur, could more easily be settled by gentle persuasion than by thundering denunciation. With his death, there ended a golden era in papal–imperial collaboration.

Looking at the cooperation between Frederick and Honorius, one is tempted to ask who really controlled papal or imperial policy in these years. Honorius' stamp seems easily identifiable in the firm but conciliatory letters that emanated from his curia. But of course there were factions in the curia that, although guided by Honorius' decisions, counselled greater emphasis on the rights of the papacy: the defence of its overlordship in Sicily, the protection of the Sicilian Church, over which Frederick was assuming his predecessors' extensive rights, the separation of Germany from Sicily. It is clear from later events that the bishop of Ostia, the future Gregory IX, privately at least, had the gravest misgivings about Frederick – not merely about his real commitment to the crusade, but about his personal behaviour, his insistence on maintaining rule in Germany as well as Sicily, and even his attitude to the Lombards. Honorius, for his part, seems to have been loyally served by the legates sent to Lombardy, who took care not to disparage the emperor.

In the imperial court, equally, there may have been divergent outlooks: a later group of publicists, virulent in their condemnation of papal pretensions, seems to have its origins in these years, for Gregory IX received a hostile press from the imperialists soon after his election. There was a newly emergent generation of aggressive propagandists, products of the University of Naples, founded in 1224 by Frederick himself, primarily as a centre of legal studies; and there was an existing tradition of ornate rhetoric at the schools of Capua. Frederick's assumption of the imperial crown encouraged him and his circle in their search for evidence that the crown carried with it universal temporal authority, based on that of Augustus, Constantine and Charlemagne. Alongside this view of Frederick's authority, there persisted in his mind a more conventional outlook, in no way incompatible with the claims to universal authority: the emperor's task was to pass down to his heir Henry an intact inheritance, which God had appointed the house of Hohenstaufen to rule; the disorders of the emperor's youth, the struggle to redeem what were now seen as his rights in Germany as in Sicily, reinforced emphasis on the *dynastic* character of Frederick's policies. The destiny of his house was as much his concern as the redemption of his rights in Lombardy or elsewhere; indeed, the two themes were insepar-able. Frederick was truly a man of the twelfth and thirteenth centuries; these were the preoccupations of Henry VI, of the Angevins who supplanted his house after his death, and of the Aragonese who in part supplanted them: to provide for one's sons, to pass on the crown, to keep intact and to enlarge further one's inheritance.

These strands of thought must have been developing further during the 1220s, stimulated, indeed, by the conflict with the Lombards. Challenges to Frederick's rights prompted more exact investigation of those rights. The Lombard conflict had effects, therefore, ranging far beyond the local issues that were, in essence, the concern of the Lombards themselves. When conflict was renewed and extended, the imperial court was intellectually prepared for the fight.

CHAPTER FIVE

THE JOURNEY TO JERUSALEM, 1227–30

I

Gregory IX: his very name was a signal, recalling that earlier Gregory who had combated so violently with the German King Henry IV, in the late eleventh century. Like Gregory VII, Gregory IX was not given to patience; and he too believed it was necessary to confront the most serious problem facing the papacy from the first days of his pontificate. For him, that problem was relations with the emperor, and the crusade was only part of a group of interconnected issues. For Honorius had not solved the impasse created by the personal union of Sicily to the empire, and the question of Lombardy's future remained uncertain. Gregory's lack of respect for Frederick's attitude to the Lombards is strikingly revealed by the casual manner in which he notified the emperor of the league's acceptance of terms: he sent an abbreviated version of the agreement to Frederick, hardly adequate after the long months of negotiation. Frederick expected to be treated with more respect. But Gregory was keen to indicate from the start the absolute primacy of his office over that of the emperor. He did not see himself as an ordinary mediator, resolving the embarrassment generated by the imperial ban on the one hand, and the Lombard refusal to negotiate with the emperor on the other. For Gregory IX, mediation represented the fulfilment of the papacy's highest task, as supreme judge on earth. With his election, cooperation between pope and emperor gave way to the idea of the subordination of emperor to pope. Gregory was all the more able to insist on these points because he was an exceptionally able orator and propagandist, 'forceful in word and in deed', as Honorius III had described his own successor. He was also, so it is believed, exceptionally old; his has been seen as the pent-up passion of a cleric long denied full expression of his powerful views. That he was an able canonist, in the tradition of Innocent III, is clear; but he was also sensitive to spiritual problems, as his patronage of the nascent Franciscan order revealed, a dozen years before his election as pope. His elevation to the Petrine throne a day after Honorius III had died was not, therefore, surprising. He was a leading figure in the curia, who had worked faithfully under Innocent and Honorius for the prosecution of papal interests. Maybe, too, the cardinals were by now less happy with the conciliatory ways of Honorius. Cooperation between pope and emperor was unfamiliar, and there may have been an assumption that Frederick would exploit papal compliance to the limit, unless a decisive figure were now elected.

For Gregory's policy was decidedly different to Honorius'. The new pope was determined to demonstrate to the world the fickleness of Frederick. His opportunity was provided by the crusade. Gregory's first letter to Frederick actually says: do not put yourself in a position where I have to take action against you; go on crusade as promised, or else. But there are signs Gregory expected Frederick to fail in his undertaking. He assumed the emperor would not depart at the promised time. In that case, it would be his solemn duty to excommunicate Frederick for flagrant breach of his oath. But by summer of 1227 Frederick's plans were advancing well. The crusade had gradually gathered a wide following, and groups of German knights, mercenaries paid by Frederick, and enthusiastic pilgrims were entering Apulia, whence the emperor was to ferry them free of charge to the Holy Land. The landgrave of Thuringia arrived with several hundred cavalry. Indeed, the dense throng may have brought disease southwards to Apulia, because by the height of summer pilgrims were dying of a virulent infection, perhaps typhoid or cholera. This in itself was a severe blow to the crusade; Frederick had not bargained for such complications. He was fully aware that he was under the strictest oath to depart; so depart he would. But he too was stricken down with the fever. None the less, he sailed from Brindisi in September. He had little choice.

It is clear that his illness was no subterfuge. Frederick's friend and colleague the landgrave of Thuringia was also a victim, and actually died at sea. Deeply discouraged, and evidently seriously ill, Frederick decided that he could not continue the voyage. What sort of leadership would a sick commander provide to the crusade? He sent a few galleys ahead to Syria, instructing the duke of Limburg and Hermann von Salza, grand master of the Teutonic Knights, to begin work in defence of the kingdom of Jerusalem. It was clear from this action that he did intend to resume the crusade at an early opportunity: May 1228 was the date he proclaimed. But he himself disembarked at Otranto and then moved across his kingdom to take a rest-cure at the baths of Pozzuoli: a fact which suggests that the worst of the illness had passed with his disembarkation. The false start evidently needed to be explained; Frederick therefore sent ambassadors to Gregory IX, to explain his illness. But Gregory did not even admit the ambassadors into his presence. It was enough that Frederick had broken his promise to go to the Holy Land in 1227. As for Frederick's attempt to travel East and his illness, these factors were not taken into account. Gregory seized on the opportunity, as if he had been waiting for it all along. He informed the Christian world that the emperor had again and again promised to go East, and finally had failed to do so; the charges and the penalty were clear. But Gregory was undoubtedly using the crusade to justify a much broader campaign against imperial pretensions. For when, in October 1227, he actually wrote to Frederick to explain the papal position, he mentioned a whole range of issues that appear only under the surface of his earlier letter to all the faithful. He complained that Frederick had been persecuting the church in Sicily showing no respect for the fiscal rights and liberties of the Sicilian Church, even, indeed, forcing into exile the leading ecclesiastics of the *regno*. (Walter of Palear may have come to mind here; this worldly prelate had fled to Venice on his own account after the Fifth Crusade, fearing Frederick's wrath at his incompetence.) All this, and yet Sicily was under the suzerainty of the Roman Church itself. What Gregory required, clearly, was recognition of this authority, and the separation of Sicily from the rest of Frederick's empire. The issue of Frederick's continued rule over Sicily, latent under

Honorius III, had now become a public source of disagreement.

The same month Gregory enlarged on his complaints in a second encyclical letter. He now moved away from the crusade to the full list of papal complaints against the emperor. Frederick's ingratitude was stressed: he had been nourished by the Church from childhood, and owed his very survival to the Church. The papacy's disappointment was stressed too: yes, there had been rich hopes of a new era in cooperation between pope and emperor; the papacy had encouraged Frederick's elevation in Germany and the empire, seeing in him the rod and staff that would support the Church. Frederick himself, it was emphasized, had taken the crusade vow at his German coronation, and the papacy had known nothing of these plans; Frederick himself had suggested that those who disregarded their vows should be excommunicated; Frederick himself had set a date, and agreed to his own excommunication if he did not fulfil his pledge by then; so the message was clear: the emperor was responsible for the penalties which had fallen on him. He alone was to blame for what had happened. Nor had Frederick's excuse of illness any validity. Gregory painted a picture of a seething mass of pilgrims forced to wait in midsummer heat, surrounded by disease – as if the emperor would not realize that these conditions would bring death and disaster to the crusade! Frederick was responsible for the death of the landgrave of Thuringia. Frederick was, indeed, a false crusader: he had not sent to the Holy Land the money and ships promised since the crusade conferences of Ferentino and San Germano. (Actually, he had: but Gregory's rhetoric took charge of the facts.)

So Frederick was excommunicated. This in itself was not the most serious problem. Excommunication was an occupational hazard of medieval emperors. Frederick I had spent much of his career in that state. What was most worrying was the obstinate refusal of Gregory IX to listen to the facts. His encyclical of October is simply inaccurate. It was impossible to come to terms with a pope who refused even to understand that Frederick's breach of his crusading vow was a technical one. It was also worrying that Gregory had so soon enlarged the area of conflict to include the state of the Sicilian Church and the history of Frederick's elevation to the German throne. While Frederick did act in Sicily as master of the Church, in true Norman fashion, it was hardly true that the papacy had protected him against his childhood enemies. Gregory IX, already in full career during Frederick's minority, was misrepresenting painful events in the past.

Stunned by excommunication, Frederick replied with a letter addressed to all those who had taken the cross, in which he tried to maintain the calmer level of debate practised in Honorius III's time. Yes, he had thought of the Church of Rome as his 'father'; he had honoured the Vicar of Christ; he had placed trust in him; but all he had obtained in return was spite. He condemned Gregory for inciting hatred – here, perhaps, he was especially worried at the effect the papal letter might have in Lombardy, where the cities seemed overnight to have gained a champion. He could prove, too, that he had indeed sent money and men to the Latin East, and had fulfilled the promise to go on crusade up to the very point when illness struck him down. Frederick was, of course, anxious to keep the debate centred on the crusade. He was angry that Gregory had intruded further issues, such as control of the Church in Sicily; he could see clearly that the pope's aim was not to achieve a crusade, but to detach Sicily from his control. There had thus emerged into the open a clash between the Norman-inspired view of Sicily, and its Church, as an autonomous entity whose ruler derived his power directly from God, and the papally backed view of Sicily as a special property of the holy see, granted (though not irrevocably) to the Hautevilles out of the patrimony of St Peter.

Not surprisingly, Frederick addressed himself to the problem of papal claims to overlordship in a series of letters to rulers whose interests were also, he insisted, threatened by papal pretensions: had not the king of England been manipulated by Innocent III, who had been his bitter enemy until the chance came to bring England under papal vassallage; had not the Albigensian crusade been used to intimidate the south French barons, in the hope that papal power in their region would be enhanced? He criticized the popes as money-grabbers, guilty of the usury they publicly condemned: an interesting reflection of the tension between moral ideals and practical fiscal needs, in an age when the Church was slowly coming to terms with the levying of interest. But the threat went deeper. Frederick accused the Church of abandoning its own founder's principles. Poverty, not wealth, was the foundation of the Church. The popes were wolves in sheep's clothing. Frederick had, of course, touched a raw nerve: Gregory IX, patron of the Franciscans, seemed so far from Francis' own ideals. Frederick's letter to England certainly gained some renown, for the chronicler Matthew Paris gleefully incorporated the emperor's words into his *Chronica majora*. Here was a marvellous assault on the hypocrisy of the hierarchy of the Church, a display of the dangers of the 'honeyed words' that dripped from the pope's mouth, a constructive exercise in anti-clericalism, demonstrating that the pure Church had been swallowed by the greed and wickedness of St Peter's would-be heirs.

Which is the truer statement of Frederick's feelings: his ex-cruciatingly polite reply to Gregory IX's fulminations, or the bitter denunciations recorded by Matthew Paris? Just as Gregory's stormy letters reveal the release of long-brewed irritation at imperial policy, so too Frederick's letters to England suggest that he had long been pondering the nature and history of the papacy, and that he had no room for the ideas of Innocent III and Gregory IX about the fullness of papal power. It is striking that his letters to France and England show a close awareness of the recent history of the papacy, particularly of the pontificate of Innocent III. Frederick was, however, aware too that papal claims to primacy must be confronted not by searching out grounds for dispute (as Gregory IX had done); pope and emperor must try to find a *modus vivendi*, for the sake of the peace of the world. It is a striking tribute to his statesmanship that the emperor remained so conciliatory towards Gregory even at this stage; equally, his intense impatience is revealed by the propagandist letters to France and England.

Frederick's case did not go unheeded, except in the papal curia. Even the citizens of Rome were active in the emperor's support: their relationship with the popes was often stormy, since they aspired to political control of the city, and played in their statements on its role as seat of empire. Gregory attempted

on Easter Day to preach against Frederick in St Peter's, and was
rewarded with a riot. He was chased out of the Church and
down the streets of Rome; he escaped northwards to Viterbo.
Mob violence in Rome only strengthened his resolve to bring
Frederick to heel: the humiliation was acute. Gregory therefore
concentrated his energy on the destruction of Frederick's fond
plan for a crusade. It is extraordinary to find a pope now forbidding the Sicilian Church to pay its crusading tithes; but there
had never before been so eminent an excommunicate organizing
a crusade. Gregory was convinced at last that Frederick intended
to go ahead with his crusade, even in a state of excommunication,
and the pope was aware that Frederick's crusade, were it to
achieve success, could damage gravely the authority of the holy
see. For here would be an imperial crusade, launched actually
contrary to the current wishes of the papacy; a sort of anti-
crusade, carried out despite papal wishes by participants who
clearly had no great respect for papal commands, who placed
their vows to God to go East before the authority of St Peter to
bind and to loose. Actually, the papacy had discovered an important fact about crusading, one that has escaped many recent
historians too: it was not really the papacy that summoned the
knighthood of Europe to fight for the faith; the crusaders were
convinced they would receive heavenly rewards for their actions
on Christ's behalf, whether or not St Peter's successor told them
so. The threat of a crusade unblessed by the papacy was a threat
to the political standing of the papacy, as organizer of holy war
and mediator, through the offer of remission of sins, between
God and man.

II
==

In any case, Frederick's crusade seemed more likely to succeed
in 1227 and 1228 than in the depressing aftermath of the Fifth
Crusade. For Frederick, unorthodox crusader that he was, had
built diplomatic ties to the sultan of Egypt, al-Kamil. In about
1226 Emir Fakhr ad-Din arrived at Frederick's court, sent by the
sultan of Egypt, who was worried by the military and political

successes of his brother, the governor of Damascus. Damascus had built an alliance with the Khwarizmian Turks of the region north of Iran, but al-Kamil suspected that his brother's real target was Egypt. The Muslim historian ibn Wasil, who later came to know Frederick's son Manfred, and who had some regard for Frederick himself, explained why al-Kamil had contacted the emperor:

> The idea of the approaches made to the emperor, the king of the Franks, and of his invitation, was to create difficulties for al-Malik al-Mu'azzam [of Damascus] and to prevent his availing himself of the help offered to him by the sultan Jalal ad-Din ibn 'Ala ad-Din Khwarizmshah and Muzaffar ad-Din of Arbela, in his quarrel with al-Kamil.

The readiness of an Egyptian ruler to treat with the leader of a new crusade should not cause surprise. The Muslims tended to see the crusades not so much as holy wars, rather more as Frankish wars of conquest in the East; and it was perfectly sensible to use the Franks as a lever against their rivals in the Islamic world. Short-term alliances between the kings of Jerusalem (and Frederick was king of Jerusalem – 'of the Franks', as ibn Wasil says) and Muslim neighbours were nothing new, either. Frederick, for his part, must have been aware that the loss of Jerusalem in 1187 had resulted from the unification of the Muslim Middle East under Saladin; it was appropriate, therefore, to exploit to the full signs of disunity among Saladin's successors. This, indeed, was the way to make his crusade succeed. He was aware of the value of diplomacy to the crusade, but earlier crusaders, even when forced to negotiate, had been slower to accept this reality: thus Richard Coeur-de-Lion had only gradually come round to the idea of negotiations with Saladin. In this sense, Frederick's view was less that of the traditional crusader, more that of the kings of Jerusalem themselves, who had understood better than newly arrived crusaders the delicacy of the diplomatic balance in the Middle East. Frederick's understanding of these problems is impressive; to some extent it may result from his links to the North African emirs across the water from Sicily, and from his acquaintance with Muslim scholars. Later, indeed, these contacts with Egypt would be used against him, in preposterous allegations concerning his love for Islam.

A second reason why 1227 seemed a good time to be planning

a crusade was the slow but promising success of the crusade army that had continued East while Frederick remained in southern Italy undergoing his rest–cure. Sidon, a city divided between Christians and Muslims by the terms of a truce, was now completely brought under Frankish control. Ports further south – Jaffa and Caesarea – were fortified. (Some of the fortifications still to be seen at Caesarea, and attributed to St Louis of France's visit in 1250, may in fact date from Frederick's reign.) The Teutonic Knights, were offered lands both in the far-off Baltic and in Galilee, where they built a base for themselves at Starkenberg, or Montfort, one of the most impressive crusader castles still to survive in Israel. These activities kept up pressure on the Muslims, and al–Kamil, aware of Frankish objectives, dangled in front of Frederick promises similar to those made during the Fifth Crusade, of the restoration of lost territory of the kingdom of Jerusalem. In return, Frederick was to attack Damascus and root out al–Kamil's brother. Conscious, however, of the shifting sands in the Middle East, Frederick also took care to ask of al–Mu'azzam in Damascus what he might offer the Franks. He replied: war. Frederick, of course, realized that his best interest lay in keeping both al–Kamil and al–Mu'azzam in rivalry, for if either gained complete victory, the Islamic world would once again be united under Ayyubid domination. Indeed, on the eve of Frederick's crusade al–Mu'azzam died, and al–Kamil's enthusiasm for Frederick died too; as ibn Wasil says, 'his brother al–Malik al–Mu'azzam, who was the reason why he had asked Frederick for help, had died, and al–Kamil had no further need of the emperor.'

Another complication occurred in April 1228, with the death of Isabella or Yolande, queen of Jerusalem, soon after she bore Frederick a son, Conrad. Frederick was now in the same constitutional limbo as John of Brienne: king of Jerusalem in right of his wife, now deceased. Frederick, with the same bravado as he had shown towards John, continued to call himself king of Jerusalem, though purists insisted that the baby Conrad must be recognized as king by right, with Frederick only as regent and titular king on his behalf. As this view spread among the often pedantic lawyers of the kingdom of Jerusalem, it began to threaten the success of Frederick's venture, not as a crusade against

Islam, but as an expedition by a king of Jerusalem bringing order to his Frankish subjects. John of Brienne, too, was still active in Italy, maintaining close links with a pope who was much keener to hear his complaints than Honorius had ever really been. Stories began to spread, no doubt with John's approval, that Isabella had been put to death by Frederick: blatant nonsense, since her death brought him not the slightest benefit, and methods of this sort are totally out of character. But Frederick, not oblivious to this, none the less continued to prepare the crusade, for that was the best defence before the world of his innocence.

Frederick seems to have found it hard to believe Gregory would launch an all-out war against him once he was away on crusade. There were signs that the pope was trying to recruit mercenaries in northern and central Italy, and Frederick would certainly expect those regions to become very turbulent while he was away: Milan, Florence and other troublemakers would be free from the danger of imperial interference. Gregory did send a legate to Germany hoping to find signs of unrest there, but there is no real evidence he yet contemplated the election of an anti-king by German princes hostile to Frederick. For one thing, there was not a solid group of princes in opposition. Frederick, for his part, still hoped to come to a settlement with the pope. He seems to have reasoned that his actual departure on crusade would call the pope's bluff. Gregory's complaints were clearly not just about the crusade; but in public eyes Frederick might be able to redeem himself, and win such wide support that Gregory would be forced to renounce the dispute. The events in Rome, when Gregory had been hounded from the city, showed how extensive sympathy for Frederick really was. So Frederick may have thought when he sent a final mission to the papal court in June 1228. He protested that he had now fulfilled his vow; by the time the letter reached Gregory he would be at sea. To no avail. Gregory was adamant. Frederick's disgrace was in no way redeemed by his departure; indeed, it was compounded, for he was an impenitent, excommunicated crusader – a contradiction in terms. It is possible Gregory had not really believed he would sail. In that case, it is even more likely that the mercenaries collected in northern Italy were not at first aimed at targets south of Rome. But once Frederick was at sea, Gregory gave way to temptation.

The kingdom of Sicily lay undefended. The false holy war of the emperor in the East would be countered by a genuine just war against the lands wrongfully held by the emperor in the west.

III

It is striking that Frederick's subjects in the Latin East were not unduly disturbed by his conflict with the papacy. Even the most hostile chroniclers of his crusade who lived in the East accepted his title to Jerusalem, though they were very doubtful about the powers the title bestowed; and they welcomed, in principle, the arrival of the crusade. They had been waiting since 1189 for a Holy Roman Emperor to come on crusade; and they had long placed their hopes for the recovery of Jerusalem on an imperial crusade. It must be stressed, therefore, that the violent quarrels which broke out in the Latin East between Frederick II and the Frankish nobility, or rather some of the nobility, had little to do with the emperor's struggle with Gregory IX. Frederick had entered another political world; and to some extent what went wrong was that he failed to realize the fact. Philip of Novara, who provides a detailed account of Frederick's visit to the East, through the eyes of an antagonistic Frankish faction, still insists that 'in 1229 the Emperor Frederick crossed the sea to come to Syria, by command of Pope Gregory'; and only once, later on, does he refer to Gregory's attempt to conquer southern Italy. The Franks of the East were rightly obsessed by their struggle for survival, set in the midst of the Islamic world; and only their Churchmen cared deeply about the emperor's excommunication.

Sailing by way of the Ionian Islands, Crete, Rhodes and Asia Minor, the emperor's flotilla reached Limassol in southern Cyprus on 21 July 1228. Philip of Novara was not, it seems, impressed by the size of the expedition: sixty or so ships, including both galleys and provision vessels. But an earlier squadron, under the imperial Marshal Riccardo Filangieri, had come out East a few months earlier. Even so, it was not exactly the vast crusading army, ready to smash for good the enemies of the Franks, for which high hopes had been held. Frederick had good reason to stop in Cyprus on the way to the Holy Land. His father Henry had sent a crown to the Lusignan ruler of Cyprus, and it was assumed therefore that Cyprus was a vassal kingdom of the Holy Roman Empire. However, the king, Henry, was a child, and the island was governed by John of Ibelin, the lord of Beirut in the kingdom of Jerusalem, himself acting on behalf of the king's widowed mother, Alice, who was technically regent, or *bailli*. The first problem, therefore, was the overlap between the baronage of Cyprus and that of Jerusalem; the lord of Beirut was one of several powerful landholders in Cyprus whose possessions also extended to the mainland. Were Frederick to develop bad relations with the Cypriot nobility this might seriously affect his prospects for success in the kingdom of Jerusalem itself. The second problem concerned the rights of the emperor over the child king. Frederick found himself in a similar position to Innocent III, when he himself had been a child. Technically he was guardian to young Henry, and John of Ibelin merely acted on his (and Alice's) behalf. So one of Frederick's first acts on landing in Cyprus was to send a courteous letter to John of Beirut, who had not come to meet him, but was in Nicosia, asking him to bring the young king to him.

John of Ibelin was alarmed none the less. For one thing, Frederick's motives were suspect: Philip of Novara, speaking for the Ibelin faction, sees the emperor as someone who spoke sweet words but committed horrid deeds. No doubt this attitude is largely the result of hindsight, but it is clear that there were Cypriot nobles who in no way welcomed Frederick to their island. For another thing, Frederick already had contact with a rival faction in Cyprus, led by Aimery Barlais and his colleagues; Aimery had awaited the emperor at the quayside in Limassol, and delivered a complaint against the powerful Ibelins the moment Frederick disembarked. Aimery and his clique offered aid to the emperor in the Holy Land. But in return they wanted action to be taken against the Ibelins. So what was at issue? Philip of Novara describes the rivalry not so much in constitutional terms, but as a struggle between the *lignage* of the Ibelins and that of Barlais and his confederates: a conflict between clans seeking power in Cyprus. Whereas John of Ibelin had to all intents become *bailli* or regent, and exercised real power in the island, he was not the supreme authority so long as Frederick, suzerain of Cyprus, remained in the kingdom. Thus to Frederick flocked the opposition, full of complaints at misgovernment, not least at the misappropriation of revenues.

John of Ibelin's followers were afraid to hand young King Henry over to Frederick. So they insisted that they would gladly proffer service in the Holy Land, apparently in the hope that, once in Syria, Frederick would cease to pose a threat to their interests in Cyprus. Indeed, in Syria there were powerful institutions, such as the Knights of St John and of the Temple, and the Italian merchant communes, that would be able to hold at bay any attempts Frederick might make to assert total command. John of Ibelin, however, persuaded his followers that they were playing into Frederick's hands. If they did not cooperate with the emperor, future generations would say:

The Roman emperor went overseas with great forces, and he would have conquered everything, but the lord of Beirut and the other disloyal men overseas preferred the Saracens to the Christians, and for that reason resisted the emperor, and did not want the Holy Land to be recovered.

So young Henry was, after all, brought to Frederick, and the emperor held a great feast in honour of his young vassal. He even commanded John of Ibelin to set aside the black robes he was wearing in mourning for his brother; this was too joyous an occasion to be marred by sombre dress.

But the feast was marred by other events. Held in the great castle of Limassol, the banquet was meticulously organized. The seating at table was arranged so that the Cypriot barons could see and hear the emperor. The lord of Beirut and other nobles of the Latin East were required to serve and cut meat for the emperor, in accordance with German imperial custom. That Frederick wished to display his special status in Cyprus, as overlord, was thus made abundantly plain. Philip of Novara, anxious to exonerate the Ibelins of any charges, insists that the nobles served the emperor 'very willingly and nobly'; they certainly wished to convince Frederick of their loyalty to him. But then all of a sudden there filed into the hall a stream of armed soldiers, wielding swords and knives, who stood menacingly around the hall. The Cypriot nobles pretended not to notice. But intimidation had begun. Frederick turned in his seat to face John of Ibelin and said loudly to him: 'Sir John, I require two things of you. Do them amiably and for good.' John of Ibelin replied: 'My lord, tell me your pleasure, and I shall do willingly whatever I hear that is right (*que soit raison*), or that which wise men would take care to do.'

There was already a note of reservation in John's reply; he would not obey blindly; he insisted up to a point on his autonomy. Even so he may not have expected Frederick's series of demands:

The first thing is that you hand to me the city of Beirut, because you neither have it nor hold it by right. The second thing is that you hand to me all the income you have received as regent of Cyprus and all that the royal rights have proved to be worth and have provided since the death of King Hugh – that is, the income of ten years – for this is my own right, according to the usage of the empire [*selon l'usage d'Allmaigne*].

John tried to resist. Frederick threatened arrest. John argued his right to the fief of Beirut under the terms of a grant of King Aimery of Jerusalem; in any case this matter must be brought before the high court of the kingdom of Jerusalem, on the soil of that kingdom. John believed that this dispute in no way concerned the affairs of Cyprus; whereas Frederick was suzerain of Cyprus, he was not suzerain in the same way over the Holy Land. His authority in Cyprus was derived from the creation of a Cypriot kingdom by Henry VI; it was the authority, as Frederick himself insisted, of the Roman emperor over a subject kingdom. But in the kingdom of Jerusalem Frederick was merely king by right of his marriage to Isabella (now, in any case, dead), and father of the child who should some day be king regnant, Conrad of Hohenstaufen. This was John's position, and Frederick was clearly guilty of a serious tactical error when he raised the question of Beirut alongside that of Cyprus. Clearly he aspired to break the power of the Ibelins, a family whose influence in Cyprus and the Holy Land was unrivalled; he suspected them of peculation; of abuse of power, accepting the complaints of Aimery Barlais. Some justice in the complaints there no doubt was. For John of Ibelin in his reply to Frederick did mention the income he had taken from Cyprus. Yes, he said, there was a lot: but it was all spent on the running of the kingdom of Cyprus;

much went not to him but to Queen Alice, as was her right, and
was spent at her will. She was the real regent, he merely her
deputy; quite likely this was simply an attempt to shift the blame
to other shoulders.

Frederick is reported to have replied in a great fury: 'I have
indeed heard before, back in the west, that your words are finely
chosen and polished, and that you are very wise and subtle in
speech, but I shall show you well that your good sense, your
subtlety and your words will be worth nothing against my force.'
Whereupon John tried to steer the angry debate towards higher
matters: the conquest of the Holy Land, for which he was ready
to render service. Frederick, however, did not press his threats
far. He agreed to take hostages from the Ibelin party, as guarantee
of their good faith, and it is clear – despite the bad press he
received from the Ibelin party – that Frederick was partially
within his rights in demanding an account of John's regency.
Frederick was guilty of a 'ham-handed and bullying attempt to
impose his own view of his suzerainty'; more than that, he had
been drawn willy-nilly into disputes among the Cypriot baronage, personal even more than constitutional, with which he
was ill-equipped to deal. Nor was compromise out of the question. Frederick was recognized by the Ibelins as suzerain of
Cyprus, but the pro-imperial barons retained control of the royal
castles on the island. The Ibelins promised their aid in the crusade.
Peace, though not guaranteed to last, had been achieved. On the
other hand the Ibelin faction was virtually ready for war against
its Cypriot rivals. Once Frederick was away, it was uncertain
whether the truce could last.

An interesting reflection on John of Ibelin is provided by his
attitude to some knights who wanted to assassinate Frederick.
John told them that the murder of their overlord would sully
their cause; 'il est mon seignor': if they wished to be believed, they
must honour their obligations to Frederick. This respect for legal
requirements is characteristic of the Ibelins. It was precisely their
attention to the law, as they interpreted it, that brought them so
bitterly into conflict with Frederick. Occasionally they seem to
have glossed over real problems (such as the management of
Cypriot affairs while John acted as regent); but their replies to
imperial demands were consistently based on the principle that

the established customs of Cyprus (in Cyprus) and of Jerusalem (in the Holy Land) must be observed. The confusion between Cypriot and Syrian rights in Frederick's speech in the castle at Limassol thus aroused their deepest concern, not merely as agile politicians but as learned jurists.

Frederick had looked at Limassol for a quick solution to several problems, concerning his rights both in Cyprus and in Syria. Partly this was because he was in a desperate hurry. The pope's plans against the kingdom of Sicily were now much clearer. Gregory was ready to launch an invasion. Thus Frederick must act quickly if he were to hold on to southern Italy. Impatience damaged Frederick's standing in the Latin East. He had asked for too much, too soon. But he needed to reach Syria, fulfil his crusading vows, and strike a blow for Christendom, as rapidly as possible. It was a daunting task. Not surprisingly, too, he carried with him to Cyprus an exaggerated notion of royal and imperial rights in the Latin East, bred in Sicily and matured in Germany and Lombardy. By 1228 Frederick was becoming more and more insistent on the fullness of imperial authority. As has been seen, he was not simply guided by the niceties of constitutional arrangements. In Cyprus it is true, he could claim authority as overlord. In the kingdom of Jerusalem, as the demand for the surrender of Beirut revealed, Frederick was tempted also to act as absolutist ruler, either because he was universal emperor, supreme ruler over all Christian lands, or because he was in any case the king of Jerusalem. He had not expected, in this puny Cypriot kingdom, such intense resistance; all had crumbled before him in large areas of southern Italy and Germany, and he had become used to the idea that his very presence would bring submission and respect. A sign that he did regard his authority as all-embracing is provided by an attempt Frederick made, while in Cyprus, to obtain an oath of fealty from the autonomous Frankish prince of Antioch and Tripoli. Anxious not to submit, the prince escaped by ship from Cyprus, where he had come to meet Frederick. Feigning illness, Prince Bohemond IV had himself borne away at speed. But once he reached refuge in Syria, lo and behold, he seemed to have been cured. Frederick's attempt to gain the allegiance of Antioch is explicable several ways. As king of Jerusalem, he perhaps argued that the Latin princes of Antioch were historically and legally his vassals; but this would have been very hard to prove. The princes of Antioch were also counts of Tripoli, and here their vassal status under the king of Jerusalem was more clearly established. But it was generally assumed that Antioch and Tripoli were autonomous entities, owing the king of Jerusalem respect, maybe aid – ties at best of a very loose kind.

Frederick reached the Latin East without a clear idea of the legal and political traditions that had developed there in the last fifty years. A series of royal minorities in Jerusalem had weakened the power of the crown enormously; in addition, the conquest of Cyprus by the Third Crusade meant that barons of Syria now held land from another king, that of Cyprus, just across the water from the Latin strongholds of Beirut and Tyre. Frederick shows confusion; he does not display much consistency. Fortunately for the emperor, there were still many Cypriot and Syrian barons who stuck by Frederick and resisted Ibelin pretensions. The appeal of a western emperor come East to recover Jerusalem was a potent one, as John of Beirut kept admitting when he said: do not let us appear to prefer the Saracens to the Christians. Frederick's hopes of uniting the baronage of the Latin East rested upon his ability to save the kingdom of Jerusalem from its enemies, and, if possible, to recover Jerusalem.

IV

From Cyprus Frederick sailed to Tyre. It was late in 1228, and the emperor's army still seemed too small to confront the forces of the Muslim world. Frederick realized that his hope of success lay not so much in battle as in diplomacy. Yet his original advantage, the rivalry between al-Mu'azzam and al-Kamil, had by now been lost: al-Mu'azzam was dead; al-Kamil's generous offer of lands to Frederick seemed therefore to have lost its *raison d'être*. As ibn Wasil says, when Frederick arrived in the Holy Land, he was an embarrassment to al-Kamil; 'al-Kamil had no further need of the emperor'. Yet Frederick had much need of al-Kamil, if humiliation were to be avoided. Events in Cyprus had not, however, created deep opposition in Syria among the Latins, at

least openly; on the emperor's arrival the Templars and Hospitallers greeted Frederick with great emotion, prostrating themselves in front of him and embracing his legs. He was, they
knew, excommunicated; but he was also the one hope in the
struggle against the Ayyubids. More materialistically, they may
have sought grants of land and rights, the more so since the
emperor's generosity to the third military order, that of the
Teutonic Knights, was well-known. Hermann von Salza, grand
master of the Teutonic Order, was one of his stalwart supporters
now and for long after. But the main business was the crusade,
and Frederick took care to send messages to Pope Gregory, by
way of his lieutenants left in Italy, informing him of his arrival
and thereby challenging the pope to lift the excommunication.
This was sensible public relations, though, as ever, Frederick
intruded into his embassy an element of cheek. One of the party
sent to Gregory was Rainald of Spoleto, lord of lands claimed by
the papacy, and of course Gregory was not disposed to deal with
him. It is possible Frederick was simply unaware, at this stage,
that Rainald now occupied a key position, defending the frontier
between the papal state and southern Italy against the incursions
of papally backed forces. Moreover, Gregory only became the
more irate when he saw that Frederick, in defiance of his ban,
was continuing the crusade amid reasonably promising auguries.
Even the patriarch of Jerusalem did not at once oppose Frederick, though it was difficult or impossible for the emperor to
participate in any Church services.

Al-Kamil spent 1228 trying to lay hands on al-Mu'azzam's
lands. These were also the lands on which Frederick had his
eyes, not least Jerusalem. Al-Mu'azzam's son, a mere child, was
rapidly dispossessed, and al-Kamil's authority in Syria was
waxing. The real difficulty al-Kamil faced was that Frederick
had now arrived and expected earlier negotiations to bear fruit;
and Frederick would not, could not, go away. Frederick, however, was in greater haste than al-Kamil ever realized. The threat
from papal armies to southern Italy was acute by March 1228.
Frederick must have been sorely tempted to return home, but he
was convinced that the crusade, if successful, would be the diplomatic victory he needed, with effects as far afield as Rome and
southern Italy. Thus al-Kamil's growing reluctance to come to

terms was deeply frustrating. Ibn Wasil portrays the emperor
refusing to return home until al-Kamil's earlier promises of lands,
including Jerusalem itself, was fulfilled. Al-Kamil tried to turn
away an embassy sent to Nablus consisting of the south Italian
nobleman, Thomas of Acerra, and of the Syrian baron, Balian of
Sidon. But Frederick's persistence knew no bounds. Attempts
were made to impress the Muslims with the emperor's deep
learning. Nor was Frederick inactive as a commander. He was
keen to show that he would engage al-Kamil's army if need be:
bluff, perhaps; but effective bluff. He marched his men south,
followed by the Hospitallers and Templars a day's journey
behind. They did not want to appear to be in league with, or
under the command of, an excommunicate. Frederick soon
persuaded them to join him by allowing his name to be omitted
from official army orders, which were to be issued in the name
of God and of Christendom. By means of this fiction a united
army was able to march down the coast of the Holy Land past
Arsuf (where the Muslims threatened) to Jaffa. Al-Kamil, however, decided that his attention was needed elsewhere, at Damascus, still loyal to the line of al-Mu'azzam. The resistance of
Damascus, the key city in northern Syria, an important economic
and military centre, made the affairs of southern Syria seem
rather trivial. After all, Jerusalem was, as a city, rather unimportant; it had some religious significance to Muslims (as did
Damascus), but less to them than to Christians or Jews. Frederick
is said to have bombarded al-Kamil with such arguments. He
told the sultan: I am your friend. You encouraged me to come.
The pope knows I am here, and if I return without gain, I shall
lose my reputation as the most powerful of western rulers (a
gross understatement of his real relations with the papacy!).
Frederick asked for Jerusalem, a desolate city, to be returned. It
was in Jerusalem that his religion was born. All he wanted was the
half-empty, meagre city; if he could have it, he could 'hold up
his head among the kings'. This attitude proved persuasive.
Frederick was finally able to convince al-Kamil to come to terms.
Jerusalem would be recovered, without a blow being struck.

Jerusalem liberated: but the abandoned city, standing now
without walls. Arabic sources say that al-Kamil imposed the
condition that Jerusalem remained undefended. Some structures,

such as the Tower of David, continued to stand, in damaged state, but in essence Jerusalem lay exposed, its tenure conditional merely on al-Kamil's promise to Frederick. Nor, indeed, was all the holy city to be in Christian hands. The Temple Mount was excluded from Frankish control, for the al-Aqsa mosque and the Dome of the Rock were among the holiest places of Islam. These mosques had functioned as churches and palaces under the twelfth-century kings of Jerusalem: but no longer. Christians could, however, visit the Temple Mount. Around Jerusalem were to remain Muslim settlements, under Muslim control. Hebron (known to the Franks as St Abraham), centre of Muslim and Jewish veneration, remained in non-Christian hands. Al-Bira, or la Grande Mahomerie, north of Jerusalem, was to be the local Muslim governmental headquarters. But between Jerusalem and the sea, there would be a narrow corridor, linking the city to the coastal towns still in Frankish hands, by way of the see of St George at Lydda. Bethlehem too was handed to the Franks, as was Nazareth. The Christians had thus regained control of the three holiest shrines of their religion, the places of the Annunciation, Nativity and Crucifixion; but all were difficult of access, reached only through strips of newly ceded territory. The frontiers were almost as contorted as those the United Nations originally bestowed on modern Israel. Frederick seems also to have gained al-Kamil's agreement in principle to the rebuilding or strengthening of the walls of several coastal cities, already in Frankish hands: Sidon, until recently divided between Muslims and Latins; Jaffa; Caesarea, where work had already begun. To some extent this was simply recognition of existing conditions: the castle of Montfort or Starkenberg, new headquarters for the Teutonic Knights, had already been established by the knights just before Frederick arrived in the East. The castle would help to consolidate the Frankish position in Galilee, though it could do little really to protect Nazareth, some way to the south.

Frederick's treaty with al-Kamil was seen both in the Muslim and in the Christian world as a betrayal. For the Christians, it was an extraordinary spectacle to have a crusading emperor arrive amid such fanfares, and then, hardly even unsheathing his sword, to have him reach agreement for the return of Jerusalem by mere negotiation. Though diplomacy was not new to the crusading movement, the crusade was always seen as a tremendous physical effort, for by the experience of danger along the way East and in battle the crusader earned divine grace. Toil, trouble and challenge, sweat, sickness and suffering, had been replaced by embassies, subtle bargaining and studied inactivity. In part this reflects a gradual change in the character of crusading: Frederick's crusade, as has been seen, was to a high degree an organized expedition from which deep fervour and mass participation were largely absent. And the emperor's objective was the winning of Jerusalem rather than the winning of glory on the battlefield. From the moment al-Kamil mentioned, long before Frederick's departure, that Jerusalem might be available by treaty, the emperor understood that he would be tested not as a knight but as a diplomat. And in this respect Frederick performed magnificently. But diplomacy means some compromise too: al-Kamil had his own public image to protect, and Frederick realized that a treaty was pointless if its result would be the collapse of the sultan's hard-won reputation in the Muslim hinterland of Syria. Equally, Frederick's impatience to conclude a deal gave al-Kamil some advantages. While Frederick later denied, in letters to European kings, that the walls of Jerusalem were not to be reconstructed, the basic point – that Jerusalem was, with or without walls, nearly defenceless – remained hard to avoid. Moreover, al-Kamil and Frederick had agreed on a ten-year truce, and al-Kamil informed his followers that, in the circumstances, Jerusalem would be an easy plum to pluck at the end of the truce: 'when he had the situation well in hand, he could purify Jerusalem of the Franks and chase them out'. He said:

We have only conceded to them some churches and some ruined houses. The sacred precincts, the venerated Rock and all the other sanctuaries to which we make our pilgrimages remain ours as they were; Muslim rites continue to flourish as they did before, and the Muslims have their own governor of the rural provinces and districts.

In Islamic law ten years, ten months, ten weeks and ten days was the normal maximum for which a truce with the infidel could be agreed. In that period, al-Kamil could hope to consolidate his hold over Damascus and northern Syria. Indeed, in Damascus, under siege from al-Kamil, there was intense mourning for the loss of Jerusalem, and it was rumoured that Muslim pilgrims were to be prevented from visiting the city. Partly, of course, the distress was aimed against al-Kamil, collaborator with the infidel. None the less, the shock was considerable.

On 17 March 1229 Frederick II reached Jerusalem, followed by many pilgrims. They at least did not avoid the company of the excommunicated crusader. His target was the Church of the Holy Sepulchre, largely a crusader structure, and untouched during the recent years of Muslim rule. According to ibn Wasil Frederick only proceeded to Jerusalem when al-Kamil had given his assent; possibly this is exaggeration. Certainly, the qadi of Nablus, Shams ad-din, was appointed by al-Kamil to play host to Frederick; he was a respected religious leader, and, full of tact, he instructed the muezzins not to make their call to prayer in the night, for fear of offending Frederick. But after Frederick's first night in Jerusalem the emperor is said to have complained to Shams ad-din, saying: 'O qadi, why did the muezzins not give the call to prayer in the normal way last night?' To which Shams ald-din replied: 'This humble slave prevented them, out of regard and respect for Your Majesty.' But Frederick is supposed to have said: 'My chief aim in passing the night in Jerusalem was to hear the call to prayer given by the muezzins, and their cries of praise to God during the night.'

He must have been very familiar with the sound of the muezzin from Sicily and Lucera. But the story is quite probably apocryphal: the Muslim sources, greatly confused by Frederick's behaviour, saw him as an emperor whose interest in the recovery of Jerusalem was rather meagre, and whose sympathy for his own religion was surprisingly – indeed scandalously – slight. Thus they also describe his harsh words of reproof to a tactless priest he encountered on the Temple Mount, entering the al-Aqsa mosque carrying a Bible. During his visit to the Temple Mount, in the company of Shams ad-din, he is said to have marvelled greatly at the Dome of the Rock, and to have tried out his wit on his Muslim interlocutors (probably in Arabic, of which he had more than a smattering). He noticed the inscription placed in the building by Saladin: 'Saladin purified this city of polytheists', and cheekily asked who the 'polytheists' might be, clearly aware they were the Christians. He asked too why there was an iron grate around the holy rock in the building, and (though the text has been the subject of controversy) seems to have remarked that it would keep out the pigs, that is, Christians. For the Muslims, 'it was clear that he was a materialist and that his Christianity was simply a game to him'. This they found offensive, on the Islamic principle that adherents of each Religion of the Book must observe its prescribed principles correctly. He gave money to the muezzins, and he paid no attention when his Saracen bodyguard, at the sound of the muezzins' call, prostrated themselves in prayer; for many, not least his Arabic tutor, were Muslims.

In other words the Muslims did not know what to make of him. They were unimpressed by his physique: as a slave in the market, he would not have fetched two hundred dirhams; and he was red-faced, going bald, had weak eyes. As for his contempt for Christianity, this may be greatly exaggerated. The Muslim historians referred also to some of his predecessors in Sicily in similar tones. They found it hard to place rulers who were, in a practical way, fairly respectful towards Islam; the norm among crusaders was profound ignorance of its tenets and lack of interest in discovering more. His love for philosophy and science, of which more later, brought him into contact, sometimes directly, with Muslim learning. This did not prevent him from treating quite harshly his non-Christian subjects in Sicily. It seems likely too that his irritation with the pope and, latterly, with the patriarch of Jerusalem, made him hostile to the behaviour of Churchmen. But this is not to say that he was lukewarm in his Christianity. His personal preference may have been for a poverty-blessed church, in which the bishop of Rome retained only spiritual functions. Yet his attitude to heretics in Italy shows clearly that he had no patience for deviant Christian belief.

On his second day in Jerusalem, well aware that patriarch Gerold was intent on preventing such an act, the emperor went to the Church of the Holy Sepulchre (excommunicate or not) and wore his crown, as Catholic emperor, conscious of the special grace by which omnipotent God had elected him to rule. That is what he says in a letter to Henry III of England, one of the European rulers to whom he sent detailed accounts of his crusade, as a demonstration of the injustice of papal hostility to his holy work. It is surprising so carefully worded a letter has given rise to such misunderstanding, then and ever after. Frederick, it is always related, went to the altar in the Church of the Sepulchre, took from it the crown of the kingdom of Jerusalem, and placed it with his own hands on his head. There was no patriarch present to consecrate him king, no act of unction. More recently, Hans Eberhard Mayer has demonstrated that Frederick's self-coronation is a misunderstanding, generated partly perhaps by analogies with Napoleon. For the emperor was performing the ceremonial act of crown-wearing, normally performed on the great feasts of the Church – Christmas, Easter, Pentecost – though also on important political occasions. He had regarded himself as king of Jerusalem at least since the oath-taking at Brindisi, after his marriage to Isabella. In no sense did his crown-wearing in Jerusalem constitute a change in his kingly status. More importantly, the letter to Henry of England indicates that Frederick wore his crown as *emperor*, as universal ruler; it was the imperial crown that God had, through special grace, bestowed on him. This was the crown of Germany and Lombardy that Frederick had (effectively) won at Mainz and Aachen in 1215, and nothing could symbolize his fulfilment of his ancient and weary crusading vow better than to appear, fourteen or so years later, in Jerusalem, crowned in his imperial majesty.

Clear evidence that this was Frederick's real purpose is provided by a speech delivered on the emperor's behalf to those present (in German translation) by the grand master of the Teutonic Knights, Hermann von Salza. Here Frederick referred to his taking of the cross at Aachen and of his difficulties in fulfilling his obligation. He was aware, he said, of papal wrath, but he pleaded for reconciliation now that the crusade had been successfully concluded. Successfully, indeed, despite the flagrant opposition of others in the Holy Land: here, perhaps, the patriarch and the two great military orders of the Hospital and of the Temple were meant. The emperor aimed to work for God, the Church and the empire, and he was deeply conscious of his own subordination to God himself, who had appointed him as vicar on earth. The speech seems to be many things: a triumphant paean; a plea for peace aimed at Rome; a declaration of the universality of his own imperial authority. It combines humility and insistence on imperial rights. It expects an answer: yes, Gregory is intended to reply, we shall together follow the path of forgiveness and of peace. It was as emperor of the Romans that Frederick entered the church, and as the emperor's mouthpiece that Grand Master von Salza delivered Frederick's manifesto. In Jerusalem, at his moment of triumph, he was strangely unconcerned with the affairs of the kingdom of Jerusalem itself, with the Ibelins and their rivalries. The air of Jerusalem stimulated grander thoughts: Frederick was the new David, appointed to bring deliverance to his people; in other words, he was the Christ-king, higher than common man, chosen to rule over the earth from end to end. This conception of his authority constituted a challenge to the idea propounded in the papal curia of the Roman pontiff as vicar of Christ on earth; thus the ceremony in Jerusalem marks an important moment in the transformation of Frederick from an enthusiastic exponent of papal–imperial peace, as in the good days of Honorius III, to an uncompromising exponent of Roman imperial universalism. The Byzantine-originating heritage of the Norman kings of Sicily may be an important factor here. In Sicily Frederick had access to an idea of monarchy that had little room for papal claims to overlordship, and that laid strong emphasis on the divine election of the king as the new David, or as Christ's vicar. In Jerusalem Frederick, already deeply conscious of his status as Roman emperor, proclaimed clearly the additional element missing from Norman ideology, the idea that the monarch has been called by God to rule *all* mankind.

But this was not the youthful *puer* who had seized in Mainz and Aachen on the apocalyptic aspirations of his contemporaries. In his mid-thirties, Frederick had acquired a more pragmatic view of his power and authority, too. The mystical calling was replaced by an awareness of legal principle: his actions in Cyprus had already demonstrated that he expected his imperial authority to be respected to the full. A tendency towards absolutism, perhaps: that at least was what his enemies, in Lombardy as in Syria, feared. The kingdom of Jerusalem, even the papacy, in some ways seemed to block his aspirations: the Ibelins with their petty rivalries, the popes with their refusal to listen to his demands for peace.

V

The reaction of the Latins in the East to his crusade deeply disappointed the emperor. First, and worst, was the ecclesiastical reaction. Patriarch Gerold, who had studiously kept clear of the crusader army, sent the archbishop of Caesarea to Jerusalem to declare an interdict, for Frederick had presumed to set foot in the Sepulchre Church, and had collaborated with the sultan of Egypt. The peace between al-Kamil and the emperor was considered in no way praiseworthy; not by such means was Jerusalem to be recovered for good. Frederick's crown-wearing was celebrated a day before the interdict was imposed, while the archbishop was hurrying to the city in the hope of preventing just such a celebration. The interdict meant that no church services could be held in Jerusalem; it was an extraordinary act to impose it on the city of Jerusalem itself, and it meant that pilgrims were denied the opportunity to earn the remission of sin they would gain from visiting the Holy Places; the announcement of the interdict cannot have endeared the pilgrims to the papacy. Frederick answered the challenge with a confident challenge of his own: he ordered the archbishop of Caesarea into his presence, to explain himself, but the prelate had the good sense to stay away.

The reaction of the clergy was hostile for other reasons too, though the complaints increased in the weeks after the treaty with al-Kamil. The newly won lands in Galilee were claimed back by their ancient lords, such as the bishops of Nazareth and Tiberias. But Frederick preferred to bestow them on those of proven loyalty, above all the Teutonic Knights. His favours to them irritated still further the Templars and Hospitallers, the latter of whom claimed rights of lordship over the German order. Thus Frederick's actions, however well-intentioned, stimulated antagonism. Another source of difficulty was the delicate relationship between the Christian merchants of Acre, Tyre and Beirut and the Muslims of Damascus, a major source of supply of luxury goods. Indeed, Acre and its neighbours were to all intents the Mediterranean ports of Damascus; and many of the Christian merchants were Genoese, Venetians and other north

Italians, who had reasons for mistrusting Frederick's Italian as well as his Syrian policy. The Arabs of Damascus deeply resented the surrender of Jerusalem to Frederick by the sultan of Egypt. The Damascenes saw the Holy Land as an extension of their part of Syria, and they saw Jerusalem as a possession of their own holy city of Damascus. Thus the merchants of Acre, and those knights whose income came from rents and taxes, were acutely worried at the possible effects of Frederick's interference in the rivalries of the Muslim world. They believed their access to the Muslim hinterland was being placed in danger; freedom to visit Jerusalem, economically insignificant, was no substitute for access to the majestic oasis city of Damascus.

The longer Frederick remained in the kingdom of Jerusalem, the deeper the antagonism to him grew. The Templars were active in support of Patriarch Gerold, and rumour had it Frederick was ready to seize the grand master and take him back to Apulia as his hostage. Once back in Acre Frederick's men seem to have besieged or blockaded the Templar quarter in the city. At any rate, the emperor had won little popularity by his agreement with al-Kamil. According to jurists writing in the Latin kingdom a little after these events, Frederick earmarked for dispossession of their lands and income a whole group of Syrian nobles, although he did not press further his claim against John of Ibelin that Beirut was not rightfully John's possession. He found in the kingdom of Jerusalem a powerful legal tradition built, it must be said, on a fictitious view of the kingdom's origins: on the view that the barons who led the First Crusade had together elected the first rulers and had acquired as of right a say in the kingdom's management; the dispossession of vassals, for instance, was a matter to be judged by the high court, containing the leading barons of the kingdom, and not by the king alone. These views had matured during the period when the kingdom was without effective leadership by a king regnant, and Frederick could not at a stroke dispense with the accumulated legal wisdom of the Ibelins and their peers: less so, indeed, since his own constitutional position, now Isabella was dead, was dubious. More than that: the Ibelins did not simply preach elaborate constitutional ideas; they held power in key areas of the kingdom, as also in much of Cyprus, and their military and political strength could not be ignored. A direct clash between Frederick's allies and John of Beirut's occurred over the lordship of Toron and Chastel Neuf. This was claimed by the Teutonic Knights, backed by the emperor and his *bailli* in the Latin kingdom, Balian of Sidon. But a rival claimant, the princess Alice of Armenia, won the support of the Ibelin faction; and, acting within the laws of the kingdom, the Ibelins withdrew their service from Frederick on the grounds that he had illegally dispossessed one of their number. This withdrawal of service seems to have occurred before Frederick returned to Acre at the end of his crusade. The emperor's hand was forced; in the end he had to agree that Alice's claim was irrefutable, and he compensated the Teutonic Order by the grant of other lands in lieu of Toron. What is clear is that Frederick found himself bound by the actions of his high court; the sanction, withdrawal of service, was a serious enough blow to force Frederick to submit to the judgement of the Syrian barons. It was thus apparent that Frederick's attempts to import into the Latin East a grander, imperial, ideal of his authority over the kingdom of Jerusalem had met with irresistible opposition.

Another sign that Frederick could not tame the Latin kingdom was provided in the last minutes of his stay in Acre. Tension in Acre was near boiling-point. The emperor, in any case, was desperate to return to southern Italy and to destroy the papal armies sent against the *regno*. His final act was to appoint a permanent *bailli* or regent in the kingdom of Jerusalem. Probably he hoped to appoint a south Italian, Thomas of Acerra, but the Syrian barons seem to have insisted on one of their own number. Meanwhile Frederick tried to steal out of Acre on 1 May, but he was recognized as he was about to board a galley standing hard by the butchers' quarter of Acre. The butchers bombarded him with offal, furious at his actions in the Latin East. John of Ibelin came hurrying after, sent packing those who had pelted Frederick – for Frederick remained king and as such worthy of honour – and, standing on the quayside, hailed the emperor's ship. Who, he shouted, has the emperor appointed as *bailli* in the Latin kingdom? The emperor called back, softly, that Balian of Sidon and Garnier l'Aleman were so appointed. It seems Frederick realized he could not impose an outsider, at least for the moment, but that two Syrian barons known for their loyalty to him would have to do instead. Frederick then sailed north to Tyre, where Balian and Garnier awaited him. John of Beirut had, none the less, scored an important point: he had shown publicly his own respect for Frederick, calling off the butchers and preventing a serious riot. A stickler for correct practice, John was able to foster the image of himself as a pillar of rectitude, as he had done when faced with a plot against Frederick's life.

Frederick's lack of success with the barons of Syria seemed to be balanced by a turn in his fortunes in Cyprus itself. Before he left Acre, Frederick sent Étienne de Botron and a squadron of south Italian knights from the Holy Land to Cyprus, demanding the surrender of all the island's fortresses to imperial authority. Leading Ibelins and their allies fled the island; John of Jaffa, later one of the leading Syrian lawyers, but now a child, was among them, and his writings reflect the constitutional struggles surrounding Frederick's journey to the east. But the result was that 'the emperor held Cyprus', as Philip of Novara concisely says. Young King Henry had to be delivered into Frederick's own hands. Frederick's coup on Cyprus meant that his return to Limassol, on leaving Acre and Tyre, had a very different character to his first visit. Aimery Barlais and his four allies were treated with honour, and were sold the regency of Cyprus for 10,000 marks: Frederick was not going to give away Cyprus for nothing. Aimery was to ensure that John of Beirut was prevented from setting foot in the island, and, to this effect, German, Flemish and south Italian soldiers were left to garrison Cyprus. Young King Henry was betrothed to a daughter of the marquis of Montferrat, whose family not long before had opposed Frederick in Lombardy; but Henry was not to wield power for some years, and the emperor was confident he could rely on the five barons and their 'Longobard' (south Italian) soldiers. What is especially interesting is the financial arrangement. Frederick's crusade had cost him a fortune; every effort had to be made to recoup expenses. Perhaps his initial demand for money from John of Beirut had been motivated by concern at the mounting cost of the crusade, as much as by a desire to stamp out corruption. At any rate, the use of diplomacy rather than arms in his crusade had offered, among other advantages, considerable financial saving.

Frederick had, however, once again miscalculated the force-fulness of opposition to him in the Latin East. Precisely because he had tried, as his final revenge against the Ibelins, to exclude them from Cyprus, the Ibelins refused to lie quietly. They fitted out some ships, sailed to Cyprus (in July 1229) and pushed the five barons northwards into the mountains around Kyrenia, Kantara and Dieu d'Amour, three strong fortresses. The Cypriot barons as a whole proved well-disposed to the Ibelins. The five barons had sought to raise the ten thousand marks promised to Frederick by extortion and dispossession of their foes. Thus considerable opposition to the barons had rapidly built up. By mid-1230 the Ibelins had gained complete control over Cyprus, and King Henry was even in their hands. Philip of Novara de-scribes his own alarming experiences on a private visit to Cyprus, threatened with death and lucky to escape from the clutches of the five barons, taking refuge with the knights of St John in Nicosia. His aim is to portray the rule of Aimery Barlais and his friends as a reign of terror; more likely, years of dispossession under John of Beirut's baillage were now being countered by acts of vengeance against known supporters of the Ibelins. In particular, the five barons needed to gain control of the castles throughout Cyprus. Their failure to do so meant that the door remained open for John of Ibelin's triumphant return.

Frederick's crusade left a legacy of conflict and disorder both in Cyprus and in the Holy Land. The imperial factions on the island and on the mainland continued for years to struggle for ascendancy; in the 1230s, the Latin kingdom was, to all intents, split between Ibelins and imperialists. What is clear from the events between September 1228 and May 1229 is that Frederick had consistently underestimated the strength of the Ibelin op-position; this strength was not merely military, but also ideolo-gical. The emperor began by assuming that it would be sufficient to proclaim his rights as he interpreted them; the Latins of the East, long anxious for his presence, would surely accept his in-structions, if only in the interests of the crusade. He found it hard to envisage the degree to which the Latin states of the East, despite the bitter threat from the Islamic world, were divided by family rivalries and constitutional conflicts. More than that, he was amazed at the lack of response to what he clearly saw as his own tremendous achievement, the recovery of Jerusalem. He had not, after all, ascended the Mount of Olives to hang his shield on an olive tree and usher in the last days of mankind; messianic fervour had proved strangely absent, amid interdicts and petty rivalries. His crown-wearing in Jerusalem, for all its Davidic associations, had not proved a catalyst; rather, indeed, had it focused opposition against him, for the imprecations of pope and patriarch had only gathered intensity. Frederick's crusade was a sobering experience. He returned to Italy more than ever conscious of his imperial rights, but also more than ever conscious that opposition to those rights stemmed from those with whom, in the past, he had hoped to work: the bishop of Rome, the Syrian barons, among others.

Frederick's Jerusalem may have flourished briefly, once in Latin hands. There are signs that a scriptorium, capable of producing a manuscript as beautiful as the Riccardiana Psalter, now in Florence, flourished in the city. The Tower of David was strengthened; whatever promises Frederick may have made to al-Kamil, the city's fortifications were gradually restored. One structure that probably dates from the period when Jerusalem was once again in crusader hands is the Coenaculum, or room of the Last Supper, on Mount Zion. It is very likely that it is thirteenth-century work, with its heavily moulded pointed windows; it stands above a more ancient structure, traditionally identified as the tomb of King David, which had already attracted the attention of Christian pilgrims. As before, however, Acre remained the commercial and judicial centre of the kingdom, rivalled more by Tyre (seat of the imperialists) than by the spiritual capital, Jerusalem. The papacy made more fuss about the disadvantages of Frederick's treaty with al-Kamil than about the obvious fact that the holiest city of Christendom had been recovered by Frederick II.

VI

==

Going fast before the wind, Frederick reached Brindisi on 10 June 1229. He returned, after a year's absence, to a kingdom in disorder. Rebellion had been fomented against him; rumours had been spread that he was dead, or a prisoner; the pope was organizing a vicious propaganda campaign against him. All seemed at risk. It is necessary to turn back to 1228, to see how effectively Gregory IX took advantage of Frederick's absence to try to destroy the emperor's power utterly. He saw in Frederick's crusade a chance to achieve the long-desired separation of Sicily from the empire; but no longer by means of a dynastic arrangement concerning the Hohenstaufen heirs. Gregory moved towards a radical solution: to displace Frederick entirely from all his thrones, to rule Sicily and southern Italy directly, since they were already under the ultimate jurisdiction of St Peter; to find a new dynasty for Germany, more amenable to papal wishes. This was seen as an act in defence of papal authority, not merely in the central Italian lands contested with Frederick's forebears, but over all Christendom.

Even before the emperor left for the East, the pope was trying to win support for radical measures. His most obvious course of action was to free the emperor's subjects from their oaths of allegiance to Frederick; this was not the same as deposition, but it was an important step in that direction. The duke of Bavaria was perhaps the only major German prince to be attracted by Gregory's plans; and the pope's failure to win much support in Germany put paid to papal dreams of a new election to the German crown, in which a compliant ruler would be chosen, willing to spearhead opposition to the Hohenstaufen. A little more interest was shown by the governments of the towns in northern and central Italy. This fact underlines the contrast between Frederick's success in gaining German loyalty, through generous grants to his followers, and his continued difficulties with the more unruly Lombard towns. But even in Lombardy there was little coordination. Actually, what the cities most wanted was the departure of Frederick for the East, for once he was away they could resume their squabbles without fear of imperial intervention. Gregory really failed to secure the support he needed in the imperial lands; he also tried to win support in Sicily, once again by releasing the emperor's subjects from their oath, a task made easier by the existence of papal claims to overlordship over Sicily. Here, in fact, his main successes only came after rumours were spread, in 1229, of Frederick's death; subversion and lies were the methods adopted by the vicar of Christ. One figure, however, stood by the irate pontiff, anxious for gain of his own: John of Brienne. Now elderly, he still saw himself as the Church's champion against Hohenstaufen tyranny, another in a line of athletes of Christ whose wars in southern Italy received papal blessing.

Gregory saw his war against Frederick as a just one, analogous to a crusade. He demanded tithes from the Churches of England, Scandinavia and France, with which he would finance John of Brienne's campaign. The target was southern Italy and Sicily, the recovery of the vassal kingdom by the holy see. In England, as Roger of Wendover reports, there was much resistance to Gregory's levies of money. In the end bishops and abbots found themselves pawning their plate, in an attempt to supply the Church of Rome with its war funds. Promises that those who gave would earn honour for themselves and papal gratitude were not enough; laymen hotly resisted the taxation. Still, a large sum was in the end brought together and transmitted to Rome. The levy of a tithe is significant for several reasons. Gregory IX tried on this occasion to harness the financial machinery of the Church in aid of a war which was not actually a crusade. For there was no promise of an indulgence, carrying remission of sins, to those who participated in the war, or to those who gave money for it. In 1228 Gregory was not yet prepared to unleash the full wrath of the Church against Frederick, even though Innocent III had already talked briefly of the war against Markward von Anweiler as a crusade; Gregory's conflict with Frederick only became a crusade in 1239 and 1240. Soldiers in the war bore not the cross on their shoulders, but the keys of St Peter. There was still uncertainty about the legitimacy of declaring a crusade against the lay enemies of the Church, in 1228; and this uncertainty was compounded by Frederick's own role as crusader, albeit under sentence of excommunication. Gregory was therefore careful not to answer Frederick's crusade, corrupted though he thought it to be, with a crusade against Frederick on Italian soil. Public reaction, not least in Rome itself, would be hostile. The war of 1228 was a sort of half-crusade, lacking the privileges conferred on participants in a crusade, but in certain other respects

– the use of the tithe, the sign of the keys rather than the cross – modelled on the existing institution of the crusade. Actually, many participants were mercenaries from northern Europe or Spain, not in any case the sort of people who could be lured to fight by the offer of heavenly rewards. Gregory's sense of righteousness was enhanced by the reaction of Frederick's devoted lieutenant Rainald, duke of Spoleto. Already the object of papal fury, because of his use of the Spoleto title, Rainald earned further obloquy by building up his armed forces in Spoleto and the area to the east, the march of Ancona. The intention was to stand in the way of any invading armies, but Rainald's lines of communication were evidently too stretched; a papal army pushed him back, despite his apparent popularity in central Italy, and exposed the frontiers of the *regno* to attack (winter 1228–9). In early 1229 another papal force marched into the kingdom of Sicily, but for two months its way was blocked by the Sicilian armies under Henry de Morra, chief justiciar of the kingdom. Morra's defeat in March led to a sudden collapse of the royalists in the area around Montecassino. From that moment, the kingdom seemed dangerously threatened. It is easy, in fact, to see why Frederick was, in the months up to March 1229, prepared to sit out the negotiations with al-Kamil without returning home. The situation in southern Italy was serious, but Henry de Morra was holding firm. Once Henry's army was routed, Frederick's need to return and organize the defence of the *regno* became acute. And that, indeed, was the course of action Frederick took. Letters survive, sent to Frederick by his officers in Sicily, urging his rapid return, and warning of plots to seize or harm the emperor. Frederick himself, according to Arabic sources, wrote to his friend Fakhr ad-din, courtier of al-Kamil and ambassador to Sicily during the 1220s; the letter is dated 23 August 1229, from Barletta in Apulia, and refers to events during Frederick's absence in the East:

As we explained to you in Sidon, the pope has treacherously and deceitfully taken one of our fortresses, called Montecassino, handed over to him by its accursed abbot. He had promised to do even more harm, but could not, for our faithful subjects expected our return. He was forced therefore to spread false news of our death, and made the cardinals swear to it and to say that our return was impossible. They sought to deceive the populace by these tricks and by saying that after us no one could administer our estates and look after them for our son so well as the pope. So, on the oaths of such men, who should be high priests of the faith and successors of the apostles, a rabble of louts and criminals was led by the nose.

Certainly the situation worsened in spring 1229. Rainald of Spoleto lost control of the march of Ancona, and John of Brienne's armies began, though only slowly, to penetrate Apulia. Insurrection among the towns was encouraged by the pope; Naples, Gaeta and other cities were offered generous privileges, granting self-government on the north Italian model in return for recognition of papal suzerainty and for the payment of certain taxes to Rome. The long-festering desire for communal auton-omy was ably exploited by Gregory. But, contrary to Frederick's letter to Fakhr ad-din (if it is at all genuine), Gregory did not intend to replace Frederick in Sicily with a new king, such as one of Frederick's two sons. He clearly aimed to disband entirely the kingdom of Sicily. Southern Italy and Sicily were to remain under the direct control of Rome. John of Brienne and his family were probably promised lands in Lecce and the rest of Apulia, but there is no real evidence that John stood to gain Sicily's crown. On the other hand, new problems were emerging which the papacy could not easily handle: a Muslim rebellion among the small Saracen community that still remained in western Sicily, hostile to Frederick but not especially keen on papal lordship either. Moreover, the costs of the campaign were frightening. Precisely because the papal armies had been held at bay so long, money with which to pay the mercenaries or to maintain supply-lines was running short. The tithe had produced enough for a good start, but not enough for a long drawn-out campaign. A quick solution was essential. The cardinals themselves chipped in with loans to the papacy. But better still was to crack opposition for good by pretending that Frederick would never return. Hence the blatant dishonesty of Gregory IX, well aware of Frederick's activities in the Latin East, through reports from patriarch Gerold and even from Frederick's ignored pleas for peace.

With Frederick's sudden return, Gregory's evil rumours now backfired on the pope. Here was the emperor, safe and victorious; rapidly, opposition in Apulia crumbled. The problematic letter to Fakhr ad-din tries to portray Frederick as the mighty ruler whose very presence is enough to sow panic among the enemy. There was probably some truth in this. Frederick restored order in Apulia, gathered together local loyalists and newly arrived crusaders, including many trusty Germans, and chased the enemy across country to the other side of Italy. Aiming for the frontier country, seized in March by the enemy, Frederick recovered control of the area around Cassino, San Germano and Sora. This last he saw as a treacherous town worthy of exemplary punishment. The city was razed and many of its inhabitants hanged or put to the sword. Frederick's brutality was not an empty act of furious vengeance. It was a considered move. A ruler who did not know how to punish treachery was not worthy of his crown; a ruler who did not know how to practise mercy, on other occasions, was also hardly worthy. As God's deputy, Frederick dispensed both forgiveness and chastisement, seeking through examples to impress on southern Italy the fate that might well await continuing traitors. It was a policy that worked well. John of Brienne was crushed by the end of October; well before this, in fact, his future had been obvious. It has been pointed out by historians that Frederick did not seek to cap his victory by pursing his enemies north of the frontier of the *regno*, into those lands recently held by Rainald of Spoleto. But Frederick did not see his task as the conquest of the papal patrimony, nor even as the humiliation of the pope, though that had already been achieved, to some degree, by his victory in southern Italy. Frederick's first priority was to wring from Gregory an acknowledgement that their long-standing conflict was at an end, and to work out a formula that would protect his own rights without disparagement of the papacy. In other words, he sought a return to the *modus vivendi* achieved under Honorius III. Frederick's second priority was the re-establishment of control in southern Italy and Sicily, for the invasion by papal armies had, as has been seen, been accompanied by rebellion; and new legislation for the *regno* was soon to be formulated. As for Germany and Lombardy, Frederick was surely struck by the loyalty of the former: here rewards were in order, in the form of further grand privileges. Lombard disunity during 1228 and 1229 had proved clearly to both pope and emperor that the north Italian cities did not pose a serious threat to Frederick once he was outside their stamping-grounds. After the irritation of his journey to the East, after the

crisis of John of Brienne's invasion, Frederick could hope for
better prospects henceforth. Gregory must be made to come to
terms, but even in negotiating with the arch-enemy, Frederick
was disposed to offer a generous bait.

VII

Making the pope come to terms proved, none the less, extraordinarily difficult. It was only in July 1230, after the intervention of
the German princes and of Grand Master von Salza, that peace
was agreed; the threat of war had been renewed, but even then
Gregory proved very resistant. It is probably right to see his
agreement to negotiate not so much as his decision, as the decision
of several prominent cardinals aware of Frederick's genuine desire
to put an end to their differences. Besides, Gregory's obstinacy
was rigid. Even the petitions of the German princes were greeted
with suspicion. Gregory knew that an agreement with Frederick
would seal Frederick's control of Germany and Sicily; it would
mark the surrender of an important principle that underlay
Gregory's initial imprecations against Frederick. But Gregory
was aware too that Frederick had by now fulfilled (after a fashion)
his crusade vows, had won much support in the courts of Europe,
and had held securely on to his power in Germany, while
Lombardy, Gregory's main source of hope, had barely lifted a
finger on the pope's behalf. In the end, then, Gregory agreed to
lift his excommunication of the emperor, and to cancel his other
acts against Frederick; Frederick, for his part, promised to permit
the Sicilian Church free elections, to exempt the Sicilian clergy
from secular jurisdiction – in other words, to renounce claims to
apostolic legatine authority within southern Italy. Frederick, as
part of this series of promises, was also to return to the orders of
the Temple and the Hospital their extensive south Italian lands,
seized after the crusade, out of wrath at the orders' behaviour
towards him in the East. In fact, a general amnesty was promised
for the pope's supporters in southern Italy.

These agreements, made at San Germano and Ceprano, are
often seen as an astonishing failure on Frederick's part to follow

through the advantages gained by his victory over John of Brienne's army. Frederick's amenability was, however, deliberate. In the first place, he had to draw Gregory towards the very idea of negotiation. In the second place, Frederick was aware that his excommunication, despite victory, remained an embarrassment, a propaganda tool for his enemies; as a Christian, he did not wish to remain in a state of excommunication anyway. In the third place, Frederick emerged from the negotiations still as German and Sicilian ruler; thus Gregory's fundamental objections to Frederick's excessive accretion of power had been set aside. In fact, the peace agreement was a victory for Frederick, not for Gregory, though it was presented in a manner which brought the pope no real humiliation. Frederick knew that the irascible Gregory must be treated with honour even in defeat; and the emperor does not seem to have minded the reaction of contemporaries who criticized him for giving away much in return for little. So long as Gregory himself could maintain that fiction, peace between pope and emperor might be made to last. The treaties of San Germano and Ceprano were a considerable act of statesmanship on Frederick's part. Moreover, Frederick had demonstrated, for the second time in two years, his diplomatic skills. With al-Kamil too he had sat and insisted and waited. Al-Kamil was in many ways an easier potentate with whom to deal.

The final act was performed in private, in September 1230, at Anagni, where Frederick, Hermann von Salza and Gregory dined together. By now papal letters were speaking soothing words about Frederick. Kantorowicz contrasts the letters of 1229, damning Frederick as the disciple of Muhammad, with those of summer, 1230, praising him as the 'beloved son of the church'. It is far from clear that the change in tone in Gregory's letters reflects a change of heart in Gregory himself. But the pope was, henceforth, on his best behaviour. He had little option.

CHAPTER SIX

LAW AND MONARCHY IN SICILY

I

Back in the kingdom of Sicily, Frederick worked rapidly and effectively towards the restoration of royal control. His victories over the papal armies rapidly brought all opponents to their knees: it was apparent that the emperor was neither dead nor destroyed, and the Peace of San Germano quashed all hopes of civic liberties in the restive towns of Campania. But the restoration of order could not, in Frederick's eyes, be achieved solely by force of arms. Another force, that of law, must be pressed into royal service. In 1231, during the summer, Frederick enunciated a new code of laws for his kingdom, presenting this code to his vassals at Melfi in the south Italian hinterland. The *Constitutions of Melfi*, containing over two hundred laws and proclamations, have been hailed by historians as the clearest evidence of Frederick's wish to make of Sicily a 'model state', well-ordered, centralized, efficient, in which all rights and obligations are subject to the ruler's whim or will. The practical requirements of reconstruction were wedded to the theoretical requirements of a highly developed concept of absolutist monarchy to create a coherent, consistent body of legislation. Such an interpretation of the *Constitutions of Melfi* is, however, based on wishful thinking. Whatever the degree of influence upon Frederick of the great Roman law-codes, of the contemporary canon lawyers, and of the newly fashionable philosophy of Aristotle, his legislation does not mark the coming of a new Justinian. The laws were not issued on the scale of the Roman codes; they did not seek to encompass the whole of human experience, but rather to deal with problems specific to a kingdom in urgent need of reconstruction. Nor were the laws profoundly original. They formed a practical combination of themes from Roman, canonist and feudal sources; elements of German common law, where thought most practical, were thrown in alongside the inveterate customs of the south Italians.

Law-codes often reveal to the reader merely what he wants to find. The *Constitutions of Melfi* have not generally been read by historians in their entirety. The search for proof of the Romanism of the Sicilian monarchy – a theme amply demonstrated in other, older sources – has distracted historians from the significance of these laws as a guide to contemporary legal conduct in law courts populated by Lombards, Greeks and even non-Christians. What will be stressed here is the link between this legislation and the political and social structure of the *regno* in the years around 1231. The antecedents of individual laws – Roman, Norman or whatever – are an issue of secondary interest. So too the name commonly given to the code, the *Liber Augustalis*, 'the Augustan book', will be avoided: a name that is the creation of those later commentators who wished to see in these laws an explicit statement of the theory of autocracy.

This is not to deny that the *Constitutions of Melfi* are filled with references to the Roman imperial past, and expound a view of the ruler as the maker of law. The point is, rather, that these themes are not consistently carried through the laws. An idea is enunciated of the nature of law, but it does not impregnate the individual laws; it does not give shape to the code of laws. Perhaps this should be expected. The laws were issued only a few months after the emperor's treaty with the pope; during that period investigators had travelled the *regno*, summoning wise men to give an account of local legal practice. No doubt these *enquêteurs* also kept an eye open for abuses of royal rights – adulterine castles, the expropriation of royal demesne land, and so on. At their head stood the emperor's closest adviser, the lawyer Piero della Vigna, one of the very few persons, apart from Norman kings and Roman emperors, to be named in the *Constitutions*. Subsequently, Frederick added a series of *Novels*, updating or supplementing the law-book of 1231. All this points to the rapidity of execution of the law-code, and its almost experimental character: the product of a few months' intensive work, it could hardly possess the smoothness and orderliness of the Roman *Digest*.

Up to a point, there is even a deep confusion about the nature of the legislative act. Frederick cited at length the laws of his Norman predecessors – generally short, emphatic statements from the assizes of Roger II, and more long-winded legislation of William the Good. The contrast between Roger's terse statements of principle and Frederick's verbose expositions (which have certainly defeated one translator into English: the original Latin is not always clear or elegant) is striking. Frederick's laws mix general statements of principle with detailed discussion of individual problems of law. Occasionally, the emperor's own hand is visible. Maybe the combination of a team of Roman lawyers, led by the redoubtable della Vigna, with a demanding and interfering master threw the law-book off balance: the attempts of the drafters to provide harmony were defeated by the particularities intruded by the emperor, and by the local problems of a kingdom whose laws were founded upon a variety of conflicting traditions.

The introduction to the law-code does, however, provide a striking view of Frederick's outlook. The first words proclaim Frederick's titles: emperor of the Romans, Caesar Augustus, ruler of the kingdoms of Italy, Sicily, Jerusalem and Burgundy. Here is the first paradox: throughout the law book Frederick refers to himself as the 'Augustus'; he mentions his 'divine predecessors' the *Augusti* of ancient Rome, or indeed of more recent times (such as Henry VI and Constance). He presents himself as emperor, and yet he legislates for a kingdom whose relationship to the empire was, as has been seen, very uncertain – a kingdom whose separateness from the Roman empire had been stressed by Roger II and apparently accepted even by Henry VI; a kingdom that in any case was a vassal state of the papacy, a fact which at once indicated that it was not a part of the empire even when ruled by the same person who ruled the empire. Frederick's law-code does not bother to discuss these niceties. In the introduction the emperor stresses that the kingdom of Sicily is 'the precious inheritance of our majesty' and that the disruptions it has suffered since his childhood make it necessary to provide for peace and justice within its borders. The legislation is expressly said to apply throughout the kingdom of Sicily, but it is not made to apply further afield. It is stated that Sicily is the kingdom under the emperor's rule in most urgent need of good rule; but throughout the law codes there are few specific references to Frederick's other kingdoms. This confusion about the status of the Sicilian kingdom was to bedevil Italian politics for the rest of Frederick's reign. It will be seen shortly that this tendency to treat Sicily as part of the empire in a certain sense, and yet as a separate entity with its own traditions, even reappears on the face of Frederick's gold coins, issued in the same period for the kingdom of Sicily.

The *regno* needed Frederick's attention: it is Necessity that lies at the root of the act of law-making. The introduction to the code begins with an account of why laws are made. God created the universe and appointed man as master over other creatures. Man was subjected to a simple primordial law, but disobeyed; by eating of the tree of knowledge man lost his immortality, and this in itself endangered the rest of creation: what was to be the purpose of lesser creatures if they did not serve the needs of the master God had created over them? At this point we perhaps see the influence of Aristotelian ideas of the function of man and the created world, an idea followed further in the analysis of the nature of and need for law. Man's transgression was potentially disastrous for creation, but God allowed man to multiply, and the spread of mankind generated new problems. Man was created virtuous, but when he became numerous he entered into conflict with his fellow-humans over the ownership of property. Hatred was itself a legacy of the sin committed in the Garden of Eden, of the discovery of the knowledge of evil. It was under divine inspiration and also under the compelling pressure of necessity that princes were created through whom crimes and disputes might be settled. Original sin was not the direct cause of the creation of princely authority: princely power stems from the benevolence of God and from the clear necessity to put to an end the strife of mankind. And what are the duties of the princes? The preservation of the Church is mentioned first. This should not be read, as it often is, as an attempt to seize the initiative in governing spiritual affairs from the papacy; the idea of the ruler (and especially of the emperor) as *gladius Christi*, defending the

Church from its enemies, was widely diffused both in imperial and ecclesiastical circles. But Frederick may well have enjoyed the opportunity to stress the seriousness of his obligation to defend the Church, at a time when echoes could be heard of the view that he was the worst enemy of the Church.

Beyond defence of the Church, indeed, resulting from that act, lay the defence of secular peace, and its enforcement through the exercise of justice. Here the *Constitutions* obliquely refer to the circumstances that brought them into existence: an emperor who had restored order within his realm, and was now under an obligation to promote *justitia*. This word meant justice not merely in the practical sense. In an elegant but mysterious phrase Professor Ullmann explained that '*justitia* is unshaped *jus*; it stands in the antechamber of *jus*'. Or, more simply, law-making should be conducted according to principles of right-ordering; laws are to be derived from ethical assumptions enshrined in God's teaching. One of the edicts in the law-book points out how the king's judges, the justiciars, take their name from the words *jus* and *justitia*. Nor, indeed, is it surprising that the great gateway erected at Capua in 1234 portrays the emperor, his judges and, in a commanding position, a statue of Justitia: righteousness expressed through good government.

It is sometimes suggested that the introduction to the so-called *Liber Augustalis* displays a striking rebuttal of accepted ideas about the nature of government. Man's sin in the Garden of Eden gives rise, over subsequent generations, to discord; rulers are the *flagellum*, the scourge, appointed by the exercise of their strictness to put to an end the squabblings of the sinful. Frederick's appeal to necessity is interpreted as a substitution of a positive natural force, beneficial in character, for the negative restraining force of government envisaged by earlier theorists. In fact, the emperor's ideas are not so revolutionary. He does not say that rulers have no duty to punish mankind for sinfulness. His ideas of government stand in a direct line going back to Augustinian ideas of the state as the corrector of man's sinfulness. It is true that Frederick intrudes notions which, at least coincidentally, have an Aristotelian flavour, stressing the function of the created world and the purpose of the ruler as a source of potential perfection or improvement within society. In other words, Frederick's introduction expounds a more optimistic view of the purpose of rulership and the ways in which government can bring society towards its most urgent objectives: peace and the exercise of righteous conduct. This optimism may have its source in a close reading not of Aristotelian texts (Aristotle's political and ethical works not yet being available in the west) but in the perusal of canon-law texts. The abstract view of monarchy's purpose, expounded in the admonitions of past popes and in the treatises of curial lawyers, now moves outside the Roman curia into the imperial court. The omission of reference to the other great 'luminary' alongside the emperor, the vicar of Christ, is not surprising. Frederick's anxiety to boost the good name of the emperor and his wish to suppress reference to the overlord of the king of Sicily meant that, on practical grounds, there was no need for reference to the pope as partner in the exercise of *justitia*. Besides, on theoretical grounds, Frederick had expounded a neat, straight-forward view of monarchy's meaning and purpose that stood autonomously – that did not depend on the saving grace of the pontiff. His explanation of the nature of political authority was based in Christian sources and upon Christian assumptions about God's relationship to man; but it was a system that subsisted without the aid or intervention of a Roman pontiff. It was not a secular idea of monarchy; Frederick's power was divinely endowed, as the introduction to the laws clearly states. But there was no sacerdotal intermediary between God and the prince.

Here lies the political significance of the introduction to the *Constitutions of Melfi*. A theory of government could be pro-pounded in which there was no need to include the saving power of the pope. It was the ruler who had the power to direct mankind to a better end, through the proclamation of good law based on the exercise of righteousness (*justitia*). This optimism must be set against the pessimism of the view that the ruler was a scourge whose power must be reined in by the vicar of Christ. In that sense, the law-book reveals important (though not outstandingly original) thinking at the imperial court – ideas to be developed further under the pressure of new conflicts with the papacy in the 1230s and 1240s. But whether the views were those of Piero della Vigna or of the emperor, and how the two men worked together, remains a mystery. It is reasonable to assume that the

learned lawyer provided the basic framework at least, while
Frederick vetted what Piero offered him.

II

In the Middle Ages, it was assumed that old law was generally
good law. Yet the *Constitutions of Melfi* combine old and new
law: the dominating theme is the need to adapt and improve law
to fit the urgent needs of the Sicilian kingdom. The German
scholar Hermann Dilcher has heroically traced the Roman,
Byzantine, Lombard, Norman, canonist, even Spanish, origins
of the laws of Melfi. But in order to do this he has had to
dismantle the laws sentence by sentence. For, though Roman
law remains the preponderant influence, the Melfi legislation
does not consist of a plagiaristic restatement of Justinian's code.
The *Constitutions* are eclectic, reminiscent indeed of the Norman
monarchy, with its enthusiastic but often inelegant juxtaposition
of ideas and practices derived from several cultures; and, just as
the Norman monarchy retained a highly pragmatic outlook, so
did Frederick in his legislation. In other words, the *Constitutions
of Melfi* are Norman government restored – not just in the sense
that the monarchy was decisively reasserting itself, but also in the
sense that a practical combination of what seemed useful in all
the legal sources available was enunciated. Norman law-making
had proceeded on similar lines.

A few examples will reveal the vigorous mixing of legislation
that underlies the *Constitutions*. A strong canonistic influence is
visible in laws denouncing heretics: the Fourth Lateran Council,
of 1215, is certainly one source, but attention seems also to have
been paid to papal legislation of the late twelfth century. Laws
against usurers combine canonistic origins with innovation:
clauses permitting Jewish moneylenders to charge ten per cent
per annum interest seem to have no ecclesiastical source. Some
laws are concerned with specific problems within the *regno*, and
have few antecedents: the requirement that the ornate 'Bene-
ventan' style of handwriting should be abandoned for a plainer
and more legible script is aimed at the notaries of Naples, Amalfi

and Sorrento, where the archaic hand remained in use; officials from that area were becoming prominent in the royal administration and there must have been a fear that the records of government would begin to be drawn up in an unfamiliar and complicated hand. A clause in the same constitution banning the use of paper for documents to be presented in the law courts seems also to be an original 'Frederician' law without precedent; its aim was to ensure that documentation was not placed at risk of easy destruction by the use of a friable medium. But extensive sections of the law-book discuss Lombard laws: an edict concerned with the violent seizure of property begins with the words, 'we choose a middle path between Lombard law and Common [i.e., Roman–Byzantine] law.' The emperor, acting in the same manner as his Norman predecessors, permitted the continued use of Lombard and 'Frankish' law among his Lombard and Norman subjects, except where it conflicted with the present legislation. But the *Constitutions of Melfi* were frequently explicit about such conflicts of laws. A striking example of this is provided by a law abolishing special privileges of the Normans (or 'Franks') in court procedure:

We desire to end the ambiguity about a certain special right, or as it might more appropriately be termed, denial of right (*iniuria*), practised by the Franks and observed in civil and criminal cases until now. Thus we desire that all our subjects should know, under the terms of this law, that we, who weigh on our scales each individual's right to justice, insist that no distinction shall be made between persons in the judgement of the courts; justice is to be administered with equal force for each person, be he a Frank, a Roman or a Lombard, be he plaintiff or defendant.

A number of precise criticisms of Frankish practice then follow. Another law takes the assumption that all have equal right to equally distributed judgement much further: Jews and Saracens are to be permitted to initiate suits, for 'we do not wish them to be persecuted in their innocence simply because they are Jews or Saracens'. So too when a case of homicide occurs and no guilty person can be found, villages and communities are to pay a compound fine, even if the victim was a Jew or a Saracen; for 'we believe that the persecution of the Christians against them is excessive at present'. This is not exactly a denunciation of all persecution, but it is legislation informed by what might be termed humane principles. It is noteworthy that the emperor insists on the rights of non-Christians not on the grounds that they are (as other legislation would make plain) his *servi* or property, but on ethical grounds.

Behind the ideal of offering good judgement to all must lie a practical problem: the emperor's standards will not necessarily accord with those of his agents. Of the greatest importance, therefore, is legislation aiming to raise the standards of conduct of government officials. The Norman office of justiciar was retained, with important modifications. These were the crown's deputies in the application of the new laws, and it is not surprising that a series of laws dealing with their duties begins by stressing that the word justiciar is cognate with the words *jus* and *justitia*. They are to take an oath that, 'with God and justice before their eyes', they will protect the needs of plaintiffs and act swiftly to bring good judgement. The emphasis on speed in giving judgement, a theme that also appears in the English Magna Carta, concerns not merely efficiency but also the prevention of deliberate and harmful neglect of the interests of litigants. A significant innovation was the decree that henceforth justiciars may not be appointed to office in lands where they hold estates. Under the Normans, it seems to have been common for the justiciars of Apulia to have been drawn from the Norman-Lombard feudal nobility; Frederick did not exclude the possibility that nobles would function as justiciars, but he sought to remove the temptation that they would be influenced by local interests. Families such as the Aquino (or Aquinas) would be made to serve the crown, not the clan. To some extent, also, Frederick clearly hoped to appoint to high office genuine civil servants, the product of his new University of Naples: a new class of officials beholden for all their fortunes to the monarchy. However, the slow start of the university and the continued appointment of nobles to major office indicates that this policy was not, and could not be, taken very far.

Underlying these laws lay the principle not so much that law was good because it was old, as that law must be watched and controlled by the ruler to ensure that it remained apt and just. The ruler, appointed by God to make and to unmake laws, decreed what was to be law by an act of will. Here we see a Roman-derived concept of law that has sources not merely in the law schools of Bologna and in the remnants of Byzantine law studied in southern Italy; the Norman monarchy of Roger II had also presented the ruler as 'emperor in his own kingdom' (to use a phrase popular with Neapolitan commentators on the laws of both monarchs around 1300), even if not emperor in the universal, Roman sense. The combination of the 'local imperialism' of the Normans with the high principles of Roman civil law was a powerful one. Paradoxically, it enabled Frederick to leave Roman law behind him, when he felt that it, or any other law code, could not achieve the practical objectives for which a law had been created, or that its moral perspective was in some way lacking.

This assertive view of monarchy's proper role is also reflected in the first sections of the *Constitutions of Melfi*, dealing with the relationship between political authority, religious belief and political or religious dissent. The law-book opens in a strongly moralistic mood; even though this mood is not sustained, the choice of initial themes is of the greatest significance: the first words, after the introduction, concern offences against God, but they are rapidly demonstrated to be also offences against the emperor. 'Heretics try to tear the seamless robe of God'; a 'sect' is (etymologically) a division, from the Latin *seco*, I cut. The law denounces with great eloquence the 'Patarines', Cathars and other groups whose members have begun to appear in southern Italy. 'We cannot contain our feelings against men so hostile to God, to themselves and to humanity.' The emperor orders inquisitions into their practices, and promises death to those who persist in their evil. Interestingly, investigation is to be conducted by ecclesiastics; indeed, the legislation against heretics was clearly inspired by the Fourth Lateran Council, of 1215, which had sought to act effectively against the spread of heresy in southern France (Albigensian country) and in north and central Italy. Some influence from Justinian's code can also be seen. What is striking is the lack of reference to papal authority. The emperor does not place himself in the role of the secular agent, anxious and able to use secular means (that is, violence) against heretics on the papal behalf; the papacy had certainly been urging such a role on the rulers of regions containing many heretics, generally to little effect. He acts autonomously, as ruler subject only to divine authority. Perhaps here we see the tension between Frederick's status as papal vassal for the kingdom of Sicily – a status he was anxious to disown – and the traditional status of the kings of Sicily as the equals of apostolic legates, assuming considerable independence in control of the Church. For the Melfi laws are often favourable to ecclesiastical interests; it has been seen that the inquisitors in heresy charges are to be ecclesiastics; and elsewhere Frederick sought to ensure that 'criminous clerks', ecclesiastics on criminal charges, should in general be summoned before ecclesiastical courts – the very issue over which Becket had martyred himself. Though the papacy accused him later, with a degree of justice, of opposition to Church interests within the *regno*, such opposition is not visible in 1231. The rider was that the conduct of the Church was, in the last analysis, subject to limitations imposed by the monarch and not by an outside force, the papacy.

Heresy, indeed, is presented as treason. Those who deny the articles of the Catholic faith implicitly deny the claims of rulers to derive their authority from God. They are enemies not merely of God and of the souls of individuals, but of the social fabric. Their questioning of religious truth involves a questioning of the monarch's command over the law; as enemies of the law, they are its legitimate targets, and the position of primacy accorded to legislation against heretics is thus entirely proper. Nor is it illogical for the law-book to move with only apparent suddenness from laws against heretics and apostates to a law of King Roger entitled, 'nobody should interfere in the deeds and plans of kings'; to question the king's decision, or even whether the officers the king has chosen are worthy, is 'tantamount to sacrilege', words themselves derived from Roman law-codes. It is interesting to see how decisively Roger and Frederick closed the traditional loophole found by the medieval rebel: my opposition is not to my king, but to the policies his advisers have adopted. In the *Constitutions of Melfi* the ruler automatically takes under his charge his officers, both commending them in this way to his subjects, and demanding of them, as has been seen, the highest standards of conduct. A judge who betrays the trust placed in him by the monarch naturally enough is treated no better than a rebel against the crown: the death penalty is threatened against him.

Nor, again, is it surprising that usury follows heresy, treason and sacrilege in the order of laws. Here the influence of canonistic thinking is plain: an opposition based on the idea that money which grows simply by lapse of time, without any contribution of labour, grows unnaturally, since it is immoral to receive money without investment of work. The papacy saw in widespread usury a threat to moral conduct and to the fabric of society comparable to that of heresy; papal denunciations of the Albigensian heretics usually included reference also to moneylenders. These denunciations began to lose their bite in the thirteenth century, as the papacy gradually accepted the necessity, even the benefit, of credit operations; Le Goff assures us that behind this acceptance lay the new doctrine that even usurers could earn the salvation of their souls by restitution at the end of life, and by the purchase of indulgences on their behalf once they had descended to the steamy realms of purgatory. Essentially, Frederick's legislation is rather conservative, here as elsewhere. He is not impressed by the world of commerce; he despises, with the true loathing of a Roman optimate, those whose fortune is made solely out of money. It will be seen that this lack of sympathy for the merchant classes was reflected again and again in his policies and statements. In leaving the Jews free to practise usury, he is consciously stressing the subordination of Jew to Christian; since, he says, they are not subject to the laws of Christianity, they may continue their usury; and no one was terribly worried about the souls of unconverted Jews. (The fact that Jewish law also forbade usury was overlooked by the emperor, as it has been by modern historians.)

From the right-ordering of society according to general principles, the law-book moves to the right-ordering of the Sicilian kingdom, in the light of the problems of Frederick's youth. Many of the laws concern the rights and obligations of the feudal barons in southern Italy, and the confirmation of the controls claimed over them by Roger II; from the laws of Justinian we move very rapidly to the local customs of Lombards, Normans and other barons. Respect for peace cannot exist without justice, nor indeed can justice really exist without peace. Not merely are rebels promised confiscation of their goods and execution, but an attempt is made to prevent future crime; law is concerned not just with curing existing ills. A law is thus issued banning the carrying of arms in a wide range of circumstances. Crimes against the person, including rape, are discussed at length. There are attempts to control rights of inheritance, the conduct of markets, the transhumance of sheep from mountain to valley pastures, the conduct of physicians, even the quality of the air to be breathed in the cities of southern Italy. It would be otiose to detail all these laws, because what they point to is a very simple and consistent theme: that all law-making is in the hands of the ruler, who respects existing law and yet has the power to rescind or restate it. He is the embodiment of law, the animate law (*lex animata*) and the giving of law entails the maintenance of the social order created by God. There is thus no contradiction between the confirmation or restatement of a wide variety of feudal rights and the essentially absolutist position adopted towards the making of law. To assume that absolutism and feudalism were two opposed options is entirely wrong, so long as the government was able – as it was – to vet the succession to fiefs, the marriage of heirs and the obligations to military service of the south Italian barons.

III

The *Constitutions of Melfi* have particular importance as the first lengthy statement of Frederick's fiscal programme, providing evidence not matched in clarity until 1239–40. It must be stressed at the outset that medieval rulers attempted to manage the economy of their realms in order to maximize their income, not in order to achieve economic growth *per se*: a concept few would have understood. Often, too, there were political advantages in favouring a particular group of merchants such as the Venetians, by grants of tax reductions or other handsome privileges. It is thus interesting to find that in the *Constitutions* native merchants were actually exempted from payment of a standard 3 per cent tax called the *dohana*, and they were charged about a third less than foreign merchants on exports of foodstuffs and of animals. The American authority James M. Powell has argued that these advantages were only superficial, because the Sicilian merchants rarely had special customs privileges from other rulers in other parts of the Mediterranean, as had the Genoese or the Venetians. Therefore the overall costs of shipping goods were about as high for Sicilians as they were for the north Italians. Perhaps in North Africa Sicilian merchants were able to benefit from special privileges; certainly in little Dubrovnik too, where Apulian merchants were granted reciprocal benefits. Frederick's reduction of tax rates for native merchants was a gracious concession, but it was not sufficiently gracious to give the south Italians any significant lead as purveyors of the kingdom's produce. Powell also points to the distinction Frederick drew between the export of agricultural produce and other exports such as textiles. Frederick's imposition of a special tax on foodstuffs could indicate an attempt, however crude, at economic regulation: an attempt to stimulate the town industries and to discourage interest in the food market, which had played so vital a role in the Norman economy. But more probable is another interpretation: Frederick knew that native merchants viewed jealously the primacy of north Italian visitors in this trade, and the inhabitants of Messina, Amalfi and elsewhere wanted some commercial compensation from the emperor for the imposition of strong Hohenstaufen rule in the cities of the *regno*. No doubt the Amalfitans, well-represented as they were in the central bureaucracy, were especially keen to benefit their relatives back home.

There are further reasons for Frederick's attitude to the export of grain. The role of the crown as an important source of grain supplies from the royal demesne needs to be considered. For Frederick traded on his own account. The king was not subject to the *jus exiture*, the royal tax on foodstuffs exported from private estates or handled by private merchants. The king alone had a truly privileged position in the food trade; and he exploited this fact. Just as the Genoese had obtained full ascendancy in the 1210s, so the crown obtained again its ascendancy in the 1230s. In 1239 he forbade the export of grain from Sicily and sent a large cargo in his own ships to Tunis, where there was a serious shortage. Later in his reign he sent food to the kingdom of Jerusalem. In each case Frederick sought not simply financial profit. In Tunis he would be able to bolster the position of the emir, who made tribute payments to the Sicilian treasury. In Acre he had many enemies who resented his interference in Syrian politics, and he needed to do all he possibly could to win more friends among the Franks.

The profits of trade reached Frederick the more securely after he established a system of state warehouses in licensed ports of the *regno*. He brought order and standardization to what had previously been an ill-organized structure of control. Indeed, the reason it was possible for him to introduce new taxes and to modify old ones, to impose bans and to confer privileges, was the tightness of central supervision throughout the kingdom. In the *Decameron* the fourteenth-century Florentine writer Giovanni Boccaccio describes the workings of state warehouses in Sicily, and the system he knew about was at least the direct descendant of that introduced by Frederick II:

There was, and perhaps still is, a custom in all maritime countries that have ports, that all merchants arriving there with merchandise, should, on discharging, bring all their goods into a warehouse, called in many places 'dogana', and maintained by the state, or the lord of the land; where those that are assigned to that office allot to each merchant, on receipt of an invoice for all his goods and the value thereof, a room in which he stores his goods under lock and key; whereupon the said officers of the *dogana* enter all the merchant's goods to his credit in the book of the *dogana*, and afterwards make him pay duty thereon, or on such part as he withdraws from the warehouse.

Although Boccaccio generalizes to attribute this system to all ports, the story in which the description features (Day Eight, Novel Ten) does concern Sicily, and the details themselves are probably close to those of Frederick II's time. Other aspects of Frederick's fiscal policies confirm the view that he was mainly anxious to extract profit from the full range of economic activities, rather than to induce economic 'growth', for instance by the creation of industries. The application of monopolies on salt, iron and other products of the soil or the sea had parallels in Byzantium and in feudal Europe, and had some precedent under

Norman rule: in the twelfth century the kings seem to have retained control over the free movement of salt, but in the thirteenth they began to assume control over its very production. The *Constitutions of Melfi* emphasized that the mineral produce of the kingdom was a reserved right of the monarch: produce that could not be made to grow by human endeavour, but rather the treasury of goods bestowed by God on the kingdom, under the trusteeship of its ruler. Such resources as iron were not limitless and for that reason they must belong to the public domain.

Frederick's attempts to maximize his income from Sicily and southern Italy can be interpreted in two obvious ways. It could be argued that he wished to raise funds to pay expenses that none of his Norman predecessors had really been obliged to meet: the cost of a crusade, of wars in Lombardy and in Germany. Undoubtedly Frederick did see the port revenues of Sicily and southern Italy as a vital source of funds. The emperor's treasury was severely strained by the 1240s, to a degree which his Sicilian ancestors had never experienced. But a second argument would look in addition to changes within the economy of southern Italy. Perhaps, indeed, the golden age of the Norman kings was at an end, for all the attempts to revive and to revise their impressive and effective institutions. Frederick was a Norman king at heart; but he did not necessarily control a Norman economy. Powell argues that grain prices fell in the kingdom during the 1230s, perhaps because the special tax on agrarian exports discouraged merchants from buying Sicilian and Apulian grain. The Genoese certainly maintained a healthy interest in Provençal and Sardinian grain, partly to compensate for the loss of privileges in Sicily, partly because any sensible communal government did try to avoid reliance on a single outlet for its vital needs – an outlet that could be suddenly closed through war, famine or, in the case of Sicily, even through royal caprice. But Powell also mentions evidence that cereal production was falling at this time and that farmers had to be exhorted to sow seeds and even to breed animals in the area around Bari. If there are no buyers, the farmers seem to be saying, why run the risk of over-production and of a consequent glut in the markets? Frederick himself, as greatest landlord of all, encouraged the resettlement of abandoned lands in Apulia and Sicily, offering plough-teams to the displaced

Saracens of Lucera and lands to the Ghibelline exiles from Lombardy; Jews were brought from the Maghrib to cultivate dates and indigo on the soil of western Sicily. Yet, despite the signs of crisis, the Venetians were keen to gain trading privileges in Apulia, and were rewarded with special commercial rights in southern Italy in 1232. They seem to have been attracted by the cheapness of south Italian grain.

It is obviously important to find a balance between the two extreme views that merchants liked to trade in the *regno* because its produce was cheap and the view that its produce was cheap because there were insufficient takers in a normal year. Obviously demand fluctuated, depending on the existence of shortages in other parts of Italy and the Mediterranean. On the evidence available it seems that there were gluts in the kingdom of Sicily and that the grain trade may not have been a very stable source of profit; at times of famine elsewhere in the Mediterranean (as at Tunis in 1239) there were very fat profits to be made from Sicilian grain exports. It appears that Frederick's reluctance to grant favoured nation status to trading partners in Genoa, Pisa and Venice was not entirely wise; the trading privileges granted by earlier kings of Sicily, and very occasionally by Frederick himself, did indeed pay for themselves not just in taxes, but in the way they provided a healthy stimulus to agricultural production. During this period there are signs of population changes which affected the grain market and also grain production. While in northern Italy the population was continuing to rise steadily, there may have been a decline within parts of Sicily. The expulsion or even slaughter of many Muslims may have led to depopulation and abandonment of the soil. This explains in part Frederick's attempts to repopulate Saracen lands in Sicily, as the Norman rulers had often succeeded in doing. The desire to maximize royal income, under the stress of war, came in time to dominate royal policy; it was this, for instance, rather than any inherent hostility to the Church, that accounted for Frederick's wish to keep vacant sees empty as long as possible, so that he could enjoy the revenues of their lands.

Certainly, Frederick recognized the need for north Italian visitors to the markets of the *regno* in the early years after the *Constitutions of Melfi*. The north Italians had not by any means disappeared in the interval between the edicts of Capua in 1220 and the fuller dispositions of 1231; the Genoese, for all their humiliations, had invested handsome sums in Sicilian trade. The opportunity to make use of the continuing needs of the north Italians in Sicily and southern Italy was indeed grasped, though slowly. He stated that he particularly wanted the Venetians to export 'those things which have their origin in the kingdom'. Unfortunately, the trading agreement with the Venetians did not prove durable, not through his own fault. He could hardly predict that, within a few years of the privilege of 1232, the doge of Venice would be a firm ally of the papacy and of the commune of Genoa, the very city which had fought bitterly against Venice over the attempt of its son Henry, count of Malta, to conquer Crete – the same Henry who became Frederick's admiral of the fleet. A feature of Frederick's agreement with Venice was his attempt to protect the commercial interests of native merchants even while encouraging the activities of foreign ones; in this respect at least the Venetian privilege was a marked improvement on previous and subsequent trade treaties, and was consistent with the legislation of 1231. Those in the kingdom who bought and sold from Venetian merchants would be freed from the obligation to pay taxes to the crown. There is a reference in the document to the Venetian practice of bringing woollen textiles (*lanas*) for sale in southern Italy, indicating how the region had become dependent on the north of Italy for its industrial supplies, while the greater towns of northern Italy were dependent on southern Italy for valuable agricultural supplies: an early sign of economic dualism, of the formation of complementary econ-omies in north and south Italy. Frederick aimed to extend his trading agreements further, to include Genoa too, but he found the Genoese still bore a grudge, and he seems repeatedly to have maintained that the substantial rights they had held in the late twelfth century were sufficient favour. One undoubted obstacle was the confirmation by Frederick of the right, granted already in 1200, of Provençal merchants to trade directly with Sicily. This involved setting aside a clause excluding southern French and Provençal merchants from Sicily that had featured in the treaties of the Norman kings with Genoa; and it involved the acceptance of Provençal rights expressed in a treaty drawn up in the very year that the Genoese had acquired a magnificent, and now deleted, set of rights of their own, from the hated Markward. But Marseilles and other Provençal ports lay in territory ruled by Frederick, the so-called kingdom of Arles or Burgundy. It is not surprising that Frederick was keen to placate his Provençal subjects with trading rights in Sicily and southern Italy, to prevent an outbreak of opposition to his admittedly very weak government in the Arelate.

Frederick could, at least, trust those ancient imperial allies, the Pisans. In part Pisan support stemmed from a negative attitude: that the Genoese and in the end the Venetians too were opponents of the emperor. But the Pisans saw Frederick as not merely a Sicilian king. He confirmed their right to trade freely in Germany; he tried to protect their interests in the Holy Land. The Pisans and other Tuscans gained the right to export large quantities of grain, but under rather strict conditions. In January 1240 four Pisan businessmen were permitted to export wheat valued at 520 ounces of gold, weighing 1,300 *salme* (a *salma* was about 263 pounds). But they had only until the beginning of March to load their ships, and they must do this either in Palermo or in Trapani. In 1239 Tuscans from Poggibonsi and even Genoese merchants were permitted similar rights, under equally tight controls. Frederick seems to have exploited his strong position as master of extensive demesne lands in Sicily – as a major grain-producer in his own right. He laid foundations for a system of controls, unique in western Europe, that survived even longer than his dynasty; the export licences of his Angevin successors around 1300 had their origins in the tight supervision exercised under Frederick II. Erich Maschke's comment is a tribute to the coherence of Frederick's fiscal system: 'the export of victuals stood at the centre of the business interests of the government.'

A certain fiscal optimism emerges in Frederick's handling of the Sicilian currency. Here he understood the need to maintain the *regno*'s place as a centre for the accumulation of foreign bullion. He accepted with delight the tribute in gold of the Tunisian rulers. In the 1220s he insisted that Venetian and other visitors must make all payments in gold – a hint, surely, that his access to adequate gold supplies was uncertain. But he also enacted that payments for business inside the kingdom must be made not in gold but in silver. Gold was to be brought in by the king's officers, and accumulated in the royal treasury. This seems to have been part of a process of royal saving, geared to a particular end: the production of a new, glorious gold coinage, the imperial *augustales*, in 1231–2.

Another possible explanation of Frederick's attitude is a shift in the main direction of Sicilian trade. Whereas in the Norman period there had been intensive exchanges with the North African towns, themselves sources of gold, in the thirteenth century trade relations with northern Europe, with a world of silver, came to the fore: the cities of northern Italy only resumed the minting of gold coins two years after Frederick's death, with the genoin and florin of Genoa and Florence: these were the first gold coins to be produced in continental Latin Europe, southern Italy and Spain apart, since the days of Charlemagne. In the years around 1230, Frederick may have been anxious to ensure continued acquisitions of gold within his kingdom; moreover, the increasing sales of European cloths by visiting merchants undermined the ability to accumulate supplies of precious metal, since more goods and less bullion were flowing into the *regno*.

Frederick wished to re-establish the money of his kingdom on an entirely new basis, contrasting royal control of the use of gold (for instance, as a means to pay crown expenses), with general use of silver. The exchange rate between the two was artificially fixed, under the direst penalties for contravention; but it is not clear that Frederick's decrees had much success. After the issue of the *augustales* he seems to have concluded that his initial work was done. The kingdom was at peace even with the papacy; a less restrictive approach to the money supply could be adopted. So he soon permitted the Venetians, in his privilege of 1232, to make payments as they chose, and to operate their own exchange tables free of royal supervision. This is either a rare instance in which the emperor believed his economic and financial objectives had already been realized, or another instance in which he recognized that artificial curbs could not mould the economy in the way that his own law-books seemed to suppose. In the previous year Frederick began to mint a grand new currency at Messina and Brindisi, bringing visible glory to his person. The very name of the new coins, *augustales*, echoed the fact that he was Roman emperor as well as Sicilian king.

The *augustalis* was a prestige issue, and its propaganda function perhaps surpassed its monetary function. Compared to the old *tari* of the Norman kings (which continued to appear), it was a coin of considerable elegance; and elsewhere in western Europe nothing like it was to be produced until the fifteenth century. It has contributed greatly to the view of Frederick as a proto-Renaissance monarch, able to recapture the spirit as well as the language of Roman classicism. Here is the profile of the emperor, wreathed in Roman fashion – less a portrait than an idealization – and, on the reverse, the imperial eagle; the inscription runs, on the obverse (*see illustration, p. 15*)

CESAVG IMPROM

that is,

CESAR AVGVSTUS IMPERATOR
ROMANORUM

and on the reverse simply

FRIDERICVS.

And the coin itself was of an unprecedented purity in Sicily, 20.5 carats fine gold, whereas the *tari* still stood at its Norman purity of 16 carats. The *augustalis* thus declared explicitly the wealth of the *regno* and the power of its ruler, who was presented, as in the *Constitutions of Melfi*, not as a mere king of Sicily but as a Holy Roman Emperor (even so, this was a Sicilian and not an imperial coinage, minted solely in the *regno*). Nor did the issue of these coins cease after their initial impact had been made. The *augustalis* continued to be struck in the *regno* throughout the rest of the reign, and was even continued by later kings. But it is possible that events in 1231 stimulated the production of the coin: the payment of tribute by the Tunisian ruler, in the form of Saharan gold brought by caravan across the desert from the gold-fields of Ghana. This gold arrived in Tunisia in the form of dust, about 20.5 carats pure, and the fact that the *augustalis* was of more or less equal purity is probably no coincidence. The tribute of 1231 seems to have come in the form of gold dust and of gold coins, and it is again no coincidence that the *augustalis* contained about the same amount of gold as the Hafsid dinar circulating in

North Africa, 4.5 grams. But the dinar was almost pure gold; Frederick's use of the gold standard set by the Saharan gold dust meant that the *augustalis* itself weighed a little more than the dinar, between 5.19 and 5.25 grams. The difference in weight was accounted for by the presence in the gold dust of naturally occurring silver and copper, making up an additional three-quarters of a gram in weight. According to Lopez, the fact that the *augustalis* weighed more, and the scrupulous fidelity of the Sicilian government to its weight, meant that the *augustalis* was more highly valued than the Hafsid dinar. Some historians have been more cautious in linking the tribute of 1231 to the issue of the new coins, pointing to the long history of such payments under the Normans and even under Frederick (as in 1221, it seems). In particular, the *augustalis* matches the gold content of the mid-twelfth-century coinage of Byzantium, and may thus also represent an attempt at imitation of an older, eastern Roman empire, now all but extinct, whose rulers had gloried in their own Romanness and whose currency had, at times, been the envy of its trading partners. Before the *augustalis* appeared, it is likely that sealed packets of Saharan gold circulated in Sicily, known as gold of paiole or paliola, so that the *augustalis* represents the formalization in coin of an existing economic reality. Also important in the emergence of the *augustalis* was the accumulation of gold brought into the *regno* by foreign merchants and exchanged on arrival – the stiff provisions from which, as has been seen, the Venetians were soon exempted. It is evident that during the 1220s the government was trying to establish gold reserves; having done so, Frederick could both issue his prestige currency and release selected foreign merchants from his restrictive monetary legislation.

Another factor in the issue of the *augustalis* was the state of the secondary, silver currency. Frederick aimed at standardization, closing the mint of Amalfi and concentrating production of silver coins at Brindisi. His attempt to ensure that internal payments were made in silver depended to some degree on the establishment of a silver currency that was widely accepted within the *regno*; again, a trustworthy silver currency would take pressure of demand away from the gold *tari* or quarter dinar, allow the monarchy to accumulate gold, and pave the way in gold for the issue of the *augustalis*. His father Henry VI had pursued what was in some respects a similar policy during his brief reign over Sicily, boosting silver but apparently aiming to hoard gold. Concern for the monetary position reflected the trend in monetary movements in the Mediterranean at this time. In the Islamic world, silver currencies were emerging after a long period of silver famine; gold itself was favoured less than before, though Italian merchants managed to suck considerable quantities of Islamic gold into Genoa, Florence and elsewhere. Frederick sought to resist the trend in countries such as Sicily away from the minting of gold, first by establishing a sound silver currency and then by establishing a gold currency that would be respected throughout the region. In other words, Frederick was acting here, as elsewhere, in a profoundly conservative spirit, by retaining and reinforcing the gold coinage of the *regno* in the face of new economic realities: the commercial conquest of Mediterranean markets by Latin merchants of northern Italy and Provence whose sales of western cloths, or exports of western silver, were slowly destabilizing the gold regimes of Sicily and the Islamic world. For this reason Frederick sought to ensure that payments by incoming merchants were made not in silver, of which there circulated sufficient already, but in gold which was in danger of being sucked out of the *regno*.

It is tempting to argue that the prohibition on the import of bullion other than gold was another factor which actually scared away north Italian merchants; nor is it likely to have encouraged native merchants trading out of the *regno*, for on their visits to Dubrovnik or Venice or Marseilles they might not find it easy to acquire gold. The awareness that the emperor wished to manage the economy for his own profit sapped the confidence of the north Italians; he seemed a capricious ruler whose interference in ordinary matters of trade brought them occasional disadvantage. The Venetians surely recognized this fact when they abandoned him for an alliance with Pope Innocent IV in 1245. They even tried to seize some of the Apulian towns for themselves, in the belief that only direct rule would really protect their commercial interests. The most blatant example of such interference was the case, already cited, of his export of grain to North Africa, because on that occasion he was prepared quite suddenly to place an embargo on all other shipping loaded with grain. His Norman predecessors had operated embargoes in time of war, but Frederick II saw the embargo as a financial tool. Indeed, Professor Powell has ranged further, to state that 'the military and naval power of the kingdom were not used to promote the interests of the merchants,' by whom he means not merely the king's own subjects but foreign visitors too. There does seem to be visible a contrast between the haphazard but generous favours granted to the north Italians by the Norman kings and the carefully circumscribed, long delayed favours granted them by Frederick II. The twelfth-century kings desired the presence of northern merchants as a matter of course, for it brought them funds and sometimes even valuable naval alliances. Frederick was more confident of his ability to stand alone, to shape the economic life of his subjects. He abandoned the loose concept of a business partnership between the Sicilian king and the northern communes, and he substituted an altogether more exacting concept of an economy based on precise and ancient laws – a 'loyal' economy subservient to his needs and adaptable to the demands of foreign wars.

CHAPTER SEVEN

'O ABSALOM, MY SON, MY SON'

I

In Sicily Frederick had asserted existing law and promulgated new law. Whether such assertion resulted rapidly in the recovery of royal authority within the *regno*, or in the appearance of a strengthened, centralized bureaucracy it is hard to say: the greatest concentration of official records from the Sicilian government dates from 1239–40, more than eight years after the enunciation of the *Constitutions of Melfi*. Contrary to the expectations of so many medieval historians, reforms of government did not produce overnight transformations. Moreover, as has been seen, the contents of the Sicilian laws were actually conservative in character, practical in outlook. Seeing Frederick as a pragmatic figure, prepared to rein in whatever idealism he possessed, makes sense not merely for Sicily. In 1231 his other territories, Germany and Lombardy, also urgently claimed his attention. He had not been in Germany since 1220, and his attempt to meet his German vassals at Cremona in 1226 had been blocked by the rebellion of Milan and its allies. What is therefore striking is that Germany had not descended into anarchy during his absence. Though Germany possessed few central organs of government to compare with those of the *regno*, the German nobility stood by their emperor to a remarkable degree, even when urged to abandon him by Pope Gregory. Frederick's analysis of why he retained such strong support north of the Alps emerges with reasonable clarity from his actions in the years 1231 to 1236. But equally clear is the existence of contrary views, propounded most significantly by his eldest son Henry, king of the Romans, resident in

Germany during the years of his father's crusade and Sicilian restoration.

Frederick relied on a regent, Engelbert, archbishop of Cologne, not so much to implement the emperor's policies as to hold together the German kingdom by persuasion and coercion. Engelbert went in fear for his life; he was a worldly man, rarely visible without his armed retainers. His principal colleague in the government of Germany from 1221 was Conrad, bishop of Speyer, and the regency council consisted in fact of princes of the Church. This was no novelty: earlier German rulers, such as Henry III and Henry IV, had also seen in the ecclesiastical princes the pillars on which German peace rested; and, as before, they were assisted by a loyal squadron of bureaucrats of relatively humble origins, *ministeriales* such as Eberhard of Waldburg, Master of the Household. It was the lay princes who found themselves less able to influence the conduct of government. So too the cities, especially those under ecclesiastical lordship, found themselves restricted in political freedom: Frederick II had, after all, earlier bestowed on the prelates privileges granting extensive rights in and over the towns. And the result of a rather one-sided regency council, composed of bishops and their cronies, was, especially on the edges of Germany, to distance the lay lords from the government of Germany. There were no longer any great royal processions to remind the king's subjects of his powers of justice and coercion. Even so, Frederick and his son Henry still functioned as a focus of loyalty; what was essential was that the emperor, and Engelbert, should manage at least to maintain that loyalty until the time came for Frederick to return to Germany and to make stable arrangements for the country's administration.

Sometimes Engelbert's grip proved too loose. It has been seen that Frederick II acknowledged Danish rights to part of the Slesvig-Holstein borderland in the far north of Germany; predictably, the lay lords who held estates in those borderlands were uneasy at this apparent sell-out. It is not clear that they suffered dispossession; they opposed Valdemar of Denmark partly because they wished to remain under the authority of the emperor, the very person who had dispensed with them. In 1223 the count of Schwerin took advantage of the arrival of the king of Denmark on the island of Lyo, for a hunting expedition, to pounce upon King Valdemar by night and take him into captivity. In effect, he was being held to ransom for the return of the lost borderlands between Germany and Denmark. Nor, indeed, did King Valdemar receive much comfort when pope and emperor learned of Count Henry's outrage. Engelbert's role consisted in an attempt to release Valdemar once Henry of Schwerin had been paid what amounted to a ransom; the territorial question was pushed on one side, for the Danes were to be allowed to recover the border counties they claimed. Frederick II's mind was elsewhere. He allowed his trusty adviser Hermann von Salza to travel to northern Germany and interview Count Henry as well as plaintiffs from Denmark. Hermann, as befitted the grand master of a crusading order (the interests of which in the Baltic were, moreover, just at this time being defined by imperial edict) bound Valdemar to travel to the Holy Land on crusade in 1226, to resign his rights to the German–Danish borderlands and to pay a phenomenally large ransom of 45,000 marks – sufficient, the grand master must have hoped, to tie the Danish king down to a penurious existence, unthreatening to German barons, not least when such other funds as Valdemar possessed were committed to the crusade.

Committing Valdemar to a crusade – and he had taken crusade vows some years before without ever fulfilling them – was not merely a way to turn his aggressive instincts to good use away from Germany. His expedition was seen as a contribution to the larger imperial crusade still being planned by Frederick II; it is possible, too, that the emperor hoped to assert *de facto* authority over Valdemar's crusade, thereby making visible the assumption that imperial power extended beyond Germany, over other European crowned heads. This, needless to say, gave the papacy the jitters, not least since Denmark occasionally recognized papal overlordship. Pope Honorius III's letters to Frederick about the capture of the Danish king reveal a familiar combination of deep unease at Valdemar's imprisonment and of ill-concealed incapacity to act decisively for his release. Honorius had, at such remove from northern Germany, to rely on Frederick's goodwill, which was available, for a high price.

Possibly, too, Hermann von Salza's interest in the unconquered

coasts of the Baltic, future domains of the Teutonic Order, influenced events. The Danish monarchy had shown great agility
in penetrating the southern and eastern Baltic coastlands; and
here a clash of interest with the German lords, and with towns
led by the great port of Lübeck, threatened to occur, whatever
the state of affairs in Slesvig. Indeed, Valdemar's release from
German captivity was followed not by a Danish crusade to Jerusalem but by a vicious war on the Danish–German frontier, for
the return to Denmark of the recently-lost lands. Henry of
Schwerin, the Lübeckers and others destroyed Valdemar's army
in July 1227; the question of the frontier had still not died in
Bismarck's day, but on this occasion Frederick had needed to do
rather little to achieve much. His wayward barons placed a triumph in his lap.

It is difficult to know how far Frederick was able to follow
events in Germany during the 1220s. It is striking that, on Engelbert's violent death (by the hands of one of the archbishop's
own kin), in November 1225, Frederick did not appoint another
prelate as regent in Germany. After several months, his choice fell
on the duke of Bavaria, Ludwig; at the same time, Frederick
tried to close his links with the German lay princes by marrying
Henry, king of the Romans, to the daughter of the duke of
Austria. Frederick's conciliation of the German nobility was just
sufficient to assure the nobles' loyalty to him during the difficult
years of conflict with Gregory IX and of absence on crusade.
Attempts by the papacy to build links with the German princes,
such as Otto the Welf, duke of Lüneburg, had no concrete results,
except in an unexpected quarter: the crisis in southern Italy seems
to have prompted Henry, king of the Romans, to take direct
charge of the government of Germany, repudiating somewhat
offhandedly his protector the Bavarian duke and his father-in-
law the Austrian duke (1228). (Henry goes by the title Henry
(VII) to distinguish him from the later Luxembourg emperor,
Henry VII.) Ludwig of Bavaria's resentment at his treatment by
Henry (VII) probably counted for more than any ill-feeling towards Frederick, now far away in the Levant; in 1229 Henry
marched into Bavarian territory, not to destroy his former
guardian but to exact from him an unswerving promise of
loyalty. Under duress, Ludwig complied; but his pledges of

devotion were no longer based on love and trust between king and prince. Henry's energy in holding together Germany during 1228–9, when the papacy would gladly have seen the princes in rebellion against the Hohenstaufen, was thus counter-productive. He went too far, using the whip even against those on whom the German monarchy had to rely if it was to achieve stability. Above all, Henry's policies went much further than Frederick II at this stage intended to go. Yet the break from the past should not be exaggerated. The German princes felt themselves coldly excluded from positions of power. Nevertheless the civil service remained almost identical in character to that created by Engelbert of Cologne: the same *ministeriales* and their kin, from the Hohenstaufen core territory of Swabia, kept the machinery of government alive. The problem was that Henry (VII) had isolated himself from the traditional decision-making groups in Germany, the spiritual and lay princes. This meant that the *ministeriales* became rather more than the executive arm of a royal council; they had direct access to the ear of the king, and prompted him to turn against the very noble families to whom both Henry and the *ministeriales* owed their survival. Worse still, their policies flew in the face of those already established by Frederick II in Germany. Whereas Frederick had always shown deep suspicion of the political aspirations of the non-imperial towns in Germany, Henry and his advisers saw in the cities a new source of support for a government that was increasingly in need of defenders. The lower Rhine towns, such as Nijmegen, received royal privileges. More seriously, the claims to authority of the prelates and lay princes, based in the former case on Frederick's *Constitutio in favorem principum ecclesiasticorum*, were now undermined. The lay princes, too, found their standing weakened when the towns under their authority received royal grants during the princes' absence in Italy and on crusade. If these were the rewards one received for helping the emperor, then Frederick must be made aware of the urgent need to restrain his son.

Henry (VII), then, can be accused of a lack of political sensitivity that his father as a young man in Germany had never displayed. In 1230 and 1231, at the Diet of Worms, Henry found himself unable to resist the demands of the princes for restoration and extension of their authority over the cities: Henry had only a very limited power base, briefly, illusorily, seeming much larger while the great princes were away with their emperor. Once Frederick had recovered control of southern Italy, the princes in Germany, almost in a quid pro quo arrangement, expected to recover their own rights on their estates. On 1 May 1231 a *Constitutio in favorem principum* was published, which reaffirmed and strengthened the rights of control of the princes within their territories. The cities had been surrendered back into the hands of the German nobility. Their communal aspirations had been suppressed as decisively as such aspirations were, in the same year, being suppressed in southern Italy, by the *Constitutions of Melfi*. When confirmed in 1232 by Frederick II, the provisions of the *Constitutio* gave the princes extensive rights of intervention in the German towns, echoing at magnified volume the rights claimed by German emperors over towns south of the Alps during the twelfth century. City governments were to exist by the say-so of the princes. Money was to be minted in the princes' name only. Indeed, we see a withdrawal from rights of intervention by the emperor himself: he promised not to interfere by, for instance, constructing towns and castles in the territories of the princes without their assent; the cession of rights of coinage, too, was detrimental not merely to the towns but to the monarchy. An attempt has been made by Erich Klingenhöfer to argue that Frederick's privileges were not so one-sided, that he took back some lost rights as well as confirming those of the princes, and above all that he reserved his position as the fount of law: it was Frederick as German emperor who granted the privileges of his own grace. Evidently, there has been excessive emphasis on Frederick's concessions and insufficient attention to what he received in return: recognition of his sovereignty. This was not just the 'abdication' Barraclough believed it to be; there was direct benefit to the crown, but its fulfilment depended on the perpetuation of a federal power-structure in Germany.

The Diet of Worms and the confirmation of Aquileia indicate that neither Frederick nor the princes was prepared to countenance Henry (VII)'s policies. It is hard to say whether Henry was an opportunist, trying to build support for a regime that had little conception of its aims, or whether there was a Henrician programme, envisaging the restoration of direct royal control

within Germany, and the curbing of the over-mighty princes.
History has been kind to Henry, for reasons that will become
plain; what more noble task than to fight for the creation of a
coherent German state, with its centre of gravity north of the
Alps, away from Lombardy, Rome and Sicily, six and a half
centuries before Bismarck? But around 1230 there were less romantic considerations: a genuine constitutional dilemma, created out
of the earlier tussles between Frederick and the papacy. When in
1220 Henry, still a young child, had been elected by the German
princes, at imperial insistence, to the throne of Germany Frederick had certainly been anxious to secure a safe succession
through the difficult years ahead, years of crusade and absence in
Sicily. In the papacy's mind lay other plans: the devolution of
royal power in Germany and Sicily to separate branches of the
Hohenstaufen family, a plan made feasible with the birth of
Conrad, son of Isabella-Yolande of Jerusalem. As has been seen,
such plans left delightfully vague the real functions of an emperor.
What practical power would he possess in Germany over the
head of his son? Frederick's answer had been given, as a matter of
fact, in Cyprus, when he insisted that, as overlord of the king of
Cyprus, he had full powers of intervention in the island's affairs.
Subsequently, in his crown-wearing in Jerusalem, he had enunciated a view of the emperor as prince of peace; and in his
Sicilian law-book he had not ceased to insist on his status as
emperor as well as king of Sicily. On the *augustalis* coins of 1231
he was displayed as AVGVSTVS IMPERATOR, even
though the coins were issued for use within the kingdom of
Sicily. Summoning a Diet at Ravenna for November 1231
the emperor emphasized that the meeting was to bring peace and
prosperity to the whole empire, particularly to troubled Italy.
The bringing of peace could not, however, simply be a question
of moral leadership. In the thirteenth century peace had to be
imposed. In other words, imperial power could not exist in a
vacuum somewhere above Henry (VII)'s head. The emperor
must use his corrective powers if he believed his son (whom he
hardly knew, after such long separation) was throwing off balance the delicate relationship within Germany between powerful
princes and an eroded monarchy. The first step in rebuilding
Germany's monarchy was precisely to avoid challenging the

princes. The further he was from Germany, the more Frederick believed this to be so. For his Italian affairs and his crusade might come to nothing if restive German princes tied the emperor up in a struggle for authority north of the Alps.

Here, then, we see a shift in Frederick's outlook, created more by political exigencies, perhaps, than by emphatic notions of universal monarchy. Up to 1220 Frederick had been prepared to concentrate heavily on German affairs, largely because his enthusiastic welcome on his first arrival had made Germany seem deceptively easy to manage. Later experience in Sicily proved that the existence of a centralized bureaucracy and of a tradition of autocratic government, in the Byzantine–Norman mould, was a more effective means to ensure respect for royal rights than a tradition of loyalty for an absentee crown. Henry (VII)'s perspective, produced entirely on German soil, was very different. He was willing to challenge the German nobility, as much out of bravado as because his support network consisted of anything substantial: Swabia and some cities, in the main. He misunderstood the limited capacity of the German crown to resist princely pretensions – not least when the king was a young man who could be played off against a charismatic father.

Frederick II reacted to the tension between his son and the German princes by promising reconciliation, at the Diet of Ravenna. In some respects the new Diet was an attempt to continue the unfinished work begun at Cremona in 1226. And, as on that occasion, the Milanese and their allies preferred to defy Frederick, blocking the Alpine passes, than to see the enunciation of detrimental legislation (which the emperor may not, in fact, have seriously intended) or the arrival of threateningly large German armies. Since Henry (VII) was summoned to Ravenna, it is most likely that Frederick primarily wished to use the meeting to bring his son's policies under control. It is usually assumed that Henry feared his father's wrath and preferred to stay away; he was still in Germany, at Hagenau, when the conference of Ravenna opened (Christmas 1231). Actually, Henry may at this stage have realized that his route to Ravenna was blocked by the Lombards: an excuse not to travel south and risk capture by Frederick's enemies. Meanwhile, the worst fears of the Lombards seemed realized when the Diet placed Milan and its friends under the imperial ban; to the Lombards, this seemed to prove that the whole purpose of the Diet was to destroy Lombard liberties. But more probably the ban was the irate reaction of an imperial court profoundly frustrated at the renewed blocking of the Alps. The Lombards had, as it were, forced their own way on to the agenda.

Henry's absence from Ravenna was compromised by the presence of his *ministeriales* at the Diet. No doubt they presented his excuses, but the fact that they, with a few of the princes, had penetrated the Alpine blockade made it plain that Henry's absence was at least half-deliberate. Moreover, it was increasingly clear at Ravenna that the king was being blamed for disruptive policies in Germany. The emperor welcomed the chance to emphasize, to those courtiers of Henry who had arrived at Ravenna, that his son was expected at a second Diet, to be held in the spring at Aquileia; and the German princes too had been trying to put pressure on the *ministeriales*, stressing the need for Henry to act in concert with Frederick.

So Henry did set out for Aquileia, arriving there in May 1232. At Aquileia the emperor seems to have made two complaints against Henry. One was that his policies in Germany were destructive of the entente between monarch and princes created by Frederick before 1220. More importantly, Frederick blamed Henry for claiming an excess of authority, that detracted from Frederick's own rights: rights that were being sold down the river, to the German cities and Henry's committed supporters. Frederick may also have suspected Henry if not of conspiracy, at least of the capacity to conspire against him (for instance, in the event of a new papal-imperial squabble). These accusations against Henry can be deduced from the description, from Henry's own mouth, of the oath he was obliged to swear before his father at Aquileia in order to avoid more extreme punishment. Henry was to defend the rights and standing of the emperor, not to harm the emperor's person or property, and was to rid himself of those counsellors who had urged on him his disruptive policies. The German princes guaranteed his good conduct. Failing good conduct, Frederick reserved the right to depose Henry; nor would Henry resist the emperor's judgement. It is interesting that the German nobility was cited in the oath. There is some evidence that Henry had defenders among the princes – not, surely, out of admiration for his past conduct, but out of acute awareness that the power of the princes depended on their capacity to hold a balance between a degraded king in Germany and a wilful emperor best kept away from Germany. The loyalty of the German princes was thus double-edged. But Frederick, apparently hopeful that he had tamed his son, was prepared to conciliate the princes still further. It has been seen already that he took this opportunity to confirm and extend their privileges within Germany, even to the detriment of royal power. This readiness to comply with German demands constituted a final slap in the face for Henry (VII). It may indicate, too, that the emperor was still not thinking of returning in person to Germany. The Lombard rebellion and the government of Sicily were keeping him very busy. Even at Ravenna and Aquileia he was occupied with Sicilian business: the ever-vexed problem of relations with Genoa and Venice, for instance, the latter of which in 1232 received a privilege for Sicilian trade (granted in Venice itself, through which Frederick passed en route to Aquileia).

For Frederick, though leaving direct involvement in German affairs on one side, was persistently pursuing one of the traditional targets of the kings of the Romans: the pacification of the north Italian lands, technically united with the German crown. Here was an area, arguably also under Henry's charge as king of the Romans, where Henry's policies had not yet added further confusion to that existing already. At least directly: the Lombards were surely encouraged by the difficulties brewing north of the Alps; imperial power was not rock-hard. And Henry, as events proved, was fatally attracted by the confusions within Italy.

II

We should not exaggerate the extent to which the oath at Aquileia compounded Henry's resentment at his father's light-handed policy in Germany. Was it more humiliating to be chastised by the emperor than it was to be a mere functionary, pursuing a policy laid down by Frederick, who possessed increasingly vague knowledge of Germany's condition? Thus Henry's dilemma. But the emperor's wishes were for the moment fulfilled. The princes were the beneficiaries of Henry's meeker conduct, exercising influence at court and receiving privileges of exemption. Neither the prelates nor the lay princes had real reason to complain of royal conduct in 1233–4; *ergo*, they had no reason to complain of imperial intervention; *ergo*, Frederick had a freer hand in northern Italy, where both he and the pope identified the most infective source of unrest. Italy had considerable influence on the relations between Frederick and Henry, and it will be necessary to by-pass the intricate complexities of Lombard politics to focus again on Henry (VII)'s role in German and Italian affairs in 1233 and 1234.

But of course it would be exaggeration to portray the German princes as united behind their reformed king. Henry was nervous at the ambitions of the new duke of Bavaria, Otto, and launched a large-scale invasion of Otto's lands in 1233; peace was made when Otto's son was dispatched to the royal court as hostage for his father's good behaviour. All this implies that the Bavarian duke had been encroaching on Henry's, Frederick's or the greater princes' rights, and it is thought the princes generally approved of the campaign against the overweening Otto. Quite possibly the encroachments concerned Swabian lands of the Hohenstaufen, for Henry doubted the loyalty of several of his Swabian vassals, and attacked them too. He was trying to maintain or restore order in the core territory of his family, but his old difficulty remained: the Swabian vassals, such as the counts of Hohenlohe, were ultimately vassals of Frederick II, their king's overlord, and it was to him that they appealed in person, in northern Italy; it was easy for them to point to 'offences' by King Henry that seemed to breach the principles of the king's oath at Aquileia, or, indeed, the edicts in favour of the princes issued with Frederick's assent. For Henry, on the other hand, his campaigns in southern Germany were precisely an attempt to defend his patrimony in the spirit of Aquileia; the young king was caught between two plausible interpretations of his duties in Germany. The old problem, that his autonomy of action was constantly being challenged directly by his father, or by appeals to his father over his head, had not vanished at Aquileia.

There was, however, a solution that cut through the Gordian knot. Henry could try to rally Germany against his own father. The prospects were not good, considering the ill-feeling his policies had generated among the great princes; but some of the *ministeriales* and townsmen, beneficiaries in the past of his actions, were behind him; so too a number of bishops (such as Augsburg and Worms), for reasons that are hard to grasp – the emperor could not, in 1233–4, be accused of undermining the papacy but rather seemed to be working closely with it. In 1234, at a meeting in Boppard, the idea of rebellion seems to have been discussed. Was it indeed rebellion? For Henry and his supporters, it was a question of defending the elected king of the Romans. But against whom? An elected king of the Romans. There are analogies here with the constitutional complexities of another of Frederick's troubled kingdoms, that of Jerusalem. But against Henry were ranged some of the greatest princes, such as Otto of Bavaria, who could call to their side their own counts and *ministeriales.* Surely a conflict between Henry and his German foes would in the last analysis be a vicious civil war between the power-holder in Swabia, Henry (VII) and the masters of the other great duchies, of whom only the Austrian duke gave Henry any support? Henry's decision to take up arms could not be effectively directed against Frederick, who was still south of the Alps; it was not supported by those, such as Gregory IX, who could exert pressure on the emperor. The revolt threatened merely to reduce Germany once again to the internecine rivalries of the days of Otto IV and Philip of Swabia. So much for Henry as the restorer of the German monarchy. By 1234 his vision of his kingdom's future had become seriously blurred by his suspicion of and dislike for his absent father.

It can be argued that Henry was afraid Frederick would dispossess him in favour of his half-brother Conrad; it is even possible Gregory IX looked with interest on the idea of Conrad (born only in 1228) as a replacement for Henry in Germany, so long as a new queen, and therefore potentially a new son, could be arranged for the twice-widowed Frederick. This putative son would inherit Sicily instead of Conrad, and Henry could expect nothing. Gregory's willingness to fall in with Frederick's plans for Germany reflects the pope's weakness in 1234, for the pope was still

reeling from the emperor's victory in southern Italy and was himself a refugee from the troublesome citizens of Rome – a fact
which itself owed something to his much-resented attempts in
1228–9 to mobilize the Romans against Frederick. Moreover,
the Lombard towns were proving as resistant to imperial armies
as they were to papal menaces, resistant even, as will be seen, to
papal attempts to act as mediator with the emperor. Gregory was
aware in 1234 that he had little to gain from proclaiming his
support for Henry (VII) or the Lombards. Indeed, he may well
have been pleased with Frederick's outlook on a number of
issues about which Gregory cared deeply: the need to curb the
spread of heresy in Italy and the empire (the subject of Frederician
legislation in Sicily in 1231, and in Lombardy and Germany a
few years later); and the need to retain freedom of action in
Germany for his Dominican inquisitor Conrad of Marburg, one
of the more revolting figures of the thirteenth century. Conrad's
power to act behind the backs of the German bishops against
those denounced for heresy aroused alarm at Henry's court in
1233; the alarm was compounded rather than dispersed when
Conrad's foes avenged blood with blood and struck him down
in 30 July 1233. For now Gregory hurled his wrath against those
German lords, including Henry himself, who had impiously
resisted the suppression of wrong belief. Lombardy, too, was
seen as a nest of heretics, and the pope did not hesitate to turn
bulls of excommunication against cities that protested, none the
less, their loyalty to the pope against the emperor. That was not
the most urgent struggle. The fight against heresy took priority.
Cathar refugees from southern France, victims already of one
crusade against heresy, had arrived in the Italian towns and, in
some places at least, they flourished, spreading extreme versions
of their anti-materialist creed among both rich and poor.

It was symbolic of Henry (VII)'s rebelliousness that he should
enter a pact with the Lombard League in 1235, against his own
father: with the enemies of the papacy, as well as those of the
emperor. The Lombards, casting about for a patron who would
fill the role taken so honourably by Pope Alexander III against
Frederick I, were unable now to turn to Pope Gregory. But
Henry saw more than the chance to build ties with another
troublesome foe of Frederick II: the Lombard League. He aimed

to act as captain of the league, some day, perhaps, leading their armies into battle; he expressed too, by this alliance, his first serious claim to authority in the Italian lands traditionally ruled by a king of the Romans. The challenge to his father intensified; and his father realized that it was only by his travelling to Germany and facing the rebels that Henry's power would be shown to be as paper-thin as, in fact, it was. Encouraging Gregory to make peace with the citizens of Rome – an irritating little conflict that tied Frederick down far from his most obvious campaign theatres – the emperor hurriedly made dispositions for the rule of Sicily in his absence. He did not even enter the *regno* to do this, calling a meeting north of the frontier, at Fano, in April 1235. Within a few weeks he had sailed from Rimini, nearby, on his way back to Germany. Could he once again enact those miracles of twenty years earlier, when his foe had been Otto the Welf, against his now excommunicate, long-rebellious son Henry?

III

It was on the power of his name that Frederick now relied, entering Germany from the south-east unaccompanied by his armies. Partly this was because he came in haste, but largely because he knew he could count on the loyalty of the princes in Germany. 1235 saw the rapid eclipse of Henry's power. Reaching Regensburg, Frederick held court with his princes, bishops and Swabian vassals, making abundantly plain the continued rights of the emperor to conduct the affairs of Germany over the head of the rebel king of the Romans. It was this Frederick sought: to isolate Henry not so much militarily (Henry's armies were busy on the Rhine, at Worms, some way away) but politically and diplomatically. A sure sign of this diplomatic triumph was Frederick's success in building ties with England, through a marriage alliance between himself and Henry III's sister Isabella (once mooted, as a matter of fact, as Henry (VII)'s bride): news that the English court was well-disposed to Frederick came to the emperor at Regensburg. Surely this happy coincidence strengthened the emperor's prestige and following: it was with him, not Henry, that the once hostile English crown sought to deal. The Welf connections of the Angevin kings of England were well forgotten.

Henry too realized that Frederick's power was too firm to be shattered by his fragmentary rebellion, whose adherents were rushing to disclaim their links with the king of the Romans. At Swabian Trifels Henry sat in moody isolation and desolation, no longer surrounded by eager supporters, but holding still the crown and vestments of the German kings. Soon he wrote to his father, begging to come to terms, which, he knew, could only mean his punishment, even dispossession in favour of Conrad his half-brother. So at Wimpfen they met: the emperor processing in state through his German domains, with magnificent pomp and display of wealth, and (no less importantly) accompanied by the great princes of Bavaria and elsewhere, thereby expressing the reality of his power in Germany; and his son the king, a prisoner, who could only fling himself prostrate before his wilful father, and beg for the forgiveness Frederick was little disposed to offer. Symbolic too, was Frederick's decision to leave judgement aside until the rebellion had been truly cracked; the imperial entourage crossed country, reaching Worms in early July 1235. This city, previously under siege from Henry's army, though largely loyal to Frederick, made a fit setting for the emperor's dictation of conditions to his son. Worms was no Canossa. Though Henry again lay prostrate for hours before his father, Frederick disdained to pay his son attention: a lesson indeed to rebels, such as the Milanese, who might ever assume they could have the emperor's ear when they wanted it. The elaborate political theatre continued when the German princes begged the emperor to pay heed to Henry's presence and the emperor then deigned to dictate his terms: acceptance of his deposition from the throne of Germany, permanently and irrevocably, including the surrender of the symbols of monarchy, the crown and vestments of the German kings, the one remaining sign that his title to the throne had any substance. Henry, never lacking in obstinacy, refused to agree, even in these desperate conditions: he had lost everything, but was he also to lose his honour? These must have been his thoughts when he continued to stand by the justice of his past acts. In earlier months he had sought to represent himself as the true upholder of peace and good order in Germany, against an overmighty nobility. His analysis of Germany's political needs was diametrically opposed to that of Frederick. He could not admit any wrong-doing; he could only stand by his royal dignity, denied though it was by all around him. The tragedy of Henry's fall, like that of Richard II's fall in England a century and a half later, lay in the king's utter certainty that he had taken the right course of action, by right authority.

Henry could expect no more than imprisonment under heavy guard. Two of Frederick's sons lived their last years as prisoners: Enzo, king of Sardinia, as enforced guest of the city of Bologna, and Henry, king of Germany, under tight duress first at Heidelberg and elsewhere in Germany, later in the *regno*. After several years spent half-forgotten in southern Italy, Henry was called to the royal court at last in 1242. Frederick apparently believed that Henry's sentence had by now been served; fatherly affection must also be expressed, a degree of mercy shown to his Absalom. This Henry did not expect. According to the generally accepted accounts, Henry was certain his father had now decided to do away with him (these were years when Frederick's reputation for brutality was being widely bandied about). Riding near Mortorano, in the south Italian mountains, on his way to his father's court, Henry seized a chance to break away from his guards and urged his horse where they would not follow him: off the road into a deep precipice, to his death.

In a famous passage from his circular letter to the Sicilian nobility, announcing (without details) the death of Henry (VII), the emperor appeared to open his heart, just as King David had after the rebellion and death of Absalom: 'Paternal grief at the death of my first-born son conquers my austere judicial sentence; a flood of tears wells up from the depth of my heart, even though heretofore held in check by the memory of the wrongs I suffered, and of the exercise of stern justice.' On the one hand, he is saying, he could not have done anything less than strip his son of his royal title and power, for if his son were allowed to maintain a rebellion against the emperor, or even if his son were only punished lightly, the law and peace of the whole empire would be placed in jeopardy. The ruler, God's representative on earth, must be the impartial exponent of pure justice. No doubt he was reminded of the great Roman heroes who had acted with even greater severity against sons who offended the state. The emperor ordered requiem masses to be said throughout the *regno*; he attended Henry's funeral, receiving tragic praise as the new Abraham who accepted the sacrifice of his beloved son Isaac. But there were other causes for reflection too. Already in 1235 he had become aware that he had only one legitimate heir, the young Conrad: Henry had disqualified himself. The death of Henry (VII) posed again the question of who was to receive the empire from Frederick. The English marriage did, it is true, produce a son, still, however, very young; his name, Henry, seemed to indicate the emperor's wish to substitute a new Henry for his disloyal first-born son.

The English marriage represented the reconciliation of the former Welf adherents to a now firmly established Hohenstaufen ascendancy. Indeed, the Welfs had not supported Henry (VII) against Frederick, and the reward they received was nothing less than readmission into the highest ranks of the empire. In summer, 1235, not long after his marriage to Isabella of England, Frederick II created as hereditary duke Otto of Lüneburg and Brunswick. It was not so much a question of bestowing new powers on the greatest of the Welfs, as a chance to bond them, by honouring Duke Otto in public, yet more securely to a crown for which, at last, they seemed to have felt respect. It was a chance, too, to emphasize at large that the emperor's rule in Germany depended on his alliance with, and trust for, the great princes. But did the programme of government have more substance than that? It must be remembered that the distracting rumble of Lombard rebellion was still to be heard. Northern Italy needed attention now Germany's prime problem had been settled. As at the triumphant moments of his rule in Sicily, in 1220 and 1231, Frederick responded to his German victories by issuing laws at a Diet held in Mainz, more modest in scale, certainly, than the Sicilian law-book of 1231, and for that reason seen by some historians as the enunciation of a draft programme, intended to lead to more substantial and centralizing legislation later on. The clearest reflection of his Sicilian legislation, and of an attempt to bring to Germany some vestiges of the Sicilian government machine, is found in Frederick's decision to create a grand justiciar to judge the appeals of the emperor's German subjects – other than the princes, of course, whose disputes would by custom have to be brought before the emperor and Diet. Yet there is a great distance between the Sicilian justiciars, or the English ones of the same period, with their extensive powers of investigation and control, and this high judge for Germany. We must not be deceived by names. A justiciar meted out justice; there is no sign that the Diet of Mainz was bringing into existence the sort of viceroy found in Sicily and England since the twelfth century.

The real emphasis of the *Mainzer Landfriede*, as its name (in Latin, *Constitutio Pacis*) reveals is the proclamation of, and defence of, public peace. The term peace is to be understood in a very wide sense: rebellion, certainly, is discussed, in passages van Cleve links to the recent experience of Henry (VII)'s revolt:

If any son violently expels his father from his castles or other properties, attacks his father with fire or by plundering raids, or connives with his father's foes, and takes the oath known in German as the *Verderpnisse* to attack his father's honour or to seek his injury or destruction, then that son shall have confiscated all rights of inheritance, shall be sentenced to be deprived of his lands and possessions for all time, and shall not be reinstated even by his father nor by any judge.

But public peace also involved the old contested problem of minting rights, the illegitimate imposition of new or evil taxes, and the preservation of episcopal jurisdiction on church lands. 'Peace' was the subject of preventive legislation, therefore, seeking to defuse possible disagreements; it was not merely a question of legislating against rebellion, robbery and dispossession (though about half the clauses in the *Landfriede* are directly con-cerned with criminal law as such). Nor, indeed, was the *Landfriede* a revolutionary assertion of new laws. As has been seen, these constitutions opposed new, unjust tolls: it was the defence of traditional rights, above all those of the princes, bishops and greater vassals, that underlaid this legislation. Old law was good law. Proclaimed at an assembly of those princes who had stood by Frederick during his son's rebellion, such law could hardly fail to respect their interests, and to confirm their central role as

propagators of peace in Germany. Without them, all proclamation of law in Germany would be merely nugatory. With
them, imperial authority certainly remained a shadow of what it
was in Sicily. We must therefore discard the enthusiastic notion
that Frederick in 1235 supposed himself in any way capable of
creating a centralized, autocratic government for all Germany.
To imagine this is to fall into the way of thinking of German
romantic historians, looking, not least in Weimar days, for the
authoritarian government which (to their ultimate displeasure)
eventually came their way. In 1235, Frederick had no conception
of a united Germany, merely of German princes united in giving
him their support. Germany was not Sicily or England, and he
did not deceive himself about this. One hint there was that
Germany had a distinctive identity: the issuing of German texts of
the laws. The purpose here was simple: to communicate. The
bringing of 'peace' was easier achieved in the vernacular, the
language of the law-courts and of the contestants, than in Latin.
This was law to be understood and acted upon. Already at Jerusalem Frederick had made sure that his speech in the Holy
Sepulchre was translated into German and proclaimed by
Hermann von Salza to his followers. The art of communication, a
sense of how to sell imperial policies, was something Frederick
and his entourage (above all Piero della Vigna) learnt to handle
very effectively.

IV

One *cause célèbre* illustrated to the emperor's German subjects the
ideals of impartiality and truthfulness in the exercise of justice.
Frederick received reports of accusations of ritual murder of a
Christian child, attributed to the Jews of Hagenau. Such accusations, growing in volume first in twelfth-century England and
then, under the influence of supposed events there, further afield,
seriously threatened the security of the Jewish communities of
northern Europe. The Jews of Germany were regarded by the
emperors as bound directly to the crown; their well-being was
thus a matter of direct concern to the crown. Yet the accusation

that Jews crucified Christian children to pour scorn on the Passion, had wider implications than the preservation of royal authority over the Jews in Germany. Frederick was aware that such an accusation concerned and affected Jews throughout Christendom. His first attempt to resolve the accusation consisted of the creation of a tribunal of spiritual and lay nobles, who were to report on the charges against the Jews. The real character of the investigation was thus not a single charge against the Jews at Hagenau, but a charge against all Jews everywhere. It is sad testimony to the ability and prejudices of the members of the tribunal that they could not unite in condemning the libel against the Jews. Frederick therefore wrote to Christian kings elsewhere in Europe, including Henry III of England, asking to be sent converts from Judaism who would have the knowledge of Jewish practice and of the Hebrew sources necessary to pass judgement on the accusation. The argument was that converts would have no compelling motive to defend Judaism, whereas the members of his tribunal had had no access to the religious literature of the Jews. The English king, founder of the *Domus Conversorum* in London, sent two converts, and the investigation they and their colleagues conducted proved conclusively that Jewish law held in absolute abhorrence any form of human sacrifice. This they reported to the emperor, whose response was equally decisive: the issue of a privilege in favour of the Jews (July 1236) in which the proceedings were described, the false accusations against the Jews condemned, and any repetition of the libel outlawed. Seven centuries later, such libels have still not died. It is noteworthy, too, that the Jews had not already been given protection in the *Mainzer Landfriede*. Frederick departed from the precedent of Henry IV of Germany by excluding them from his declaration of a land-peace; the special status of the Jews as outsiders in a Christian society necessitated a special decree in their favour. In fact, Frederick used the opportunity given by the judgement in favour of the Jews to describe them in his privilege as *servi camere nostre*, 'serfs of our chamber', thereby claiming more extensive rights over them than had his predecessors. Even so, such claims proved hard to enforce, not least on the estates of the great princes.

The question of Frederick's tolerance towards non-Christians will need fuller discussion elsewhere. But the emperor's actions should not be seen as the product of a Renaissance enlightenment, unparalleled among his contemporaries and subjects (some of whom were decidedly perplexed by the news of a privilege 'in favour of' the despised Jews). Among contemporary rulers, his namesake Frederick II, duke of Austria, whose links with Henry (VII) have been mentioned, issued privileges encouraging the Jews to settle; the Viennese-Jewish community owes its origins to this Babenberg patron. Innocent IV, a pope whose career was dominated by the struggle against the Hohenstaufen, condemned the blood-libel while at the same time praising the book-burnings in Paris that saw manuscripts of the Talmud consigned to the flames. Actually, the Talmud was one of the main sources used to vindicate the Jews of the accusation in Germany; yet the Church was beginning to see in the Talmud a work that had transformed Judaism from the religion of Temple times into a Jewish heresy. Interestingly, Innocent's letters defending the Jews against the blood-libel are directed against Germany a mere ten years after Frederick's court of enquiry. Frederick had not, indeed, quelled even his greater subjects; whether or not they believed the accusations against the Jews, they gladly pillaged the defenceless community so long as its protector was tied down south of the Alps.

Perhaps, rather than enthusing naïvely at Frederick's tolerance and far-sightedness, we can draw the following conclusions from the Hagenau incident. Frederick seized an opportunity to demonstrate both to his German subjects and to the world beyond the practice of impartial justice, the bringing of *pax* not merely to his Christian subjects but to those who, as chamber serfs, were entirely at the mercy of his will. He quite probably did not believe the accusations from the start; his energy in handling the case suggests he was not prepared to accept at face value the testimony of the denigrators of the Jews. And in this he was perhaps guided by his upbringing in Sicily, in a land where the non-Christian was a much more familiar sight. (Frederick even encouraged new Jewish settlement in Sicily, though with some reservations.) Behind his appeal for well-informed converts lay also his curiosity. Frederick's interest lay not merely in the final conclusion, whether or not the accusations had any merit, but in the way the conclusion was reached, through an investigation of the (to him) closed world of Hebrew scholarship. In fact he knew a little about the Jewish religion: he once asked a Jewish philosopher whether the complex purification rituals of the red heifer, described in the Torah, did not find their origin in Indian religious practices, a question that betrays an interest in other cultures and faiths that was unusual even in the Christian borderlands of Sicily and Spain. And, finally, on a very different level, he could not but be conscious of the problems of public order that would arise if the issue were not settled in favour of the Jews.

That the emperor was not the free-thinker, contemptuous equally of Moses, Jesus and Muhammad, for whom generations of historians, since his own time, have taken him was demonstrated a couple of months before he issued his privilege to the Jews. He led the ceremonies for the translation of a new saint, Elisabeth of Thuringia, to her shrine at Marburg. Just as at his coronation in Aachen he had laboured alongside the workmen to re-inter the body of his forebear Charlemagne, so at Marburg, splendidly attired in his coronation robes, he helped place the saint's body in a gold and silver plated tomb, surrounded by his princes and a vast gathering of hundreds, even thousands, of his subjects. The skull of St Elisabeth was removed at some stage in the proceedings, and was covered by a crown, the gift of the emperor; the whole reliquary was then worked into a chalice, also offered by Frederick; it still survives, in Stockholm.

If we ask who Elisabeth of Thuringia was, we are a little nearer to understanding what was happening. She was the widow of Frederick's former colleague, the same landgrave of Thuringia who had fallen ill and died at sea off Brindisi when Frederick first attempted to leave on crusade. She was thus the wife of his second cousin. She had led a life of excruciating holiness after her husband died, sufficient to hurry her rapidly to her grave. In a letter to his friend the Franciscan general, Elias of Cortona, Frederick stressed his kin-relation with Elisabeth; and the desire to win for the imperial house, even by the adoption of a second cousin's wife, a saint and cult centre must have been a powerful motive in Frederick's patronage of St Elisabeth's cult. It is possible, too, that Frederick had known her personally. But beyond the desire for a royal saint, reflecting on the glory of his dynasty and of the Roman empire, lay humbler objectives. 'Holy devotion' also bound him, he told Elias of Cortona, to pay respect to St Elisabeth's remains. A fascination, maybe, for the life of grinding hardship, renouncing worldly goods: spirituality bound to voluntary poverty, a view of the Church so very different from the picture presented by politician popes and disloyal bishops.

But sometimes historians are too credulous. Are we to believe that Frederick II would ignore the translation of a saint whose canonization had recently won acclaim in Germany, who was (or whose husband was) formerly known to him, whose translation would, moreover, be attended by several princely families, including that of Thuringia, as well as the leading prelates of Germany? Frederick could not ignore such an occasion. His place was at the head of the ceremonies, before even the surviving children of the saint. And in crowning the saint, he crowned also himself, figuratively, once again as true lord of Germany.

PART THREE

CHAPTER EIGHT

═══

CULTURE AT COURT

I

══

Few medieval rulers have gained so impressive a reputation for the cultural activities at their court as Frederick II. For Charles Homer Haskins, writing in the 1920s, Frederick was a worthy successor to Roger II in the patronage of science and philosophy; the 'brilliant and precocious culture of his Sicilian kingdom' was partly a Norman legacy, and partly a result of his own almost inexhaustible curiosity about the natural world. The precondition of this cultural activity was the physical position of Sicily itself, the crossroads of Greek, Arabic and Latin influences, a land of three or more civilizations under a single autocratic ruler. What worried Haskins was that the evidence for scientific activity was actually rather scanty; moreover, the court of the Hohenstaufen clearly had to be placed in the context both of Sicilian cultural traditions of the twelfth century and of other European rulers of the thirteenth, in Castile and Aragon, who displayed similar interests. Seen this way, Frederick's court begins already to lose its reputation for uniqueness; but no matter, since at the heart of its activities we detect the moving spirit of 'one of the most remarkable minds of the Middle Ages', Frederick II himself. Later German historians were to elevate the emperor's cultural attainments still higher than Haskins. The *stupor mundi*, the precocious Renaissance prince, the rationalist and sceptic: this was the figure historians wanted to see, and they seemed to find ample confirmation in the tales of contemporary writers: Matthew Paris in England, or the shameless gossip (and friar) Salimbene in Italy.

The argument for continuity from the Norman period to Frederick II was taken for granted. Van Cleve listed in his biography of the emperor the impressive output of the south Italian schools and monasteries – the medical college at Salerno, the abbey of Montecassino; and he straightforwardly assumed that what had been achieved anywhere in the *regno* during the twelfth century was a basis for yet greater glories in the centralized thirteenth. Clearly there was a considerable recession of cultural patronage during the emperor's youth; even so Kantorowicz conjured up a kindly centaur who taught the young king of Sicily the secrets of the universe. The historian's inspiration lay in Greek mythology, not in recorded fact. Frederick was well-educated, but not by a centaur, nor by the learned rabbis and imams of Palermo. When he was in his prime, a century had elapsed since Roger II had entertained at court the ambassadors of the Fatimid caliph and had patronized the scholarship of Idrisi and Doxopatrios. The court of Sicily had already become heavily Latinized by the reign of William the Good, and Muslim scholars were rarely to be seen in the royal entourage. Nor was Sicily in any way as great a centre of Jewish learning as was Castile or Egypt in this period: Sicily contained neither the vociferous enemies nor the enthusiastic followers of the controversial Maimonides. The question is, therefore, whether Frederick II revived and enlarged upon the cultural interests of his forebears. And the answer has to be no.

In the first place, the cultural mixing attributed to the Norman court is not visible under Frederick II. The Muslim element now consisted solely of a bodyguard of Lucera Saracens, whose cultural attainments seem to have been nil. They were soldiers, not scholars. There were Muslim visitors, certainly, such as the ambassadors of al-Kamil, and Frederick maintained a fitful correspondence with Islamic scholars as far away as Ceuta. He seems to have understood Arabic, as events during his crusade make plain. Yet the Arabs of Palestine whom he met on crusade were not the standard-bearers of Muslim culture; what he learned from them was the art of seeling the eyes of falcons. Nor was Frederick the recipient of fawning verses in his praise written by Arabic-speakers of Sicily, Malta and North Africa. The Greek element was also very small in scale. Possibly Frederick understood some Greek, but he did not bring many Greeks to court. The principal work in Greek to emanate from Frederick's court was in fact a Greek version of the *Constitutions of Melfi*. The native Greek culture of Calabria and eastern Sicily, evinced in the Greek charters of contemporary Messina and in the Greek churches of Rossano, touched the court but little. John of Otranto and George of Gallipoli, Greeks from the heel of Italy, wrote poetry in Frederick's honour, but the great rhetorical pieces of Roger II's day would have been understood by very few at court. A Greek see in the mountains of Calabria, at Rossano, stood for the survival of Orthodox learning, but Frederick had no real interest in the Greek Church of Italy or of the Byzantine world. Constantinople had ceased after the Latin conquest of 1204 to act as the international centre of a cosmopolitan culture whose reserves of knowledge were unrivalled in the Christian world; where Roger had envied the Komnenoi their Roman imperial crown, Frederick wore a different imperial crown of his own, and the Latin emperor of Constantinople was accorded none of the status that even westerners had recognized the Roman emperors of the East to possess. Frederick kept on good terms with the Lascarid emperor of Nicaea, ruler of a rump state that resisted Frankish conquest, but this was just one element in a Mediterranean policy whose emphasis lay elsewhere.

Moreover, Frederick's court was an itinerant one, partly because the imperial lands of Germany and northern Italy were traditionally ruled by an itinerant emperor with no single capital or base; partly because the strains of war kept Frederick on the move in Lombardy and central Italy for long periods in the 1230s and 1240s. When in 1239 he slowly moved south from Parma to the *regno* he was not going to a final destination; he was moving from one transit camp to another, in a ceaselessly itinerant life. Naples and Messina became important administrative centres of the *regno*, but Frederick preferred to take solace (his word) in the hunting-lodges of Apulia; after his youth he had no time to visit the island part of the kingdom. This travelling court was not and could not be a match for Roger II's magnificent capital city of Palermo. In 1239–40 Frederick issued orders from afar to his courtiers, to prepare sugared violets and to look after his beasts of prey, but the animals and the confections were not with him. He carried with him, it is true, some remarkable animals – an elephant, camels, falcons – as well as his crown jewels and part of his library. Much of this was seized by his Lombard enemies at Parma. Had he been able to live at peace with the Italian towns and the papacy he would very probably have spent larger sums on books, animals and entertainments; even under pressure of war he gave these interests high priority. His court officials, notably the poets who formed the *scuola Siciliana* of vernacular lyric poetry, were in touch with contemporary trends in European culture, though their poetry is but a pale imitation of existing Provençal work: more of this shortly. There is, however, little room for the classic image of the emperor at leisure among his Arab, Greek, Jewish and Latin men of genius, brilliantly casting doubt on the tenets of each monotheistic faith and exploring the universe in tandem with iconoclastic men of science. The accusation that he talked of Moses, Jesus and Muhammad as the 'three impostors' has no validity; it was a stock accusation against disbelievers in the west well before he was born.

A further problem in Frederick's reputation as a great patron of cultural activity is the tendency to attribute to his influence every exciting intellectual development between 1200 and 1250. Leonardo Fibonacci of Pisa, who worked hard for the recognition in the west of the value of arabic numerals, first wrote on the subject in 1202, when Frederick was seven or eight. It is true he met the emperor many years later, apparently while Frederick was at Pisa, and provided Frederick's court with a new edition of his *Liber Abaci* (as it was called) in 1228. But Fibonacci was by origin a Pisan trader in Tunis, where he learned some Arab mathematics; he was a product of the mercantile culture of Tuscany more than of the court of Frederick II. Frederick read the work, but by then the use of Arabic numerals had already spread in Italy. A Genoese notary was using them within a few years of Fibonacci's first treatise. Or, to take a second example, Michael Scot, the dominating figure among Frederick's scientists, spent much of his working life in Toledo, and came to the emperor with experience as a translator and man of magic. He imported to Frederick's court the Arabized science of Castile, and this fact points to an important feature of the court culture patronized by

Frederick. The major cultural advances of the early thirteenth century were being made by Jews, Muslims and Christians working side by side in the translation of Greek and Arabic texts, not in Sicily but in Spain. Frederick's court was culturally dependent on that of Castile.

Taking the Jewish translators at Frederick's court, we find that they are very few in number and that they are not even south Italians. It was from Provence, with its close links to the Sephardim of Aragon and Castile, that came members of the illustrious ibn Tibbon family, one of whom, Jacob Anatoli, worked alongside Michael Scot, and another of whom, his brother-in-law Moses ben Samuel ibn Tibbon, also helped produce translations of Arabic texts. This family was of Spanish origin, but had fled from the invasions of the fanatical Almohad Muslims in the mid-twelfth century; the ibn Tibbons came to southern France with a knowledge of Arabic language and philosophy that was unusual even in so cultured a Jewish community as that of Languedoc. Anatoli's works included translations of the commentaries of Averroës, the great student of Aristotle from Moorish Spain, and of Ptolemy's *Almagest*. It is especially interesting to find the latter work appearing in a new translation, because it had already been rendered into Latin in Norman Sicily around 1160. The Norman version was a translation from the Greek, but Anatoli worked from an Arabic text, itself a paraphrase of a Syriac translation of the original. In Spain and southern France, this was the preferred mode of translation, and it is easy to see why. In the first place, few in Spain understood Greek anyway. But in the second place, these were very difficult texts to those new to their ideas, and the Arabic versions did much, with varying degrees of accuracy, to make Greek philosophy intelligible; they came accompanied by commentaries, of later Greek philosophers such as Apollonios of Aphrodisias or Muslims such as Avicenna and Averroës, all of which helped elucidate the texts. A good deal of the meaning of the ancient original was lost, but the thirteenth-century translators were not modern classical philosophers anxious to elicit the exact thought-process that went into each statement. Their version of Ptolemy had to make sense within the framework of an existing post-Hellenistic, Islamized epistemology. It was hard, therefore, for Latins of Sicily fully to comprehend the translations from either Arabic or Greek, but the latter came in undressed state, and the translators were often perplexed by unfamiliar terms and concepts; this left the translations from Greek full of infelicities and misunderstandings.

Of all the translations made in southern Italy in Frederick's reign, the most important was surely that of a work originally written in Arabic but then put into Hebrew, whence it reached the court of Sicily and the scholars of Naples. Moses ben Maimon, also known as Maimonides, or Rambam, sought in the *Guide for the Perplexed* to reconcile the world-view of Aristotle with the dictates of Jewish religious teaching. His most fervent modern admirers tend to ignore this work in favour of his more orthodox works that had no such impact outside Judaism; he is thus a cult figure both for the orthodox and for the anti-fundamentalist wings of modern Judaism. But the *Guide* had among its early readers the scion of a south Italian noble family, well-liked at court, Thomas Aquinas, and he too, like Maimonides and Averroës, was to attempt the reconciliation of Aristotelianism with his faith. Michael Scot may have had a hand in the translation from Hebrew, but in fact his Hebrew, though he knew some, seems rather faulty, at least in surviving manuscripts. As with the translations from Arabic, this must have been team-work, with Jew, Christian and where appropriate Muslim sitting together and communicating in the vernacular romance they had in common. Certainly, Frederick's court was not packed with Jewish scholars. Frederick brought Jews to his kingdom of Sicily to help cultivate the soil, but expressed reserve about allowing in too many or permitting them greater religious freedom than canon law assigned them. Scholars were to some extent above these rules, but Frederick was no enthusiastic philo-Semite; he shares the attitudes of his more educated contemporaries, and no more. Set against the saintly, hysterical Jew-baiter Louis IX of France he easily appears a man of sense and moderation, but similar views to his could be found even in papal circles, and influenced his own outlook. Not to deny that occasional Jewish scholars were presented at court: the ibn Tibbons and Judah ha-Cohen certainly knew Frederick personally, and were on good terms with Michael Scot. At the very highest rung of the intellectual ladder there were scholars of all three religions who were willing to

confront together problems they shared, in science or even religion, such as the proof of God's existence or the eternity of
matter. Although the court of Frederick provided some opportunities for this work, that of Castile was a more effective
pestle in which ideas could be ground together; it really did
contain representatives of the three religions and enjoyed readier
access to the texts of Arabic learning, many themselves first
written in Spain.

Frederick compensated in part for the upheavals of a gypsy life
by sending letters to foreign scholars; Frederick's cultural activity
consists largely in a correspondence course in science and philosophy with Jews of Spain, with Muslims of Egypt and with his
own courtiers, absent as they sometimes were from Frederick's
presence. Judah ben Solomon ha-Cohen received letters from the
emperor in Castile and visited Frederick in northern Italy later. It
was Michael Scot who provided the main link between this
youthful mystic and scientist and the Hohenstaufen court. Al-
Kamil, sultan of Egypt, maintained contact with the emperor
after Frederick's crusade by exchanging views on the nature of
the universe, offering replies to elaborate questions of mathematics and even sending over an astronomer who was to instruct
Frederick as well as to serve the needs of diplomacy. Such
combinations of diplomatic and philosophic tasks were by no
means unusual in this period; the Norman Sicilian Aristippus
secured manuscripts from Constantinople even when he could
not secure a peace treaty. Frederick too sought to raise the esteem
of his Mediterranean neighbours for him by appearing in their
eyes as a man of learning of whom it might be said (as it had
been of Roger II) that but for his religion he was the intellectual
equal of any Muslim prince. This was partly a diplomatic game,
but Frederick played it with vigour; his cultural interests were no
sham, and his intellectual interests were much broader than those
of contemporary colleagues on the throne of England or France.
But this does not mean he maintained a particularly glittering
court, nor that he had time to delve into the abstruse necromantic
studies his enemies attributed to him.

Thus in the early 1240s Frederick, with a clever eye on diplomatic advantage, wrote to the Almohad caliph in Morocco, and
sent a list of philosophical questions which were eventually

answered by a prominent man of learning from Ceuta, ibn Sabin. Similar questions were sent to Muslim philosophers in the Middle East, as far afield as Yemen. Probably they were first dressed up in Arabic by his court philosopher Master Theodore, of whom more shortly. In any case, the questions failed to impress ibn Sabin. He made it plain that the emperor had not grasped the basic terminology of philosophy, and implied that the only real answer lay in a commitment to the Islamic faith. Were Frederick to receive this irascible philosopher, ibn Sabin would instruct him adequately. This was not a demand for a pension, as so often occurred; ibn Sabin actually refused to accept the purse Frederick sent him. As for the subject-matter of the questions, it seems Frederick was already infected by Aristotelian ideas, though it is hardly surprising that he was perplexed by them; they were new and unfamiliar in a world still dominated by Plato's theory of forms, and there really was a problem in reconciling these novel truths with received opinion. To ask ibn Sabin how Aristotle was able to demonstrate the eternity of matter reveals both a general knowledge of Aristotle's views and a lack of access to or understanding of Aristotle's detailed arguments; other questions, such as the immortality of the soul, are also known to have worried Maimonides and Averroës. Thus we find an intellectual trying to come to grips with half-heard and vaguely transmitted ideas, whose dramatic implications for theology had yet to be resolved. Questions to other philosophers were often rather less ambitious; Judah ha-Cohen was asked to resolve some geometric puzzles, while the court of al-Kamil was set to work on the emperor's behalf to explain, *inter alia*, why a stick partly immersed in water will appear to be bent.

Haskins brought to light a further series of questions, put this time to his Scottish astrologer and physician, Michael Scot; whereas in the earlier examples it is hard to know whether Frederick or his agent is posing the problem, now, if Scot's word is to be believed, we hear the emperor's own voice. Frederick required nothing less than a description of the universe from its foundations to the uppermost reaches of heaven. These, Frederick said, were the central questions of existence; often the emperor had heard about the stars and the natural world of earth – the peoples, animals and minerals of the familiar world. But there were secrets beyond the stars: paradise, purgatory, the inferno. Where do they lie and who rules them? 'In which heaven is God in the person of His Divine Majesty and how does He sit on His throne, and how is He accompanied by angels and saints, and what do they do continually before Him?' In addition there are questions about the waters, salt water and fresh, that are found on earth; these probably find their connection to the earlier questions in the belief, propounded in *Genesis*, that the earth itself is suspended between 'waters'. Another of the four natural elements, fire, issues from the earth at Etna and in the Lipari islands off Sicily; Frederick requires an explanation of volcanoes, geysers and other similar phenomena, based in part, no doubt, on his observation of the Sicilian volcanoes.

The jump from the description of the heavens to an analysis of the nature of salt water or of Stromboli is a small one, for the heaven of which Frederick speaks is a material reality with substance. The soul itself in some sense participates in the laws of physics and does not stand on a different plane of reality. A concrete view of the universe was being actively propounded by those theologians and philosophers who in the twelfth century began to identify purgatory as a place, and not simply a condition in which the soul might find itself after death. The universe, as Jacques Le Goff has maintained, acquired now a detailed map, with impressive repercussions for the theology of sin and even for the economic organization of earthly society. Frederick's questions arrive at a time when the idea of purgatory as a place is becoming widely accepted, and in that setting they are not unusual. Above all, they are not the questions of a sceptic. 'Where is God?' he is asking; and a religion that posits a God who can take human shape and eventually ascend to heaven has to face the implications of the idea of divine corporeality and of divine location. Frederick was not one to take comfort in the standard argument of men of religion that there are unknown and unknowable things; his was a concrete rather than abstract mind, interested in the facts of the material world. He was not a philosopher in any modern sense; his concern was exact information, applied to the realms of God as to those of man.

One manuscript of the questions contains additional material that one would like to think genuine. 'Tell us whether one soul in the next world knows another and whether one can return to this life to speak and show oneself,' and, later: 'How is it that the soul of a living man which has passed away to another life than ours cannot be induced to return by first love or even by hate, just as if it had been nothing, nor does it seem to care at all for what it has left behind, whether it be saved or lost?' This passage has always excited comment; yet it may be a later interpolation. If not, it perhaps reflects a feeling and loving Frederick whom the historian finds it impossible generally to reach: the Frederick whose first wife, Constance, gained his love more than any later wife, and whose enemies too (such as Gregory IX) inspired in him a loathing that outlasted their death; whose son Henry brought despair and tragedy to the imperial dynasty. Such questions about the soul also perhaps inspired the preposterous stories that spread in contemporary Italy; the foul-tongued Salimbene records that Frederick placed a condemned man in a barrel and closed it tightly so that the prisoner suffocated. The intention was to test whether the soul could be observed leaving the barrel. It is highly unlikely that Frederick indulged his scientific interests this way.

Michael Scot was not one to avoid such questions, even though his intellectual capacity was not quite what he himself liked the world to think. 'If it is asked, where resides the God of Gods, and Lord of the rulers of the universe of earth and heaven? we reply that, although He is everywhere potentially, yet He is substantially in the intellectual heaven'; and there seems some confusion in Scot's work whether this intellectual, or empyrean heaven, is at the centre or in the south of the heavens. He compiled for the emperor descriptions of the material world, works on astrology and alchemy, all of which reveal a dependence on classical and medieval predecessors, but some originality too. His description of the causes of rainbows seems novel, though it is now known to be inadequate. Scot was vain about his work, and proudly proclaimed that he had indeed witnessed the transformation of copper into silver, or that he could vouch for the veracity of learned Muslims of Majorca and Tunis; still, he was a pioneer alchemist, introducing to the west, with the help of Jewish colleagues (normally wary of the discipline), an elaborate experimental chemistry one of whose ends was intended to be the creation of cheap gold. And, as a translator of texts of Aristotle, and as a devotee of the Arab astronomer al-Bitrûgi, Scot was helping in the transmission of the learning of Muslim Spain to the Christian west (his translation of al-Bitrûgi actually antedates his arrival at Frederick's court). A Scotsman trained in Toledo, he was the link between the imperial court and the more active centres of translation in Spain; and he became a great help to Frederick in the emperor's own researches into the habits of birds. For Frederick, Scot's most important works must have included his translations of Aristotle on animals (*De animalibus*), and of a shorter work on the same subject by the Persian philosopher Avicenna (ibn Sina). These books were to influence Frederick's views on, and method in approaching, the science of falconry.

Scot was also the court magician and astrologer. He arrived at court some time between 1220 and 1224, and remained with Frederick during the late 1220s and early 1230s, dying, supposedly, when hit by crumbling masonry in church, around 1236. Thus his career at court was relatively short; he had earlier moved in papal circles, under Honorius III and Gregory IX, taking advantage of the peace between papacy and empire to gain favours from each. He was even offered as reward for his eminence a non-resident benefice at Cashel in Ireland, which he very honestly resigned on the grounds that he knew no Erse. He was thus a figure of note in Italy, a scholar reputed to have probed the inner secrets of the universe in the company of the magicians of Toledo, a magician himself. Magician or not, he professed to cure the emperor's illnesses, with varying success, and showed a detailed interest in physiology, even in gynaecology. His astrological theories were put to the test by Frederick. It was generally assumed that the stars and planets provided a guide to human behaviour; they did not determine behaviour, but acted as an impartial scientific guide to it. They were a perilous source of information, for, as Scot insisted, the emotions of the astrologer himself, and many other factors, could produce wrong readings; but Scot was prepared to try his hand at, for instance, the prediction of fortunes in the Lombard war:

I began, as the custom is, to seek the lord of the ascendant on behalf of the enquiring emperor and the lord of the seventh house for the hostile party, so that I might know from their positions in the signs and in the *figura* what would be the outcome between the interrogator and his enemies.

Fortunately for Frederick the lord of the ascendant was mighty Mars, but the mistress of the seventh house weak Venus; the enemy would surely petition for peace. 'So this conjunction signified victory of the prince from fortitude over his adversaries, and promptly, without delay.'

Scot's analysis of the natural world is built on similar certainties. If you wish to know whether a pregnant woman will bear a boy or a girl, ask her to extend a hand. If she puts out her right hand it will be a boy; if the left a girl. Similar old wives' tales still make the rounds. There is an obsession with prediction, visible in Scot's description of the significance of sneezes; it is easy to dismiss these comments lightly, but Scot was surely trying to reduce to order a little understood universe, seeing rational connections between behaviour at one level (the stars) and another (the human body), which in combination betrayed the actual fortune of the individual. Astrology was inherently *scientific*, because it sought to express exact rules about the performance of animate and inanimate objects; its basis was an assumption that the universe is harmonious, that everything exists in an interrelated state of order, or rather in an intricate mechanism binding the motion of the spheres to the moods of man. We now know the assumptions about the planets and stars to be entirely wrong; but in a universe constructed on what might be called thirteenth-century lines the value of astrology seemed patent.

Frederick had his doubts, nevertheless. Once he asked Scot to measure the distance from the top of a church tower to heaven. This Scot managed to do. Then Frederick lowered the top of the tower by a few inches without telling Scot, and before long told Scot to measure again. Scot did so, with the comment that either heaven had receded a little from earth or the tower had shrunk. Needless to say the emperor was tremendously impressed. Scot's elaborate theories of seven heavens need to be analysed in the context of Jewish, Christian and Muslim ideas current in the thirteenth century (the Kabbalists talked of no fewer than twelve heavens around this time), but it is clear that the necromancer believed in God and saw his task as the description of God's creation. There is thus little distance between the emperor who questioned Scot about the dimensions of the universe and the philosopher whose whole mode of thinking assumes the reasonableness of questions of the type Frederick posed. Ibn Sabin felt no such comfort about Frederick's concept of the universe. Expressed differently, one could say that the questions to Scot reveal that Frederick is under the intellectual spell of Scot, asking the sort of question that Scot has taught the emperor to ask.

Scot was succeeded as Frederick's astrologer by Master Theodore, probably a Christian from Antioch. Much less is known about this figure, and he did not accompany Frederick on all the emperor's travels. Like Scot, he was as much a physician as a soothsayer, and his confections of sugared violet for Piero della Vigna and the emperor were apparently thought to have some medical value. At any rate he wrote a work on hygiene for the emperor, basing himself on a text wrongly attributed to Aristotle. His expertise in Arabic earned him responsibilities that Scot lacked; in Theodore's hands was placed correspondence with the ruler of Tunis, an exchange of letters in which the main concern was delicate diplomacy towards a tribute-paying Muslim king. The nephew of the Tunisian ruler had fled to Italy; the pope believed him to be seeking baptism but Frederick was holding him under guard without showing interest in converting him. Scientific questions may also have had a place in this correspondence with Tunis. Frederick's choice of Theodore as court astrologer suggests that the emperor felt the loss of Michael Scot; but Theodore may have lacked the experience of Spanish scholarship that gave shape to Scot's work.

Frederick's patronage of astrologers was far from unusual; had not Michael Scot found favour at the papal court itself? His allies and rivals, such as Ezzelino da Romano, had their own astrologers as a matter of course. Where Frederick is less typical is in the lack of extensive patronage of traditional Latin learning at his court. Apart from medical works, and the legal studies that culminated in the *Constitutions of Melfi*, there is little. The University of Naples, founded by imperial fiat in 1224, had a fitful existence; its greatest alumnus, Thomas Aquinas, found glory in Paris and elsewhere. There was some study of natural philosophy under Arnold the Catalan and Peter of Ireland (Petrus de Hibernia) but the basic aim of the university was to train notaries and judges for the royal or lesser service; it was an intensely practical institution, whose founder believed in the importance of practical training, and its intellectual vivacity was thereby restrained. The medical school at Salerno was controlled by royal interference in its examinations after 1231, and rapidly began to lose its primacy to schools further north (notably at Montpellier in the lands of the crown of Aragon) which were less conservative in their teaching, and prepared to add to the strictures of Galen new knowledge acquired through Jewish and Muslim inspiration or by empirical observation. The school of Salerno kept only its reputation, which lasted into the sixteenth century; but, just as the emperor's heavy hand had suffocated the mercantile vitality of such towns as Salerno, so too did his interference in the medical regime have dire consequences. Like his Norman predecessors he seems in any case to have preferred to employ for his own use physicians who had not passed through Salerno – Scot, Theodore and perhaps also some of his Jewish philosophers.

Haskins sought to show that Frederick's court was a major centre of Latin letters, but his case was based on sixteen examples spread over the whole of Frederick's life, such as Peter of Eboli, who had lauded Henry VI, and Leonardo Fibonacci, who also began work long before Frederick's patronage was available. Some of Haskins' names are those of translators from Arabic – Scot and Theodore; one is the Latin poet Henry of Avranches, a notable figure, but his three poems in praise of Frederick are a small part of his oeuvre, which was also addressed to patrons in France, England and at the papal court. Despite the reputation of Naples as burial-place of the magician and poet Virgil, there were few Latin poets who worked within southern Italy during the early thirteenth century; Jacopo da Benevento translated into Latin the moral maxims of the vernacular poet Schiavo di Bari, and probably wrote original pieces of his own, while Riccardo di Venosa, an imperial civil servant, dedicated a verse comedy to Frederick around the time of his crusade. A few more examples can be added, but it is not an impressive output, especially when compared to that of Frederick's Angevin successors on the throne

of Naples. Frederick was cool to religious literature, and there is
no evidence that the emperor stimulated the writing of sermons
and saints' lives as earlier and later kings of Sicily chose to do.

There was one important way in which Latin letters at Frederick's court were developed to a high pitch. Piero della Vigna
and his secretaries gave further impetus to the study of rhetoric
by composing florid, but for their time very accomplished,
orations and letters. The barbs of della Vigna were feared at the
papal court, and Frederick's civil servants were unique in Europe
in the ease with which they could match the elaborate style of
papal letters and propaganda with elegant missives of their own.
It has to be remembered that the study of rhetoric was by now
widespread in the schools and universities of northern Italy (della
Vigna may have attended the great university at Bologna); in
Cremona, Arezzo and elsewhere model letter-books, and treatises
on the rhetorical art were much in vogue. A new civil service,
required for the complex needs of city government, as well as for
the Sicilian and papal monarchies, was trained in Latin letters;
Frederick's court was only participating in a wider movement.
And southern Italy, especially Capua, was already established as a
centre of rhetoric before Frederick's time; the career of Thomas
of Gaeta, or of Cardinal Thomas of Capua, who died in 1229,
suggests that late Norman southern Italy was a centre of Latin
studies around the time of Frederick's birth; from such an aca-
demic background came the Amalfitan and Salernitan civil servants who were to dominate Sicilian administration under
Frederick and his successors. Much attention has often been paid
to the foundation in the 1220s of the University of Naples, the
first university to be established by a king; but its existence was
largely sustained by Frederick's ban on Sicilian attendance at the
University of Bologna; and its origins must in any case be sought
in the existing schools of rhetoric in and near Capua. All this is
not to deprecate the achievement of Piero della Vigna, Terrisio
di Atina and other rhetoricians, who not simply wrote on Frederick's behalf, but composed satirical and philosophical letters,
many of which were still being circulated to admirers of their
prose in the fourteenth and fifteenth centuries. It was not the
concise, even dense Latin of a new Cicero, but a baroque, allusive
style that depended for its success on the fact that it was an

excellent example of the style already preferred by north Italian rhetoricians. In other words, Piero and his colleagues were not initiators but imitators, whose work surpassed that of their masters in Bologna and Capua. A few lines of the original Latin give a sense of the style; here is the body writing to the soul, bewailing the separation of death, remembering pleasures carnal and glories martial:

Ubi est uxor pulcherrima velud stella cum qua cotidie lecto florido amplexibus et basiis delectabar? Ubi sunt equi arma et indumenta serica deaurata quibus cum militibus decorus cottidie apparebam?

Once the body had delighted in a beautiful wife and had ridden in silken cloth-of-gold accompanied by a squad of knights. But now the body suffers great torments under the icy earth. There are cheerful pieces too, and the height of satire is reached in a bogus address of Pope Gregory to his hierarchy, sent to 'fornicacioni vestre', 'your Fornication', instead of 'fraternitati vestre'. Both letters cited belong to a collection of *exempla* made by a notary of Ischia, probably named Iohannes de Argussa, and they are another product of the lively Capuan school of rhetoric. As late as 1400 a Latinist at Lübeck copied the Ischian letters, proof of the enduring quality of this prose.

The prohibitive cost of magnificent display meant that Frederick's court was, contrary to general assumption, a pale shadow of the opulent Norman court, and a less grandiose affair than under his Angevin successors. There were marvellous animals, to be sure, but little was spent, unless danger of decay decreed otherwise, on palaces and the fine arts. A few of the mosaics of the great cathedral at Cefalù on the north coast of Sicily may date from Frederick's reign, but the great Sicilian mosaic cycles were no longer produced; partly, this was because there was no longer the challenge of Constantinople, which had fired the Normans to imitate the great churches of the East; partly it reflects Frederick's lack of interest in gifts to a Church from which he had suffered much; partly it reflects the cautious spending of his reign. The exceptions are a few hunting-lodges, castles and the great gate of Capua, of which more elsewhere. Much was spent on fabulous gifts to Mediterranean rulers; the sultan of Egypt deserved fair exchange for the gorgeous planetarium, said to be worth 20,000 marks, that he sent in 1232; what better than to raid lands far to the north and present him with a polar bear (assuming it was not simply an albino bear – rare enough in either case)? The planetarium moved; it was a clock as well as a map of the heavens, and no more suitable gift to Frederick can be imagined. Apparently even in Damascus his interest in natural science was recognized.

Yet there was one subject that had a special place among the emperor's scientific interests, the life of birds, and especially of falcons. Here a passion for hunting was combined with a spirit of enquiry that led Frederick to produce one of the great works of ornithology of all time. To falconry it is now necessary to turn.

II

For the house of Hohenstaufen falconry was a passion similar in intensity to the love of horses displayed by the house of Windsor. Frederick was matched by his illegitimate sons Manfred (later king of Sicily) and Enzo, king of Sardinia, in his love of hunting with birds; Manfred revised the text of the emperor's great study of the falcon, while Enzo was dedicatee of a French translation of the hunting-book of Yatrib, originally written in Persian. In fact even earlier, under Roger II, a royal falconer had prepared a now-lost treatise on the subject, so Frederick's interest may have been a continuation of an established Norman one. It is said that when the great khan of the Mongols wrote one of his tiresome letters telling Frederick to submit to his might or forfeit his crown, Frederick remarked that he might gladly resign his throne if he were allowed to become the khan's falconer. Moreover, the unusually dense administrative records for 1239–40 indicate that his falcons took second place only to the cares of government in Frederick's daily business; forty documents in the register concern falcons, and more than fifty royal falconers are named. Frederick arranged for the capture of falcons on Malta, a good source; he ensured a supply of Arctic gerfalcons via Lübeck; he even reported on and asked about the prey – there are letters describing the capture of cranes in the region of Gubbio, and he expects his

justiciars in south-eastern Italy to give their time to the capture
of live cranes which are to be used in training sessions. He is
anxious to hear of the recovery from illness of a falconer in
southern Italy. From Greenland to the Dar al-Islam Frederick
sought his falcons and information about them: he gave Master
Theodore the Syrian astrologer the task of translating the *De
scientia venandi per aves* of the Muslim Moamyn, and while
waiting during the interminable siege of Faenza Frederick went
through the manuscript, apparently correcting Theodore's text.
If so, this is a tribute to Frederick's knowledge of Arabic, of
which he certainly knew a little.

Frederick's own book *De arte venandi cum avibus* must be seen
on two levels; it is a guide for the hunter, but it also offers precise
ornithological information not merely about falcons but about
their prey. In writing the book Frederick was inspired by Aristotle, and particularly by the *De animalibus*, which had been
translated at court. Yet he sought to apply Aristotle's methods to
the nth degree: observation, empirical study, was the basis of the
book, and if that meant, as it often did, that he had to correct the
erroneous observations of Aristotle himself, the Master of Them
That Know, so be it. This ability to apply the philosopher's rules
and yet not to be in awe of Aristotle is one of the main reasons
why the *De arte* must be seen as a considerable intellectual and
scientific achievement. Frederick did make extensive use of other
'books of philosophers', and he also took care to read contemporary hunting books; but the preponderant source for the work
is what he saw with his own eyes, or what he learned from his
staff of falconers. His aim, he said, in reproof to Aristotle and
other authorities, was 'to show those things that are, as they are'
(*manifestare ea que sunt, sicut sunt*), and this phrase has often,
perhaps too often, been taken as the motto of his whole reign.
The observant falconer is thereby transmogrified into the dedicated realist, whereas in fact Frederick could be obstinate in the
face of political reality and emphatic about rights that he could
hardly hope to enjoy. Inconsistent in his politics, he was nevertheless quite consistent in his biology, and the *Art of Hunting with
Birds* is a thoroughly remarkable piece of science, describing in
exact and unadorned detail the nesting habits of falcons and their
prey, dismissing contemporary hocus-pocus, the product of

experiment and long thought. Thus Frederick examined the stories that barnacle geese were hatched not from eggs but from barnacles in the sea, or from trees; he had pieces of wood bearing barnacles brought to him, and argued rightly that there was a confusion between the shape of barnacles and that of the geese, but no biological connection. Do vultures find their prey by sight or by smell? The answer must lie in experiment: Frederick seeled the eyes of his captive vultures, and proved that they operate by sight.

The book survives in two versions, one which is made up of six books, and is apparently all the work of Frederick, and a revised version, of books one and two only, with additions, mostly small, by King Manfred. A manuscript of this in the Vatican Library, gorgeously illuminated with meticulous paintings of the birds, is rightly considered one of the library's greatest treasures; but there once existed in Frederick's own possession a very beautiful copy of this or another hunting book. In 1264 or 1265 a citizen of Milan offered Charles of Anjou, count of Anjou and Provence, and soon to be king of Sicily, a copy of the book captured with the emperor's treasures at Parma; in it could be seen an illumination of the emperor seated on his throne, and magnificent illustrations of dogs and birds. This may in fact have been not his falcon book but a second work, on hawks as a whole (of which the falcon is a sub-species). In any case, Manfred searched out Frederick's additional notes deposited in the castles of Apulia before setting to work on his revision of the falcon book, and it seems that Frederick had been accumulating notes and drafts for over thirty years. Sections of the falcon book on the diseases of birds are now lost, and even so the work is a very substantial one; the Vatican manuscript is only 111 folios, but the six-book version reaches 589 folios in a fifteenth-century copy prepared for a later claimant to the throne of Sicily.

This was not simply a work of science, bred in the atmosphere generated by Michael Scot and Master Theodore. The underlying notion is that falconry is worthy of such study because it is the sport of kings. 'Cranes are the most famous of all birds which birds of prey are taught to hunt, and the gerfalcon is the noblest of the birds of prey and the bird which captures cranes better than other falcons and best goes after them.' The aim is to perfect a noble sport, and to gain the fullest satisfaction from hunting;

this means training the falcons to reach their maximum natural ability. Nature endows falcons with extraordinary skills; to participate in these skills is to observe nature as much as it is to enjoy sport in the ordinary sense of the term. The fullest potential of the falcon can be tapped; we are on the edges of an Aristotelian world where activities, human and animal, are described in the light of their function.

But Frederick did not spend all his hunting days in contemplation of the sport's deeper meaning. In Apulia, Frederick erected hunting-lodges, of which the most famous is that of Castel del Monte, with its simple octagon shape. Frederick was a real hunter, and his love of falcons in particular left him free to hunt in all his domains, from the Black Forest to Apulia and Sicily, even in Syria, where he learned much about the training of his birds. Konrad von Lützelhard, Teutonic knight, seems to be the author of a work on hunting the stag that appears to have circulated in imperial circles in Germany. A day spent hunting was eventually to wreak havoc when the imperial camp at Victoria, near Parma, was left unguarded. Cheetahs graced the travelling court, not just for display in a menagerie but for use in the field. 'In another age,' it has been said, 'he might have stalked big game in Africa or explored the fauna of the Upper Amazon with the energy of a Theodore Roosevelt'; had he been faced with Roosevelt's small bear, he would no doubt have saved it (and seized it) too, but more out of scientific enquiry than out of compassion.

III

In traditional historiography, Frederick's II's claim to be 'wonder of the world' is based not merely on his scientific interests and on the high drama of his conflict with the papacy. He earns constant plaudits as the founder of Italian lyric poetry. Tracing their origins to the Hohenstaufen court, the thirteenth-century Italian poets were labelled 'the Sicilian school'; Dante, conscious of the improvements and shifts of emphasis that had been made by his immediate predecessors in Tuscany (above all Cavalcanti) marked off the Sicilians from the *dolce stil nuovo* of his own day. But

Italian love poetry was seen by Dante as a relative novelty, coming to the Sicilian court only in the first half of the thirteenth century – that is, a good century after the poetic career of Guilhem de Peiteu, duke of Aquitaine, and apparent founder of Provençal love poetry. Such was the power of the Provençal tradition even in Dante's time that Dante Alighieri considered writing his *Divine Comedy* in Provençal rather than in Tuscan; whether the result would have been the immortalization of Provençal or the obscure burial of his greatest work cannot, of course, be said. Nor did Dante regard the 'Sicilian' dialect in which the first Italian lyrics were written as especially refined. He was more impressed by the patrons of the poets than by the language of the poetry:

But those illustrious heroes Frederick Caesar and his highly favoured son Manfred, displaying the nobility and righteousness of their souls so long as fortune was favourable, followed what is human, disdaining what is bestial: wherefore those who were of noble heart and endowed with graces strove to attach themselves to the majesty of such great princes; so that in their time whatever the best Italians produced, first appeared at the court of these mighty sovereigns.

Dante's remarks raise a number of problems. Was this poetry Sicilian (or at least south Italian) in origin, character and expression? Or did Frederick II merely attract to his court poets of diverse origins – Lombards, Tuscans, Ligurians, even Provençaux, as well as natives of the *regno* – who have been crudely classified as 'Sicilians' because their patron was ruler of Sicily? Was this poetry original in themes or technique? Or did it owe much, maybe everything, to the great Provençal troubadours, the German *Minnesänger* and the north French *trouvères*?

Allowing for the disappearance of great amounts of the poetry of the 'Sicilians', some clear answers can be provided. Giacomo da Lentini, born in Sicily, an imperial notary and member of Frederick's court, seems to have invented the fourteen-line poem known as the sonnet. E. F. Langley, editing Giacomo's work in 1915, remarked that 'in the sonnet form Giacomo had no predecessors that are known to us'; twenty-five out of thirty-five Sicilian sonnets known to Langley were at least attributed to Giacomo da Lentini. Even if he did not invent this verse form, its

origins appear to lie among the Sicilian lyricists. Nor are
Giacomo's origins among the Sicilian population unusual. Most
of the poets who surrounded Frederick II were genuinely Sicilian,
and many of them came from Messina or the east coast: Stefano
Protonotaro hailed from the Messina region; so did Guido delle
Colonne, Odo delle Colonne, Rosso Rosso (lord of Villa
Sperlinga and Martini and creditor of Frederick II), Mazzeo di
Ricco and others. Iacopo Mostacci is described both as a Mes-
sinese and as a Pisan, but this is no problem: many of Messina's
inhabitants were of north Italian origin by the early thirteenth
century. Maybe the prominence of Messina reflects accidents of
manuscript survival, but in fact it seems that the bustling, pros-
perous port with its large settler population provided an ideal
environment for the importation of north European fashions –
not merely fashions in textiles, but fashions in speech and literature. It was in eastern Sicily, too, that the largest accretion of
Latin settlers was to be found, as a result of attempts to occupy
abandoned lands, to deprive the Muslims of their estates, and to
turn Sicily into a primarily Christian island. Iacopo Mostacci was
certainly not the only 'Sicilian' poet to descend from mainland
forebears. What the settlers brought with them was their own
jumble of romance dialects, all new to Sicily; in some remote
villages of the eastern Sicilian interior distinctive dialects close to
those spoken in Liguria or elsewhere have survived into the
twentieth century. By the early thirteenth century, however, it is
possible to talk of Italian as one of the languages of Sicily,
alongside the Greek of the Byzantine population and the Arabic
of the Muslims and the Jews. Not that this Italian was a coherent,
fused dialect; the poets themselves stylized and standardized the
speech of eastern Sicily, interlacing it with rhetorical devices of
Latin derivation to create an elegant, if stilted, literary language.
But the Provençal troubadours had acted in much the same way;
their poems were declaimed in a formalized language that no one
really spoke, but that any princely court could understand and
appreciate. The later history of the poems penned in Sicily adds
further complication to this process. For many of the surviving
manuscripts are Tuscan, and reflect the interest of later generations of poets in the apparent founders of their craft. Again and
again, therefore, the language of the poetry has been Tuscanized,

its orthography and even vocabulary altered from the original to conform with the dialect of late thirteenth-century Tuscany. This has left literary historians with formidable tasks of reconstruction, when trying to recover the Sicilian original.

The literary language of the Sicilian poets was further enriched (or confused) by the presence at Frederick's court of non-Sicilians: mainly south Italians such as Rinaldo d'Aquino, Folco di Calabria and, most famous of all, Piero della Vigna himself, author of excruciatingly leaden verses. The Genoese Percival Doria may have had contact with the Sicilian poets; he certainly had political links to Frederick II. A few Sicilians originated away from the east coast: the distinguished poet Cielo d'Alcamo, and one or two poets perhaps from Palermo. The great majority of poets can be shown to have enjoyed offices under the emperor, or under his son King Manfred. Giacomo da Lentini seems to have been entrusted with the care of some mainland castles in 1240; he is mentioned a few times in the single surviving imperial register. Ruggero de Amicis was sent to Egypt in 1241 as Frederick's ambassador, and was involved in the conspiracy of 1246 against the emperor. Iacopo Mostacci earned Frederick's favour by serving as one of the emperor's falconers; but he was also a jurist, surviving the changes of regime in the 1260s and 1270s with remarkable agility. And as for Rinaldo d'Aquino, it is not clear whether he was indeed St Thomas Aquinas' brother; but it is clear that he belonged to a powerful and favoured Campanian family with access to the emperor's ear.

Thus we find a group of poets bound to the emperor, engaged in other, and important, activities alongside the writing of poetry. In this respect they are unlike some of the early Provençal troubadours: Cercamon and Marcabru, for instance, had earned their keep at the courts of Languedoc, in the mid-twelfth century, purely as poets and singers. The fact that Frederick's court was the principal or single focus of lyric poetry in the *regno* comes as no surprise. The poetry of the Sicilian school, like the patronage of science at Frederick's court, did not strike deep roots on Sicilian soil; the person of the emperor was the focal point of the circle of poets. It is self-consciously courtly poetry, drawing little on popular tradition within Sicily, modelled, in fact, on the lyrics of the troubadours and their own German imitators. It is poetry written to entertain the court, or rather the emperor's closed group of familiars; it was not intended to mark the creation of a great European literature, though Italian literary scholars can be excused for reading it in such a light.

To explain the ideas at work behind the creation of Frederick's circle of poets, it is necessary to move back in time to the origins of the Provençal love lyric, and to compare the impressive range of literary production in twelfth-century Languedoc with the much narrower range found at Frederick's court. For the Sicilian poets left out a good deal; and this explains much about them. The first point to emphasize is that the origins of the courtly love lyric remain mysterious; Moorish tracts on love, Ovid's poetry, popular tradition, even Cathar heresies in secret code, have been cited to explain the appearance in southern France, around 1120, of the first 'troubadours'. Traditionally, the founder of their craft was Guilhem de Peiteu, or William of Aquitaine, a brutish warlord who somehow managed also to produce a few delicate lines on love, and many more lines that even modern readers, inured to such themes, might find very explicit. Contrary to common belief, the early troubadours did not idealize or 'platonize' love; carnal success was the object of the exercise, and the process by which the lady was raised on to a pedestal was a gradual one. But the germs of such ideas are already there in William of Aquitaine. Standard motifs emerged in the twelfth century that played on the agony of separation between lover and lady: the separation might, for instance, result from a knight's vow to go on crusade, leaving the object of his love in Languedoc; or he might find the lady of his desire in Syria, only to have to return to the west and abandon hope of seeing her again. Needless to say, a knight would often idealize a lady who was not his wife; a cult of adultery emerged that met with strong disapproval from the Church. It is no coincidence that the Albigensian Crusade helped put an end not merely to heresy but to the cult of love in southern France; or rather, the leadership of the cult of love moved northwards to imitative courts in the Île de France and the Rhineland, where Provençal was abandoned for French and German.

Among the most illustrious, if not the most talented, north European love poets were the two foes Richard Coeur-de-Lion and Henry VI of Hohenstaufen. And it has been seen that the duke of Aquitaine is credited – rightly or not – with having invented the fashion. The presence of well-born poets alongside low-born *jongleurs* is an important feature of this love poetry; and, because few historians (as opposed to literary specialists) have been let loose on this material, the significance of princely participation has been ignored. No doubt, as Peter Dronke has argued, the Provençal love lyric has roots in popular love poetry that has played on similar themes since time immemorial (he cites the example of the love lyrics of ancient Egypt). But what was new in twelfth-century southern France was the sudden transformation of the status of the poet; a prince, the duke of Aquitaine, sat before his court and performed lustful lyrics; the texts were preserved in writing; the love lyric increasingly took as its theme a feudal society, in which the knight finds himself at odds with rules of social status (his lady is often in a higher social stratum), with current mores (for instance concerning adultery), or with his own knightly duties (as, perhaps, a crusader who has vowed to fight for Christ, but prefers to fight for his lady). Princes and knights became the controlling influence in the production of lyric poetry; if they were not the authors and performers, they were at least the patrons and audiences.

And indeed by the end of the twelfth century, in north and south France and in Germany, the ability to write love lyrics in the vernacular had become a mark of fine feeling that any ruler worth his salt made efforts to display. The grossness of the early lyrics gave way to conventionalized, but entirely respectable, imagery. Whether or not Frederick's father Henry wrote the following lines – and the sentiments expressed seem remote from the Henry we otherwise know – is hardly of consequence; such themes were becoming quite standard:

Kingdoms and countries are under my rule when I am with that lovely lady; when I leave where she is, all my power and wealth are gone. Then longing and grief of soul is all that I count as mine . . . She seems to me so good and so beautiful that, sooner than give her up, I would give up my crown.

One thing is sure: the lady in question is not the Empress Constance. And, whether or not Frederick II read his father's poetry, he could not help being aware of the *Minnesänger* during his rise to power in Germany. Walther von der Vogelweide was not just the author of *Under der linden*, 'Under the Lime Trees'; he was also a political commentator of influence, and indeed the struggle between Otto IV and his Hohenstaufen foes was followed with rapt attention by the court poets. Nor was this a uniquely German phenomenon. The Provençal poets had cultivated satire and political diatribe as well as love poetry. Peire Vidal, an outstanding Provençal troubadour around 1200, travelled to Sicily and composed poems in praise of his Genoese patron Henry, count of Malta, future admiral of Frederick II's fleet.

But in twelfth-century Sicily too there were poets. Roger II's court attracted Arabic and Greek writers; mixed with the florid and perhaps insincere praise of the Norman king we find love poetry in the North African or Byzantine tradition. The royal court seems to have been the main focus of versifying, but there were satellite courts too, such as that of George of Antioch. French visitors must have brought their own fashion to Palermo. None the less, it is impossible to demonstrate continuity. The Arabic and Greek poets were not the main influence on the 'Sicilian school'; the impulses were all Provençal, German and Latin – because the elegant models provided by Ovid and late Latin lyrics counted for much in a court dominated by the rhetorician Piero della Vigna.

A great amount of nonsense has been written in attempts to date the poems of Frederick's court, or to link individual poems, such as those with crusading motifs, to exact events, such as Frederick's crusade itself. But such motifs were part of a common fund, and were not cited solely when personal experience made them appropriate. The poems are not precise historical documents; they are intended to be elegant, moving exercises in an unused vernacular. To assess them on aesthetic grounds is not easy, given the different tastes that Dante and his successors have generated in the European reader. But something honest needs to be said about their quality – not just by quantifying the clichés and mistakes in metre with which the verses abound, but by looking at them as intended objects of beauty. And the place to start is surely the group of poems attributed to Frederick II himself. This attribution has caused endless headaches, but it is safe to say that two poems really seem to be by his hand, and maybe three more:

Alas, I did not think that separation from my lady would seem so hard. Ever since I went away it has seemed that I must die, remembering her sweet companionship. I have never endured such anguish as I did when I was on board the ship. And now I believe that I shall surely die if I do not return to her soon . . . Happy song, go to the flower of Syria, to her who holds my heart in prison. Ask that most loving lady, in her courtesy, to remember her servant, who shall suffer from love of her until he has done all that she wills him to do. And beseech her, in her goodness, to deign to remain loyal to me.

Nothing in this poem attributed to Frederick to cause surprises, except the use of Italian as vehicle for the ideas. Though sometimes linked to Frederick's crusade, the poem is merely a restatement of the classic separation motif. It is not a bad poem; but it is not at all original. What is pleasant in Frederick's poetry is the delicate handling of a beautiful language:

Secondo mia credenza
non è donna che sia
alta, si bella, pare.
nè c'agia insegnamento
'nver voi, donna sovrana.
La vostra ciera umana
mi dà conforto e facemi alegrare;
s'eo pregiare – vi posso, donna mia,
più conto mi ne tegno tuttavia.

'Peerless lady, there is, I believe, no woman alive who can match your worth and beauty; and none can compare with you for courtesy. Your kind and lovely face comforts me and gives me cheer; and I appreciate your qualities more every day, lady – at least as far as my capacities allow.' ★

Poems thought to be the work of his sons Manfred and Enzo rise to greater heights, and here at least real events played a part: Enzo's long imprisonment in Bologna left him only the freedom to compose elegies on love, and on his own unenviable position:

Va, canzonnetta mia,
e salute Messere,
dilli lo mal ch'i' aggio:

★ I would like to thank Virginia Cox for her help with this translation and the translation of 'Va, canzonetta mia'.

quelli che m'à'n bailìa
si distretto mi tene.
ch'eo viver no porraggio;
salutami Toscana,
quella ched è sovrana,
in cui regna tutta cortesia;
e vanne in Puglia piana,
la magna Capitana,
là dove lo mio core nott'e dia.

'Go, my song, and salute my lord for me. Tell him how I am suffering: for the power that holds me keeps me in such close confinement that it will surely be the end of me. Greet the land of Tuscany for me, the queen of the lands of Italy, where courtesy reigns supreme; and go thence to the plains of Apulia, and to the broad Capitanata, where my heart still is.'

There is no reason to doubt that Manfred and Enzo, illegitimate but favoured sons of Frederick, acquired their taste for poetry at their father's court. They travelled often with their father and he felt more for them than for his heirs Henry and Conrad.

Less plaudits for Piero della Vigna as a poet; his verses seem stiff and formal by comparison with those of Enzo. It is Giacomo da Lentini and Rinaldo d'Aquino who seem to rise to the greatest heights, not because they say anything that the troubadours might have missed, but because they show a sensitive and rhythmic handling of Italian:

Però prego l'Amore
che mi'ntende e mi svoglia
come la foglia vento,
che no mi faccia fore
quel che presio mi toglia
e stia di me contento . . .

sings Rinaldo: 'therefore I pray to love who fills me with desire and sweeps me away like a leaf on the wind, to hold back and not to take from me what, gone, will take away my good name.' Or there is Giacomo da Lentini's dialogue between lover and lady, where the lover says (in the surviving, Tuscanized, text):

Ed io basciando stava
in gran dilettamento
con quella che m'amava,

bionda, viso d'argento.
Presente mi contava,
e non mi si celava,
tutto suo convenente;
e disse: Io t'ameraggio
e non ti falleraggio
a tutto'l mio vivente.

'And I, sharing kisses, took great pleasure in her who loved me, she of the blond hair and silver face. Openly she spoke to me, concealing nothing, and saying: "I will love you and never betray you my whole life long."' Not surprisingly, there is a husband elsewhere; the troubadour motif of illicit love, physically expressed, reappears in standard form.

Indeed, it follows from this description of the Sicilian school of poets that very much Provençal lyric poetry must have been read and discussed at Frederick's court, even if very little was composed there in Provençal. But certain types of poem, not least the satirical *sirventes*, hot blasts of air against ill-advised rulers or badly-conducted princes, are entirely absent from the Sicilian repertoire. Frederick's court was not a place at which to indulge in free criticism of the emperor and his advisers. The poetry of the court was therefore confined to a single, even if dominant, strand in the European tradition of the lyric: the love poem, generally expressed in gentle, unexaggerated tones. The poetry of Frederick's court – whatever its influence on subsequent generations of poets in Tuscany – must thus be seen as profoundly conservative. Only the language has changed; in other respects, we find a close and competent imitation of Provençal and German models of the end of the twelfth century, limited almost entirely to themes of love. A great literature may indeed have its roots in exact imitation: that is how Latin literature was born in the Roman republic, based on translations and imitations of Greek models. But outstanding claims for the quality of Frederick's poets should not be made; nor, as has been seen, was the presence of the ruler among the poets in any way unusual. His absence, indeed, would be the real source of surprise. Frederick's claims to originality lie elsewhere: his scientific studies, concentrated on birds and on the mechanics of flight, remain his principal claim to fame as a man of culture.

IV
=

Frederick II has been hailed as a great builder, who adopted the classical styles long abandoned in Europe; the *augustalis* coins were thus a miniaturized statement of what was proclaimed yet more forcefully in his great Capuan gateway, in his hunting lodges and in his castles. It seems, however, that his contemporaries were less impressed than modern historians have been. Charles of Anjou, on winning Frederick's former kingdom, grumbled at the insignificant size of nearly all Frederick's buildings, and proceeded to build at Naples a French-style donjon that in scale and defensive security outclassed the works of the Normans and the Hohenstaufen. A second factor to be emphasized is that Frederick was engaged more often in the restoration or extension of existing castles erected by the Normans, or even by the Byzantines and Arabs, and that the castles at Bari or Gioia del Colle (for example) must be seen as the product of slow evolution, in which Frederick himself played a secondary role. A third point is that Frederick spent little money on buildings in the period when his finances are most open to examination, 1239–40. During those years he is found instructing his provincial deputies only to make essential repairs to castles which were suffering from (say) the intrusion of rainwater. He was firmly opposed to wasteful expenditure that went beyond minimal maintenance of the fabric. Finally, there is some doubt whether the architectural styles favoured by the emperor are really to be seen as a self-consciously revived classicism, and not, as Ferdinando Bologna and others have maintained, an intermediate stage in the development of the Italian Gothic style.

Against these arguments, there are the buildings themselves. The evidence that Frederick was a builder emperor turns on four principal sites, three in the *regno* and one in Tuscany. The great gateway and castle at Capua, torn down by the Spaniards in 1557, is known from drawings, descriptions and from the survival of much of its remarkable sculptural decoration. Frederick's hunting-lodge at Castel del Monte still stands on a high point overlooking the otherwise endless Apulian plains, and contains what appear to be classical motifs in its architecture and sculpture. In Sicily, Frederick's major monument is the Castello del Maniace at Syracuse, a truly massive construction in a port that others, not least the Genoese, eyed covetously. Finally, there is the Castello dell'Imperatore at Prato to the north of Florence, a single example of Frederick's 'classicizing architecture' north of the kingdom's borders. These are buildings which are presumed to speak for the imperial ideology of thirteenth-century Sicily; the arrangement of the statues on the Capuan gate has been the subject of lengthy discussion, on the easily demonstrable ground that the statues appear to make a statement about the nature of government.

This is the place to begin. The identification of the main statues is not entirely certain, even assuming that they were intended to be portraits of living individuals. That they were placed over the entrance gateway so that visitors from the north, crossing the river to enter Capua, passed right beneath them is clear. There was a large head of *Justitia* and a smaller figure of the seated emperor (most probably) that now survives headless. Two large busts are traditionally identified as Taddeo da Suessa and Piero della Vigna; in any event they represent judges or ministers whose authority has been delegated to them by the emperor. The most likely arrangement of the sculptures, to judge from surviving drawings, was as follows. The two judges were placed in niches to either side of the entrance arch, in space left vacant by the curvature of the arch. The figure of *Justitia* could be seen in a larger niche directly above the arch. Above *Justitia* was a false arcade containing in the middle the emperor on his throne and on either side of him two youthful female statues; higher still was a yet more intricate arcade containing further sculptures of uncertain subjects in a similar style. The ensemble was contained between the heavy towers of the fortress proper, built in an unusual style of chamfered stonework, elaborately worked and almost certainly expensive to produce. Much of the stone may have been retrieved from local Roman buildings; some shows signs of having been reworked (*see plan, p. 282*).

The Capua gate was begun in 1234, when Frederick was still able to enjoy some financial ease; that it was a costly enterprise is clear from the care with which the materials were worked: it was

Reconstruction of the first-floor room of the left-hand Capuan tower, excavated in 1930

Architectural plan of the Capuan archway and towers

Engraving of the statue of Frederick II
from the Capuan archway

Ground-plan of the excavated Capua Gate

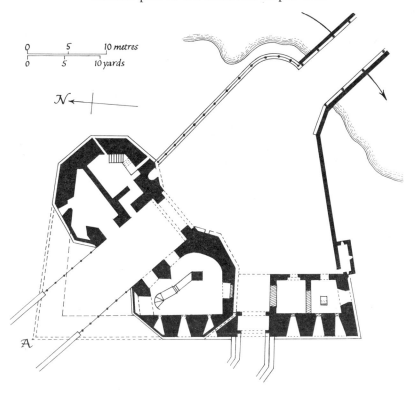

intended to act as a reminder of the nature of royal authority and of the power of the monarchy to those who entered the first large town of the *regno* on the way south. In a sense, it was a visual commentary on the *Constitutions of Melfi*, depicting *justitia* as the guiding principle of government and stressing that the emperor was the living expression of *justitia*, the spokesman for that power of justice that is intermediate between God and the world (to cite thirteenth-century Castilian laws). In other words, '*Justitia* was an Idea or a goddess,' as Kantorowicz maintained; the Capua Gate was a statement about the special function of the monarch as the human law-giver who bestows on mankind the type of law that the spirit of *justitia* determines as truly just. Just as the Martorana mosaic had provided a clear statement about the derivation of royal power from God, in the Byzantine mode, so the Capua Gate offered an interpretation of kingship that accorded with the views of Roman lawyers, and that had strong parallels to opinions circulating in the papal curia about the function of the pope as mediator between God and man, guided in his political and moral judgements by attention to *justitia*. Frederick's presentation was not therefore entirely novel: the ideas were familiar, though their visual expression was a novelty; and their application to a secular ruler, though rare in western Europe, was a feature of Norman Sicilian kingship in the twelfth century. Roger II too had been the *lex animata*, the law incarnate, working through the agency of *justitia*.

It is hardly surprising to find that the artistic language used to express these views was that of the classical world. For the Capua sculptures are carved in a neo-classical style. It is no longer believed that any of the major pieces is in fact a genuinely ancient statue put to new use, but it is clear that the sculptors kept a close eye on Roman models. They betray their thirteenth-century hand in the manner of working the stone, which is more comparable to the earliest Greek sculpture than to classical models the artists might have known; yet the treatment of the hair of Taddeo and of Piero seems to reveal an interest in classical bronzes, while the handling of their beards is not in accord with surviving Roman models from the amphitheatre at Capua. This really suggests that the Capua heads are an attempt to return to classical styles, but not necessarily with the help of classical methods, some of which were not clearly understood. The result was a series of majestic sculptures which impressed contemporaries with their Romanness, but which can be seen by a modern eye to be a little less than Roman. Clumsy workmanship, as for example the carving of the cheeks of Taddeo da Suessa, suggests that thirteenth-century sculptors were still – not surprisingly – inexperienced in the imitation of classical models. But it must also be remembered that the microscopic treatment of modern art historians fails to convey an idea of the appearance of these works to visitors to Capua. Not concerned with fine details, the visitor could see an unambiguous advertisement for the Roman imperial monarchy whose restoration had been the aim of the Hohenstaufen dynasty since the middle of the twelfth century: its *Romanitas*, and the principles on which it operated, were there for all to see.

Nor can the influence of local styles from the south of Italy be discounted. The neo-classical lions that grace the entrance to the cathedrals at Trani and elsewhere, the flowering of Apulian Romanesque since the time of the Norman conquest, had meant that an affection for classical motifs never disappeared. The way the Capuan sculptures were set in what was to all intents a heavy late Romanesque gateway with a slight tendency to Gothic-style detail should also be remembered: the gateway was not an imitation of Paestum or Segesta, but a true medieval bastion in which apparently classical figures were liberally inserted. The interior of the bastion contained large rooms with decorated columns along the walls and crisscross rib-vaulting, anticipatory in many ways of the interior of Castel del Monte, and signifying the slow adaption of what would be regarded later as typically Gothic features. But the inspiration lay elsewhere than Frederick himself. It is likely that the Cistercian monasteries of central and southern Italy, at Fossanova, Casamari and Santa Maria di Ferraria, provided the imperial court, and Frederick in particular, with new ideas about architecture, in particular the ribbed vault: 1222 saw Frederick staying at Casamari, and 1229 brought him to Santa Maria di Ferraria. Perhaps Frederick was inspired too by the construction methods visible in the magnificent castles of the Latin kingdom of Jerusalem; the stonework of the Capua gate may owe something to the crusader East. By the 1220s he may

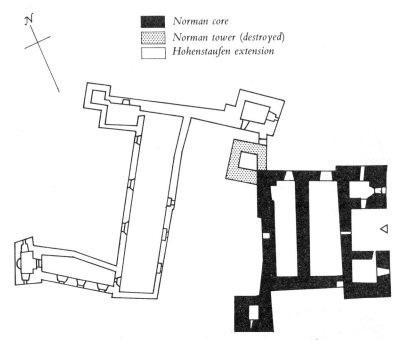

Norman core
Norman tower (destroyed)
Hohenstaufen extension

Ground-plan of Frederick's castle at Melfi

Section through the castle at Lucera, based on the drawings of Jean L. Desprez

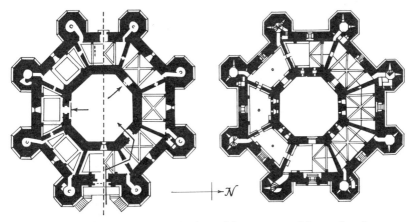

Castel del Monte: ground-plan of the upper and lower levels

Ground-plan of the castle at Bari

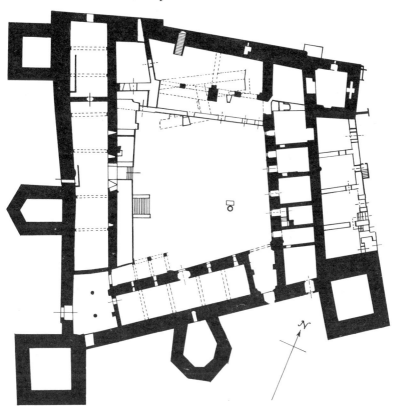

have had a team of architects at work on a number of projects, and by 1240 the fashion for Gothic styles had triumphed, both at Castel Maniace in Syracuse and at Castel del Monte.

Castel del Monte is best described as a hunting-box. It was small, reasonably but not especially strongly defended, and unusually regular in construction: there are two floors, each containing eight rooms, organized to form an exact octagon. The interior of the building is remarkable for its ribbed vaults, but it is a singularly unexciting place inside; once you have seen one room you have seen them all. Relief is provided by some remaining pieces of sculpture, lions in the neo-classical style of southern Italy, and by a simple pedimented doorway. If Frederick's architecture has one truly distinctive theme it is in the use here and at Prato (for example) of rectangular entrances surmounted by pediments and surrounded by Corinthian pilasters: here, perhaps, a self-conscious classicism re-emerges, but it is not of a part with the rest of the building, whose unadorned style is more reminiscent of Cistercian proto-Gothic than it is of the classical past. Shearer was certainly right to insist that 'in Castel del Monte we see the culmination of his art, an almost Burgundian Gothic construction, in which classic and antique elements play only a secondary part.' The same applies to Castel Maniace, built around the same time.

And it must be stressed that there is no evidence Frederick made extensive use of Castel del Monte. It was begun in 1240 and completed only around the time of his death; the hunting-box was not one of Frederick's residences, much as he may have hoped to use it for his sport of falconry. Nor was the hunting lodge at all sizeable. The upstairs rooms measure 11.5 by 7 metres, which has been called 'unusually small and cramped, as compared even with thirteenth-century standards'. A similar picture emerges from his castle at Lagopesole. That the castles were furnished in some luxury emerges from the British excavations at Lucera, where the pottery unearthed included rare pieces of Chinese celadon ware. But Lucera, with its Muslim staff, was no doubt more like an oriental palace than any of Frederick's castles.

As with other aspects of Frederick's career the degree of artistic innovation and the scale of building operations must not be exaggerated. Frederick was not easily dissuaded from placing falconry near the top of his list of priorities, and so the construction of a new hunting-lodge could go ahead in 1240 even when ready funds were very short; the impoverished generally take all the more care over their favourite luxuries. But the same period sees a reluctance to spend large sums on buildings, and his reign as a whole sees little spent on the patronage of new church building or on mosaic cycles comparable to those his Norman grandfather had begun. Some work at Cefalù may date from his reign, that is to say the loggia-like façade and the beautiful mosaics of soaring angels at the entrance to the choir; but the artistic glories of Norman Sicily did not extend into his reign. Even his magnificent sarcophagus had in fact been prepared not for him but for Roger II. Frederick did understand the propagandist use of a building programme, and it would be a mistake to go to the other extreme and deny the significance of the classicism of the Capua sculptures. Even here, however, the classicism belonged to a tradition that existed since the eleventh century, in Rome and in Rogerian Sicily. Frederick was not a great builder; but his buildings, such as they were, expressed his attitude both to the task of government and to the delights of leisure.

CHAPTER NINE

THE END OF CONCORD, 1235

I

Already at the Mainz Diet Frederick made public a programme of action south of the Alps: he urged the German princes to join him in a campaign against the major group of traitors still in rebellion after Henry (VII)'s humiliation: the Lombard opposition. This in itself reflected his optimism that the few remaining foci of revolt in Germany would soon be extinguished: the Babenberg duke, Frederick of Austria, held out until 1241 before coming to terms, but the resistance around Trifels and elsewhere in Swabia was not fierce enough to delay the emperor's return to Italy. The German princes declared themselves pleased to help Frederick in Lombardy; the emperor was optimistic enough to write in August 1235 to his ally the pope, announcing that he had made preliminary arrangements for an expedition to Lombardy. For Gregory IX, Frederick's apparent assumption that the Lombard problem could be settled by war and intimidation gave rise to serious worries. The pope urged both the emperor and the princes to desist. Had he not sent legates to the Lombard towns, who were desperately trying to draw up terms of settlement? In August 1235 Frederick was playing a delicate game: knowing that Gregory was still anxious for a peaceful settlement in Lombardy, himself keen to see a rapid end to Lombard resistance, Frederick encouraged war talk in the hope that the pope and his mediators would be hurried to conclude their business in Lombardy. To Frederick's advantage was his newly reinforced strength in Germany, visible in the staunch loyalty of many of the princes who had resisted Henry (VII).

Aware, too, that Gregory had cooperated in the excommunication of Henry (VII) and some of the Lombard towns, Frederick remained confident that he would win his way. Thus the war plans in Lombardy did not exclude a continued search for a peaceful settlement.

Indeed, the emperor even made known his terms, in 1235. He wanted a settlement by Christmas of that year, probably so that he would have ample time to cancel the arrangements with his princes for the levy of an army. He demanded a 30,000 mark fine of the Lombards, a sum which probably reflects the belief that the regalian rights in Lombardy were a major source of wealth to the north Italian towns; the fine also indicated his continued displeasure at their alliance with Henry (VII), for it had first been mooted (at two-thirds its new value) as punishment for their encouragement to Henry. Frederick also demanded that the pope should excommunicate those Lombards who did not come to terms by the date the emperor had set. Gregory cannot have been pleased to have an emperor tell the pope whom to excommunicate and when. But the papacy took Frederick's demands seriously. The legate in Lombardy was urged to work at full speed; the Lombard cities were reminded of the emperor's threat to unleash war against them, a point which only revealed the pope's incapacity to stand in Frederick's way. But Gregory tried to show willing, in his letters to Frederick, for he saw that successful mediation would reflect on his own reputation and that of the papacy, as highest judge on earth. So he encouraged Frederick to trust in his mediation, telling him that he should order his own delegates to travel down to Rome, for a peace conference to be held in December 1235. Frederick selected the obvious person, his old companion Hermann von Salza, grand master of the Teutonic order, who had, moreover, met Gregory before, and who had maintained close contact with the pope even from Germany over the state of the negotiations.

But it was the Lombards, once again, who made a settlement well-nigh out of the question. The representatives of the Lombard League reaffirmed their resistance to the emperor in November 1235, solemnly confirming the pact of mutual assistance that bound them together. A new member, Ferrara, posed a particular threat to Frederick's interests. It lay blocking access from north-eastern Italy, where Verona (under the redoubtable despot Ezzelino da Romano) and still friendly Venice supported the emperor, to central and southern Italy, thereby cutting Frederick off from his other kingdom. Gregory IX, for his part, must have reflected with irony on Frederick's ultimatum to the Lombards. He and his legate were expected to achieve solid results in a few months, while not many years before Frederick had constantly demanded more time to plan his crusade. An army against Lombardy was being raised with enthusiasm; an army for the recovery of Jerusalem had always been low on the emperor's agenda. It was to Jerusalem, again, that Gregory therefore urged Frederick to go with his troops, and there is evidence that Frederick was willing to fall in with the proposal, but only after the Lombard cities had been quelled.

In fact, Frederick's attempts to raise a German army met with only limited success. The delays in Germany – lengthened further by skirmishes between Frederick's allies the Bavarian duke, the Bohemian king and other princes and the troublesome Frederick of Austria – meant that the Christmas deadline was passed without Frederick taking up cudgels against the Lombard League. It was still several months before serious campaigning could begin, and the squadron of knights to be sent down to Italy, to Verona, left only in April 1236. But the delays strengthened rather than weakened Frederick's resolve to turn an army on the Lombards. He had dealt mercilessly with the treason of his own son. Was he, at the prompting of papal mediators, to deal any less severely with rebel towns, whose very method of government contradicted his own perception of what good government was? The treason of Milan obsessed Frederick from 1235 onwards. But it was not just political rebellion; it was rebellion against God. His *Constitutions of Melfi* had already linked heresy and treason. In northern Italy there were heretics aplenty. Having encouraged the suppression of heresy in Sicily and (passively at least, during the Conrad of Marburg affair) in Germany, the emperor announced to the world his mission to eradicate heresy in Lombardy too. Matthew Paris, the English chronicler, reports Frederick's own description of his priorities. No, he had not forgotten the Holy Sepulchre, but in Italy 'the weeds are beginning to suffocate the wheat'. Here were enemies of Christ who needed his chastisement even more urgently than the Muslims in the East. He would conquer northern Italy and turn to good use against the Lombard heretics its money, arms and horses. Such words were a faithful echo of those of the papacy itself when it unleashed a crusade against the protectors of the Cathar heresy in southern France nearly three decades earlier. And his addressee on this occasion was Gregory IX himself. But Gregory's priorities were clearly very different. He once again wanted Frederick to absent himself in the East not, apparently, in the hope of trying to unseat him from the *regno* but in order to restrain him from intervention in Lombardy. The papal and imperial view of what needed to be done had indeed converged, between 1230 and 1235: but Gregory had hoped, by bringing a compromise peace to Lombardy, to limit the emperor's influence there and in the rest of northern Italy; while Frederick, never really prepared to compromise with those he saw as traitors, had seen an alliance with the papacy as a way to cow Lombardy into submission. Gregory had, in other words, aspired to the sort of settlement achieved by Alexander III when Frederick I came to him, on his knees, at Venice in 1177, a settlement that enhanced the standing of the papacy and guaranteed, under much-ignored restrictions, the liberties of the Lombards. It was a goal worth striving to achieve, and Gregory had thrown himself enthusiastically into the task, excommunicating his former friends and shunning a potential ally, Henry (VII). Once Frederick began to insist that the papal policy of mediation had no chance of success, Gregory was bound to lose interest in a common course of action. In effect, Gregory had failed; he was determined, as before, that Frederick and not he should pay the price of failure. First the emperor's war plans, and then the announcement of a Diet, to be held in the emperor's presence at Piacenza in July 1236, set the seal on the divergence of views. Yet Frederick made plain his own wish to comply with Gregory's plans, up to a point: crusading was on the agenda for Piacenza, but so was the re-establishment of peace in Italy – both the taming of the Lombard League and the announcement of new provisions for the government of northern Italy under imperial aegis. On this occasion at least, exasperated by a decade of Milanese opposition, Frederick did not mind letting it be known that he wanted to impose tighter controls over the liberties of the wilful communes.

Obsessed by their assumption that conflict between pope and emperor underlay every communication between them, from the eleventh century to the death of Frederick II, historians have failed to see the significance of this emperor's period of peaceful relations with his former enemy, Gregory IX. The suspicion generated by the attempt, at the start of Gregory's pontificate, to destroy Frederick and to seize the *regno* was never entirely dissipated: the propaganda war, soon to erupt between pope and emperor, dwelt at length on the differing views of Frederick's conduct while on crusade. But there was also a striking willingness to work together after the peace of San Germano, different in tone to Honorius III's more indulgent relationship with the emperor. Honorius, and Frederick throughout the period before 1236, seemed to be aiming at interdependent concord between the two highest authorities on earth: collaboration in the cause of peace. Gregory IX acted with greater political deliberation. Like Frederick, he was profoundly concerned to uphold the rights and dignity of his office. He was impressed, too, by Frederick's conciliatory approach from San Germano to the moment when he announced his Italian expedition. But he had less faith in the permanence of good relations than had Frederick, who too easily assumed he could make Gregory accept the necessity for his Lombard wars. One explanation lies in the lack of unity of thought in the papal curia, as compared to Frederick's entourage. There were powerful voices favouring not Frederick but the Lombards among the cardinals. Later events show that Sinibaldo de'Fieschi, from Genoa, nurtured an implacable hostility to the emperor. Another cardinal ill-disposed to Frederick, and particularly to Frederick's solution of the Lombard crisis, was the cardinal bishop of Palestrina: of him more in a moment. In imperial circles, clearly, there were some sceptics on the Italian question. Gregory's appeal to the German princes does not seem to have brought explicit support for the papal outlook, but the princes were little enthused, either, at Frederick's requests for troops to take down to Italy. Hermann von Salza stood by the emperor, and was handsomely rewarded with privileges for his military order, and with Frederick's trust; yet he also managed to retain some respect at the papal curia – an Armand Hammer of the thirteenth century. Meanwhile Piero della Vigna, the jurist and classical revivalist, became the eloquent, even extreme, spokesman for Frederick's policies, expressing a conception of the emperor's office deliberately calculated to challenge and offend the papal theorists. Frederick was, as a matter of fact, actually aware of the divisions of opinion at the papal curia, and some of della Vigna's most rousing letters, written under the emperor's name, consisted of attempts to win over influential cardinals by stating that it was well known their collegiate power equalled that of the pope himself: to no effect, however.

James of Palestrina was pushed, willingly, to centre stage in summer 1236, when Gregory relieved the patriarch of Antioch of his post as legate in Lombardy, appointing the bishop of Palestrina in his place. James's first task was to block the Diet of Piacenza, his own native city. At his prompting, the Placentines abandoned the imperial side, and it became obvious that the Diet would have to be moved elsewhere. Of course, there were still plenty of pro-Hohenstaufen towns in Lombardy – the commune of Cremona, the despotism of the da Romanos at Verona, for instance – and the present Lombard League was far less inclusive than the pan-Lombard alliance that had successfully stood firm against Barbarossa. The signals from the papal curia were, however, clear: Gregory was looking for friends among his own recent foes; they, after the crushing defeat of Henry (VII), were also looking for a patron who might carry real weight. Frederick saw the appointment of the bishop of Palestrina as the end of any serious attempt at mediation. Expressed differently, he saw James of Palestrina as an agent sent north to work with the Lombards against his own plans. And, given the emperor's absolute commitment to war against the Milanese, this meant James could not possibly work out an acceptable formula for peace between the emperor and the Lombards. Frederick wrote to the English and French kings complaining at this turn in events: he saw himself under an obligation to resist Lombard pretensions, which were an offence not merely to the empire but to the Church. This is surely an allusion to the existence of heresy in many of the Lombard towns; it also refers to his idea that, as God's representative on earth, he must treat rebels against his authority as rebels against God himself. The holy task of destroying disbelief in Lombardy could and should be followed by a crusade to the East; he explained his Lombard campaign as a prelude to a crusade, not a distraction from it. Interestingly, there are parallels between this approach and that adopted at the papal curia in the thirteenth century (mainly after Gregory IX's death) to the wars against the Hohenstaufen: the struggle within Italy was the first stage in a campaign that would culminate in a crusade to Jerusalem.

Gregory did not need to turn back very far in the papal archives to find material for his propaganda war against Frederick. His reply to the emperor's complaints about James of Palestrina says nothing very new. It invokes the Donation of Constantine to argue that the papacy retains ultimate suzerainty, even in things temporal; it insists on the primacy of the spiritual realm (and thus its master on earth) over the temporal; it reminds Frederick that the papacy had chosen to crown Charlemagne emperor, implying that what could be chosen could also be unchosen. But the reply also uncovers a number of specific grudges concerning the emperor's treatment of the Church (an answer to his claim to be a hammer of heretics) and his intervention in the papal state. This was not the sort of letter Gregory would expect Frederick to digest with humility. It was a throwing-down of the gauntlet: come with your armies to Italy and you can expect nothing less than my outright, vocal support for the Lombards. Concord had failed.

II

It may still be wondered whether, in late spring of 1236, Frederick II anticipated a lengthy and bitter war with the Lombards. In the past his great victories had been political and diplomatic (as on crusade); he was not a brilliant commander in the field. He left southern Germany in July 1236 accompanied by only about a thousand knights, plus a few thousand foot-soldiers. His appeals for aid were met with a growing reluctance among the princes to commit German resources to a struggle that could and should be paid for by using armies from the pro-imperial towns of northern Italy and, if necessary, further levies from southern Italy. The princes' analysis made sense up to a point: the Lombard allies of Frederick were sufficiently scared of the Milan-led league to commit their own resources, in great number, to the war; they did not, to their credit, see the emperor as a *deus ex machina*, whose duty was to take on his own shoulders the entire burden of the struggle. Moreover, Frederick had already sent half the present number of knights ahead to Verona, to meet his formidable ally Ezzelino da Romano and to await his own arrival.

Ezzelino ranks with Frederick II as one of the most heavily maligned figures of the thirteenth century. Papal abuse against him knew no limits. At least in part the reputation was deserved: by 1250 he was consorting with heretics, unleashing great brutality against his opponents, and making public his scorn for the Church, not least by outrages committed in church. When in 1254 Pope Innocent IV launched a crusade from Venice to destroy Ezzelino, the war gained widespread support within the towns and among the petty nobility. In 1254 he stood out as the living symbol of rotten government: a tyrant who had supported the Hohenstaufen and had suppressed civic liberties. His opponents claimed to stand for the defence of the city-state against an insidious trend towards despotism in northern Italy. These accusations carried some weight by 1250, but in 1235 Ezzelino did not seem to be a liability to the emperor. He was a powerful feudal lord in north-eastern Italy, controlling the key city of Verona, which gave access via the Adige valley and the south Tyrol to southern Germany. Verona was an ideal military base from which to penetrate the lands of the Lombard League: Brescia and Milan lay on the plains to the west. Moreover, Ezzelino was a capable general, as his subsequent victories made plain; this aspect of his reputation must have made him acceptable also to the Lombard cities that supported the emperor. But Ezzelino's prime drawback was his rivalry with a second north-east Italian *signore*, Azzo d'Este, who competed for control of the towns in the hinterland behind Venice – Vicenza, Treviso, Ferrara. It was Ezzelino's success in building ties to the emperor that decided Azzo to seek fortune in the Lombard camp: even so, Azzo had long maintained links with Frederick and was not irrevocably committed to the opposition. Both Ezzelino and Azzo had their own power in mind, so that, if opportunity arose, they would reconsider their alliances. Azzo has certainly won a better press, as the friend of the Lombard communes in their struggle against tyranny. It is therefore right to point out that his aims were not very different from those of his rival: the establishment of lordship over large areas of north-eastern Italy; it was precisely because each wanted the same, more or less exclusive, lordship that their interests clashed so violently.

But in 1236 Azzo seemed poised to strike at the heartlands of Ezzelino's domain. Faction-fighting in Vicenza had culminated in the appointment of Azzo d'Este as controller (*podestà*) of the city. From Vicenza Azzo's armies pointed towards Verona itself; Frederick's arrival in Italy in August 1236 was therefore well-timed from Ezzelino's point of view. Even so, Frederick did not stay long at Verona, heading westwards away from Ezzelino's front line towards the loyal city of Cremona. Azzo, the Lombard opposition and the Vicentines pitched camp by the Adige river, awaiting a confrontation with Ezzelino's men but thankful that the imperial army had vanished from the scene. Alas, it was all a ruse. A fortnight later the imperial forces, suitably refreshed and reinforced, turned east again, aiming for Azzo's camp. The Italians did not wait to see what would happen. They ran away. The road to Vicenza was now open. The city was besieged and refused to surrender. But its defences were too weak: the imperial army clambered over the walls and sacked the town, most of which was burned to the ground amid great pillaging. There are signs that Ezzelino, not yet perhaps the bloodthirsty tyrant he became, tried to hold back the German plunderers. Vicenza's value to him, militarily and financially, would be all the greater if the city remained reasonably intact; and, though a resisting city could rarely expect much mercy once stormed, it seems that there were factions in Vicenza favourable to da Romano interests who should not be alienated. Perhaps for this reason Frederick regarded the burning of the town as punishment enough; for the rest, he was content to place the city under his own governor. The main object was to create a cloud of fear in north-eastern Italy in which the cities, aware that they could save themselves by abandoning the league, would avoid Vicenza's fate and ally with the emperor. Excessive brutality, on the other hand, might only harden the resolve of the resisters.

An anecdote about Frederick and Ezzelino, if true, suggests that the emperor had a clearer idea how to manage the cities than did Ezzelino. Walking together in the fields outside Vicenza, the two started talking about how Ezzelino could restore his authority over the town. The emperor said, 'I will show you how,' and unsheathing a sword he lopped down the longest blades of grass (or the heads of poppies standing above the grass). The removal of powerful rivals in the cities was the way for a *signore* to establish his control for good. It was a recipe that Ezzelino and other despots came to follow widely.

Frederick was impressed at the rapid success of his close alliance with Ezzelino; he was convinced, too, that the victories at Vicenza would push the Lombards to submission. He was still, in November 1236, relying to some extent on a political solution to the Lombard rebellion. Milan and some other cities would be hard nuts to crack by these or any other means. But less enthusiastic opponents of the emperor now began to reconsider their position. A particularly valuable new ally was Ferrara whose lord was a redoubtable old *signore*, Salinguerra, anxious to sustain the city's trading position in the face of Venetian hostility. His links to Frederick II brought some prosperity to Ferrara (and, in consequence, much popularity to Salinguerra), but Venice was peeved to find Ferrara reasserting its control over the river system of eastern Lombardy, and winning privileges for trade in Frederick's kingdoms. Thus, in the complex rivalries of Italian city politics, the winning of one ally to the emperor might often result in the loss of a friend. Venice during the 1230s made a complete volte-face: the imperial privilege of 1232 was discarded in favour of alliance with Milan and Venice's recent bitter enemy, Genoa.

But Frederick was confident enough at these rapid successes to leave Italy entirely by the end of November. The Italian campaigning season was effectively at an end; moreover, he did not intend to go so far from Italy that he would be out of touch with new developments. Winter and spring saw the emperor processing through Austria, reimposing imperial overlordship over large areas and isolating Duke Frederick at Wiener Neustadt.

Handsome privileges were bestowed in early 1237 on the Viennese, confirming and extending the laws of earlier dukes of Austria. In Austria, too, Frederick was able to re-establish contact with the prince electors to the throne of Germany. He was keen for Conrad, his second son, to be raised to the crown in succession to the deposed Henry. The princes went so far as to recognize Conrad both as king of the Romans and as future emperor in succession to Frederick, on Frederick's death; thus Frederick was very anxious to tie down the arrangements for the succession at a time when a potential rival, the prisoner Henry, was still alive, and when the papacy, newly hostile, might once again try to interfere in the affairs of Germany. The election was announced by Frederick as an expression of the special role of the princes in providing for the safety and prosperity of the empire, a role inherited by them from the Conscript Fathers of ancient Rome. The idea that the princes could create an emperor, and even choose the next emperor in his father's lifetime, struck forcefully at the papal theory of empire, according to which the pope made a German king emperor by the acts of unction and coronation; moreover, the German princes were being asked to accept that the Hohenstaufen dynasty would become hereditary emperors, though not by simple right of primogeniture – Henry (VII) having earlier been dispossessed. Frederick thereby made it plain that he expected and trusted the princes to stand by him whatever crisis might occur in relations with modern, papal Rome. The election of Conrad concerned not the future alone, but also immediate events: a grand occasion when the emperor could surround himself by and declare his confidence in the great princes. Frederick of Austria's continued resistance seemed of little moment compared to this success.

Frederick's absence from Italy was also calculated to defuse his difficult relations with Gregory IX. The salvos of the propaganda war had not been followed by decisive action on Gregory's part. Indeed, James of Palestrina was quietly dropped as legate in Lombardy; he was rushing things too fast. Thomas of Santa Sabina and Rinaldo of Ostia, cardinals of less extreme outlook, were sent to northern Italy in his place. Their brief was to persuade the Lombard rebels to discuss peace; symbolic of Gregory's insistence that he still had a part to play in north Italian affairs was the summoning of the Lombards to a conference with the legates at Mantua in Spring 1237. Frederick too was keen to reopen discussions: it was a sound objective while he was out of Italy settling his German business, for he could now test whether his brief foray to Vicenza had indeed created the right mood among the rebels. Hermann von Salza, predictably, and Piero della Vigna were appointed to meet the legates and the Lombards; the release of two such important figures from duties at the imperial court reveals that the emperor was not taking this chance to negotiate a settlement lightly. A meeting was held not at Mantua but at Brescia, in late July, but the mood among the imperial delegates was increasingly bullish. They knew that the German princes were fed up with the impudence of the Lombards, and were pressing the emperor to settle the conflict by war: this was the just penalty for their rebellion. Nor, indeed, were the two cardinals prepared to punish the rebels. They argued that it would be enough for the Lombard League to be disbanded under promise not to unite again in opposition to the empire. But instead of fines or the imposition of imperial governors, their only serious obligation was to consist in the provision of crusading armies. These terms reflect well the thinking of Gregory IX: his renewed anxiety for the safety of Jerusalem, now that Frederick's ten-year truce with al-Kamil was near expiry; and the feeling that Frederick's power in Lombardy must not be allowed to grow any further than the events of 1236 had allowed already. The cardinals fed these thoughts with reports of the misery of Lombardy under the influence of the emperor and Ezzelino. Mutilation of prisoners, abysmal treatment even of widows and orphans, the desecration of churches: all the horrors of war, whether accurate or simply derived from Lombard propagandists, were reported back to Rome. These were not, then, the conditions in which permanent peace was easy to achieve through negotiation. This does not mean that the pope and emperor were raring to bite each other's throat. Even the Lombards, long confident of their ability to withstand Frederick, were now aware that they could not hope to retain their league, with its military command structure, in any negotiated settlement.

One reason Gregory was renewing his requests for serious

discussion was the news that the emperor did not intend to dally in Germany. Partly because the German princes were impressed by Frederick's early successes at Vicenza, partly because his favours to them in Germany at last began to elicit real rewards, a larger imperial army was now made ready to cross the Alps. With the help of his Italian allies, such as Cremona and Ferrara, as well as Ezzelino, he now posed a more formidable threat even than before. Some aid was also arriving from southern Italy, not least the much-feared Saracens of Lucera. By mid-September Frederick had reached Mantua and the Lombard rebels were also armed for war. Once again, at the start of November, the pope urged him to put first the highest of priorities, the defence of Jerusalem; by this stage the pope's letter perhaps expressed not so much a plea for alternative action, as a document for the papal files which would demonstrate in due time that the emperor had obstinately stood in the way of peace and the cross in order to pursue his vendetta against the Lombards.

Having tricked the Lombards into misunderstanding his movements in 1236, Frederick repeated his act in 1237. By November 1237 Frederick seemed to be drawing his troops together to spend the winter at Cremona. Autumn weather had arrived and the Lombard plains were becoming damp and boggy. The Lombards decided that there would be no great battles this year after all, and, apparently imitating the emperor, broke camp at Pontevico on the Oglio river. While the Lombards moved northwards along the left, easterly, bank of the Oglio they were shadowed, unwittingly to them, by imperial troops moving parallel to the right bank, through Soncino to Cortenuova. It was here that the Lombards began to cross the river in order to reach their own winter stations at Milan. Frederick's army was some way behind the Lombards, however; and when scouts brought news of the Lombard crossing at Cortenuova, the emperor realized the urgency of action. On 27 November a detachment of the imperial army hurried forward to close in on the enemy; the intention at this stage was not to engage in battle. But in fact the imperial detachment collided with a group of Lombards; battle began; the Lombards were pushed back to the positions of the main rebel army. Even a relatively small number of imperial troops had proved able to defeat a Lombard squadron.

But the two main armies had not yet engaged. Frederick hurried on the heels of his advance guard, delighted to discover that they had already won a clear victory. But the Lombards stood resolute around the *carroccio* of the Milanese, an ox-drawn cart bearing saints' relics and sacred banners, solemnly drawn into battle by the Italian cities, a symbol of the divine protection they craved and a source of morale to the troops. And, inspired by their *carroccio*, the Milanese and their allies stood firm, amid awful slaughter, until nightfall, when further fighting was barely possible. The armies disengaged, but settled down for the night breathing down one another's throat; battle was to be resumed next day. Or so the imperialists believed. In fact the Lombard rebels began to melt away before dawn. They tried to carry off the relics and the cross on top of the *carroccio*, but even that was left behind when their wagons became stuck in the mud. For the rains had come and even flight from the enemy was hard work. The Lombards had suffered humiliating defeat. It has been suggested that about thirty-five thousand men were on the Cortenuova battlefield, about nineteen thousand under imperial banners, the rest fighting for the Lombard League; and Frederick informed the English royal family that ten thousand of the enemy died or were captured. We may consider these figures exaggerated; what is clear is that the Lombard League had committed its best resources to the struggle, that Frederick's own Lombard allies had raised plentiful troops too, and that help from the Germans and the Saracens confirmed the imperial supremacy. Milan reeled under the impact of Cortenuova: its *carroccio* gone, its *podestà* (a Venetian) in captivity and many of its nobles, and those of allied cities, dead or in chains.

Frederick's propagandists went rapidly to work. They made sure that Cortenuova became prominent news in the European courts; for they were aware that even Cortenuova might not be sufficient warning of the emperor's strength to quell Gregory IX's demands. Piero della Vigna rejoiced in the opportunity to describe to the world how the Caesar Frederick had left the enemy dead in piles. A carefully contrived triumphal procession into Cremona was arranged, to consolidate Frederick's victory. The centre point of the procession was the enemy *carroccio*, hauled by an elephant from the emperor's menagerie – the *carroccio* broken and desolate, the elephant topped by a wooden tower bearing Frederick's pennant. Recalling the triumphs of the ancient Roman emperors, there was a great procession of captives, including the *podestà* of Milan, Pietro Tiepolo (the doge's son), who was shackled to the *carroccio*. It is difficult to know what made the most impression: the precise attention to Roman imperial triumphal procedure; the visible signs of Milanese degradation; the sense of relief in Cremona at the defeat of its ancient rival; or indeed the elephant. Chroniclers as far afield as the Rhineland heard of and eagerly reported Frederick's triumphal entry.

One letter Piero della Vigna must have particularly enjoyed writing. Pope Gregory was reminded by della Vigna of the imperial glories brought to new life by his master Frederick. As subtle as any of Piero's literary allusions was the decision to offer to the citizens of Rome the captured Milanese *carroccio*. This was not classical revivalism gone mad, but a chance to place on the Campidoglio a needling reminder to the papal curia, at the Lateran nearby, that the restoration of imperial authority was real. The Ghibelline annalist of Piacenza reports that Gregory 'grieved to death' at this gift to Rome; since the annalist is a spokesman for Gregory's foes, there is no need to believe him, but Gregory was certainly displeased at the emperor's decision to pay court to the commune of Rome. His relations with the city government were, as has already been seen, extremely poor; in the past he had had to rely on Frederick's aid against the Romans. He hardly wished Frederick to give aid to the Romans against him. He was being pushed, deliberately, into a tight corner. The inscription placed with the *carroccio* on the Campidoglio, reminding the reader that the trophy 'makes plain the triumphs of Caesar' (*triumphos Caesaris ut referat*), expressed a joy in which the pope could not participate. All this was accompanied too by rococo nonsense from Piero della Vigna, promising the Romans that in conformity with the practice of antiquity the city's ancient nobility would again be restored: a big promise, considering that the German princes had already been assured that they were the real Conscript Fathers. (Sometimes the political promises emanating from Frederick's court were wrapped thickly in woolly verbiage.)

In Lombardy the predictable occurred now. The Lombard

League began slowly to dissolve. Lodi, long a victim of Milanese aggression, was easily taken (12 December 1237) by the imperial armies. Milan must sit out the winter, until the new campaign season, with the emperor on its doorstep. Its allies were one by one suing for peace or disowning the league. Its hoped-for patron, the pope, was incapable of standing up to Frederick. The answer was simply to follow where the other Lombards led, to negotiate with the hated enemy.

Yet it would be wrong to overstate the strength of Frederick II after Cortenuova. The battle had revealed the superior resilience of the imperial army. It was an army very composite in character, made up of Ghibelline devotees as well as Sicilian and German subjects, but in 1237 Frederick's links to his allies remained firm. Yet Frederick still had to make plain his intentions in Lombardy: whether to impose a central government, whether to confirm communal liberties; and he still had to placate the pope. Once again, the test the emperor faced was not so much military as political.

III

Frederick counted too heavily, in the weeks after Cortenuova, on the terror that his victory would create. He was encouraged to find that Milan rapidly decided it had to open negotiations; predictably, of course, the Milanese offered little. The bargaining began in December 1237 when a mission from Milan proposed terms of settlement quite similar to those already suggested by the papal legates: acceptance of Frederick's sovereignty without loss of the communal and territorial rights of Milan; the provision of as many as ten thousand soldiers for a crusade; possibly, too, a money fine. In advancing these proposals the Milanese were surely aware that they would have Pope Gregory's backing. Unfortunately, they offered too little. Frederick countered by demanding the total surrender of Milan. The city must place itself before his mercy; at his will the fate of Milan would be decided. Whether Frederick expected Milan to accept such terms it is hard to say. He may still have hoped to impose on the city an imperialist *podestà* or an imperial military governor, after exacting a massive fine and seizing the property of the rebel leaders. But the Milanese (and maybe they read his mind accurately) remembered the levelling of their city to the ground by Frederick I seventy years before. They were convinced that Frederick II, too, would wreak vengeance on Milan for its treason towards the empire. They may have hoped that the emperor's ill-feeling would be moderated by his advisers. But there is no reason to suppose the Cremonesi, and the other Ghibelline cities, encouraged Frederick towards compromise. So, seeing Frederick's counter-proposal as the end of negotiations, the Milanese reiterated their defiance of the emperor, and notified him that his reply to their mission was totally unacceptable; they began to gather their strength for renewed war.

Frederick's attitude to communal liberties was in many ways similar to that of his grandfather. He certainly resented the claims of mere merchants to exercise sovereign authority within cities, whether in Germany, Sicily or Lombardy. To say he was unsympathetic to the commune is not to say that he ignored the necessity to work with it. He did not expect to sweep it away in northern Italy; even in Germany he had given his assent to the dismantling of the communes on the princes' estates without actually suppressing the liberties of several imperial towns. He was in a sense anti-commune (we may compare some modern politicians in their attitude to the trade union); but he believed he could come to a compromise solution based on a rigorous interpretation of the Peace of Constance of 1183. Thus the inhabitants of Cremona, Reggio and the other staunchly loyal cities were not forced to submit to tight imperial control. Indeed (as under Frederick I) their loyalty won them confirmation of their liberties. A different arrangement was needed for cities that had been brought more reluctantly into the imperial fold. Padua, a da Romano conquest, and Lodi, taken by Frederick's own forces, fell under the authority of an imperial *podestà*. This did not mean major interference in the internal affairs of the cities, once the Guelf opposition had been dispossessed and purged and once the citizens had been bullied into acceptance of the emperor's suzerainty. Such cities, like the loyal core, would be expected to provide armies in aid of the Lombard campaign. There was no plan to garrison the cities with German armies; but the imperial *podestà* in the conquered cities was, by 1240, often a Sicilian baron. Even this, however, refects gradual developments in Frederick's thinking. As his conflict with the Lombard rebels and with the papacy intensified, he decided to impose tighter control in the areas where future loyalty might be at risk. And even this move must not be seen as an attempt to force Lombardy into the Sicilian mould of centralized, bureaucratic government. A vicar-general for Lombardy, his son Enzo, king of Sardinia, was appointed in 1239, but his main task was to coordinate relations with the allies, with each imperial *podestà* and with the German armies; Enzo was in no sense a Lombard copy of the Sicilian king. His powers of arbitration between cities and as appeal judge for their inhabitants were hardly revolutionary in character. Nor did his authority to appoint judges and notaries, and exercise other traditional regalian rights, necessarily detract from the authority of the loyal cities; they actually needed a higher authority who could perform these essential functions on their behalf. Many of the Lombard cities, anxious that such powers should be exercised, had accepted these claims. When the cities rebelled against the Hohenstaufen, they still needed a higher authority that could provide these services; and so, in the twelfth century, the Lombard League, acting collectively, and (to a lesser degree) Pope Alexander III took on such duties, while in their struggles with Frederick II, the league, Pope Gregory and, latterly, Henry (VII) had aspired to function this way. Townsmen abhorred a vacuum: even if the commune were 'free', it stood under the suzerainty of a higher power, pope, emperor or other prince; the open question was not whether such higher power existed, but what the rights of the higher power were. Moreover, the existence of several claimants to that power, in the form of Gregory IX, Frederick II and, briefly, Henry (VII), enabled the Lombard Guelfs to shift their loyalty around. But the Milanese, even then, did not deny that the emperor should be their overlord; they argued that his tyrannical acts had forced them away from the exercise of all obligations of fidelity; and that in any case they owed fidelity only, and not revenues or citizen-levies. Only Venice laid explicit claim to independence from the authority of empire, papacy or other higher ruler, after centuries spent playing off successfully the demands of German and Byzantine emperors against one another.

The withdrawal of the Milanese from the imperial court did not mean that Frederick expected to have to lay siege to Milan. He continued to act with slow deliberation, building up his military forces again not so much for conflict as to sap still further the morale of the Milanese. By June 1238 Frederick had been joined in Lombardy by Lombard, Sicilian and German troops, the last under the command of the new king of the Romans, Conrad. The Cremonesi were spoiling for a fight, and were generous in providing aid. News of the war, spread by Frederick's letters to the English, French and other courts, brought to Lombardy many knights from lands well beyond Frederick's own jurisdiction: Frankish Greece and the Spanish kingdoms, as well as Hungary, France and England. Some of these knights were sent specifically to aid Frederick, such as a hundred English knights from the court of Henry III, the emperor's brother-in-law. But many were young knights in search of a good war. A decade earlier, such men might have joined his crusade; a decade later they might have volunteered to conquer Andalucia from the Moors. It will be seen shortly how significant for the emperor's relations with the papacy was Frederick's appeal in lands as far afield as England. And yet, throughout this period, the emperor continued to state emphatically that he hoped for a negotiated settlement. Pope Gregory was, indeed, being held in a vice: so tightly that the pope's resentment at Frederick's successes grew red-hot.

What Gregory needed was a turn in the emperor's fortunes in Lombardy. His prayers seemed answered in the summer of 1238, when Frederick became bogged down in the siege of Brescia. An attack on Brescia made considerable sense. Lying to the east of Milan, Brescia, once captured, would act as a bridge between the emperor's power base in eastern Lombardy, around Verona, and his target of Milan. When Brescia fell, surely Milan would once again beg for terms. Brescia itself was judged to have weaker walls than Milan, and, to ensure victory, Frederick moved up to Brescia a terrifying assortment of catapults, battering-rams, siege engines and mining engineers. Alas, the enthusiasm went too far. One of these engineers, a Spaniard named Calamandrino, fell into enemy hands and was persuaded by handsome gifts (a house and a wife to go with it) to fight for Brescia. The trouble with professional soldiers is precisely that they are very liable to change sides. Calamandrino advised the Brescians to remarkable effect, teaching them to build catapults of their own, powerful enough to damage Frederick's siege-towers. The besieging army then had no compunction in tying Lombard prisoners-of-war to the front of the siege engines, in order to prevent the Brescians from harming their kin. Savagery begot savagery. Imperial prisoners in Brescian hands were lowered from the battlements in the direct path of Frederick's battering-rams. So the siege dragged on. By October the Brescians seemed to be scoring all the points: a night raid killed many snoring Germans and reached the edge of Frederick's own quarters. Frederick took advantage of deteriorating weather and the end of the campaign season to pull back to Cremona, but there was no concealing the fact that Brescia had defeated him. An indication of the effect the Brescian victory had on morale is provided by the behaviour of the Brescian Ghibellines who despaired that the emperor would re-establish them in power in their home city, as he had all too easily promised; the emperor offered as compensation lands in Sicily, around Corleone, where they are supposed to have settled in their hundreds with other Ghibelline exiles.

More importantly, Frederick's ability to keep Pope Gregory under restraint was destroyed by the failure at Brescia. As it was, a new papal representative in Lombardy had been appointed, Gregorio di Montelongo, in summer 1238. He was to remain a source of irritation to Frederick for a dozen years. Gregory IX saw, even before Brescia's resistance proved successful, that he must strengthen his own position in Lombardy. If Frederick defeated Brescia, the pope would have to work hard to draw the emperor into the vague but serious plans for a new crusade, taking him away from Lombardy in a campaign publicly seen to be conducted at the pope's behest. If Frederick were defeated by Brescia, the pope would wish to place himself before the Lombards as their long-lost champion, checking Frederick's advances through strategic alliances and forcing the emperor to withdraw from Lombardy – maybe, indeed, on the much-vaunted crusade. In other words, Gregory still saw himself as a peace-broker, but

as a peace-broker ready to go to war. If the emperor absolutely
refused to come to terms with the Lombards in a way entirely
satisfactory to the pope, then Gregory could take Frederick's real
hostility to the papacy to be confirmed; the peace of San Germano
would be at an end.

1238 saw other tensions between pope and emperor. It became
obvious to Frederick that Gregory was watching his every move
in Italy, and challenging him all too vigorously. News that the
Genoese had broken with Frederick in autumn 1238 was little
surprise; since 1220 the Genoese had nursed ill-feeling at the
emperor's abolition of their trade privileges in Sicily and of their
rule over Syracuse. They had continued to trade in Sicily, but
were irked by higher customs dues and limited influence at court.
Nevertheless, to rebuff Frederick (by informing him that they
would not renew their fealty to him, when asked to do so) was a
difficult, dangerous step. It placed Genoa alongside Milan in
rebellion against the empire. The emperor could interrupt their
trade to the Levant, which passed through Sicilian waters; he
could also be expected to give his support to the Pisans in their
endless feud with the Genoese, fought out in almost every corner
of the Mediterranean. Frederick, as titular king of Jerusalem,
could even influence Genoese fortunes in the Near East. The
Genoese reaction therefore reflects the feeling, enunciated by the
city's *podestà*, that the emperor would make intolerable financial
and naval demands on the city, quite conceivably suppressing the
city's ancient liberties. It seems that Genoa's stand was not at first
prompted by the pope; but Gregory heard the news with glee,
sending urgent messages of support and suggesting that the time
had come to unite forces with Genoa's second inveterate enemy,
after Pisa, Venice. This was a master-stroke on Gregory's part.
The only security at sea Genoa could hope to gain, in opposition
to Frederick, would be that guaranteed by its greatest commercial
rival. Before Christmas the two cities had already, with extreme
speed, worked out an agreement assuring protection to each
other's ships. Genoa and Venice together would resist anyone
endangering their free passage around the coasts of Italy: the
Sicilian fleet is clearly intended here. Both Genoa and Venice
promised to support the pope against those who disobeyed his
authority: this without having even entered a formal pact with

the papacy (only achieved in July, for Genoa, and September 1239 for Venice). Genoa and Venice promised also that they would not make an agreement with Frederick before 1247 unless the pope gave his approval.

Genoa had important secondary interests which coincided with the papacy's own secondary interests. One clause of the agreement between Genoa and Venice is revealing here. Traffic between Sardinia and Genoa was to be protected by both parties. Venice had no direct interest in Sardinia, but for Genoa the island was the source of much bitterness. The Genoese had courted Pope Alexander III in the twelfth century in the hope that he would recognize their title to the island, seen as an important potential source of grain, wool, silver, even slaves. In other words, the Genoese recognized Alexander's title as overlord of the island and in return hoped to be confirmed in their possession of parts of the island – the north-west and west; they knew that even a papal grant would not expel overnight their rivals, with strong bases in north-east Sardinia, the Pisans. The Church's claim to overlordship, a long but largely ineffective tradition, clashed with a rival claim from Frederick I, who favoured the Pisan interest in the island. By the 1230s the island was divided among contending Genoese and Pisan-dominated factions; even the local rulers, 'judges', were closely tied by marriage to the two republics. A delicate balancing-act brought Gregory IX temporary acknowledgement of his suzerainty from the northern Sardinian princess Adalasia, mistress of Torres and Gallura; when, soon after, she was widowed, the pope dreamed of replacing her former Pisan husband with a close ally of his own, a certain Guelfo de Porcaria. But Adalasia was on the international marriage-market. Poor Guelfo's virtues were overlooked when an illegitimate son of the Holy Roman Emperor was known to be available and ready. Adalasia married Enzo, who was created king of Torres and Gallura in Sardinia – an office from which his duties on the north Italian mainland, and his subsequent imprisonment at Bologna, deprived him of any joy. And Frederick's creation of a new kingdom within the empire, in lands claimed as of right by the papacy, was a source of deep offence to Gregory IX. Frederick had actually promised to defend papal rights in Sardinia and Corsica before his return from Germany to Sicily in 1219–20. Moreover, Sardinia and Sicily had an important feature in common, in papal eyes. To deny the ancient authority of the papacy in the one was surely implicitly to deny that authority in the other; the Donation of Constantine was taken as proof of papal rights in the Mediterranean islands; Gregory's claims to overlordship over the king of Sicily were being set aside in the same breath that the emperor declared Sardinia a kingdom. Nor was Frederick inclined to give way. Sardinia, he said, had always been part of the Roman empire. Having promised to restore the empire, as the whole world knew, he would not slacken his efforts. Yet of course in enforcing imperial rights to Sardinia he lost more than he gained. The island was remote and of little use in his struggles in Lombardy (later the popes tried to recruit knights there, to little apparent effect, for the struggle against Frederick). His policy in Sardinia helped confirm the Genoese in their suspicion of the emperor, since their ancient settlements at Alghero, Castelsardo (or Castelgenovese) and Casteldoria lay in the ambit of the 'king of Torres and Gallura'. Interference in the affairs of the Sardinian Church was cited against Frederick by the papacy as a sign of his contumacy. It was a strange counter-achievement for Frederick to help push Genoa and Venice into each other's arms over a whole series of issues; their enmity had recently been as bitter as that between Frederick and Milan.

In 1238 pope and emperor were jostling for position. This is far from saying that an intense propaganda war had broken out. Diplomatic contact had to continue: each side, however strident the mood, wanted to be able to show the world that it was the other which had been unreasonable. It is therefore regrettable that historians have intruded later evidence, of 1239 and even 1243, into their discussion of events in 1238. One cannot cite the white-hot propaganda of a papacy determined, once again, to destroy Frederick II when describing the careful, suspicious waiting during the siege of Brescia and its aftermath. Each side was, certainly, storing up abuse: Gregory was undoubtedly taking an interest in reports of Frederick's treatment of the Sicilian Church; of Frederick's supposed immorality and cruelty; of his conduct, ten years earlier, on crusade. Piero della Vigna was sharpening his pen while reading the classical rhetoricians on whom he professed to base his ornate style. Each side knew that conflict in the open would test their skills at winning and holding support to a very high degree.

IV

Winter came, and a long residence by the imperial court at Padua, itself a symbol of the triumphant progress of Frederick, Ezzelino and the Ghibellines through north-eastern Italy. It was a time to try, by diplomacy, to extend the gains of war. And the most obvious target of attention was the rivalry between Ezzelino da Romano and the house of Este. Knowing that Azzo d'Este had already, over two decades, swayed between the emperor and the Guelf opposition, Frederick sought to tie him at last to the imperial camp by marrying Azzo's son Rinaldo to the daughter of Ezzelino's brother Alberigo. Unfortunately for Frederick Alberigo was no less wayward than Azzo d'Este; his own loyalty was primarily to self-interest. But Frederick's suspicion of Alberigo was pressed too far: he sent Rinaldo and his bride to southern Italy as hostages for their parents' good behaviour. They lived in considerable discomfort, accentuated by Alberigo's realization that he and Azzo d'Este had a common interest in opposing the emperor. Should the pope declare war on the emperor, Gregory could count on their friendship.

Frederick could already anticipate the next move of the papacy. Attempts to woo the people of Padua by way of della Vigna's ornate flattery of the city's merits consolidated Frederick's hold over originally reluctant subjects. But the direction of such praise really lay beyond Padua. It seems likely that Frederick knew Gregory wanted once again to excommunicate him; later, the emperor insisted that there were cardinals of non-Lombard origin (and, no doubt, some well-disposed Lombards too) who opposed the pope's will. Such dissension in the papal curia must have come to his ears. But it was not sufficient to deter Gregory from imposing his dreadful sentence on Palm Sunday, 1239. What is striking is not that the sentence was imposed but the explanation given to the world for it. Lombard affairs play little role in the

complaints made against Frederick's conduct in the bull of excommunication. He was stated to have grabbed lands of the
Church in central Italy and to have blocked the free passage of
papal legates; however, the latter complaint seems to have
referred to his detention of legates travelling south from England
rather than to interference with the legates in Lombardy. He had
deliberately not lifted a finger in defence of Jerusalem: this complaint had tangential reference to Lombardy, since it was his
duty, the papacy had for several years been insisting, to give the
fate of the holy city priority over his vendetta with the Milanese.
But some clauses really appear remote from the underlying,
unstated *casus belli* of Lombardy: Frederick's neglect of warnings to
give free passage to a Tunisian prince, held by his officers in Sicily,
was quite unrelated to the Lombard crisis; it was, rather, a move in a
delicate balance-of-power game whose purpose was to keep the
rulers of Tunis cooperative – they paid the kingdom of Sicily a
handsome tribute in pure gold. Gregory maintained, however,
that Abdul-Aziz had fled from Tunis to undergo baptism, thus implying that Frederick was preventing the conversion of Muslims
to Christianity. This was a preliminary salvo in a papal programme of pouring discredit on Frederick's Christian adherence.

No less important a sign of Frederick's scorn for Christianity
was his treatment of the Church in Sicily. The greater part of the
bull of excommunication actually dwells on his crimes in the
regno. Once again, it was a subject on which the emperor had
been amply forewarned. His insistence that clerics were liable to
contribute to the increasingly heavy war taxes in the *regno*, his
use of revenues from the churches in Sicily during (deliberately
prolonged) vacancies in episcopal sees and other offices; the
seizure of Church property – these were the signs that he was an
inveterate enemy of Christianity. His legislation favouring the
judgement of clerical crimes in Church courts was not, of course,
cited in his favour. And, while he was seen as the instigator of
unrest in the city of Rome – no doubt Gregory had in mind here
the gift of the *carroccio* – his help to the papacy against the
Romans, during the years of papal-imperial peace, was naturally
ignored. Pybus and Powell have in fact shown that the Sicilian
Church was not despoiled by Frederick, even though he was not
a particularly generous benefactor; he confirmed the privileges of

exemption of several great abbeys and sought to avoid conflict over ecclesiastical matters, aware from his predecessors' experience, and from brief incidents in his youth, how damaging such conflicts could be to royal power and to papal-Sicilian relations. The mosaic of Thomas Becket in the apse of Monreale cathedral was ample reminder of the troubles in store for kings who clashed with their clergy; Frederick's clergy contained very loyal supporters such as Berardo, archbishop of Palermo and the Franciscan luminary Elias of Cortona. And yet one of the problems created during Frederick's minority had been the wholesale endowment of the leading ecclesiastics in the *regno* with lands and rights; as he did with the Genoese and the Germans, so with his bishops Frederick refused to confirm these generous grants of the popes and their agents in southern Italy. And so it was easy for the papacy to cast him in the role of despoiler of church lands, instead of that of restorer of royal lands, briefly ceded to the Church. On the question of the Sicilian Church, the papacy's grievances were of course very ancient. The control traditionally exercised by the kings of Sicily over their Church, on the basis of Urban II's grant to Roger I in 1098, continued to be seen as a major source of conflict. Empress Constance's renunciation of her predecessors' rights did not restrain Frederick from assuming tight control over the Church in Sicily. Equally, the papacy never lapsed from its insistence that the kingdom of Sicily was a papal fief, entirely detached from the Roman empire, and that the internal affairs of the *regno* were a matter of constant, close concern to the papacy.

But this time Gregory would be following a very different strategy to that during the war of the keys at the start of his pontificate. He knew that, for all his complaints at the emperor's conduct there, the kingdom of Sicily could not easily be subverted. It is true that he made plans with the Venetians and Genoese for an invasion of the *regno* (July and September 1239), but even these agreements envisaged a two-front war, in which the emperor would be contained in Lombardy long enough for the fleets of the republics to ferry vast numbers of troops to south Italy. There was a frantic optimism: the troops would be found for both wars, in Lombardy and Sicily. But from where? Here too Gregory adopted a different solution to that he had

experimented with in 1229. The war of the keys was now presented as a real crusade; but, as will be seen, this was a gradual
process, to some extent determined by Frederick's own response
to the excommunication and other pressure against him. The
legate Gregorio di Montelongo, according to the Ghibelline
annalist of Piacenza, proclaimed a crusade against the emperor at
Milan in 1239, but this was almost certainly a localized attempt
to stimulate the Milanese to new heights of enthusiasm, especially
after the blows to morale at Cortenuova. More immediately
helpful to Gregory's cause was the sending of friars through the
imperial lands, warning Frederick's subjects of the papal ban and
urging them to renounce their loyalty to the emperor (as a matter
of fact, by canon law they would automatically be absolved
from bonds of fidelity to him if he remained excommunicate on
Palm Sunday of 1240). Aware of this campaign, Frederick tightly
closed the kingdom of Sicily to those coming from the papal
curia and banned the circulation of the pope's accusing letters.
The clergy was forbidden to heed the papal interdict on Church
services in the *regno*.

Alongside practical counter-measures, there was a need to
shout back. The papacy, by means of legates at the European
courts and by the deft use of the friars, could spread its message
fast and effectively. Gregory's hope was to raise money and
troops from as far afield as England, Hungary, Scandinavia.
Frederick must counter by emphasizing to fellow-rulers the threat
that papal interference in Sicily and the empire posed, by implication, to every crowned head: to his brother-in-law Henry
III (a papal vassal, as a result of King John's submission to Innocent
III); to his neighbour, a figure of increasing influence in the west,
Louis IX of France. Louis proved very resistant to Gregory's
requests for aid against Frederick, largely on the grounds that the
pope had gone too far in his attempts to bring the emperor
down; had Frederick been condemned by a Church council, he
said, he might see the matter differently. Solidarity among rulers
was clearly a principle that appealed, remarkably consistently, to
Louis of France in his dealings with Frederick II. Henry III of
England was more complaisant to the papacy, fearing, according to the English sources, that the papacy would unleash
threats against himself too. Preaching and collecting of funds in

England was therefore permitted, but it aroused little enthusiasm. It should not be forgotten that some English knights had actually aided the emperor against the Lombards only a couple of years before. There was sympathy for Frederick; and the emperor complained that his brother-in-law was studiously ignoring their kin ties by favouring the papacy.

Louis IX's assessment of the situation mirrored, unconsciously no doubt, Piero della Vigna's first major defence of his master against the bull of excommunication, in the form of a public oration delivered in the Palazzo Comunale of Padua. Frederick, he said, had not acted unjustly but had been unjustly attacked; the emperor would have gladly confessed his errors if in fact he had ever committed them. Punishment cannot be imposed on someone who has not acted wrongly: 'It is right to bear patiently suffering that is deserved; punishment imposed without justice produces sorrow instead.' The words were Ovid's, not Piero's (*Heroides* 5.7–8) but they (rather than any sacred text) were used as the basis of the orator's speech. And that Piero could rival the most eloquent and resounding epistles of the well-practised papal curia was proved in April 1239 when he unleashed, under Frederick's name, an encyclical appeal to the rulers of Europe, rich in colourful condemnation of the impure priest, the unjust judge, the unseeing prophet, Gregory IX. He warned the crowned heads of Europe: 'When a fire rages in your vicinity you must hurry with water to douse your own house also,' in other words, once my power is broken the subjection of all other rulers will be made easy. Under his own name Piero della Vigna went even further. Casting Frederick in the role of Jesus before his accusers, he pictured the 'Pharisees' gathered together in conclave against their Lord the Roman emperor, terrified at his triumphs and fearful that a complete victory over the Lombards will be followed by the uprooting of all their kind. Wait no longer, then: 'they said: let us attack the enemy, let neither our tongues nor our arrows lie concealed; let them rather come forth, to strike; strike so as to wound; let him be wounded so as to fall; fall so that he cannot rise again, seeing thereby the emptiness of his dream.' Piero's startling pursuit of an analogy with Jesus' own career was to be reformulated again and again in the propaganda battle. Such language emphasized the place of the emperor as

God's agent on earth, implicitly attributing to him, and not the false priest Gregory, the status of vicar of Christ. These thoughts were not, in their basic content, so innovatory: since the eleventh century the German kings had stressed their status as God's representative on earth, in the face of strident papal claims to primacy. Such statements, dressed in a thinner costume of classical and biblical allusions, already formed part of the propaganda dossier of Frederick I. More importantly, in the kingdom of Sicily surviving ideas of monarchy, under strong Byzantine influence, stressed the ruler's function as God's mouthpiece on earth. Indeed, as has been seen, the Martorana mosaic went even beyond Byzantine practice in depicting, a hundred years before these events, king and Christ with an identical face.

The forcefulness of della Vigna's propaganda elicited a purple, and purple-faced, response from the papal curia. The thirteenth-century popes used the most extreme language in their struggles against the Hohenstaufen, and here, as elsewhere, the apocalyptic language is difficult to assess. Did Gregory really recognize in Frederick the 'forerunner of Antichrist', a monstrous Leviathan roaring blasphemy from a lion's mouth, formed like a panther but with the feet of a bear? Metaphor was heaped on metaphor: the panther was also a 'wolf in sheep's clothing' (fairly standard language, this), a scorpion. But this is merely the proemium to a sustained and consistent attack on Frederick's person. Not his policies alone, but his evil character from which stem those policies, have become the target of the campaign. And, whereas Frederick can abuse the pope by decrying his faith and justice, Gregory abuses the emperor by trying to portray him as a deserter of Christianity. Not enough that he should have robbed the Church of its rights and possessions: he has condemned Moses, Jesus and Muhammad as 'three impostors', has mocked the idea of the Virgin birth and has led a life of notorious immorality. The immorality charge had been aired in 1238 already; he had been abused as a sodomite on top of everything else, an accusation entirely unproved. The charge that Frederick spoke of the 'founders' of Judaism, Christianity and Islam in such dismissive terms is almost certainly pure fiction: as has been seen, as early as the eleventh century apparent unbelievers had been supposed to state such things. In any case, the papal propagandists also accused

Frederick of being too friendly to one of the religions he was said to condemn, Islam.

Frederick hastened to issue a reply, penned by Piero della Vigna. The notion that he was an unbeliever was laughed off. The emperor countered with the charge that it was the pope who conducted himself contrary to Christian norms. The very act of heaping abuse on the emperor, in these circumstances, was a self-condemnation by a papacy that had no sense of humility. Maybe there are hints here of the view that the see of St Peter should return to a state of pristine poverty, leaving the battlefields of the world to the prince of peace on earth, the Roman emperor (and it is worth noting that the controversial Franciscan general, Elias of Cortona, was an associate of the emperor, and may have pumped some such idea Frederick's way). But in the end Frederick's reply to the pope settles on a more moderate doctrine. The priestly and the imperial power coexist on earth, neither impinging on the other – no more than the sun ever obstructs the moon can the spiritual power take away the light of the temporal. Nor, Frederick explained in a further broadside, did he ever allow past his lips a description of Moses, Jesus and Muhammad as the three great impostors. He stood firmly by the Catholic creed, acknowledged the glorious role of Moses in the giving of the Divine Laws to the Children of Israel, and he knew perfectly well, as did any other knowledgeable Christian, that Muhammad was an enemy of God and that, while his body had been dispersed by devils into the wind, his soul underwent eternal torture in hell. This was all eminently orthodox stuff, in the thirteenth century. But it was Gregory who belonged in the company of Muhammad, he implied. Not Frederick but Gregory is the real Antichrist, but much else too: a false prophet, like Balaam, an enemy of peace, like the red horse in the Book of Revelation. We may wonder whether this rich and fervent prose won Frederick any more friends than did Gregory's fiery letters. Louis IX, Henry III and indeed the rulers of the Italian communes were aware that, beneath the visions of impending doom, lay a real world in which the struggle for primacy between pope and emperor, the survival of urban liberties, the defence of ecclesiastical property, the future security of the Holy Land were the fundamental issues. The thirteenth-century chroniclers were rarely swept along by the rhetoric of the papal–imperial quarrel; the Italian annalists, for instance, occasionally cite letters but they show little interest in the argument that the last days of human history are now dawning. They know that the conflict is most likely to be settled, and then perhaps only briefly, by a resounding victory for one side, on the battlefield or at the walls of one of the great cities: Milan, or Rome itself. In Gregory IX, certainly, we do see a passionate commitment to the destruction of Frederick, that is carried through to his successor Innocent IV. But whereas Innocent is an organizer, cajoler, politician, Gregory is mainly a thunderer. He cannot be much else: his cardinals do not all believe in him; he is isolated from his Lombard allies; the senate and people of Rome dislike him; the kings of Europe have heard him enough already. Against all these odds Pope Gregory set out to prove, by defeating the emperor, the justice of his case.

CHAPTER TEN

REMOTE CONTROL

I

Those who wish to see in Frederick II the exponent of rationalism, an intelligent practitioner of coherent government, look not merely at his attitude to the papacy and his subjects in Lombardy and Germany. His management of Sicilian affairs after 1220 is supposed to reveal to the highest degree the skills of bureaucratic, autocratic central control. It has been seen, however, that the *Liber Augustalis* of 1231 barely lives up to its grandiloquent name; as a manifesto of autocracy it is slight. For much of its emphasis lies on the rights of the monarch over his feudal vassals. Yet something is known about the day-to-day government of the kingdom of Sicily in the late 1230s and 1240s, owing largely to the seven-hundred-year survival of part of a government register of Frederick II; and additional evidence comes from fragments of other, long-lost, registers, copied into the records of later rulers of southern Italy anxious to find precedents for the rights they claimed over their subjects. Much more, in fact, would be known were it not for the sudden end that came to most of these documents in 1943, when descendants of the emperor's German subjects gratuitously destroyed virtually all the medieval documents in what, till then, had been one of the most magnificent archives in Europe, that of Naples. The Archivio di Stato di Napoli had ranked with the Public Record Office in London, the archives of Barcelona, Genoa, Venice or Dubrovnik as one of the great repositories of medieval government documents, mostly in the form of transcriptions entered into large paper registers; well over a million documents survived in this form, from the reign of Charles of Anjou, the great enemy of the Hohenstaufen, and his fourteenth- and fifteenth-century successors as kings of Naples. And among them there was a single 116-page register from 1239–40, the years of Frederick's bitter struggle against Gregory IX's crusade. Clearly this was itself a tiny fragment of a much larger Hohenstaufen archive; further echoes of the lost records of the period before 1266 survived in a late copy of a Norman military register, the 'Catalogue of the Barons' (also destroyed), and there were undoubtedly many detailed fiscal reports, filed by provincial officials, that went up in smoke centuries ago.

The circumstances of the destruction of this archive were these. Not long after Italy declared war on the Allied Powers the most precious documents of the Naples archives were moved to safety to a country-house inland; it was feared that, in time of war, Naples itself would suffer bombardment. The decision made sense. But by 1943 the Naples area was the front line of the advancing allied forces. The Germans had taken control of much of Italy; the partisans were busy performing their duty. When some German officers were killed by the partisans in the Naples countryside it appeared that once again the local population would suffer the barbaric reprisals in which the Nazis delighted. A junior officer took his revenge in a different way, and it has to be said that, insofar as it did not lead to loss of life, it was indubitably a preferable way. But it was still an act of barbarism, consigning to oblivion the detailed and irreplaceable records of the past. It was decided to destroy the stored archives. When the custodian objected on the grounds (among others) that here lay the priceless register of *your* emperor, the great Frederick II, he was given a few minutes to remove a precious item or two, but with everything packed in cases there was no chance of recovering what was there. And so the archives went up in smoke.

Yet Frederick's register still remained accessible, after a fashion. As early as 1786 a Neapolitan archivist, Carcani, copied it carefully and published the text as an appendix to an important edition of the *Constitutions of Melfi*. His transcriptions were not perfect, and there were sections, at the start and the finish, that he found impossible to read, because the manuscript had already deteriorated. Nor, indeed, was Carcani's edition widely diffused throughout Europe. The British Museum, the Bodleian, the John Rylands Library never acquired it, though one reached Cambridge in Lord Acton's superb library. Within a hundred years the French scholar Huillard-Bréholles had decided to edit every single charter from Frederick's court, and naturally he included the documents from the register in his *Historia Diplomatica*, a massive work which remains the cornerstone of the subject. But Huillard-Bréholles did not print the texts as they appeared in the register, where the government scribes had incorporated standard abbreviations ('he wrote to the same person', 'Similarly to so-and-so', 'Similarly throughout', etc.) and had omitted the grandiloquent invocation at the start of each document. He also re-ordered the texts, which were not in exact chronological order – the register had been wrongly re-bound, though the mistake was clear to a reader of Carcani's text. So Huillard-Bréholles bravely produced a reconstruction of what had originally lain before the government officials when they transcribed the letters and decrees that were to be included in the register. What was lost was not merely an exact picture of the register, but a sense of the register in its entirety: as a record of certain types of government business consistently pursued over several months in 1239 and 1240. Though itself undoubtedly a small fragment of a much vaster archive, lost well before 1943, the register of Frederick II provided a remarkably clear statement of the emperor's priorities, not merely in the government of Sicily, so long as it was read as a whole.

Aware of the faults of Huillard-Bréholles' method, German historians, long before the Second World War, decided it was their bounden duty to the emperor's reputation to re-edit the register, correcting Carcani's mistakes, identifying the myriad individuals mentioned in the text, cross-referring to other records of Frederick II where similar issues were treated. Some of the documents in the unique register had in fact been copied in the late thirteenth or fourteenth centuries into the registers of the Angevin kings of Naples, and this meant close checking of alternative texts preserved in Naples, Marseilles and elsewhere. At this sort of work there are no better specialists than the scholars of the *Monumenta Germaniae Historica* in Munich. To Eduard Sthamer was entrusted the high task of re-editing the register.

Since Sthamer could not complete his work in Naples only, a microfilm was made of the manuscript. Then came the war, and the destruction of the register, with Sthamer's edition incomplete; and then too came Sthamer's death, no one the wiser about the whereabouts of the microfilm. It was only a few years after the war was over that a trunk containing the effects of another German historian, Wolfgang Hagemann, was recovered from Italy and examined by German colleagues. To their delight, it contained, unlabelled, the now very precious microfilm. To Wolfgang Hagemann was now entrusted the same high task of completing the edition; he had already set to work on a rough reconstruction of the manuscript after the war, and had proposed to base himself on the notes left by Sthamer and by other scholars. Now he could hope to cast a full edition in the same mould as Sthamer's work. Hagemann's expertise in this field could not be doubted. But the bottle won the battle. His career ended in dipsomania. The edition remained incomplete. To describe this as a scandal is to be gentle. Were it not for the continued devotion to the project of several German historians, it would seem unlikely that the nation whose soldiers destroyed this record might ever atone for the act by producing the much-awaited edition. Meanwhile in Naples one can consult the ghostly photographs of the register, copies made from the nearly lost microfilm; even these photographs are treated, as they have to be, as the most precious possession of an archive bereft of its real treasures. And the photographs do suggest that Carcani's original edition was quite competent, though not perfect – usable, without a doubt.

The register of Frederick II is very different in character to the contemporary papal registers still preserved in the Vatican. The papal registers contain copies of privileges to petitioners (such as monasteries worried about their rights), of letters to foreign rulers, of instructions to legates, such as those organizing resistance to Frederick in Lombardy and Germany. By no means all the output of the papal chancery was recorded in the registers, and petitioners might have to pay handsomely for the extra guarantee of their rights accorded by registration. Occasionally, a coherent item of business, such as the affair of Frederick II or the organization of a crusade, would be separated from the main text and recorded separately in an appendix. Although there was some attempt to group material by subject in the main text, the order of documents was, in general, roughly chronological. The papal registers record what might be called the public face of the papacy: its summons to arms against enemies and infidels, its attempts to control wayward prelates, its desire to offer effective arbitration in disputes lay and ecclesiastical throughout Europe. Frederick II's register is nothing like this. It is not in fact an *imperial* register: it concerns the kingdom of Sicily; even where Frederick's other kingdoms are mentioned, such as Jerusalem, it is in the context of ties with Sicily and southern Italy. Second, Frederick's register contains many letters intended solely for his officials: instructions to repair this or that castle, to provide for his hunting needs, to sell or purchase grain or salt. There are circular letters to the royal justiciars, where an administrative decision concerns all or much of the *regno*; there are many instructions to provincial officials on behalf of individuals, such as creditors to the crown, or Lombard captives seized at Cortenuova and Parma. The main character of the register is that of a private government record, mixing domestic and wider affairs, containing even a few 'state secrets'; these are the decisions of the inner group of Frederick's intimates, addressing the bureaucrats and royal servants upon whom the emperor depended for the smooth operation of an autocratic government, explaining his concerns, great and trivial. The language is not the resounding, classicizing Latin of the papal chancery, nor of Piero della Vigna at his most eloquent; it is straightforward, reasonably clear, notarial Latin that would have shocked Cicero, and yet often it is Piero della Vigna himself who is the author.

Another significant characteristic of this letter-book is that many of the documents it contains were written outside the *regno*. The documents date from between October 1239, when Frederick stood near Milan, to May 1240, by which time he had travelled south through Lodi, Sarzana, Pisa and the central Italian cities on Gregory's doorstep, to reach Foggia, Lucera and Orta. Only in March did he enter the Sicilian kingdom again; only about one fifth of the register contains documents drawn up in the *regno*. Thus what we have is government by remote control. But control is the word. Frederick seems as busy with his instructions when in Milan as he is in Foggia, and the range of concerns, from bank loans to naval supplies to hunting leopards, is much the same. Evidently, the delays in contact between northern Italy and Sicily meant that instructions on urgent matters could take weeks to arrive. But the fact is that Frederick's officials in Sicily continued to bombard him with demands for a final decision on long lists of problems. It seems, then, that Frederick expected to govern the *regno* as closely beyond its borders as when he was resident on its territory; in that respect the fact that so many of the documents were issued outside the *regno* does not change the register's character greatly. More complicated is the question whether the months from which the register survived were typical of Frederick's government of Sicily in the 1230s and 1240s. Analogous letters, the copies made by later kings of Naples from other registers of Frederick II, suggest that there may have been a gradual tightening of control, especially over financial assets, in the late 1230s and 1240s, but in essence the concerns of Frederick's government in 1239–40 were not greatly different from those in other years of conflict with the papacy: an ever present need for funds, and a barely satisfied desire to turn his back on the problems of politics and to ride out instead with his falcons.

Finally, there is the question of authorship. Was Frederick II directly in charge, or was it in fact Piero della Vigna, Taddeo da Suessa and his other 'familiars' who made the decisions that mattered? Historians have been very ready to assume that Frederick was the master-mind of Hohenstaufen politics, with the undoubted advice and assistance of his lawyer-bureaucrats. The voice that comes through the pages of the register is, at times, that of Frederick. The passion for hunting, amid the troubles of war, seems occasionally to dominate what might now be thought weightier business. Here and there occur flashes of imperial anger – against the illiterate merchant Matteo Curiale, who has wrongly attained high office in Salerno; or of solicitude, for a sickening valet in charge of his falcons. Rarely, but powerfully, Frederick expresses his pained fury at the conduct of the papacy, writing, for instance, to the archbishop of Messina, a possible mediator. It really seems likely that Frederick was worried about problems of agricultural production, about the state of the flocks in Apulia, even about his reputation as a debtor who repaid loans promptly and reliably. No doubt the routine varied: when the emperor was heavily involved in Lombard or German affairs, he had to trust the good sense of his civil servants; but when enforced leisure, at the siege of Parma for example, left him free to think about Sicilian affairs he was happy to provide very detailed answers to questions about the minutiae of government. The wording of these answers he of course entrusted to his deputies – 'by imperial mandate made through Master Piero della Vigna Angelus de Capua wrote to Riccardo de Pulcaro' (the example can be multiplied).

It is clear that there were other registers kept for other purposes: there are references to the 'great registers' (*quaterniones grande*) which suggest that something similar to the papal registers also existed, books in which the major public acts of the reign were recorded. There were short financial reports, too: accounts sent by portulans charged with the levy of taxes on merchants; accounts detailing the cost of repairs to a castle; registers listing the taxes and rights of the crown in different parts of the kingdom, such as one for eastern Sicily mentioned in the register. All this suggests elaborate record-keeping on a scale rare in Europe at this period. The administration of England, Provence and (though very slowly) Aragon began to acquire similar concern with accurate record-keeping and transmission of information. The problem in Sicily and southern Italy was, however, the absence of the ruler from the traditional bureaucractic centre, Palermo: Frederick sought to govern his kingdom without daily access to large archives, and this meant that his decisions tended often to be *ad hoc* ones, determined partly by reports of established precedent from his officials, but partly by immediate pressures, political or financial, and expressed through the medium of commands to his civil servants.

II

To gain an idea of the concerns of government in 1239–40 it will be necessary first to look at some of the letters in Frederick's register that give a clear idea of his outlook. Then it is worth isolating several consistent interests of Frederick, themes repeated again and again throughout the register, and in his other documents. Finally, it makes sense to look at a few days only, to see how business great and small was handled by the itinerant court. For it is precisely the vast range of royal concerns revealed by the register that is so significant.

In February 1240 Frederick was at Foligno, in central Italy, working his way slowly southwards. The register records his reply to enquiries from the archbishop of Messina, who had been trying to act as go-between in the struggle with Gregory IX. Frederick reveals his disbelief that this pope is genuinely interested in making peace once again. Against Gregory's continuing fulminations the emperor hastens to remind the archbishop that, at the very moment he had been active in Christ's service, and risking his life, the pope had invaded the *regno* and tried to keep it in his 'greedy hands'; thereupon Frederick had not pressed his advantage, but had tried to bring Church and empire into accord, only to find the same pope fomenting discord in Milan and elsewhere. The tone of the letter is pained, loading on the papacy all blame for the breaches that had occurred; yet there is also a menacing tone at the end, when Frederick promises to recover control of the duchy of Spoleto and of the marches, areas which he now claims the papacy had seized from the empire. Since Frederick's armies had long been active in the duchy, and since indeed he was now passing through the Spoleto region, these were not vain threats but a statement of reality – some at least of these lands were already under imperial control. There is little remarkable in the instructions to the archbishop, for Frederick's attitude to the papacy on this occasion fits well with his public statements in, for example, his letters to the English and French kings. What reveals more closely the impact of his struggle with Gregory on the government of Sicily are his letters concerning denunciations of barons in the *regno*, or of ecclesiastics, for adhering to the papal cause. Jacopo Sacerdote from the Abruzzi was denounced for stating that Frederick's deeds and commands were of no worth since he was an excommunicate. 'It is not right for our Excellency to tolerate such bold presumptuousness'; therefore an investigation will have to be made by the justiciar of the Abruzzi, and, if the accused is found guilty, he is to be expelled from the *regno* and all his goods are to be appropriated by the royal fisc. Adenolfo, a canon of the church of San Panfilo at Sulmona, also in the north-east of the *regno*, was accused of inciting the whole city of Sulmona to swear oaths of fealty to the pope during the war with Gregory IX; he too was to suffer expulsion and expropriation, if guilty. Frederick welcomed denunciations of traitors by local subjects, and the motive of those who denounced is not always far to seek: no doubt they were loyal to the emperor, but some, like Sinibaldo de Fossasecca or Tommaso de Venafro hoped to win favour or the return of lost lands. The struggle between pope and emperor had been expressed locally in vengeful seizures of the property of rivals, but by early 1240 it was clear that the papalists would lose not merely what they had just won, but all that they possessed. The major beneficiary was Frederick's treasury. But there were political uses for these disseized lands, too, since they could be used at little pain to Frederick's purse to reward willing helpers in the anti-papal war.

It was the cost of the war that worried Frederick as much as the outcome. Again and again the register states that the emperor needs to maximize his income: 'especially since money is now necessary to us for the current struggle in Lombardy', Frederick says. There were two obvious ways to raise funds, apart from the dispossession of traitors. One was to request loans from the pro-imperial bankers of Rome, Cremona, Parma, Poggibonsi, even Venice and Vienna. What is clear is that Frederick was very conscious of the need to repay loans fast, to avoid excessive interest payments. He was not prepared to mortgage his resources or to break faith with the bankers, as later European rulers were so often to do. Frederick's borrowings came at a time when it was still unusual for rulers to make extensive use of loans; short-term borrowing, to cover immediate needs, was widespread (witness King John and the Jews), but under Frederick II the problem was still one of the shortage of ready cash rather than of an outright shortage of funds. One royal page could not be provided with funds to pay for the two squires and three horses he needed, 'since in our Chamber there is not at present enough money to pay his expenses', yet the sum involved was a mere four ounces of gold. This was to be paid instead by Crescio of

Amalfi, the master chamberlain of the Abruzzi. It is certainly hard to believe no-one could find this relatively modest sum at court, but the imperial army had now reached Tuscania (Toscanella) in the Roman countryside, on its way south, and Frederick seems to have waited until he entered the *regno* before replenishing his coffers. Once in southern Italy, he also ordered several bankers who had been returned their capital but no interest to be paid what was still owing: a scrupulousness which none the less also suggests that money was hard to come by at his court and in the provincial treasuries.

In fact, the loans Frederick received from the north Italian bankers were all, so far as can be seen, to be repaid in the *regno* by the provincial treasuries, either in money or, occasionally, in kind. The method he adopted was to raise loans in Lombardy and Tuscany against future repayment in southern Italy, which the merchants still saw as a wealthy kingdom with revenues that would amply repay their loans. In November 1239, while Frederick was still at Lodi, loans totalling about 2,270 ounces of gold were granted by twenty partnerships of Roman bankers: 'about' 2,270, because the loans were apparently made in Venetian silver against a promise of repayment in ounces of gold, and the value of the repayment must include a service charge and probably a small interest payment. Without such funds, Frederick could not pay his troops, including many mercenaries; and he gave orders that his son Enzo, king of Sardinia, should also receive funds to enable him to pay his soldiers. Certainly it is impressive how many bankers from Rome remained unpersuaded that Gregory IX could crush Frederick II. These bankers were themselves of good, even *papabile*, family: the Pierleoni, the Sinibaldi, the Cenci; and the citizens of Rome had already shown the pope that he could not rely on their support against Frederick II. The presence of bankers from imperial Cremona is no surprise, either. More unusual is the presence of the Viennese merchant Heinrich Baum, who provided Frederick with 1,000 silver marks in money of Cremona and Cologne, as well as accommodation for the ambassadors of the Russian ruler during their visit to Vienna. At Arezzo in January 1240 Frederick acknowledged a debt of 1,400 ounces of gold, a sum he was hard-pressed to repay, especially since half of the

loan had reached him only a month before at Parma. He thus
proposed a novel method of repayment. Baum was to be permitted to export 4,462½ *salme* of wheat (over 1.1 million pounds
weight), enough to fill two large ships, from Apulia, to be carried
anywhere but hostile Venice. The wheat was to be supplied by
the government, from new stocks, and no export dues were to
be levied. The notional price of the wheat was to be one third of
an ounce per *salma*, so that the Viennese exporter would be receiving wheat worth 1,487½ ounces (he would also be saving at
least 300 ounces in taxes), and his debt of 1,400 ounces would be
repaid with interest. In fact, ten *tari* per *salma* was quite a high
price to pay for wheat, so Frederick was not doing badly out of
the deal either. Baum may not have been entirely happy to lend
money and receive in return goods at an artificially fixed price,
goods too for which the market was unpredictable. Even less
well fared some merchants of Poggibonsi who were granted the
right to export 1,000 *salme* of wheat from Palermo or Trapani,
for thirteen *tari* per *salma*. Frederick granted the privilege in
November 1239 at Cremona, but the export was to take place in
February 1240. In other words, he was taking their money in
northern Italy, to use for his war needs; and he was repaying
them in kind, in Sicily, out of the royal grain stocks. But unlike
poor Baum, they do not seem to have had the arrangement
forced on themselves.

Frederick saw in the grain supplies of Sicily and Apulia an
essential source of war funds and of war provisions. For the grain
was required for the royal fleet in Sicilian waters or (in the form
of biscuit) for the Sicilian garrisons in the Holy Land. But best of
all, he could mobilize any remaining surplus to make money,
and transmit the profits to his camp in northern Italy to relieve
the endlessly pressing penury. In December 1239, while at Pisa,
he sent instructions to Sicily for the better management of the
Sicilian grain supplies: royal grain should be sent to North Africa
and Spain, because it fetches a better price there; the beach at
Eraclea should be fitted out to permit easy embarkation of boats.
But in February 1240, Piero della Vigna was able to write on
Frederick's behalf to Nicola Spinola, the Genoese admiral of the
Sicilian fleet, commending him for a plan to sell 50,000 *salme* of
grain for 40,000 ounces of gold in Tunisia, which was desperately

short of food but, as terminal of the gold caravans from West Africa, was relatively rich in gold; that is, a price was being charged of no less than 37.5 *tari* per *salma*, nearly four times what Baum had to pay. This was an enormous coup for the Sicilian crown, and it was necessary to close the ports so that no merchants could take out grain before Frederick's grain ships sailed; Nicola Spinola perceived that there was still a danger private merchants would undercut the Sicilian crown in Tunisia. The Genoese had already been seen by his agents buying grain in Sicily and then carrying it not homewards but to the king of Tunis. Frederick, still irked by Genoese ill-will, felt no reason to permit his sometime enemies to make a profit that could, with firm management, come his way. And his loyal Genoese admiral saw no reason to favour his compatriots, either. It may be true that Spinola's initiative was not typical of royal involvement in the grain trade, and that the emperor rarely imposed such strict embargoes; what is clear is that grain was seen as a financial asset, and that war exacerbated Frederick's need to use grain to mint money. The continuing emission of *augustales* was made possible by the continuing arrival of African gold, under the new conditions of famine.

The register contains clear instructions to Frederick's officials about taxes on grain: the value of one-fifth of the cargo in Apulia or Sicily, where grain was abundant, but one-seventh in the less endowed regions of Calabria or Abruzzo. These instructions were given in response to enquiries from portulans who were unsure about the exact rules. Should native merchants pay as much as foreigners? Could native merchants export to Venice, even if others (not least Venetians) were prevented from doing so? The portulans of Garigliano were instructed that a tax of one-seventh should also be levied on horses and mules: as well as grain, livestock and meat and salt were closely supervised. Behind these clarifications of government policy lay the urgent motive of maximizing income from the kingdom. The export trade had long been a major potential source of revenue to the crown, and the early years of Frederick's rule in Sicily had seen the expropriation of royal rights of taxation by the Genoese and other freebooters. At a time of military emergency Frederick was determined to extract every last ounce of gold from his portulans.

Careful orders were given for the transmission of revenues to a central location, often the treasury in Messina, sometimes the itinerant court instead. Rumours that provincial officials in, for instance, the Abruzzi were not making proper returns of revenue from trade were a source of worry. And sometimes, indeed, the orders seem almost superfluous: in May 1240 Frederick reminded his deputies in Sicily that a one fifth-tax should be levied on foodstuffs passing through Augusta and Milazzo, but the duty of the royal officials to provide him with these revenues was patently obvious from earlier orders. Any sign that the system was breaking down was carefully noticed at court, and warnings or reminders were rapidly issued.

In October 1239 Frederick issued his *'Ordinance concerning the new ports in the kingdom from which foodstuffs are to be exported'*; this was duly copied into the register. Eleven ports were added to the existing list of official ports (such as Palermo or Bari) from which grain could be exported by sea, and in which the portulans were to supervise the movement of goods. The idea was to reduce restrictions on the movement of commodities which could produce handsome income for the crown. It has to be said that few of the new ports had a distinguished future. Trapani was to emerge, though really after 1300, as one of the major grain ports of Sicily, ideally placed for access to Africa, Sardinia, Spain and the coasts of France and northern Italy. Augusta too — whose very name heralded an imperial revival — had a bright future. Pescara was well-placed for Adriatic commerce. But others, such as San Cataldo in Apulia, were only subsidiary stations outclassed by the traditional centres. In these ports, as in the traditional centres, the portulans were expected to keep busy counting the cargoes, checking prices and recording the information (and revenues received) in their own registers, all of which are now lost. They were charged with some discretion too: the carriage of goods to Venice was not absolutely prohibited to Frederick's subjects, so long as it did not become common knowledge — though how such information was to be kept from the Venetians it is hard to say. Only natives of the *regno* were to ply this trade to Venice, however. It seems the lure of lucre took precedence over Frederick's ill-feeling towards his erstwhile friends in northern Italy.

Salt was another commodity in which Frederick took a strong interest. Here we see attempts at price fixing. The monarchy had gained extensive control over salt production since 1231, and had built up stocks of salt for sale within the kingdom. But sometimes the price was set too high, and Frederick was prepared to shift his stocks at lower prices when his officials warned him that the goods were not moving. 'Do your best for us,' was his answer: yes, the price could be lowered, if that meant the royal treasury would actually receive the money it so badly needed. Frederick was more circumspect in dealing with livestock, however. Slaughtered animals could of course be exported for profit (especially since a fair quantity of royal salt would be needed to prepare the food for its journey); live animals were another matter. There are constant instructions to prevent horses being exported from the *regno*, to encourage the breeding of war-horses for eventual enrolment in the imperial army: horses were exceptionally precious items, but so were mules. To compensate for a shortage of pack-animals Frederick requested that horses and donkeys be encouraged to mate and to bear young mules; he also imposed levies on different districts in southern Italy, requiring them to send small numbers of mules across the frontier to his army. Here too there is an attempt to avoid unnecessary waste of money, for the alternative was to compete on the open market for animals that the enemy too sought to obtain. Oats were to be sown in the Capitanata, providing fodder for essential animals. Thus the whole cycle of the breeding and raising of horses and mules was supervised from afar by the emperor. Other animals too came within his purview: flocks of sheep, in the possession of a Saracen rustler, were to be expropriated by the crown; there was to be a large-scale slaughter of pigs in the area round Messina, partly because of a shortage of acorns and partly because a group of eminent crusaders, lodged in the region, needed to be looked after until the time came for them to sail to the Holy Land. Leftover meat was to be processed into bacon, of which eastern Sicily had for some time been an important producer. Nor were draught animals forgotten. The Saracen community of Lucera was to receive one thousand cattle, both tamed and untamed, and a list was to be made of the Muslims who received a gift. The idea was to bind the Saracen colony to the soil, 'as was the

case in the time of King William' – to transform a settlement of
restive, transplanted rebels into industrious peasants who could
perform the same agricultural tasks as they had done when
resident in Sicily. It was not, therefore, simply a question of
improving revenues from the region of Lucera; there were
important political motives at work, too. Great care was in fact
to be taken that Saracens on the mainland could not cross back to
Sicily, where there was still trouble among the few Muslims who
remained, though the justiciar of western Sicily managed to reach
an accord with them by the end of 1239.

Although the Saracens had largely been forced out of Sicily,
there still arrived immigrants from North Africa: not Muslims
but Jews. Frederick was anxious not to lose the agricultural expertise of the Islamic world, and he had little to fear from Jews,
who had no political organization of their own and no loyalty to
a rival ruler. The register indicates these concerns clearly. Jews
from North Africa, possibly from the island of Jerba (which was
held, on and off, by the Sicilian crown), were to plant and tend
date plantations, as well as to introduce the cultivation of indigo
and 'other various seeds which grow in North Africa and yet are
not now seen to grow in Sicily'. Contrary to common assumption, Frederick's Sicily was not, or not yet, an island of oriental
gardens and palm groves. Half of the Jews' produce was to be
paid to the crown, and, like other Jews, they were treated as
'serfs of the chamber'; they were liable, as were the Lucera Saracens, to the poll-tax of Muslim origin, and to taxes on wine and
on 'knives', which must mean the kosher slaughter of animals by
the use of a sharp knife. Yet there were doubts: the North African
Jews seemed to have trouble with their Sicilian brethren,
probably over questions of ritual, and the court reluctantly
conceded them the right to have a separate synagogue. But rather
than a new building, the synagogue was if possible to be an
existing, disused synagogue somewhere in Palermo which they
could rebuild and refit. This was a decision closely in accord with
recent ecclesiastical decrees and with Roman law: new synagogues could not be built, but old ones could be maintained in
good shape. Frederick's statement distantly echoes the decisions
of his remote predecessor Justinian. The *secretus* of Palermo,
Uberto Fallamonaca, was worried that Sicily might attract too

many of these immigrants, and their future was made none too secure: their palm grove was to be leased to them for no more than five or ten years. The royal court evidently wished to keep a close eye on the situation. There was none of that spirit of tolerance for which the court is constantly praised. The issue was one of what benefited the ruler's interests the most: the court was to be kept informed of the revenues received from the new Jewish settlements. Moreover, other settlers, not apparently Jewish, were required: Riccardo Filangieri, the imperial representative in the Holy Land, was to be asked to send two men experienced in sugar plantation to Sicily, to revive another industry that had probably suffered severe decline after the expulsion of the Muslims. The vineyards of Messina, too, were not producing as much as the court required, and here investigations were ordered; this area, long Christian, and specializing in a commodity little favoured by Muslims, was not free of economic troubles either. But it must be stressed that Frederick's concern was fiscal more than economic. Some concern was shown that the burden of taxation should not fall on the poorest; but the aim was to find the most ingenious means of increasing revenue and of cutting costs.

Thus it was with some reserve that Frederick's justiciars and castellans asked for funds to help repair their castles; they too knew that the budget was extremely tight. Frederick could see clearly the necessity of strong defences on the northern frontier of the *regno*, and did not begrudge this expenditure, so long as it was kept under control. While the emperor was at Foggia, in April 1240, he received the castellans of Bari and Trani, who reported that the Apulian castles were suffering from severe neglect; there were rooms and buildings quite open to the sky, at risk from heavy rains – but all this damage could be avoided 'without great outlay of money'. So indeed repairs should go ahead, but without extravagance. No doubt the massive Norman castles of the late eleventh and twelfth centuries were beginning to show their age, while smaller inland structures were often in a state of some decay. Frederick extended and improved many Apulian castles, such as Goia del Colle or Bari itself, but necessity, at least by 1240, was the reason at least as much as design. And although money could only be spared for important works on the castles, Frederick did not lose his enthusiasm for other costly constructions: the completion of the famous gateway to the city of Capua; the repair and completion of his 'places of solace', hunting-lodges and palaces in Apulia and Sicily.

For his priorities were not absolutely entirely the conservation of funds for the war effort. He intended also to live like an emperor. It is impossible to say how much of his income was given over to the luxuries of court life; it is clear, however, from his register that he continued to give much thought to his relaxation even while confined to the battlefield (and during long sieges there was often time for agreeable hunting). So the letter-book contains instructions to his officials in the *regno* that they should buy black slaves and train them in the trumpet and trombone; they were to be aged between sixteen and twenty, and they were to be sent to the emperor in Lombardy as soon as possible. There were instructions about the arrival of camels brought by Enrico Abbate, Sicilian consul in Tunis, from North Africa to southern Italy. It is possible some of these camels were destined for Lucera, where Frederick was anxious to establish Muslim camel-drovers and also Muslim musicians (including dancing-girls). Away from the battlefields of Lombardy, Frederick could indulge his tastes to the full; in March 1240, at Foggia in northern Apulia, he requested for use at court Greek and other sweet wine and fish of the best quality, prepared in an aspic jelly. It has to be said that such culinary requests are not found elsewhere in Frederick's register. But the register shows that he did enquire of his 'philosopher' Master Theodore about the supply of special syrups and of a violet-coloured confection, intended either for medicine or for a sweet tooth.

More than any other pleasure, that of hunting or of the hope of a speedy return to the hunting-field, kept Frederick happy. His preferred style was to hunt with falcons, of course, and the register indicates how widely he sought his birds of prey: in the islands between Sicily and Africa, such as Pantelleria and Lampedusa, and especially on Malta; but also from the far north, as his contacts with merchants trading through Lübeck reveal. While Frederick was at Arezzo he learned with regret that Carnilevario da Pavia, one of his falconers in Apulia, had found it impossible to secure reimbursement of his expenses from an unreliable provincial administrator; and his concern for his falconers was also revealed when he learned that one of them was sick. Even from afar he tried to keep an eye on the well-being of his falcons, though he also took great delight in hunting with cheetahs – he even asked that six hunting leopards be sent to him at Pisa in December 1239, and as he approached the Sicilian frontier a few months later he was especially insistent that he wanted leopards and their handlers to come to him. It seems that the animals were based in Apulia, and probably at Lucera; the handlers themselves were doubtless Muslims, just as the source of supply for the beasts was the Islamic world.

The business of a few days in February 1240, as the emperor moved south via Foligno to Viterbo, gives a clear idea of the relative significance of some of the themes touched upon here, in the day-to-day management of Sicilian affairs. On 8 February there were letters written concerning denunciations of adherents of Gregory IX and concerning the mating of horses and donkeys, the latter intended partly at least 'for the convenience of our subjects'; inefficient management of the royal warehouses at Messina, where munitions were probably stored, also required an urgent letter to the *secretus* of eastern Sicily. The question of supplies for the garrison in the Holy Land was to be dealt with by the dispatch of a ship loaded with grain from royal stocks to Tyre, the headquarters of Riccardo Filangieri, 'legate of the holy empire across the seas, *bailli* of the kingdom of Jerusalem, marshal'. Bartolomeo de Bessis was entrusted with the defence of Taranto in the heel of Italy; his predecessor (whose name Frederick's court did not have on record) was to be sent packing, not so much for his faults as because of Bartolomeo's virtues. Money worries were not absent from the day's work: the portulans of Porto Garigliano were sent their instructions about taxes on exported livestock. They had asked Frederick's court what rate should be levied on horses and mules, and the reply came that they had no business permitting such animals to be exported; in the case of other animals, they were to follow existing instructions (a levy of one seventh). Horses and mules were in fact requisitioned the same day by the imperial court, from the Justiciar of Terra di Lavoro and of Molise. Finally, 740 ounces of gold were assigned to Simone de Ursone of Capua, who was to settle debts owed to Roman bankers; as usual Frederick's method was to require his officials south of the border to provide funds to settle a debt incurred north of the border.

This readiness to use the resources of the *regno* to pay for wars outside its frontiers undoubtedly gave rise to severe resentment in the 1240s. The register itself records the levy of the *collecta*, the emergency war tax that became a regular annual levy. There is little sign of unrest in the register: apart from strife between sailors of Savona and Genoa in the streets of Messina, and apart from the frequent denunciation of past traitors, the register suggests that the absent emperor maintained a striking degree of control in the *regno*. Even the Saracens were at last quiet after half a century of rebellion. Frederick's solid network of *secreti*, justiciars, portulans, castellans had proved mainly reliable: often enough new men, citizens of Amalfi or Salerno who entered the royal service from studies at Naples, lawyers rather than ecclesiastics or barons. Those officials who failed the emperor were more likely guilty of peculation than of outright treason. Gregory IX's second attempt to subvert the *regno*, at the period when the register was compiled, was even less successful than his first. But to maximize revenue from the *regno* for wars in Lombardy was not so simple. Unrest could be stimulated by taxation for outside uses. More than that, the capacity of the kingdom to continue production of wheat, salted meat and other foodstuffs was increasingly in doubt: the loss of the skilled Muslim agriculturalists meant the loss of special expertise, and it could only in part be compensated by the settlement of Jews from North Africa. In fact, Sicily and Apulia would remain great Mediterranean granaries for centuries to come, but Frederick's reign saw them depopulated and thus unable to produce to peak capacity. He saw the need to settle not just Jews but Ghibelline adherents from northern Italy; he knew that the cultivation of the soil was the key to his financial solvency, and thus to his political success. But his Norman predecessors had commanded much greater wealth, and Frederick's recourse to Roman bankers – while itself a notable victory over Gregory IX – revealed that he was delicately balanced on the edge of the abyss of insolvency. He was to leave a legacy of financial uncertainty to his successors, who placed control of the kingdom's resources more completely in the hands of the Tuscan bankers, and stimulated internal unrest by their constant demands for funds.

CHAPTER ELEVEN

A DIFFERENT PROCEDURE, 1239–45

I

In 1239 Frederick's hopes for a victory were still centred on the Lombard battle-fronts. Rather as his stunning success in 1229–30, in southern Italy, had forced Gregory IX to come to satisfactory terms at San Germano, so, he imagined, a sustained triumph in Lombardy would bring the pope to a settlement ten years later. He had some confidence in the college of cardinals, where several restive figures pressed for renewed negotiations – Thomas of Santa Sabina, for instance. These cardinals were not necessarily friends of the imperial party, but they saw that Gregory was risking the future security of the papacy to pursue his vendetta against the emperor; they were less interested in grandiloquent statements about the nature of Petrine authority than in the practical preservation of that authority in and around Rome. To sustain his case, Frederick must actually achieve marked success. It was this that eluded him at first, and stimulated a rethinking of his plan of action. He and Ezzelino did, it is true, nibble away at the Guelf fortresses of north-eastern Italy. But they failed to seize Treviso in summer 1239, when they lost the sympathy, only briefly held, of Ezzelino's rival Azzo d'Este. The loss of Venice's support for the emperor was keenly felt: the privileges of 1232 had not convinced the republic that its prime interests lay in an alliance with a figure who threatened to domi-nate the entire hinterland behind Venice. A more ambitious scheme was that dangled before Venice and Genoa for a papal invasion of southern Italy and Sicily. Why bargain with the emperor for access to the *regno* if, by allying with the pope instead, you can take and keep what you want of southern Italy? The Genoese were even promised Syracuse again, the city they had dominated for two decades until Frederick first asserted himself in 1220.

A renewed attempt by the imperial army to reach Milan, in September 1239, met with studied refusal by the Lombard rebels to come out and fight. Frederick saw little hope in a siege of so vast and well-protected a city, and was forced by the sheer in-activity of the opposition to withdraw, moodily, southwards. But he still had his firm allies in the Lombard plain: he called in on Cremona, and was pleasantly instructed that Como had decided to join the imperial side; it was a city with a long history of ill-feeling towards Milan, and its acquisition certainly strength-ened the imperial position in Lombardy. Even so, it is hard to describe Frederick's position as better than stalemate. Moreover, Frederick recognized the fact. He had already begun in summer 1239 to elaborate 'a different procedure', which he described in the letter to the archbishop of Messina, preserved among his admi-nistrative orders for the *regno*; its two central points were the threat of force rather than negotiation as a means to end the conflict; and the assertion of imperial rights in central Italy, in the duchy of Spoleto and the march of Ancona. The archbishop, who counselled peace with the pope, was thus left under no illusion that the conflict had entirely changed its character once Gregory had imposed his ban on Frederick. Even so, we may doubt whether Frederick had now turned his back on negotia-tion; he saw war as the only possible means to an end, not as the only desirable means to that end. Indeed, the purpose of war was to force the enemy to come to terms. Neither now nor later did the emperor propose the complete humiliation of the papacy, as achieved sixty years later by Philip IV of France over Boni-face VIII, in the 'outrage at Anagni'. Preliminary moves by Enzo, acting as Vicar of All Italy under Frederick's mandate (July 1239), had already brought the emperor significant gains in summer 1239: Jesi, the city of his birth, was recovered for the empire, an achievement that was more than symbolic, given its proximity to the northern borders of the kingdom of Sicily.

It was, however, Frederick's presence that was needed to cow the region into submission. The failure against Milan was swiftly followed by a progress southwards to Ghibelline Pisa, where the emperor spent Christmas 1239 thinking not so much about his Lombard strategy as about the recovery of central Italy. In other words, he sought to cajole, coax and, if need be, conquer the cities of the papal state laboriously built up by Innocent III and his successors – isolating Gregory in Rome, whose own loyalty to the pope was proverbially unreliable. Late winter and spring of 1240 saw the emperor's plan achieve remarkable success. Although some of the cities in the higher ground of the Umbrian interior remained firmly Guelf, the towns closest to Rome submitted: Viterbo, an important centre, often used as a papal residence, Corneto (now called Tarquinia), Sutri at the gates of Rome, as the emperor processed southwards. And Rome itself was Frederick's target, for, with Piero della Vigna's high-sounding prose announcing his coming, the emperor foretold the restoration of Roman imperial glories in their native city. Briefly, he may have dreamed of making Rome his capital. For he was gradually beginning to integrate his Sicilian and Italian administration into a loose unit, using Sicilians as *podestà* in the north and allowing his high court in Sicily to judge cases north of the border between the *regnum Siciliae* and the *regnum Italicum*. In early spring of 1240 the emperor could optimistically assume that his 'different procedure' had achieved its desired effects smoothly and rapidly.

The remaining problem was the submission of Rome and the taming of the wolf Gregory. Here too there were grounds for hope. Frederick's campaign was partly financed by loans from Roman bankers, as the government register of 1239–40 reveals; here were Gregory's own Roman subjects funding the conquest of Lombardy and central Italy. Divisions between factions in the college of cardinals, over local politics as much as imperial, accentuated the impression that Rome would not withstand the sight of Frederick's armies. Indeed, as he approached Rome the Ghibelline sympathizers went around with the cry: 'Let the emperor come and receive the city!' To Gregory, Rome's salvation had, however, added significance. This was the holy city of Sts Peter and Paul. Another holy city than Jerusalem was under threat. Having wreaked havoc in Jerusalem, Frederick would unleash devastation on Rome. On 22 February Gregory made his appeal to the city, and to the world. It took remarkable form. A great procession wound its way from the papal palace at the cathedral of St John Lateran across the city to the shrine of St Peter in the Constantinian basilica at the Vatican. Culminating point of the procession was the display of the relics of Sts Peter and Paul (apparently in the form of their skulls), and an impassioned speech by the aged pope, urging the Romans to protect the liberty of the Church. If the Romans would not defend their city, let the two saints act instead; he removed his own tiara and placed it over the skulls to emphasize the point. The war against Frederick was a holy war, justly proclaimed for the defence of the faith; those who participated were no less than crusaders, certain of the joys of heaven if they died truly fighting for the Church's cause, protected by all the privileges of a crusade. Crosses of cloth were distributed among the crowd, or improvised by enthusiasts for Gregory, to be sewn on the garments of those who were willing to join the papal army. Despite the continued opposition of the Ghibellines in Rome, Gregory had conjured to his side a large and vociferous body of support. The Romans had been proved to be fickle in their admiration for the emperor; but they might equally prove fickle in their adoration of the pope.

Frederick did not challenge Gregory. Rome's walls defended the vast city well; Frederick wanted to enter it not as a warrior but as a prince of peace. Now Gregory assumed that role, preaching that distinctive type of peace, the crusade, the holy war for the bringing of ultimate peace to Christendom. As ever, Frederick was reluctant to put to the test his military skills. In truth, they were not very well developed. Nor did Frederick wish to hand to the pope a propaganda victory, by storming Gregory's palaces and showing himself an enemy of the Church. On the other hand, he could see that Gregory had few troops at his beck and call. Those towns near Rome that still supported the pope, such as Velletri, would be easy prey for Frederick's army, and could never supply Gregory with the level of armed support he needed. Gregory did, it is true, extend his appeal for knights to join his crusade against Frederick right across Europe, but as yet the campaign to win support was very slow-moving;

its main aim was to impress potentially sympathetic rulers, such as Henry III of England, who, as a papal vassal, might be expected to supply funds or men to resist the emperor. From all this — visible, indeed, to Frederick — we might conclude that Frederick made a serious mistake in not attempting to break the will of the Romans. Would they really stand firm once the memory of Gregory's histrionics had faded?

Actually, Frederick was still consistently adhering to a plan of action. The use of force, prophesied in his letter to the archbishop of Messina, was intended to achieve a political result: the settlement of the emperor's differences with Gregory through negotiation. But the negotiations would be more than ever under Frederick's terms, if the emperor's current strategy in Italy came to fruition. In 1240 Frederick withdrew from Rome only to gather together larger forces, from southern Italy; he continued to run circles round the city. Perhaps the papalists remembered that Hannibal had done the same, to no effect. Frederick believed, too, that the time had come to negotiate with the cardinals in the first place; if he could win their sympathy, he might be able to neutralize the pope politically — not merely this pope, but future popes who should, as his letters had earlier hinted, be subject to the control of the college of cardinals. But how could he even approach the cardinals, many of whom were in the blockaded city of Rome? Frederick did not stand in the way when the German princes urged the grand master of the Teutonic knights to hurry to Rome and speak with the cardinals. This was no longer Hermann von Salza — he had died the day Gregory excommunicated the emperor — but Conrad of Thuringia, who was little less sympathetic to the imperial cause. What in fact was happening was an attempt to reopen contact on new terms without giving rise to embarrassment. The pope, who continued in public to insist roundly that he had no intention ever of coming to terms with Frederick, was simply not part of the negotiating team.

Among the cardinals who recognized the apparent hopelessness of the papal stance was one, Giovanni Colonna, who represents many of the problems of Rome itself. His family stood at the head of one of the two great city factions; their rivals, the Orsini, also commanded great influence in Rome, where Matteo Orsini was trying to establish tight control over the city government. When the Colonna favoured the emperor, then, they favoured a protector of their fortunes in the city. And, as lords of vast estates to the south of Rome, the Colonna were naturally sensitive to the presence around Rome of large imperial armies. They had ample reason to hold pope and emperor apart, at the very least; and according to Matthew Paris, the English chronicler, the pope quarrelled violently over Giovanni Colonna's conciliatory attitude towards Frederick. He accused Colonna of drawing him towards an ignominious truce with one who was, and had always been, his mortal foe. Frederick enjoyed having a stranglehold over the Colonna, and used it to good effect. As the months went by, they openly identified with the Hohenstaufen cause, in exasperation at Pope Gregory's obstinacy. More important to Frederick was the growth in feeling that a general council of the church needed to be called at which the aggrieved parties could submit their complaints for settlement. This plan echoed significantly the correspondence of Frederick II with the European kings, especially Louis IX: the pope had been blamed, since the act of excommunication, for not permitting the case against Frederick to go for judgement. Yet who was to judge it? The cardinals well knew that a council at which the motif was reconciliation between two aggrieved rivals would only succeed if there existed an authoritative mediator. Since both pope and emperor claimed the power of a universal monarch, with the right to judge all on earth, the mediator must be a panel of lesser arbitrators composed largely or in part of the cardinals themselves. (By the same principle, the cardinals, though less than the pope, had the power to elect a pope; the German princes, on similar lines, had the power to elect a king of the Romans; or, indeed, a cathedral chapter to elect a bishop.) Naturally, Frederick was only amenable to the idea on condition that his own voice was heard at the council, for instance through the mouth of the German spiritual princes. Gregory, equally, expected the Lombard rebels to be well represented, and saw a council only as an opportunity to condemn the emperor in the presence of a loyal following from Italy and the rest of Christendom. For him it was not simply a means to peace, but a means to victory. Thus what had begun as a serious proposal for a peace conference, not unappealing to Frederick himself, became a direct threat to the emperor, an expression of Gregory's staunch refusal to contemplate compromise.

So Gregory rushed in to announce a council for Easter, 1241, without letting the ponderous negotiations between the cardinals and Frederick's representatives reach any conclusion. He had cleverly taken the wind out of the cardinals' sails. But he had not impressed Frederick. The emperor reacted with hostility to the very idea of a council that did not represent his interests. He refused to guarantee the safety of those travelling to Rome for the meeting. This did not merely mean that he banned his Sicilian, German and other subjects from attending. Such bans on travel to Rome were nothing new, in the long history of papal conflict with the rulers of Europe. To hint that even those from outside his jurisdiction might not be safe was also not entirely new; he had detained other kings' emissaries to Rome in the past. What was new was that he really intended to prevent the event ever taking place.

But the cardinals and bishops who set out for Rome from northern Europe and Lombardy did not suspect how real the threat was. In Spring 1241 they sailed together under convoy from Genoa, carrying with them, it seems, much of the money collected from England and elsewhere in answer to Gregory's appeal for financial aid. Adorned with red crosses on their white sails, the ships served as a visible reminder of the crusading cause in which their passengers travelled. Yet crusader crosses could not guarantee immunity, especially against a renegade Genoese admiral in command of a Sicilian and Pisan fleet. Old rivalries, between Pisa and Genoa, between the great Genoese clans, and between pope and emperor were fought out on 3 May 1241 when Admiral Ansaldo de Mari swooped on the Genoese fleet off the coast of Tuscany. At the sight of the enemy, many of the Genoese sailors rushed to enter into crusader vows; an intense atmosphere of devotion was briefly and rapidly created. But pious acts did not save them. They were overwhelmed, and many were slaughtered without mercy: that in itself was almost unexceptional in the bitter Pisan-Genoese wars of the twelfth and thirteenth centuries. More importantly, from Frederick's point of view, there was plenty of booty on board: live booty, in the form of dozens of delegates to the Rome conference, two cardinals and many bishops. Among them, the cardinal bishop of Palestrina, who least of all could expect mercy from the emperor. The captives were, at least according to papal accounts, treated appallingly, both at sea in the aftermath of the naval battle, and in prison in Tuscany and in southern Italy. But we should not believe the sources too literally. A second cardinal, Otto of St Nicholas, was won over to the emperor's case while held in southern Italy. It seems that Frederick's treatment was conditional on the degree of cooperation he found (or formed) in his captive. Yet his ugly attitude to the cardinals and bishops who fell into his hands would not be out of tune with thirteenth-century ideas. What was spectacular was the size and number of the fish he had netted. As has been seen, those whom he thought to be enemies of his empire (such as his son Henry) could expect no mild sympathy once in his hands.

They were hostages: punishment was not the real aim (though James of Palestrina probably suffered the most), but bargaining, on his terms. He did not want his captives dead of jail-fever or neglect, though some did die of ill-treatment and disease before ever they reached southern Italy. The new policy of the use of force only led this far, though. The next stage was to compel the pope to negotiate. In fact, the immediate result was, rather, to isolate Gregory further: he had lost the support of a council, for most of the delegates never arrived; he was being urged by several cardinals to sue for peace; he was even being urged by the captives themselves to end the struggle. But Gregory also had his inner core of determined supporters. When the brother of Henry III of England, Richard, earl of Cornwall, tried to mediate between the emperor and the pope he found he could make no progress; he was suspect simply as a peace-maker. The abusive hostility to Frederick II pervaded Gregory's circle: Sinibaldo de'Fieschi, Rainier of Viterbo and a few other cardinals gave no ground.

Frederick's capture of the cardinals did not, however, compensate for his defeats in the north-east. Away from the Veneto, he was unable to hold down several of the key strongholds of the imperialists: Ferrara, under Salinguerra, was betrayed in 1240; and the real victors turned out to be the Venetians, whose interests lay less in the political strife of commune and emperor than in the establishment of commercial mastery in the upper Adriatic. So in late 1240 Frederick found himself back in the north-east, struggling to hold down the borderlands between the *regnum Italicum* and the areas over which the papacy claimed a nebulous authority. Here Ravenna (lost in 1239), Bologna (inveterately hostile) and Faenza, on the main roads to the south, were key objectives. A six-month siege of Faenza culminated in April 1241 with the hungry city's submission. It was a practical way to spend a winter: it was not good weather for pitched battles; patience was demanded, and Frederick whiled away the time studying scientific texts on a much-loved subject, falconry. All this boosted the emperor's confidence, and, even before the prelates had been captured at sea, Frederick decided to show his charming side to the world by pardoning Faenza. As before, he was probably guided by the requests of the city's Ghibelline exiles, who were anxious to return to rule a city that was still worth something. But the emperor also knew that a balance had to be sought between mercy and terror. As the papal propaganda machine gathered momentum, abusing the emperor as a friend of tyrants, he must demonstrate by his acts how remote from reckless tyranny he actually was. He was scrupulous, too, at the siege of Faenza in ensuring adequate payment of his mercenaries. Bullion ran out; his funds were stretched to the limit. He therefore minted, or rather printed, leather tokens which were later redeemed against silver – a proof of his good faith to those who trusted his promises.

Effectively, though, much of Italy was now open to him, in the sense that he could pass freely from north to south. He was back in the Roman countryside in summer 1241, building close ties with Giovanni Colonna. That the cardinal wanted help in ousting the Orsini from control of Rome was not the point. Frederick needed local help in easing his own way closer to Rome. He was able to bottle Gregory up in Rome during the hot summer. But, immured in Rome, the pope was inaccessible, even to the pleas of the moderate. Then, in August, Gregory IX, resisting to the last, and sapped, it is said, by the summer heat, fell ill and died. He had not defeated Frederick; but neither had Frederick defeated him.

Gregory IX ended his pontificate engaged in the struggle with which he had opened it. Even insisting, as we must, on the long interval from 1230 to 1238 when relations between pope and emperor were correct, even cordial, it is impossible to escape the view that this pope was obsessed by the spectacle of Frederick's excessive power – of the emperor's dual monarchy in Sicily and Germany, of his supposedly wilful treatment of the Church in Sicily, of his neglect of the true interests of the Holy Land, of his interference in the papal states and his influence even at times within the walls of Rome. The Lombard question was to some extent a *casus belli* rather than a substantial grievance; Frederick's occasional successes in northern Italy signalled the danger that the empire would recover its authority in yet another region, perhaps building on its conquests a real suprastructure of government. There were certainly suspicions that the target was not Lombardy alone, but Tuscany, the Adriatic provinces and the Roman campagna itself. But Gregory's approach went beyond the territorial question. The issue in the last analysis was the relative standing of the pope and the emperor: the right of the pope to command in moral affairs, and the duty of the emperor to follow the pope's guidance. There was a clear and emphatic notion of papal-imperial cooperation, but its basis was the dependence of empire on papacy, the empire receiving its light from the papacy as did the moon from the sun. The cooperation of the years 1230 to 1238 was not conducted in this spirit; it was seen by this pope as a period of humiliation, revealing the practical powerlessness of the papacy in the face of the emperor. Thinking in these terms, Gregory adopted a mood of confrontation. His duty was to redeem his office from the tutelage of San Germano. Future peace could not be realized on those terms; San Germano looked like peace, but it was merely a truce. By 1237 or 1238 Gregory IX began to see that the troubles in Lombardy could indeed be turned to papal advantage. Cautiously, gradually, the pope encouraged a shift in alliances, away from Frederick, and towards those who in any case never ceased to insist on their loyalty to the holy see, the Lombard rebels.

In other ways Gregory was also a remarkable figure. His patronage of the Franciscan Order in its earlier days was of crucial importance in winning the curia's approval for the eccentric, ascetic Francis of Assisi. His legislation and his work on the Roman law-codes (the Decretals, a collection of canon law texts of capital importance) was noticed even by his Ghibelline enemies. As a canon lawyer, he was extremely capable; it was his understanding of the legal rights of the papacy and the Roman Church which, however, steered him towards collision with a younger but rival tradition: the revived Romanism of the Hohenstaufen empire.

II

The death of the pope did not remove at a stroke Frederick's differences with the papacy. Disunited though the papal curia was by 1241, it also contained some cardinals who were favourable to Gregory's great cause. Frederick himself could only express a hope that the next pope would be a friend of God, someone keen 'to correct the errors and to right the wrongs of his forerunners'. His most pressing need was, therefore, to influence the next election in this direction. Frederick possessed three cards: the cardinals James of Palestrina and Nicholas of Ostia were in his hands, while Giovanni Colonna was now an ally. However, the emperor still found himself unable to break Rome itself. The Orsini remained dominant under their senator Matteo; and he was desperate to steer the papal election in his own favour. That meant the election of a pope who would maintain resistance against Frederick and his Colonna partners. Matteo Orsini's methods were no more polite than Frederick's had been, after the capture of the prelates at sea. Closely guarded, even for a time shackled, the cardinals present in Rome were conducted to a tumbledown palace, the Septizonium, where they were immured in the most beastly conditions. Their guards, stationed above the ceiling, are said to have used the roof of the cardinals' chamber as their lavatory (this was standard practice in attempts to coerce cardinal electors). The rains came; into the chamber itself through the many cracks and holes. Conditions so terrible, indeed, that the English cardinal Robert of Somercote fell ill and died. The two cardinals in Frederick's hands were not, by now, living in worse conditions. At one point Matteo Orsini threatened to hurry the proceedings by exhuming the body of Pope Gregory IX and placing it, in full process of decomposition, in the middle of their chamber. Fortunately this threat did not materialize.

The problem was that – for all Matteo's methods – the cardinals remained divided. The emergency facing the Church was far more serious to them than their own extreme discomfort. The diehard opponents of Frederick, including Sinibaldo de'Fieschi, wanted Romano of Porto as pope; he was one of the cardinals who had stood by Gregory IX. Including Romano, this group numbered four. Five electors stood out for another cardinal, Goffredo of Santa Sabina, making a group of six. Among them was Giovanni Colonna, who had been readmitted into the city specially for the election. These cardinals were, relatively speaking, the 'moderates' – less favourable to Frederick, as a whole, than Giovanni Colonna, but certainly keen to negotiate effectively for an end to the conflict. Even so, there must have been endless jockeying of position and trading of votes as the weeks dragged by. What was plain was the inability of the cardinals to come to a clear decision; they were even reluctant to think of a compromise candidate, counting, no doubt, on outside support (from Matteo Orsini, the emperor or other interest groups) if only they could swing the election their way.

Although living under disgusting conditions, the cardinals were not sealed off from the world. Papal elections in the Middle Ages may have craved secrecy, but they rarely achieved it. In fact, it became obvious that an appeal to the outside world was necessary if they were ever going to resolve their differences: the two absent cardinals in the emperor's hands must be admitted to the deliberations, in the hope that, with their votes available, a united choice could be made. Here the cardinals played their hand well. Frederick might be reluctant to send James of Palestrina to elect an enemy to St Peter's throne; but Otto of St Nicholas was a much more amenable figure, and the emperor was keen to have him elected pope. The threat that Romano of Porto would ascend the throne led Frederick to conclude that the release of his captured cardinals might prevent a dangerous foe from being elected pope; it was a gamble, but some cheating also seemed permissible. If Matthew Paris is to be believed, the cardinals were actually told that they must elect Otto of St Nicholas pope, if they wanted him and James of Palestrina to be released from custody. Otherwise, they would remain Frederick's 'guests'.

This was too much for the cardinals to take; rebuffing such interference, they now turned their mind to outside candidates. It is possible that Humbert of Romans, a powerful force in the Dominican order and an able canonist, was actually chosen. But Matteo Orsini did not want an outsider. He wanted someone who was physically under his own control. This brought the college back to its earlier dilemma. It seems Romano of Porto had blackened his own reputation by persecuting scholars in Paris University; there were even salacious rumours of his unseemly conduct in the presence of the French queen mother. (Once again, the source is the Englishman Matthew Paris, a distinguished predecessor of the Fleet Street gossip journalist, for all his other qualities.) Matteo's insistence on the election of Romano or one of his associates only proved counter-productive. It prodded the cardinals at last into unity of action. The cardinal deacon of Santa Sabina was declared elected, and he took the name Celestine IV.

He had little chance to make peace with anyone. The one significant act of his pontificate was the excommunication of Matteo Orsini. For, less than three weeks after his election, worn out, no doubt, by life in the pig-sty of a palace, he had followed Gregory to the grave; a new election was called for. Nor was this easy to arrange: once out of confinement, most of the cardinals had fled from Rome to the summer residence of the popes at Anagni. Giovanni Colonna was left behind in the Orsini prisons, but only Sinibaldo de'Fieschi and one or two others dared hang on in Rome itself. Not to forget, too, that the emperor still held captive his own pair of cardinals. Even to bring together the cardinals would demand careful diplomacy: there was some feeling that Rome was no longer a safe place for the election, and that in emergency it would be permissible to elect at Anagni. However, the cardinals still in Rome, perhaps under Orsini in-fluence, were loath to leave the city, arguing that they were effectively under siege by Frederick II. Were they to follow James of Palestrina to the dungeons of southern Italy? It was obvious that James's future was seriously impeding further action. So long as he was held captive the cardinals at Anagni refused to proceed to an election. They also requested Frederick to lift his blockade of Rome (as he did), so that their brethren in Rome could join them for the election. At least this signified a re-sumption of negotiations between the princes of the Church and the emperor, even if the matter in hand was arrangements for the new election. So Frederick tried to extend the discussion further, insisting that the papal legate Gregorio di Montelongo be withdrawn from Lombardy. Then only would James of Pale-strina be released from captivity. The cardinals made vague promises to do something about Gregorio, but continued to extend the debate by urging the emperor to restore what he had taken from the Church and purge his guilt. Clearly the cardinals were not simply prepared to make peace without elaborate conditions of their own. So it was less the prompting of the cardinals, and more the poor press that the emperor began to receive throughout Christendom, that led him, after intolerable delays, to release James of Palestrina. He was increasingly por-trayed, even in France and England, as the single figure who was doing most to prevent a papal election. By summer, 1243, the scandal of the vacancy had turned to the emperor's detriment. The role of Matteo Orsini had been largely forgotten; the blame stuck on Frederick instead. There was no advantage to him now in trying to negotiate for peace with the cardinals: their priority was not, as he had briefly hoped, the seizure of the power to guide the Church in the absence of its pilot; they were aware that the Church was in a weaker state without its pilot. Moreover, Frederick's ill-treatment of the cardinal bishop of Palestrina sug-gested what perils lay in waiting for the cardinals if they lacked at their head a far-sighted, hard-bargaining leader able to call Christendom to witness against the emperor's excesses.

In other words, Frederick seriously miscalculated. It was not enough to flatter the cardinals with insistence on their authority to govern the Church with or without a pope at their helm. Curial thinking of the thirteenth century did not contemplate a headless monster at the helm of the Church. Nor did it give way to imperialist claims for the comparability of power of pope and emperor. The question in the minds of the cardinals was not so much whether the canonists and theologians had overstated the nature of papal power; it was whether recent popes had used that power wisely. It was a question either of reviving Honorius III's more diplomatic approach, or of continuing Gregory IX's unflinching confrontation. The nearest they would move to Frederick's position was to elect a more conciliatory pope, but even so the emperor deluded himself if he expected a quick return to peace. Aware of the growing hostility to his interference (by holding James of Palestrina captive) the emperor announced after all that he would release his prisoner (Spring 1243). He hoped this would show that his first concern was the peace of the Church, not the defence of his own dignity, and that it would be seen as an act of the purest selflessness and clemency.

But it was too late; 25 June 1243 saw the election of Sinibaldo de'Fieschi, Genoese aristocrat, canon lawyer of the highest intellect, long-time associate of Gregory IX. He took the name Innocent IV. He was the last person Frederick can have wanted as pope, the more so since Frederick's previous opponent in the college of cardinals, Romano of Porto, had died. Historians have wondered at, and even been deceived by, the 'great joy' that Frederick declared he felt on receiving news that a new pope had been elected. Piero della Vigna, Taddeo da Suessa, Ansaldo de Mari (surely not terribly welcome), the grand master of the Teutonic order, in other words the very highest officials at Frederick's court, were instructed to form a negotiating team: the emperor did not see how the new pope could avoid peace talks. Frederick, then, was still convinced that the way to peace lay in a negotiated settlement. So far from trying to overwhelm Rome and the Orsini, he had withdrawn his troops from the outskirts of the city when requested to do so. He wanted at last to be heard; Gregory IX had consistently refused to listen. By bestowing on Innocent IV his congratulations and by expressing his hopes for future cooperation, Frederick wished to prove that he could work alongside even an adherent of the doctrines of papal supremacy. Such thoughts were naïve.

III

Seen from the point of view of the staunch papalists, Innocent IV's task was this. He must hold the ground gained by Gregory IX, such as it was: not physical territory, but some fine successes in the propaganda war against Frederick II. He must continue to give comfort to the beleaguered Lombard rebels, the more so since for two whole years they had been deprived of a patron. But Innocent must also capitalize on the change of popes, and on Frederick's mistakes of the last two years, to present to the world a less irate, less menacing papacy – a papacy justly aggrieved by Frederick's captivity of the delegates to the Rome council, by his seizure of lands until recently under papal rule and by his insistence on impossible terms of settlement. This was not a Machiavellian plan to undermine the Hohenstaufen through 'disinformation' or misrepresentation, though within three years it became that too; the party of Pope Innocent genuinely believed that Frederick II had turned his back on God and the Church, and that his occasionally stunning demonstrations of fidelity to the Church were in reality subterfuge. There was, too, confusion in Rome, indeed in all Europe, about the most urgent priorities facing Christendom. The defeat of the Hohenstaufen was seen by Louis IX of France as a mischievous distraction from a higher purpose, the renewal of the war for the recovery of Jerusalem. The entire holy city was lost to the Khwarizmian Turks in 1244, in an easy victory against which neither the Hohenstaufen, the Franks of Outremer nor the Muslims of Egypt could lift a finger. Moreover, the Mongol invasions were now hitting eastern Europe hard; Hungary was ravaged and Tartar armies threatened even the Adriatic; Germany too was seriously threatened, and the German princes wanted and expected imperial help against this horrendous menace. Frederick issued an encyclical against the Tartars, but words alone brought little comfort. All this meant that Innocent IV's emphasis on a war to the death between the papacy and the Hohenstaufen was seen in many quarters as a further contribution to the ruin of Christendom: 'a nation divided against itself shall fall.'

Innocent was, however, keen to gain time and favour by opening negotiations with Frederick. A papal mission reached Frederick's court within a few weeks of the new pope's election. The terms of its recommendations were vague, avoiding abuse of Frederick but insisting on the good faith of the papacy: there was talk of reparations for the wrongs committed by the emperor (with emphasis on the capture of the prelates at sea), a denial that the papacy had committed offences of its own, and a suggestion that – should Frederick insist on his innocence – the question of his guilt and of reparations be referred to a commission of spiritual and lay princes. It has been pointed out, however, that Innocent sought to include the Lombards in any final settlement, describing them now openly as 'friends of the Church'; there was little intention of abandoning them to imperial wrath. Indeed, the papacy renewed the commission of Gregorio di Montelongo as legate in Lombardy; the papal register of the period is chock-a-block with instructions to Gregorio, urging him to win friends and influence people in the north of Italy; Frederick's own complaints at Gregorio's behaviour were turned aside. All this reveals a double-edged approach to Frederick, in the papal curia. On the one hand Innocent could not be accused of unreasonable refusal to re-open discussions; on the other hand, Innocent's actions offended imperial honour and dignity, and offered the emperor no certainty of reconciliation to the Church. For it was perfectly possible that Innocent's commission would insist on terms that the emperor was unable to accept, such as his abdication from at least one of his thrones. Frederick, as Innocent knew, would not lightly agree to disarm himself completely for combat. Nor was the pace of negotiation speeded by problems over the credentials of the emperor's ambassadors sent to the papal court. As associates of the excommunicated emperor, the legates too were said by Innocent to share in the ban; they could not be admitted. It was only on the third request for admission that these legates were granted audience.

Delays on one front, then, deliberately contrived. Meanwhile, on other fronts, attempts to gain a stronger bargaining position. Here, to be fair, Innocent was led, rather than chose to lead. His tempestuous adviser Rainier of Viterbo, of all the cardinals perhaps the most determined enemy of Frederick II, had personal interests in the conflict of pope and emperor. His home city, to

the north of Rome, had been under imperial control since the
dark days of winter, 1240, when the emperor marched south
towards Rome. Rainier took advantage of grumbles among the
Guelf families of Viterbo to organize a *coup d'état*, bringing together Viterbesi, Romans and mercenaries to restore Guelf rule
in the city. They pounced on the imperial garrison and suddenly
took charge of the city, neatly and effectively. Only a small
group of imperial soldiers, under the command of Frederick's
podestà, held out in a strong-point within the well-walled town.
But imperial control over Viterbo had been lost and – as in
Lombardy and the Veneto – the vulnerability of Frederick's
friends to Guelf conspiracy had been embarrassingly revealed.
The emperor's reply was to park an army outside the walls of
Viterbo, besieging the Guelfs while they besieged his *podestà*
(September 1243). But Viterbo had (and still has) magnificent
defences, and Frederick had brought only a moderately sized
army. The nut was too hard to be cracked. By November he
gave up, and even agreed to a papal plan for the safe conduct of
the imperial garrison within Viterbo out of the city; this really
meant complete surrender to Rainier and his cronies. It seems the
emperor hoped thereby to convince, if not Rainier, at least Innocent of his own moderation: he was in a mood to compromise
on all sorts of matters, if only the pope would move faster to the
conference table. The pope, however, could promise, not guarantee, the safety of Frederick's men. When they did leave their
strong-point, together with part of the emperor's army, they
were pounced upon and savaged by the jubilant Guelfs. The safe-
conduct was worthless: many lost their life. This, too, despite the
presence at these events of Cardinal Otto of St Nicholas, sent to
supervise a smooth withdrawal. Throughout the 'Viterbo affair'
Rainier's hand is visible. It is of a part with his generally unre-
lenting, unforgiving opposition to Frederick II. Whether that
hatred was guided by adherence to the principles of papal primacy, or by a personal involvement in the affairs of central Italy
and especially Viterbo, it is hard to say. He certainly wrote of
Frederick in the language of an extreme 'papalist'. Did he draw
Innocent IV to his outlook? Innocent IV did offer to finance the
mercenaries used in 1240 against Viterbo; he certainly knew of
plans for the city's seizure. But he spoke of a payment of 2,500

ounces of gold, a very large sum, destined more likely for a well-organized military campaign. Cardinal Rainier preferred to combine the hire of troops with conspiracy, bribery and subversion. In the end, he used the pope's money, as well as his own and the proceeds of loans in order to achieve his target. It is arguable that he presented to Innocent a less complex plan of action than in fact he followed; but even then it cannot be argued that Innocent was unaware of the decision to grab Viterbo from Frederick's hands. He preferred to leave the business to his associate, taking neither praise nor blame, but winning considerable moral and tactical advantage in his dealings with the emperor. Frederick, more hard-pressed, could be offered yet tougher terms of settlement; more aggrieved than ever, too, Frederick might seize the chance to take up arms against Rome and the papacy. Though this might place Innocent at risk, it would also expose to the world what the pope and his counsellors were convinced Frederick's real aims must be: physical domination over the city of Rome and the papal patrimony, indeed over the whole Italian peninsula.

Yet Innocent's hopes that he could capitalize on apparently independent events at Viterbo were dashed by the near massacre of the imperial soldiers as they left the town. This placed the pope in an embarrassing position; nor is there reason to doubt Innocent's good faith when he promised a safe-conduct to Frederick's men. The Viterbesi, egged on, perhaps, by his cardinal, had overreacted. Innocent therefore hastened to honour the terms of his agreement with Frederick, by insisting on the restoration of Ghibelline property recently seized in Viterbo and on the release of imperialist citizens of Viterbo. The Guelfs were hardly disposed to listen. Indeed, Rainier of Viterbo was ordered to go with Otto of St Nicholas to enforce restitution. Probably he encouraged his allies to do as little as possible. Innocent was aware, too, that Viterbo would become volatile once again if its Ghibelline citizens were restored to their rights and property. Reluctant to see the city collapse in disorder – maybe, indeed, collapse into Frederick's lap – he decided to do nothing for the Ghibellines. After all, they were his enemy's allies.

It was by nibbling away at Frederick's influence in the area round Rome that the papacy could hope to achieve advances during this long drawn-out series of talks about talks. But the pope still avoided an open declaration of hostilities. He was well aware that the mood outside his curia and the cities of the Lombard League was not cooperative. Gregory IX had already met with sullen refusal in most areas of Germany, when he tried to organize resistance to Frederick; the English barons hated Henry III's compliance towards the popes on this matter; the French king talked of the need for a crusade. And the last years of Gregory IX's pontificate had seen the gradual erosion of Frankish control over Galilee and the corridor to Jerusalem, mastery over which was gingerly held as a result of periodic minor crusades under the ruler of Champagne and Navarre (1239–40) and under Frederick's acquaintance Richard, earl of Cornwall (1240–41). Louis of France insisted on the urgency of a full-scale crusade, and Innocent, despite his obsession with the Hohenstaufen, was also keen to see something done. It was not that he had no enthusiasm for a crusade; it was merely that his enthusiasm was torn in two, by the two conflicts he had to manage – the crusade and the struggle with Frederick, not to mention a third struggle, that against the Mongols, which was a further major source of worry. However, the virtual stalemate between Innocent and Frederick made it possible, in 1243–4, to give further thought to the crusade. It was clear that the papacy's interests would be served best if the crusade were led by Louis of France himself, and if it consisted of a predominantly French army. However, another plan was being mooted: an imperial crusade, redeeming the errors of 1228–9, based on Sicilian, German and, ideally, Lombard resources. Of this idea, more later.

In winter 1243–4 serious negotiations between pope and emperor at last started to move. Piero della Vigna and Taddeo da Suessa were, predictably, the emperor's representatives. After several months, on Maundy Thursday 1244, the terms of an acceptable peace arrangement were announced in Rome, at a grand conference of the papal curia, Frederick's representatives, the Lombards and other interested parties. The agreement steered a careful middle course between competing claims. Thus the disputes over lands in Italy, seized by partisans of one side or the other, were to be settled by a simple act of turning back the clock to Palm Sunday 1239, the day of Frederick's excommunication by Gregory IX. This would, on balance, favour the papacy; the recovery of Viterbo, for instance, must be ruled out by the Ghibellines. On the other hand, it would still leave the emperor with a strong hand in parts of north-eastern Italy, and would not extend the authority of the pope or of the Guelfs into some areas over which they might press claims. Frederick would not receive immediate absolution, but for the moment must show some respect for the sentence of excommunication; that is to say, he must not order services to be held when they contravened the decree of excommunication, and he must restore those properties of the Church dispossessed by him. Clearly this restoration involved both acquisitions since Palm Sunday 1239, and the settlement of claims, in Sicily and Benevento for instance, that went back much further in time. Restitution for his offences against the captured prelates was another *sine qua non*. Beyond restitution lay contrition, and he must display this by proper acts of charity; he was increasingly regarded as mean to the Church and so he would have to show his devotion by constructing new churches and hospitals. Forgiveness to his enemies was another virtue the papacy enjoined on him: he was to cease pressing his claims against the pope's allies – here the Lombard rebels are clearly intended, in first place – and he was even to ensure that Guelf property was restored to its rightful Guelf owners, whether or not, as was common, it had been taken over by Ghibelline claimants. Such questions of property bedevilled the Italian city-states, for claims and counter-claims often went back several generations; in consequence, attempts at restitution generally did more to inflame passions once again than to assure internal concord. Two, more general, clauses of the agreement stand out. In one the emperor had to accept the primacy of the holy see in spiritual affairs; his enemies at the papal curia had read enough of della Vigna's diatribes to realize that the Hohenstaufen were developing startling ideas of a Roman imperial revival – ideas visible already under Frederick I ninety or so years earlier. The second of these general commitments is perhaps even more revealing, cryptic though its phrasing is. The emperor was to engage to give aid in men and money to such Christian princes as the pope might think appropriate. The main thrust of the clause was surely to promise help to the German princes and the

Hungarian king, against the Tartar hordes, and to King Louis IX, on his forthcoming crusade. Such help to the French king was doubly appropriate since Louis had long been using his good offices to bring about a compromise agreement of this sort. Symbolic, too, of the crusading interests of the papacy at this time was the presence at the negotiations of the Frankish emperor of Constantinople, desperately in search of aid against his Greek and Slav neighbours who were working efficiently to whittle away the inglorious Latin empire won by the Fourth Crusade in 1204. Gregory IX had already promised aid to the Latin emperor of Constantinople; Innocent IV took interest in missions and campaigns aimed at the schismatic Greeks, Bulgars and Vlachs. This figure would thus be a beneficiary of the imperial–papal pact, the more so since Frederick preferred to cultivate links with the Greek rather than the Latin princes who ruled the remaining fragments of Byzantium. Possibly, too, it was a mild propaganda point for the papacy to be able to show that one emperor, the 'emperor of Romania', obeyed its will even if the other, the Holy Roman Emperor, had been refusing to do so.

Frederick II was well-disposed to this agreement, even though it seemed to make him lose face. In truth, he had never enjoyed the status of an excommunicate. He was even prepared to admit that he had acted badly towards the intolerable Gregory IX, though this acknowledgement was wrapped in the excuse that there had been errors on both sides in the use of accepted procedure. But the emperor gladly announced to Germany that the dispute between papacy and empire was, to all intents, at an end. They were hard terms, Frederick must have known; they limited his freedom of action in Lombardy. The Lombards, though represented at the peace conference, were likely to remain a source of trouble, and it is difficult to see how the emperor could go back on his firm promises to deal resolutely with the treason of Milan. Actually, peace was everything to him at this time. His motives included some more material ones, certainly. The high cost of his Italian wars was forcing him to turn to the Italian bankers for war loans. Although he generally managed to pay back his advances promptly, and was thus a good customer to the banks, he did so by squeezing his Sicilian subjects, demanding of them regular war taxes which were deeply resented. And the imperial register of 1239–40 indicates with glaring clarity how concerned Frederick was that his resources were running dry; there simply were few funds to hand to meet war costs. Fortunately his papal foe was little better off, despite the appeals for money and men to all Europe. The continuing emergency in eastern Europe was another problem. His failure to bring rapid aid to the German frontier-lords undermined confidence in him north of the Alps; the Tartar threat seemed far more serious there than the republican ravings of Milan.

Yet the agreement with Innocent IV also posed difficulties. What was envisaged was a gradual disengagement: withdrawal from occupied positions, restitution of property, visible devotion to the Church, all culminating in Frederick's absolution by the pope. The arrangements were actually vague. Who was to show willing first, the pope or the emperor? Innocent IV, seeing the agreement as a virtual act of submission, expected the lands in the papal states, the papal enclave of Benevento and other territories to be restored forthwith. The emperor could not show his devotion to the Church simply by professing his faith, or fulfilling selected parts of the agreement. Frederick, however, wanted signs of movement on the papal side as well. Indeed, Frederick's legates were barely back with Frederick when Innocent wrote to insist on the return of occupied Church lands and to remind the emperor that the peace agreement must cover the Lombard rebels as well as central Italy. And indeed, looking at past history of Guelf–Ghibelline rivalries, it is hard to believe the Lombard rivalries would or could be settled by this agreement: there were too many purely local issues in dispute, over property, rights to a say in city government, and there were undying blood feuds among the city clans. Clearly, however, Innocent feared continuing military action by Frederick's allies in the north. But for Frederick all this went too far. He was being asked to complete his side of the bargain while leaving the pope, possessor of the power to bind and loose, free to absolve or not to absolve the emperor at the end of the process. For Innocent, this expressed nicely the nature and reality of papal power. For Frederick, it smelled of continued mistrust, even treachery. So he requested instead rapid absolution, to be followed by detailed negotiation on the rights of pope and emperor in central Italy.

There are signs that this view commanded support in the college of cardinals; the Latin emperor of Constantinople, seeing all hope of aid evaporate, also urged the quick absolution of Frederick: he wanted some of those troops badly. Innocent's cast of mind was revealed when he countered the arguments of the cardinals by adding to their number a further dozen cardinals, nearly all of whom were likely to support his handling of the crisis. As under Gregory IX, we find the pope strikingly isolated from his curia, which is faction-ridden to an alarming degree. Cardinal Rainier of Viterbo was in no way typical of the college, but he shouted loudest and most vociferously what the pope wanted to hear.

As the emperor began to see that his hopes of a trial peace were over-optimistic, his mind turned back to the events of 1230. He had managed to deal with the obstinate Gregory IX face-to-face. It made sense to assume that he must adopt the same approach now. Besides, he had something tempting to offer. Yes, he would hand over the disputed lands in Central Italy and Benevento. But he must see the pope; and, once in Innocent's presence, he would certainly request the long withheld absolution. They would meet, it was decided between them, at Narni, north of Rome (rather than south of the city as Frederick had suggested: that seemed too dangerous to Innocent). What Frederick wanted, then, was to seal at a single blow the whole agreement. Blind to Innocent's view, the emperor seemed to assume that a desperate plea for the cause of peace would end the conflict.

In June 1244 pope and emperor began to converge on Narni. Innocent sent ahead one of his cardinals with a dour message. Beneath the issues discussed at the Rome conference (he said) lay a 'hidden sickness', the problem of Lombardy; it was on that, really, that peace depended. Such a message was hardly calculated to increase Frederick's confidence that his meeting at Narni would achieve firm results. Frederick saw no reason to allow the papacy an automatic say in Lombardy; he had (as he saw it) honoured the papacy by inviting it to mediate in Lombardy under earlier popes. But now Innocent went to the limits of the papal argument, by assuming the right to dispose order in an imperial territory above Frederick's head. This went far beyond disinterested arbitration. Worse news was to follow. The pope had indeed travelled north from Rome, but had turned back at Cività Castellana, to reach Sutri. He entered Sutri in disguise with a tiny retinue, and then crossed country to Civitavecchia, on the coast. There Innocent boarded a Genoese ship, which hurried him north to his home territory of Genoa where he landed on 8 July. Meanwhile, his cardinals scattered: some to Genoa, some to the Alpine foothills, a few, such as Rainier of Viterbo, to the Guelf power bases in central Italy. The brief of these cardinals was to resist encroachment by Frederick's forces.

All of which suggests premeditation, and a well-guarded secret. The Genoese were waiting for the pope at Civitavecchia; the cardinals were briefed as to their future duties and itinerary. That Innocent did not want to meet Frederick at Narni is plain. But what made him flee from central Italy is less plain. 'A curtain-raiser for the Avignon papacy', this event is often called, the more so since Innocent's destination was not Genoa but Lyons, an imperial city near the south-eastern edge of St Louis' kingdom. Just as the fourteenth-century popes sat for nearly seventy years across the river from France, so did Innocent find refuge away from the turmoil of Italy a few miles from the French dominions, in a city where the word of the French king carried more weight than that of the emperor. Yet the issue is not so simple. St Louis forbade the pope entry to French soil proper, loyal to Frederick as ever, but also fearing that the pope would challenge his power in France. A contrast indeed to events in the 1160s, when Alexander III resided as guest of the French king during his conflict with Frederick I. But Alexander was in conflict also with a rival pope, backed by the emperor. Innocent IV had no reason to fear a rival pope; he was on the verge of receiving from Frederick II a personal avowal of the emperor's good faith, expressed in the return of some of those lands disputed between pope and emperor long before either was born.

Maybe it was this very prospect that alarmed Innocent. Narni had the makings of a Canossa: the pope would be forced to accept Frederick's profession of faith, and would be pushed into a tight corner. Apparently Innocent did not see the agreement worked out at Rome as a viable or satisfactory settlement. Innocent may also have suspected Frederick of plotting to seize his person. Earlier kings of Sicily had made a practice of this, and one of the issues then as now had been the problem of the Church lands in the papal enclave at Benevento. Matthew Paris reports gossip that 300 knights were being sent to capture the pope. But this looks very much like an *ex post facto* argument. Groping for analogies, historians have summoned up not merely the residence of the papacy at Avignon, but the outrage at Anagni that preceded Avignon, the capture of Pope Boniface VIII by the men of King Philip the Fair of France. Innocent is then seen as the pope who escapes his Anagni, or rather Narni. But although the propaganda war under Innocent IV and under Boniface VIII has several striking similarities, we still have to remember that Innocent fled from peace talks, whereas Boniface was seized at a time of continuing, bitter conflict between pope and lay ruler. Nor had Frederick ever laid hands on Rome. The idea that Innocent feared the emperor would renew his siege of Rome and beat the papacy into submission to his own peace terms only works if the past history of Frederick's relations with Rome and the popes is set on one side. Frederick knew he could not hope to impose his will on Rome, nor afford to spend funds on an army to blockade the city; he wanted peace, and was prepared to go to extraordinary lengths to achieve it. War brought the prospect of financial disaster before Frederick's eyes. The imperial register makes this abundantly clear. Really, the explanation of Innocent's flight lies in the pope's fear of peace; in other words, his own terms of settlement were more extreme than those announced on Maundy Thursday 1244, but he had been pushed to a less exaggerated position by his cardinals and by the sheer impetus of bargaining. Bargaining was not what he wanted at all. He knew what needed to be done. Compromise was out.

Of course, it is also possible that Innocent misread the signals. He may have believed in the three hundred knights sent to seize him, and he may have heard wild rumours of Frederick's continued obstinacy, concealed beneath a conciliatory façade. The forward planning necessary to have Genoese galleys waiting at Civitavecchia gives the lie to this interpretation. Several weeks would be needed to send for the galleys, and for them to travel to Civitavecchia. Even if, for some reason, the galleys were by chance to hand in June 1244, there are other signs of advance planning that point in a similar direction.

In Genoa, after a stormy voyage, the pope fell ill and was obliged to wait three months before he could set out again. But he was among friends, delighted at his presence, their morale much restored after their crushing defeat by their treacherous son Ansaldo de Mari and the Pisan–Sicilian fleet. Not surprisingly, the papal chancery, such as it was in Genoa, churned out letters describing in renewed detail the rigours suffered by the captured prelates since 1241; the clear implication was: if this happens to dozens of bishops, even some cardinals, what might happen to the holy father himself, or to any Churchman? And then from Genoa the pope slowly processed, actually across the emperor's own territories, to Lyons, where he was ensconced a few weeks before Christmas. There, on 27 December, the pope announced to his congregation the calling of a general council of the Church, to be held on 24 June 1245 in Lyons itself, and to include in its business the issues the captured prelates had been supposed to handle at the council to which they had been travelling. Among these issues, the relations of Frederick and the papacy had a high place. Ominously, the emperor was merely described as a '*princeps*', a prince or ruler, a word which implicitly denied or detracted from the legitimacy of his royal and imperial titles. Equally, however, the triple problems of the loss of Jerusalem (now a reality), the threat to Latin Constantinople, and the Mongol invasions stood high on the agenda.

Nonplussed, the emperor continued to plead for peace and absolution. Was Innocent's flight a victory over Frederick, or a carefully stage-managed defeat of the papacy? In 1244 it was still too early for anyone to say.

IV

=

Frederick's response to the flight of Innocent IV was to stand by his policy, seeking once again the sympathy of those cardinals who were likely to restrain the pope from further condemnation of the emperor. He was even prepared to guarantee the safety of delegates bound from Italy to the Lyons council, an act of generosity which had a hollow ring, given his earlier seizure of delegates to the Rome council. More significant was the emperor's continued insistence that the agreement very nearly concluded a few months earlier should still serve as the framework for peace. It is even possible that, around the time Innocent announced his forthcoming council, Frederick was giving further ground: suggestions seem to have been in the air that the emperor would promise to go East to fight the infidel for at least three years, handing over control of the empire, maybe even the crown itself, to his son Conrad. Naturally he would also return lands seized from the Church too. It has been objected that such self-denying terms of settlement must have been mentioned only to discredit Innocent, to suggest that the pope was not even prepared to accept an 'abject surrender'; Frederick's armies were in fact still hard at work around Rome enforcing imperial authority in the face of Rainier and the Guelf opposition. Therefore (the case continues) he cannot seriously have intended even to hand back the papal lands his cronies had grabbed, let alone to have resigned the imperial throne. But this argument misses the point. Frederick's policy was double-edged: it was based on the premise that negotiation would be made all the more desirable to Innocent if the pope could see his political strength in the Roman countryside constantly being undermined. Unfortunately, such actions so close to the holy city also provided fuel for the papal propaganda machine: more of that shortly. It is fair to state that, had Frederick's armies stood idle in central Italy, the Guelfs would only have taken advantage of their enemy's inactivity. To maintain political and diplomatic momentum, continued activity in the field was essential. To that extent the conflict could never be settled by negotiation: the rivalry of pope and emperor had been so vigorously exploited by the factions in the central Italian, as previously the north Italian, towns that a negotiated settlement between Frederick and Innocent could no longer provide a guarantee of peace in the region. In a certain sense, pope and emperor had become irrelevant to the real conflict. Just as in northern Italy and Tuscany, for over a century to come, the labels 'Guelf' and 'Ghibelline' lost close connection with the disputes between popes and secular rulers, so in central Italy the real motor of conflict was faction and feud in the towns, over which higher loyalties to pope or emperor were superimposed.

More lives were lost in the struggles of the factions than on the battlefields of Frederick II; and, to the citizens of the small hill-towns, more was at stake: the horizon did not extend beyond the next range of hills.

Frederick's prospects of making peace at the Council of Lyons were bleak for other reasons than these. The tone of Innocent's verbal summons to Lyons left him in little doubt that he was to be condemned. A stream of invective letters, many from the pen of Rainier of Viterbo, portrayed him in blood-curdling apocalyptic language as the fourth beast in the vision of the prophet Daniel, a destroyer and devourer, iron-toothed and brazen-clawed, believing himself able to transform those things that are set, to direct the course of history away from its path. The atheistic emperor was seen as a new Herod, a Sadducee, and much else (a nicely chosen reply to della Vigna's characterization of the curia as a bunch of Pharisees). Frederick was trying to steal the pope's powers, or at least to deny them, representing himself as the real vicar of Christ with plenitude of power over the Church and the lay. Here, again, there may be angry echoes of della Vigna, who delighted in the picture of Frederick as God's chosen, born in the new Bethlehem but also suffering the savage taunts of godless priests; echoes also, perhaps, of the high-flying ideas of kingship preached and practised since the reign of Roger II in Sicily. But in the main the papal propaganda machine concentrated on less obscure allusions. Here was the false crusader, friend of Muslims, enemy of Christian belief, capturer of cardinals, foe to the death of Gregory IX, usurper of papal lands and rights. Whether Innocent sanctioned the wording of many of these attacks it is hard to say. It seems likely that his friend from Viterbo spent much time stoking up the fire; acting in the pope's name, he may have deliberately fanned the flames higher than Innocent himself originally intended. On the other hand Innocent certainly needed to win the propaganda war if his Lyons council were to produce anything but fine words and heroic gestures.

Rebuffed, Frederick all the same sent Taddeo da Suessa to Lyons. The emperor had made it plain that the terms still offered by the papacy – completion of Frederick's side of the bargain agreed at Rome before the papacy would even consider the emperor's absolution – were not terms at all. He felt as the

Milanese had felt in 1237–8. He was being asked to surrender to the will of the pope without any guarantee of the outcome, as he had asked Milan to surrender to him. But Frederick could at least use the Council of Lyons to present his case. Even for him such a potentially hostile gathering had some propaganda value. Taddeo da Suessa was a skilled lawyer who had for several years participated closely in the emperor's affairs. He was an excellent choice as imperial spokesman. His audience would be mainly French, Spanish and English, for the German attendance was not large; the emperor's own subjects realized that the council was not the place to be seen. But there were also some potential mediators present: among lay lords, the count of Toulouse, Raymond VII of Saint-Gilles, a subject both of Louis IX and of Frederick; the Latin emperor of Constantinople, who could be relied upon to stress the various needs of the eastern lands. It is thought, in fact, that the number of patriarchs, archbishops, bishops and abbots present was no higher than 150, making rather a small gathering.

In the cathedral of Lyons on 28 June 1245 Pope Innocent rose to speak on the words of Jeremiah: 'Behold, and see if there be any sorrow like unto my sorrow.' Coming from the Book of Lamentations, such words conjured up images of the desolate city of Jerusalem, ravaged by a new Nebuchadnezzar, the Khwarizmian Turk. The need to aid the Franks in the East was a major topic of the sermon. But the image of fallen Jerusalem and its persecutor was a flexible one. Frederick II, false crusader and persecutor of the Church, was not spared the slightest mercy. The list of complaints adds nothing really new: the recent propaganda campaign had gone much further already. Here was the lover of Saracen company, female and *horribile dictu*, male also; the denier of God; the destroyer of churches, whose treatment of the Sicilian Church was especially notorious. The emphasis on Sicily, even more than central Italy, is striking: the papacy insisted, of course, that Frederick was a papal vassal for the kingdom of Sicily; but it is noticeable how, from now on, Innocent pushed Sicilian problems to the fore. Aware, no doubt, of the difficulties in presenting a case that hinged on the Lombard crisis, the papacy focused on issues that had to all appearances been rather secondary during the years of estrangement and failed negotiation: Frederick's 'tyranny' in Sicily could be presented as a warning example of the ambitions the emperor harboured towards the rest of Italy, Germany and Burgundy. Moreover, the papacy was aware that without subverting Frederick's power base in the *regno*, Frederick could never be broken. More of such attempts at subversion shortly.

The contents of the attack by Innocent were so predictable that Taddeo da Suessa had no difficulty in presenting a coherently prepared, cogently argued reply. He spoke at the council of a very different emperor: compliant, contrite, cooperative. As before, he was anxious to stress the emperor's wish to comply with the terms of the Rome agreement, clearly expecting, however, absolution in the process. If there were any chance of making Innocent agree to grant absolution simultaneously with Frederick's abandonment of central Italy, it was now, when the pope's fury at the emperor might be constrained by moderate cardinals and delegates. Better still, Taddeo made the offer to end all offers. Frederick himself would turn against the three enemies in the East, concentrating his energies on the war against the Mongols in Europe, on the recovery of Jerusalem and on the restoration of 'Romania', Greece and adjacent lands, to the Roman obedience. Here was a direct plea to the emperor of Constantinople, seated next to the pope, for help in arranging a final peace. There were also delegates from the Latin states in Syria whose ear Taddeo hoped to catch. Appeals were made in other directions, too. Knowing St Louis' attitude, Taddeo emphasized that Frederick could only be condemned for heresy if publicly examined for it; then alone could his heart be unlocked. If the emperor employed Muslim soldiers, was this not in Christian interests, since in battle their blood would be spilled rather than that of Christians? (A delightful piece of sophistry, this: the papal complaint was precisely that Christian blood was being spilled in Italy at the hands of Frederick's infidel subjects.) But Taddeo revealed that the imperial court was wounded by the accusations of immoral conduct with Muslim women, when he bothered to answer the charge with the claim that the women were dancers and acrobats. In fact there is little reason to doubt that some were Frederick's concubines as well as his variety entertainers. Altogether, however, this was an effective reply. It exposed

Innocent as the unbending, partisan pontiff that he was. For what Taddeo was really saying was this: even if your charges carry some weight, they are of such seriousness that the emperor cannot simply be prejudged. He must be allowed a proper chance to defend himself, even in person. Moreover – and here was a point that made just as much impact – he had plans for restitution and for a future life of devotion to the Church that cannot simply be swept aside. When Innocent tried to ignore Frederick's generous offer of terms, the pope argued not against the terms but against Frederick's good faith. He informed Taddeo that Frederick might promise all this, but who would hold him to it? Was it not likely that the emperor would again find, as he had found when bound to go on crusade, that completion of the bargain had to be delayed, the terms altered, or their meaning disputed? No problem, said Taddeo: let the English and French kings act as guarantors. They are good choices given the close papal and imperial links to Henry III and the growing reputation of Louis IX. No again, said the pope, and for Matthew Paris a major reason was Innocent's fear that Frederick, Henry and Louis would gang up against him. Even so, Innocent was well trapped. Taddeo's arguments pushed him to an admission that the emperor must indeed be summoned to Lyons. Until the accusation of heresy was settled in public, no more, apparently, could be done. The case against Frederick was prorogued.

During early July Innocent and his advisers apparently sought a way out of the trap. They were aware that, were Frederick to appear, he would gain immediate advantage; the very act of humbly submitting to judgement would be a propaganda coup, and his presence at Lyons would make it much harder to refuse his peace terms and absolution. This does not mean Innocent's party knew the charges, colourful and scandalous as they were, to be false. They believed, rightly, in some of the accusations: the issue of the Muslim dancing-girls has already been cited; the seizure of papal lands was a fact; Frederick's treatment of the Church in Sicily had assumed the continuation of Norman rights ceded earlier by his mother. The question was not the accuracy of these charges. Frederick himself was even prepared to admit several serious errors of conduct towards the Church. The question was how far to press punishment for the charges. The emperor had already shown an unexpected degree of political masochism, accepting humiliating terms in return for peace. And peace was what some of the delegates at Lyons had thought they were coming to achieve. Peace tied to the crusade to the East was an irresistible package, as Innocent well knew. But he did not trust Frederick; he feared his presence; he believed he must be destroyed. The pope had not fled from Frederick at Narni to meet him at Lyons, even though he was undoubtedly in less physical danger at Lyons than in central Italy. Nor would the proposed settlement remove for good the underlying problem that concerned the pope's own right to judge all mankind. Agreement or compromise with Frederick, even if advantageous to the pope, still represented a sort of defeat. The pope must make plain to the world that his task was not to bargain with bullies, but to restrain them of his own accord, out of the plenitude of his power. In other words, the pope could not really reconcile himself to the idea of negotiation. The core issue was the nature of his authority as vicar of Christ. By stressing moral charges – the emperor's misconduct with his dancing-girls, his supposed scorn of orthodox belief, and so on – the papacy sought to bring him entirely under its jurisdiction, and to move away from the political issues (especially Lombardy), which contemporaries tended to see as a matter for compromise and diplomacy.

So there was only one course of action: to condemn Frederick forthwith, before he could arrive and plead his case before the papacy, the Church and the world. Frederick was moving north through Piedmont; his arrival at Lyons seemed in prospect when, on 17 July 1245, Innocent proclaimed sentence against the absentee defendant. The charges were reviewed in detail, with heavy stress on Frederick's personal life, his conduct in the *regno* and his infamous treatment of the captive cardinals. His inability to come to terms was construed as a sign of his unwillingness to do so; which was nonsense, but an effective enough way to counter Taddeo's viewpoint. Long excommunicate, the emperor was already technically subject to the terms of the decree *excommunicamus* of the fourth Lateran Council (1215); this provided that an excommunicate ruler's subjects were released from their bonds of allegiance if the ruler remained under the ban of the Church for a year and a day. Frederick had, as a matter of fact, been excommunicated far longer. Anyway, the pope announced that Frederick's subjects no longer owed him allegiance, neither in Sicily nor Italy nor Germany. Most controversial of Innocent's acts was his declaration that Frederick was now deposed from the imperial and all other thrones, and stripped of all his titles and dignities.

The deposition of an emperor: several popes had argued that they possessed the authority to remove the emperor (whom they created, according to the same argument, by the act of unction and coronation in Rome); Innocent III, in more ways than one a model for his namesake of 1245, had thrown Otto IV overboard, so that the same pope who crowned him disposed of him. Moreover, the papacy had long argued that other rulers, such as kings of Germany, duly elected by the princes but never crowned emperor, were subject to the will of the supreme pontiff. Several kings were papal vassals, and with them business was easier, at least in theory: kings of England, Sicily, Aragon and so on. As king of Sicily Frederick could be said to be subject to the corrective power of the papacy; here the argument was easier to present than to enforce. Innocent's party was not, then, making a major theoretical advance. It was the practical implications that were startling. How would other crowned heads react to interference in the rights of kings? Louis IX had already revealed his deep unease on several occasions. Yet Innocent's action would have to be explained to them; the pope could not afford to look ridiculous by imposing a sentence that most of the world rejected or ignored. And in what way did the 'deposition' affect the substance of Frederick's power? In July 1245 Innocent may have hoped to win support from rebels inside the empire, from gallant knights in England, France and Spain (whose preference would lie, however, with wars against the Saracens), maybe even from Frederick's Sicilian subjects, groaning, supposedly, under the weight of taxes, brutality and suppression of the Church. But the fact was, as Innocent perfectly well knew, that the 'deposition' was a renewed declaration of war; the imperial armies would revive their assaults on central Italy, maybe Rome itself, and on Lombardy, while the papacy's sympathizers would risk being ruthlessly destroyed.

What the 'deposition' changed most, therefore, was the mood

of the conflict. Negotiation seemed dead. War was renewed, with enthusiasm by the pope and the Guelfs, but with frustration on the part of Frederick. The emperor did not abandon interest in plans for a negotiated settlement; but he no longer expected much from them.

CHAPTER TWELVE

AN UNENDING CRUSADE, 1245–50

I

Thwarted from his plan to present himself and clear himself at Lyons, the emperor reacted with fury to the news of his deposition. He was waiting at Turin to cross the Alps, and his crowns were packed for the journey. But he ordered a treasure chest to be opened, took out a crown; and, with his eyes blazing, placed it on the head where it belonged, roaring: 'I have not yet lost my crown, neither will pope or council take it from me without a bloody war!' This was not blind fury, then: he saw clearly the obvious consequence of Innocent's action. Probably, too, long pent-up doubts about the nature of papal power received new impetus. The della Vigna arguments in favour of a blessed Church of the poor, in which the pope's functions remained purely spiritual, came to appeal to the emperor more and more. Indeed, unless he explicitly challenged the over-extension of papal authority in his own letters to European rulers, he would be made to seem, by his enemies, an unrepentant rebel against God, guilty of an abuse of power no less shocking than that of which he accused the pope.

There were still attempts to reach a negotiated settlement, but the main enthusiast henceforth was Louis of France. He was mindful not just of Frederick's warnings that his deposition was a blow to the power of all kings in Christendom. Louis was disturbed to see that Innocent showed more enthusiasm for the crusade against Frederick II, henceforth preached with vigour even in imperial lands, than for the crusade to the Nile delta to which the king of France was passionately committed – let alone the war against the Mongols. Innocent had the sense not to press his crusade preaching against Frederick very far in France, but each soldier recruited for the coming struggle against the Hohenstaufen was conceivably a soldier lost from the Nile crusade. At the end of November, therefore, Louis IX travelled to Cluny to meet the pope, begging him, over a period of several days, to accept Frederick's profession of good faith; neither now nor on the occasion of subsequent appeals did Innocent give ground. Frederick, for his part, allowed himself to be examined for heresy by some of the leading Churchmen under his rule. The examiners were convinced of the emperor's orthodoxy, and sought to convince also the pope. But Innocent was suspicious of them: when they sent an embassy to him in Burgundy, he rightly surmised that they were trying to stimulate into life wider negotiations between pope and emperor. The pope told them that the unauthorized, private examination they had conducted was not at all what was needed. Only the pope could examine Frederick on these charges and shrive him; even then, Frederick must come virtually alone, without his armies, at the behest of Pope Innocent. Underneath this already forbidding answer lay other considerations: having condemned Frederick out of hand at Lyons, Innocent was not prepared to admit that he had himself been in error. To some extent the idea that both sides had erred had been present in the provisional Rome agreement; but now the notion was greeted with horror.

What hope did the papacy have of defeating an enemy who controlled or at least ruled, Germany, the eastern bank of the Rhône, part of Lombardy and the Veneto, large areas of central Italy, as well as southern Italy, Sicily and (in theory) Sardinia and parts of the Latin East? The summoning of the faithful to fight the deposed emperor was one option; in 1245 the more fanatical members of the curia may have assumed this would achieve results. Political extremists are notoriously incapable of appreciating the indifference and hostility that their demands for self-sacrifice engender among those they seek to mobilize. But there was also a short-cut that would save human lives, at least Christian ones. Frederick's exercise of authority must henceforth, in papalist circles, be deemed illegitimate. A deposed emperor who continued to wield arbitrary power was, in the fullest sense, a tyrant: a *de facto* ruler whose power was based on violence and oppression. Thus Frederick was bracketed with Ezzelino da Romano and the other north Italian 'tyrants'. The papalists could argue themselves into a position where tyrannicide was justifiable. There is no need here to look at the lively discussion, conducted in the twelfth century by such figures as John of Salisbury, and in the thirteenth by Frederick's former subject, the brilliant Aquinas, on the legitimacy of tyrannicide. For the papal curia had good hopes that the blood of the deposed emperor would be upon Frederick's Sicilian subjects. It was apparently common knowledge that the Sicilians were irked by the regular imposition of war taxes, *collecta*, intended to fund the war in northern and central Italy. The papacy, as overlord of the *regno*, had long complained at Frederick's levying of imperial taxes year in year out (by the late 1230s, at least). In southern Italy and Sicily there was growing unrest; restrictions on economic activity, such as embargoes on sailings or tighter controls over markets and the money supply, were keenly felt in town and country. There was renewed agitation in the hills of western Sicily, where a small knot of Muslims who had evaded deportation to Lucera took up arms in 1246: an event which gave the lie to Innocent's argument that Frederick loved Saracens, and they him.

But the greatest threat to Frederick came from a conspiracy against his life, hatched by Bernardo Orlando Rossi, the pope's brother-in-law but also, until early 1246, a confidant of the emperor. His associates were leading government officials, south Italian bureaucrats who had served Frederick as imperial vicars in central Italy, or in one case as *podestà* of Parma, and as administrators in the *regno*. They were representatives of that group of well-born but dependent loyalists, created by the emperor as a result of his reorganization of the *regno* since 1220. Guglielmo di Sanseverino, for example, was a major landholder in Apulia and member of a family that gave loyal aid to the rulers of southern Italy throughout the thirteenth century; Giacomo di Morra had administered the march of Ancona for the emperor, while his father had been one of the emperor's inner circle of advisers twenty years earlier. It was an over-ambitious conspiracy, however: news leaked to the household of the count of Caserta, a son-in-law of the emperor. While Frederick was at Grosseto, in

Tuscany, on his way southwards, the plot was unveiled to him. Whoever told Frederick may also have told the conspirators that the game was up. Two plotters, Pandolfo di Fasanella and Giacomo di Morra, escaped from the imperial court before hands could be laid on them. Their destination is revealing: Rome, where Innocent's representatives sheltered them without qualms. Other conspirators were already in southern Italy. For them the failure of the plot meant a grimmer fate. They tried to occupy the strong-points of Sala and Capaccio, determined to resist to the end. Maybe they vainly hoped that the whole of southern Italy would explode in wrath behind them. The fall of Sala and eventually of Capaccio brought the conspirators the expected fate. Guglielmo di Sanseverino and his friends were horribly mutilated, burnt or cut to pieces. The bodies of the traitors were sent to the south Italian towns to remind Frederick's subjects of their abject crime. There did survive pockets of resistance for a time, for instance among the Saracens of Sicily, but the plot had fizzled out with only the murmurings of rebellion. In 1246 the emperor spent several months cleaning up such opposition as there was, mostly not so much generated by sympathy for the conspirators or the pope, as by ill-feeling at the growing tax demands of an increasingly penurious government. It has sometimes been stressed that the troubles of 1246 mark the beginning of a road leading to the much more violent outbreak of rebellion in 1282, known as the Sicilian Vespers; there again resentment at over-taxation and over-government lit the fuse. Predictably, however, the emperor's response to the grumbles of 1246 was to tighten the screws of government rather than to loosen them; a new master justiciar in charge of the whole kingdom, with powers to deputize for the emperor, was created in 1246. There was a feeling that the imperial court must keep close watch on the *regno*; its loyalty, and even that of its leading officials, could no longer be assured. Frederick's awareness of the fickleness of his courtiers affected him profoundly. The conspiracy, and subsequent defections, proved successful in one sense: he felt more isolated; his confidence in his ability to organize and sustain resistance to Innocent IV was sapped.

Yet he was convinced that the conspiracy did not simply have its origins within the *regno*; nor in Parma where the rebels

obtained further succour and recruits among the Guelf opposition. It was not a tax revolt; it was (he believed) a papally
inspired assassination attempt. There is no doubt that Innocent
IV approved of the conspirators: he actually wrote to congratulate Pandolfo di Fasanella and Giacomo di Morra on their
escape from the emperor, and later on seems to have expressed
the hope that the rebels at Capaccio could be freed with the help
of Roman troops. He assured the cardinals still in Rome that
they were right to protect the conspirators. Whether Innocent
IV knew of and encouraged the plot to murder Frederick is
another matter. He may have wished to keep his hands clean. He
and his cardinals in Rome were certainly anxious in 1246 to raise
money for an attack on the *regno*. However, it is difficult to see
whether this formed part of a wider plan for the takeover of
southern Italy, by invasion, rebellion and subversion; or whether
the pope was attempting to coordinate his moves with those of
the conspirators, so that the Romans would head south on the
news of Frederick's assassination. Plans for an invasion of the
regno were not new – Gregory's links with Genoa and Venice
reveal as much – and they did not die even when Frederick
discovered the plot against his life. Evidence cited by Hampe
supposedly implicating Innocent in the plot, in the form of an
enigmatic letter from one of the Roman cardinals to the pope,
actually postdates the plot's exposure; the letter seems to talk, in
convoluted language, of the liberation either of the entire *regno*
or of the conspirators holed up at Sala and Capaccio in defiance
of the emperor. In reality, the main evidence that Innocent was
behind the plot is provided by Frederick himself, who is not the
most reliable source for events at the papal court; moreover,
Frederick is very guarded in what he says. He informed Henry III
of England that he was safe, but that the conspiracy had its roots
in the wild promises of him 'who is known to be our enemy',
one whom it was better not to name, though all knew of his
complicity in the affair. Innocent had, Frederick believed, lured
members of the imperial staff to his side by dangling high office
or other rewards in a conquered southern Italy. This is quite
possibly true: within a brief period, Innocent was to win some
allies in southern Italy by promises of lands and privileges to
adherents of the papal cause; but these were people who had

already shown their dislike of Frederick, even fleeing from the *regno*. More importantly, Frederick insisted that captured rebels said they had opposed the emperor for the sake of Mother Church; surely, Frederick argued, this was evidence that the pope stood behind their actions? Actually, rebellion in the name of the Church could signify something else, no less discomforting to Frederick: the act of deposition and the long propaganda war had undermined the emperor's support in southern Italy; and it does not follow from the rebels' stand against Frederick that they were all involved in a murder plot, merely that they saw in Innocent's decrees a licence to take up arms against their deposed overlord.

Thus it has to be concluded that, while the pope would have liked the conspiracy to succeed, he was not necessarily its instigator. More probably, he made no effort to stop the plot once he heard of it from his agents in central Italy. He had already washed his hands of Frederick in 1245. The taking of the life of the heretic ex-emperor was not a matter for disapproval. Aware, however, of the criticism that open encouragement of assassination would generate, he kept as far as possible out of the affair. The cardinals in Rome were the prime agents. Yet there was certainly talk in Burgundy of the fate that was supposed to await Frederick. A German bishop seems to have picked up gossip at the papal court to the effect that Frederick's own courtiers would before long turn against their master and kill him; when this talk came to Frederick's ears, he assumed that this was further proof of Innocent's wicked designs. More probably, it was wishful thinking on the part of the pope's followers, anxious to persuade an imperial bishop that there was no point in Germany standing behind this Babylonish despot, whose days were clearly numbered.

II

The other way of trying to destroy Frederick was to preach a crusade against him: a slow process with uncertain outcome, especially now that the French king was stressing the priority of his own crusade to the East. But the idea of a crusade against the lay enemies of the Church within western Europe posed other problems, too. The papal curia had always argued that Jerusalem was only one of the legitimate targets of the holy war in defence of Christendom; to the war against the Moors in Spain and against the pagans of the Baltic had been extended, since the twelfth century, the same privileges as were granted to crusaders bound for the Levant: indulgences promising remission of sins, the protection of the property of those absent on crusade, and so on. By 1200 canon lawyers had much to say on the status of the crusader as an armed pilgrim under the protection of the Church. Even quicker to develop, among the knighthood of western Europe, were ideas of a holy duty to defend Christ's inheritance, or the Mother Churches of Spanish Christianity, and to extend Christianity by the sword in eastern Europe. Frederick II and Gregory IX both gave full support to the crusade of the Teutonic Knights against the Baltic pagans; but the focus of knightly outlook tended to be the crusade to Jerusalem. The summoning of a crusade against the Albigensian heretics in southern France, in 1208–9, and the threats of crusades against lay leaders such as Markward von Anweiler, made ample sense to the theorists of crusading in Rome; but insofar as the Albigensian war did attract crusaders, many of them were fortune-seekers interested in lands in the target area, Languedoc, or knights who, having taken crusade vows already (say, to liberate Jerusalem) were anxious to redeem those vows more easily by offering the requisite forty days' service in southern France. Few stayed beyond that time to help the leader, Simon de Montfort, in his attempts to uproot heresy and to consolidate a new order. Vituperative criticism of the conduct of this war from the Languedoc troubadours – themselves not heretics, it must be stressed – damaged further the image of the crusade against the internal foe.

Against this, there were the curialists, aware that the arguments used to justify the shedding of blood by Christians did not refer solely to the war for Jerusalem, southern Spain or the Baltic. The theologians pointed to the discussion of how to treat heresy in Augustine's *City of God*: 'Compel them to come in.' The canon lawyers argued that violence was a final sanction where an offender refused to accept the judgement and jurisdiction of a just authority (a modern analogy would be the right of bailiffs to use a reasonable amount of coercion in the removal of a debtor's goods). In the wake of Gregory IX's studies of canon law, the 'Decretalists' debated the nature of just and holy wars; prominent among them were Hostiensis and Sinibaldo de' Fieschi – the latter familiar already as Pope Innocent IV. F. H. Russell has remarked, 'when Innocent in practice and Hostiensis in theory called all Christians to the aid of the Church and freed imperial vassals from their oaths of fidelity, they were demonstrating the judicial theory of wars waged on direct papal initiative for the sake of the faith.' Indeed, it was Hostiensis who argued that the *crux cismarina*, the crusade within Europe, was even more just and reasonable than the *crux transmarina*, the crusade to the East. The gangrene of heresy or disobedience to the Church threatened to putrify Christendom from within; it was (as the papal letters often stressed) in more urgent need of cure than the threat from Islam; nor could Islam be faced effectively while Christendom itself was in ill-health. Such ideas have already been encountered in Innocent III's appeals for a crusade against Markward von Anweiler. They underpin Innocent IV's obstinate refusal to listen to St Louis' pleas for peace: Innocent IV appreciates King Louis' desire for success in the Nile delta, but believes that the threat from the enemy of Christ rampaging in Italy is far more pressing than that from the sultan of Egypt. In the second place, Innocent stands by his authority as overseer of all Christians. The crusade launched by Innocent IV against Frederick II was firmly rooted in the principle that the pope had the right to dissolve the bonds of fealty that tied Frederick's vassals to him, to depose Frederick from his kingdoms and to declare as God's work the war against him. In the same years the canonists were adducing arguments of this nature to deal in their treatises with supposedly hypothetical cases of contumacious rulers. But they were certainly aware of the applicability of their views to the Holy Roman Emperor.

To understand Innocent IV's approach to the problem of an anti-Staufen crusade we must return briefly to the pontificate of Gregory IX. For it was then that tentative steps were taken in the direction of such a crusade. It has been seen that the war of 1228–9 was not preached as a crusade; the sign of those who fought Frederick's forces was the crossed keys of St Peter, but not the cross; indeed, to their consternation, the soldiers of the keys found themselves facing professed crusaders, wearing the crusaders' cross, followers of a crusading emperor. The confusion of the war of the keys was not repeated in 1239–40. Gregory's insistence that Frederick consorted with Saracens at the Muslim colony of Lucera was one propaganda point intended to show Christendom that the Saracen foe lived in Italy as well as Syria or Spain; it was one plank in the crusading platform Pope Gregory was trying to build. The second plank was the argument in defence of Rome as a holy city, in some respects comparable to Jerusalem; the exhibition of the relics of Sts Peter and Paul at the height of Gregory's struggle with the emperor was calculated to impress this point on the Romans at least. But it has been seen that even the Genoese sailors who accompanied the ill-fated prelates south towards Rome took the cross in defence of the Church when battle loomed. A further plank in the platform was the decision to appeal to the monarchs of Europe for aid against Frederick II. Gregory's war, and the extension of crusading privileges, was to a large degree conditional on the pope's ability to finance an effective campaign. In England, foreign clergy holding benefices were ordered to pay one-fifth of their revenue to the pope; the English clergy too was asked for a handsome subvention. All this met strenuous opposition: Matthew Paris portrays Henry III cringing before papal demands with the words, 'I do not wish or dare to oppose the lord pope in anything.' As on the other occasions, it was objected that the emperor had not been condemned by a Church council. There was also a fear of creating an evil custom, since the English Church had already, reluctantly, made contributions to the war of the keys in 1228, on the understanding that such demands would not in fact be repeated. Some of the English money collected in 1239–40, such as it was, may have been aboard the Genoese ships seized by the Sicilians and Pisans in 1241.

A further means to turn the crusade into reality was the preaching of the cross in areas where the papacy might hope to win sympathetic ears: Lombardy, most notably. The privileges normally associated with those who abandoned their homes and property to fight for Jerusalem were dangled before the citizens of Milan; their own willingness to fight was not, perhaps, in doubt, and this was as much a way to boost morale as to boost recruitment. More ambitious was an attempt in 1241 to organize the preaching of the cross in Hungary. Giovanni de Civitella, Gregory's legate there, permitted Hungarians who had vowed to go to Jerusalem to commute their vows and to direct their energies instead against Frederick II. They would have to surrender the sum of money they would have spent travelling to and from the Holy Land, upon which a new indulgence would be issued in their favour. It is possible, therefore, that they were not actually being asked to join the anti-imperial armies; it was the funds that the pope was keenest to have. The Hungarians, however, were more worried about events in the East than about Frederick; the East was coming perilously close, too, as their country felt the first waves of the Mongol advance into central Europe. Preaching campaigns in Germany met with no greater success; quite apart from the hostility of the princes, it was difficult for the friars to preach disaffection or a crusade to a population at best indifferent, at worst openly critical of papal meddling in imperial politics.

Thus under Gregory IX the anti-Staufen crusade was not, in fact, preached very widely. What is significant is the gradual move from a 'war of the keys', modelled on the crusade, fought in defence of Rome and the Church, to a full crusade whose hallmark was the granting of the special privileges of a crusader, the indulgence for remission of sins and the wearing of the crusader's cross. It is under Innocent IV that the range of the preaching greatly enlarges. From the Council of Lyons onwards, the crusade is preached vigorously in Germany and northern Italy; again and again it is stressed that those who join the campaign will acquire the privileges normally associated with the journey to the Holy Land. For the papacy was aware that Jerusalem still held the greatest appeal; the crusade within Europe against the papacy's enemies (generally called by modern historians the 'political crusade') needed energetic sales techniques. Though seen by the canonists as perfectly legitimate, it was, in practical terms, a novelty, and audiences must be convinced of its desirability and urgency. Success was quite limited in Germany. In 1248 the pope was pressing a group of Frisians who had vowed to join St Louis' crusade to commute their vows and join instead the war against Frederick II: 'For this they receive the same indulgence as if they were going to Jerusalem.' But many or most of the Frisians demurred. It was to the East they wanted to go, and Innocent could not in the end stand in their way. In November 1247 Innocent wrote to his legate in Germany to express his glee at the recruitment of fifteen German knights and five French ones who were willing to commute their vows, and fight Frederick rather than the Egyptians. No names are given; there is no indication that the crusaders are knights of special distinction. Excitement at the recruitment of twenty volunteers in the war against Frederick suggests that knights were not coming in great numbers to aid the cause of the Church. As early as 1246 the cross against Frederick was also being preached in Denmark and Poland, but there is no sign that this produced troops keen to serve in Germany against the emperor.

Greater success was met, as before, in Lombardy. Gregorio di Montelongo put much energy into the preaching of the cross among the Guelfs; as before, too, this only involved confirming the adhesion of those already well-disposed to the papal cause. A significant by-product of the preaching was, however, the formation of Guelf confraternities, for example at Parma: groups of knights and citizens who were granted some of the privileges of crusaders; and swore to pursue the struggle against the Hohenstaufen and against heresy. Such confraternities helped tighten the grip of the papal loyalists over the government of the Lombard and Tuscan towns held by Guelf factions; but it should be stressed that, as ever in north Italian affairs, their interest lay as much in settling scores with Ghibelline or other rivals as it did in pursuing the struggle with Frederick II. Interesting, too, is the stress the confraternities laid on the suppression of heresy. In part, this was a reaction to the pope's characterization of Frederick II, Ezzelino da Romano, Uberto Pallavicini and other war-lords as heretics and church-destroyers. But the mood of the Lombard League was increasingly hostile to heresy within the town walls – popular heresy such as Catharism, which Frederick himself had worked hard to eradicate, and which he had told Gregory IX was the real menace in northern Italy. Since 1233 the Milanese began to persecute heretics in their midst. The Lombards, as would-be allies and then real allies of the papacy, were anxious to eradicate anti-papalists within the cities; and the enthusiasm of the Guelfs in the struggle against heresy probably did more in the next decade to destroy Catharism and other movements in north and central Italy than the Albigensian crusade had achieved in its forty-year history. Florence, once a great centre of Catharism, now bristled with confraternities, ceased quarrelling with Rome, and embarked on a devoutly Guelf career.

To England Innocent looked yet again for another type of aid for his crusade: money. Henry III's position as papal vassal and imperial brother-in-law was uncomfortable. In the summer of 1246 King Henry gave way to the bitter opposition of his spiritual and lay barons, and forbade the export of funds in aid of the Roman Church. Matthew Paris relates that the king had recourse instead to covert action in aid of the papacy. Some of the bishops agreed to defuse the crisis by supplying, in secret, small groups of knights – five to fifteen per see – who would join the papal armies and be maintained at the expense of their English patron for a whole year. If knights could not be sent, money would be dispatched in lieu. But even if ten or twelve bishops and abbots participated in the scheme, it could hardly have produced many soldiers. Nor was Innocent helping his vassal the king of England. Henry's involvement in Sicilian and imperial affairs as defender of papal rights was to turn sour in the 1250s when the English barons reacted with fury at half-baked and high-costing plans to place his infant son Edmund on the throne of Sicily. The demands from Rome in 1228, 1239 and 1246 helped set Henry III on his disastrous course towards bitter political and constitutional conflict with his barons.

The decision of Pope Innocent IV to take much further Gregory IX's appeals for a crusade against Frederick was of momentous importance. It represents the first large-scale attempt to use the crusade as an instrument for the defeat of the papacy's political enemies within western Europe. It is true that, as with the Albigensian crusade of 1209, the papacy emphasized the threat from heresy. But now the heresy was not a fairly widespread popular movement; it was the reputed, unproven, scorn for the papal keys and for Christian tenets of a ruler who contested the theory of Petrine supremacy and who had laid hands on papal lands in central Italy, who was a wilful vassal as king of Sicily and a known friend of Muslims and disbelievers. Alongside Frederick, Ezzelino da Romano and Uberto Pallavicini were also cited; their blasphemies and outrages against churches and human beings were not difficult to document. Frederick's own conduct might or might not add up to heresy, but his attempts to clear himself of the charge had been dismissed out of hand. Yet it is noticeable how the papacy, still unsure of the response its appeal would receive, loaded on board its pleas for a crusade many of the traditional arguments used in the preaching of more 'conventional' types of crusade. The war against the emperor was a war against Muslims, for the Lucera Saracens had played a major role in the central Italian campaigns of the Hohenstaufen; was it not frightful that the infidel, once upon a time cleared from the soil of Italy, could now parade within sight of Rome? The war against Frederick was also part and parcel of the war against Egypt: did he not correspond with the sultan of Egypt? Was he not known for his alliance with al-Kamil, under the terms of which he had conducted his own parody of a crusade? Actually Pope Innocent also corresponded with the sultan of Egypt, hoping to isolate Frederick in the Mediterranean; but Egypt was also the proposed target for St Louis' crusade, and this was just the moment to fling mud at Frederick, accusing him of subverting the French king's plans. Frederick could then be presented as the obvious first objective of any serious attempt to re-establish Christianity in the central and eastern Mediterranean. Mud may be flung, but it does not always stick. Louis IX's attitude remained detached. But the papal curia remained fascinated with the idea that Jerusalem could not be redeemed until its enemies in southern Italy and Sicily were destroyed; the argument became a central one in the planning and preaching of further political crusades against the Hohenstaufen and, later in the thirteenth century, their Aragonese successors.

Alongside the crusade, with its promises of spiritual reward, there were other good offers available to those the papacy tried to woo in the 1240s. Remission of sins was vaguely promised to those who supported the pope in Germany by backing rival claimants to the throne; rewards were material too. The large number of papal letters addressed to Germany and granting plaintiffs the right to marry within the prohibited degrees of kinship reflects an attempt by the curia to gain support among the German nobility. One early beneficiary of this policy was Henry Raspe, landgrave of Thuringia, soon to become leader of the opposition to Frederick II. But individual contacts of this type could only be achieved gradually and piecemeal. Nor did the lure always work: the nobles gained what they wanted, but were not necessarily keen to do the pope's bidding once the wedding was over. In southern Italy, Innocent won allies by promising to return or enlarge the estates of exiled barons, such as the conspirators against the emperor, or by granting franchises to the towns. But many of the beneficiaries were enemies of Frederick already; most of the towns ignored what was on offer, much as their citizens would have valued communal freedom. In central Italy, too, the pope heaped favours on real or potential supporters: towns were exempted from provincial taxes due to the holy see, or their military obligations were reduced in a carefully judged attempt to ensure their loyalty as volunteers in the papal cause; this was no different a policy to that adopted by Frederick in Lombardy, towards Ghibelline cities. Towns such as Spoleto were promised a share in the trade of southern Italy, which in 1245 Innocent still hoped to conquer; besides, as overlord of both the duchy of Spoleto and the kingdom of Sicily, the pope was in no doubt of his ability to issue such privileges. Yet turning them into reality was more than he could manage. Most peculiar of all was Innocent's wooing of the port of Ancona, which in 1245 received from him trading rights not merely in Sicily but in the Latin kingdom of Jerusalem. Innocent instructed the bishop of Acre to ensure that the rights of Ancona in the Levant were respected, but in fact it had never been a prerogative of the pope to exempt Italian merchants from the taxes of the kingdom of Jerusalem, whose king was not regarded as his vassal. It is possible that Innocent assumed responsibility over the kingdom of Jerusalem on the grounds that its king, Frederick's son Conrad of Hohenstaufen, was an absentee and an enemy; but it was an ambitious extension of papal rights, none the less. Even so, this and other grants brought some of the central Italian towns more decisively into the papal camp.

No more phoney wars then, no more jostling for position

while negotiations (in which Frederick at least placed some hope) were kept half-alive. In 1245 Innocent IV sought to organize the whole of Christendom in support of his struggle against Frederick II. He did not see himself as a mere refugee, precariously living on the edge of Frederick's territories, forbidden from crossing into France. What remained to him was his power to command. Innocent could not believe that Germany, Italy and Sicily would spurn him.

III

The crusade against Frederick was evidently no more than the means to an end. Innocent IV's correspondence leaves little doubt as to that end. In Germany, the Hohenstaufen dynasty was to be swept aside. In Sicily and southern Italy, papal suzerainty was to be turned into reality: either by direct rule or through the agency of a loyal vassal. Even in 1245–6, Innocent was issuing decrees for the kingdom of Sicily (such as the trade privileges just cited) on the assumption that supreme authority reverted into his hands on the deposition of the secular ruler of the *regno*. In northern Italy the Guelfs were to be encouraged to swallow up their many rivals – Ghibelline factions within the towns, Ghibelline towns and regions under the rule of Ezzelino and other 'tyrants'. Then, with a new order established in Europe, the business of the Church in the East could at last receive serious attention. It was a massive programme, and attempts at its realization shaped the next hundred years in Italy and the empire.

In Germany the pope met with considerable ill-feeling against his interference. He miscalculated if he thought the German princes would submit to a higher authority and agree either to the deposition of one they had chosen, or to the election in his place of a ruler slavishly loyal to St Peter. They had struggled for centuries to assert their own rights as makers and unmakers of emperors; the fact that the pope eventually crowned their choices in Rome was, to them, of less significance than their original act of choice. Only some of the Rhineland electors, the archbishops of Mainz, Cologne and Trier, gave solid support to the pope in his attempt to make real Frederick's deposition. The Rhineland was a trouble-spot of Frederick henceforth, but the degree of opposition must not be exaggerated. The emperor believed that a rapid campaign would be sufficient to quell opposition. Moreover, the ecclesiastical princes could not elect one of their own number to a throne; in consequence they had to find lay nobles willing to support the pope's venture. Nor was this easy. The bullying of the German clergy, and the bribing of minor princes, lay and spiritual, achieved slow results: an evaporation of positive enthusiasm for the Hohenstaufen, but not a major revolt against the emperor. The pro-papal electors settled on the landgrave of Thuringia, Henry Raspe, as their leader and he was solemnly elected king of the Romans in 1246. He even scored a victory over Frederick's son Conrad at Frankfurt in August, 1246. But this was a battle between the most committed supporters of either side, and indicated nothing about the future allegiance of the greater princes. And when the hireling Henry died suddenly in 1247 his lands passed in any case to Frederick's allies of the house of Meissen. Precarious indeed, was the strength of the rebels. Were the emperor to appear in person, the papalists might well pack their arms and flee. In 1246, too, Frederick took advantage of the death of his namesake the duke of Austria, whom he had long been trying to tame, and placed Austria under direct imperial rule. Though Frederick Babenberg may well have been impressed by the papal propaganda directed at the German princes, he had played no serious part in the resistance to Frederick of Hohenstaufen. The only effect of the papal attacks on the emperor had been to make the duke of Austria think twice about a plan for marriage alliance with the Hohenstaufen; his niece was to marry the emperor, a widower for the third time. The marriage never took place, but Frederick II still secured his ends, obtaining control of Austria by these more direct means.

It can thus be seen that imperial policy in Germany, more or less consistently sustained over thirty years, paid off well. The greater princes were not disposed to overthrow one who had granted them extraordinary rights of exemption, bringing towns and revenues under their control. Even the bishops saw advantages in the continuation of Hohenstaufen rule, a few Rhenish exceptions apart. For it was they who had been the first beneficiaries of Frederick's generosity in Germany, and they wanted to keep papal interference in their own affairs to an absolute minimum. Even to be asked to contribute to the costs of the anti-Staufen crusade was embarrassment enough; they were being urged to compromise their loyalty by the surrender of their funds, but there was no guarantee of a return on their investment. If there was one problem that threatened Frederick's standing in Germany, it was of a quite different nature. The Mongol hordes were uncomfortably close to the lands of the German princes; they wanted and expected the emperor to lead his armies against this tremendous peril. His campaigns in Italy irked them. But their irritation was primarily expressed in their reluctance to send large numbers of troops south of the Alps. Frederick was no Otto the Great, able to convince his German subjects of his right to rule by a massive victory over the enemy in the East – in the tenth century the enemy had been the Magyars, in the thirteenth it was the Mongols. But equally the German princes could gain little comfort from a pope who placed the proposed civil war in Germany above the war for the defence of Europe against the Tartar menace. However, the threat from the Mongols reached its peak between 1242 and 1244; by 1245 the immediate emergency was over. The princes could still feel aggrieved that help had not come when they demanded it, but there was no chance, either for an anti-king to seize the initiative by attempting to lead an army against the Tartars at political expense to Frederick.

Failing to win Germany, Innocent continued to nurture plans for a takeover of power in the *regno*. Here he could try to fan ill-feeling towards a powerful, demanding bureaucracy, anxious to raise war taxes in support of the emperor. The failure of the 1246 plot revealed how narrow Innocent's support base in southern Italy in fact was. But it is clear that he still hoped for an invasion of the south by the Romans, Genoese, Venetians and other Italians. In 1248 we find the pope legislating for the unconquered kingdom, revoking the acts of Frederick II concerning the Church in Sicily and southern Italy, and stressing the extensive rights of exemption of priests from the secular courts of the kingdom. Even cases of high treason were to be dealt with by ecclesiastical courts if the defendant were clergy. Moral offences by laymen, such as adultery, were to be judged by ecclesiastical courts. The attempts Frederick and the Normans had made to revive Byzantine marriage legislation, bringing marital affairs within the realm of secular courts, were soundly rebutted. All this amounted to a blueprint for an ecclesiastically directed state in which the ruler would be carefully circumscribed, treated as a mere agent of his suzerain the pope. No doubt Innocent hoped also to impress the Sicilian bishops and abbots by appearing to offer them powers that Frederick had long denied them, at least in practice. However, the south Italian clergy was in large measure unimpressed. Many were the emperor's placemen anyway. Berardo, archbishop of Palermo, was among the excommunicate's constant companions.

Innocent's blueprint provided that spiritual lords who did not hold property or rights from the king of Sicily were not to be liable for oaths of fealty to the king; some of the great monasteries, such as Montecassino itself, might thus find themselves in an advantageous position, becoming virtually autonomous principalities dependent directly on Rome. But another implication of this provision is that the *regno* would still need a lay ruler once conquered. Innocent may have toyed with the idea of direct rule, and in some respects was still proposing it – in the form of direct control over important legislation and potentially over extensive Church lands – but in essence he followed the lead of his namesake forty years earlier. A papal champion was needed who would act faithfully at Rome's bidding, guaranteeing the safety of the holy city from which St Peter's successor was now a refugee; who would prosecute vigorously the crusade in Syria, Greece and Africa and repress rebellions by sympathizers of the Hohenstaufen. It is known that in winter 1249–50 the pope made inordinate efforts to charm Richard, earl of Cornwall; Henry III's brother was summoned to the papal court at Lyons for discussions, and aroused the unquenchable curiosity of Matthew Paris. The chronicler talks of long, secret sessions between pope and earl and suggests elsewhere that Innocent's ambition was to seat Richard on the Sicilian throne; approaches were certainly made to him twice after the death of Frederick II. Richard's wealth and energy qualified him for the post of papal champion; the mood at Henry III's court had, besides, turned against Frederick with the arrival of persistent tax demands from the Roman curia, accompanied by vitriolic attacks on the emperor himself. Moreover, Isabella had now died, and Henry III may have felt less disposed to support Frederick as his brother-in-law; in any case, the English court could not point to clear advantages gained from a marriage alliance that had, if anything, proved an embarrassment in relations with the pope. It is therefore not inconceivable that Earl Richard was highly tempted by Innocent's offer. It has been objected that the activation of such an offer would have involved the dispossession of Richard's nephew, Henry, son of Isabella, whom Frederick hoped at this time to have as successor in the *regno*; the boy had still not been baptised, and Frederick was to use this fact as bait to the papacy – more of this in a moment. It is also known that Frederick and Richard had in the past seen eye to eye over the need to draw up a negotiated settlement between papacy and empire. Matthew Paris himself suggested that Richard could not have wanted to supplant his nephew: '*inhonestum videretur nepotem suum Henricum supplantare.*' What is quite possible is that Innocent offered to back Richard in a conquest of southern Italy in which Henry would be declared king of Sicily, but Richard would act as the boy's guardian, and as regent deputizing for the papacy. For, although the pope would occasionally demand the extinction of the whole race, or *stirps*, of the Hohenstaufen, he was also prepared, as later events revealed, to make use of Frederick's close relatives if that seemed the quickest road to success. We should not expect great consistency in the pope's actions, anyway. His determination to win a struggle for which, as he was well aware, the holy see was ill-equipped led him to experiment with all sorts of possibilities. What was consistent was not the method, but the goal: to turn into reality the declaration of Frederick's deposition at the Council of Lyons.

IV

Frederick's success in suppressing conspiracy and rebellion in southern Italy, during 1246, released him for urgent tasks in northern and central Italy from which he had been distracted.

Winter was not yet over when, in 1247, he crossed the borders of the kingdom of Sicily and moved northwards through the papal state. He was reluctant to linger there, not because he feared the threat of papal armies, but because he identified Lombardy as his target. He proposed to cross the Alps, meet the German princes, confirm their support, and organize from there his major campaign for the suppression of his foes. In other words, he did wish to draw together subjects from all his dominions in a once-for-all assault on the allies of the papacy. In the duchy of Spoleto there were, it is true, papal troops under the leadership of two cardinals, Stephen of Santa Maria in Trastevere and Rainier of Viterbo, but they had already suffered serious defeats as early as 1246. In Lombardy too Enzo of Sardinia was keeping the Guelfs under serious pressure; the Guelfs of Parma, sympathizers with the recent conspiracy, were scattered (or captured), and imperial power seemed re-established. The emperor knew, however, that the maintenance of this position must depend on his ability to counter papal moves; if the pope did stir up Germany, for instance, this would act as a direct signal to the Guelf rebels in Lombardy. The situation was, then, promising but still precarious.

Frederick's awareness that his ascendancy could not yet be assured was one factor that made him receptive to further peace calls from the ever-hopeful king of France. Besides, the emperor's feeling that true peace could only be established by sincere agreement between himself and the pope had never been thrown away, merely put in store. Frederick rejected in his correspondence with King Louis any notion that he would not respect the spiritual authority of the pope. He insisted he was still ready to send his representatives to Lyons to discuss peace terms, though it sounds as if the emperor was reluctant to make a move before he had met his German princes. He knew well that their visible support for him, even if expressed in no more than a public meeting with one whom they continued to see as their ruler, would strengthen his hand in dealings with the papal curia. Frederick continued, too, to hope that the less fanatical cardinals would temper Innocent's fury. Frederick even claimed he had allies at the papal court who were predicting a real peace, which would culminate in the baptism by the pope himself of his son Henry, titular king of Sicily. This sanguine approach is visible

again in late 1246, when Frederick seems actually to have envisaged a journey across the Alps to Lyons, for face-to-face
negotiations with the pope. It is clear that the French court lay
behind these hopes. It is probable, too, that Frederick bruited
about reports of his peace terms, which were almost impossibly
generous. He would leave Europe for the Holy Land and spend
the rest of his days there, if only the pope agreed to crown
Conrad as emperor in his stead and to revoke the excommunication of Frederick, as well as to pardon all his supposed
crimes or to dismiss them as mere rumour. Matthew Paris, in
reporting these terms, insists that King Louis of France was in-
furiated by the pope's rejection of these demands. What more
could Innocent want of him? Actually, the pope was convinced
that Frederick aimed to impose his will on the curia at Lyons, by
brute force. Louis IX was urged to protect the pope from seizure,
and the French king, ever anxious to maintain his neutrality,
agreed that he would not tolerate the occupation of so sensitive a
border town as Lyons by an imperial army. But he was by no
means prepared to fight Innocent's wars for him.

Innocent's approach to the problem of negotiations was unbending. He insisted that he could not negotiate if Frederick, or
indeed Conrad, continued to ignore his act of deposition and his
other bans against the Hohenstaufen. He would discuss terms
with an ex-emperor only. In saying this, he of course acknowledged indirectly that he had not succeeded in deposing Frederick
from his *de facto* position as emperor. In the winter of 1246–7,
therefore, Innocent had to work very hard to make sure his arch-
enemy stayed south of the Alps. This could best be done by
stirring up Lombardy to such an extent that Frederick was
tempted to stop there and combat the rebels. But it was a risky
ploy: would the Lombards, faced by an imperial army, wish to
act as front line in the papacy's war? In the past, at Cortenuova,
they had cut and run. In Cardinal Ottaviano degli Ubaldini, a
youthful and worldly prelate, Innocent found the war-lord he
needed. The cardinal earned his standing at the papal court from
his great personal influence in Tuscany, where his family held
extensive estates, rather than from his expertise in law and
theology. He fancied himself as a general, though his military
skills were to prove much more limited than his diplomatic. He

was not one on whom to rely; he would save his own skin before he saved the pope's, if matters came to a head. And indeed his grand entry into Italy in summer 1247, with a decent following of troops, failed to bring military glory. Having reached the mountains of Piedmont he discovered that the local princes were newly favourable to Frederick II; Frederick's bastard son Manfred had recently married a princess of the house of Savoy, and the lord of Montferrat, the most powerful landowner in north-western Italy, had followed Savoy into the imperial camp. So poor Ottaviano was bottled up in the western Alps, and the authority of the imperialists could now be seen to stretch right across the Alps towards the Rhône and – in the far distance – Lyons itself. It seemed that the Italian princes were clear in their mind that Frederick was the impending victor in the contest.

What helped Innocent IV far more than the cardinal's mock heroics was the ancient Guelf–Ghibelline rivalry in Lombardy. Although Parma was known to be pro-imperial, the city's loyalty had never been assured: the papacy, acting through Bernardo Orlando Rossi, had managed to cause an upset there during the conspiracy of 1246 against the emperor's life. Further funds sent to Parma and the Parmigiano won back the adherence of the city's Guelfs. The result was that Gregorio di Montelongo found Parma an easy prize; it fell smoothly into papalist hands and tied itself in alliance to the Lombard League. The blow to Frederick's influence was the greater since Parma lay in a key position between the Cisa pass, giving access to the Arno valley and Tuscany, and the wide Lombard plain, giving access to the emperor's prime Lombard foe, Milan. As a matter of fact, Frederick's son Enzo had been keeping an eye on Parma when it fell; he was away from Parma when the papal army arrived there and could do little more than appeal urgently to his father for help. Meanwhile he sought to isolate the city from further papal reinforcements, by imposing a blockade; Ottaviano degli Ubaldini, for instance, had at last reached the Lombard plain, but he again was blocked. This time Ezzelino da Romano was there to prevent him proceeding further. In any case Ottaviano was believed to be in contact with the enemy; whether through caution or through treason, the cardinal seemed content to remain stuck. He took little advantage of such opportunities as presented themselves to break through to Parma.

Gregorio di Montelongo realized that the blockade around Parma was likely to suffocate the city. He resolutely remained within. It has been seen that during this period the Guelf confraternities began to organize themselves in defence of the city, blessed with special privileges analogous to those granted to crusaders. After several weeks of siege conditions, the Parmesans began to wonder whether it was all worth it. Gregorio di Montelongo is said to have resorted to ruses to keep the complaints at bay. For instance, he summoned the principal citizens of Parma to dinner; during the meal there arrived a dusty-footed messenger from afar; weary from his journey, he delivered a letter informing the legate that help was on its way; Gregorio joyously read out the letter to his guests; and soon the news was all over Parma. But in fact Gregorio himself was author of the message, and he had simply ordered a retainer to appear at his lodgings under pretence of having come from beyond the city. The letter had the value of Billy Bunter's promise that he would shortly receive a large postal order. There were no armies on their way, just as there was no postal order.

And then, in late summer of 1247, the emperor himself came to supervise the siege of Parma. He had truly been kept south of the Alps, and for that Innocent could only be grateful. His solution to the problem of Parma suggested no comfort to the city's inhabitants. Parma's history was to come to an end; a new city, more splendid, and evocative of his impending triumph, was to be built nearby: its name was Victoria. Here was the emperor, within sight of Parma, fulfilling his functions as highest ruler on earth with the foundation of a replacement city, Roman in street plan, an imperial capital for this region of Italy. It is hard to believe that Victoria was ever so magnificent as generations of chroniclers wished to portray it: in one summer and autumn many of the proposed public buildings can only have been marked out on the ground – the cathedral of St Victor, the palace with its court of justice, its administrative wing, its harem and its menagerie of exotic animals. Elephants, camels, lions and cheetahs were among the first inhabitants of Victoria. It is clear from subsequent events that Victoria was not adequately fortified: it was a camp, organized on a Roman model; a city in the making, but not yet a brick and stone capital. But, as the centre of

Frederick's operations in Lombardy, it had been chosen as place of deposit for the imperial war-funds; for the imperial treasure (including the imperial crown) and robes; for *matériel de guerre*, not just arms but the vast transport army of horses, mules and oxen; for provisions, in the form of livestock and other foodstuffs; even for the imperial library, including a beautiful manuscript of a hunting-book written by the emperor himself.

And indeed Frederick had left Victoria to indulge this passion for hunting when the Parmesans struck. A false sortie by some of Parma's soldiers led the imperial garrison of Victoria out of sight of the new city. Meanwhile the rest of Parma's army, indeed most of Parma, male and female, young and old, rushed the short distance to Victoria and overpowered its remaining defenders. The imperial camp was laid waste. The emperor's quarters were raided: gold, silver, jewels, fine cloths were found in amazing quantities, and at once seized; even the imperial crown was stolen, and brought in victory to Parma cathedral. Judging from Salimbene's description, this was probably the massive crown made for Otto the Great and now preserved, along with many of Frederick II's vestments, in the Hofburg at Vienna. Off went the magnificent manuscript of his hunting-book, too; by 1264 it was in the possession of a citizen of Milan, who offered it to the mortal enemy of the Hohenstaufen, Charles of Anjou. But the worst loss was that of an individual, Taddeo da Suessa. He was seized and mutilated; his hands were cut off and then he was dragged away to an unceremonious end in Parma's prisons. It was the sort of death that the Guelfs always said Ezzelino, or indeed Frederick, liked to mete out to their victims. But Guelf standards were certainly no higher. For the emperor, the loss of Taddeo was hard to bear. His loyalty to Frederick had never been in doubt. He was a man of considerable ability, less bombastic than Piero della Vigna, but no less insistent on the basis of imperial authority in the 'revealed truths' of Roman law. He had served Frederick well as negotiator with the papacy; his appointment as imperial spokesman at Lyons in 1245 is the clearest proof of the common thinking and intense trust that bound Frederick and Taddeo.

Frederick, says Salimbene, reacted with the fury of a 'she-bear robbed of her cubs in a forest'. He returned to Victoria to find his new city smouldering and empty. But he was back again on 22 February 1248, a mere three days after the victory of the Parmesans. His sudden, confident reappearance paid off, when the joyous Guelfs panicked, leaving behind loot and captives taken at Victoria. Anxious to show that Victoria had not been totally abandoned, Frederick gathered together his forces in the vicinity of his old camp and held a 'great council' with his advisers. The council of war saw that there was no tremendous advantage to be gained in rebuilding Victoria or renewing the siege of Parma. Frederick and his generals had the foresight to realize that, if the effects of Parma's return to the Guelfs could be counteracted, the defection of Parma itself would carry little significance; and indeed the destruction of Victoria would have little strategic value to the Lombards. For the point about Parma, as has been seen already, was that from there access could be gained across the Apennines to Tuscany. The imperial forces therefore made a move south to the Cisa pass, and were able to guarantee the future free passage of Frederick's armies. In the process Orlando Rossi, former ally of Frederick, subsequent arch-conspirator, fell into the hands of the Ghibellines. The pope's brother-in-law met an end no less nasty than that of Taddeo da Suessa. The imperialists could rejoice to have out of the way a powerful and able rival.

Frederick keenly felt the insult at Parma. It was a blow to his pride and, not least, to his pocket. He was not finding it easy to raise war funds, and it was galling to see a large part of those funds fall into enemy hands. He, like his enemies, depended heavily on mercenaries, and the size of his armies was therefore directly related to the capacity of his purse. By summer 1248 he was levying an exceptional war tax in Sicily, on the Churches as well as on the laity, which was precisely the action that the papacy had long been condemning him for. Yet it would be wrong to conclude that Frederick had suffered irreversible defeat at Parma. The Guelf victory certainly gave heart to his enemies in northern and central Italy; his power seemed fragile and some towns were convinced it was crumbling already. But in fact Parma was far from sufficient a victory for the Guelfs to bring Frederick down. The war in Lombardy was still spasmodic and localized. None the less, it revealed the indifferent military management of the imperial army; the understanding of tactics, subterfuge, intelligence and basic rules of defending a position was primitive. Military judgements were haphazard and inconsistent. The war was to be won through making an impression no less than by effective military manoeuvres; Frederick was aware of this, but he neglected the military side at the expense of the political. A reluctant soldier, he had to admit after the events at Parma that even political success would now depend on striking military successes, sufficient to turn into gloom the glee of the joyous Lombards. The Parma defeat made Lombardy the urgent focus of attention. Germany, let alone Lyons, could not be visited until northern Italy was again in fear of him.

V

1248 was a year for counting losses and gains. Frederick was still smarting from events at Victoria; Innocent had still not succeeded in mobilizing Christendom. In Innocent's favour, however, was the departure during the summer, from the newly built port of Aigues-Mortes, of King Louis of France; the would-be mediator was now well on his way to Cyprus and Egypt, where delays, defeat and captivity would tie him down for several years. This left the pope freer to press ahead with his own crusade, that against Frederick. It has been seen that many, such as the Frisian crusaders, were reluctant to commute their vows to travel east into vows to fight Frederick; but henceforth Innocent's audience would be those European knights who had already decided that St Louis' crusade was not for them. Yet Innocent saw that the war against the Hohenstaufen could not be won in Germany. He tried to focus his efforts on central and southern Italy, organizing exiled Sicilian barons into an opposition force by promising them lands and titles, winning back (in the wake of Parma) some wavering towns on the south Italian frontier. A symbolic victory here was the recovery, by Rainier of Viterbo, of Jesi, where the hated emperor had been born.

The personnel of the conflict underwent major changes in 1248 and 1249. Rainier, now very aged, was unable to continue his duties as legate charged with the consolidation of papal authority in central Italy. It was clear that he would not be the right person to arrange the long-planned invasion of southern Italy. But he remained in the region, and his fanatical expertise in fanning opposition to the emperor was no doubt still appreciated. He was to die towards the end of 1250. In Germany, a new leader for the rebels was found in 1248, several months having elapsed since the early death of Henry Raspe. Count William of Holland was not a prince of high rank, and could command only patchy support in the Rhineland and parts of the Netherlands. He was constantly urging the pope to obtain more knights in his aid – the Frisian crusaders, for instance – but he never aroused great enthusiasm. He was conscientious, but hardly likely to win the support of the prince electors who were not already committed to the pope. His main interest seems to have been the incorporation of Zeeland into his patrimony of Holland; even on the Rhineland he made rather little impact. On the imperial side, too, there were important changes: King Enzo of Sardinia early in 1249 was seized in battle at Fossalta, where the Cremonesi and Modenesi were fighting the staunch Guelfs of Bologna. He had been an effective commander of Frederick's troops in northern Italy, notwithstanding errors that had left strong-points ill-defended. His liaison with Ezzelino da Romano and the other war-lords was close and valuable. The Bolognesi immured him in a fairly well-appointed prison in their Palazzo Comunale, and there he spent the rest of his days, despite constant attempts to secure his release. Such an unhappy fate at least proved a source of inspiration to the poets.

But the most dramatic fall from power was perhaps that of Piero della Vigna. Isolated already after the conspiracy of 1246 and the execution of Taddeo da Suessa, Frederick II seems to have grown increasingly suspicious of his diminishing group of close advisers. On della Vigna he had relied for over twenty years, in the formulation of his laws and policies, for the publication of his diatribes against papal injustice and for delicate diplomatic negotiations. It is often hard to be sure whether it is della Vigna's voice or the emperor's that can be heard; he was certainly seen by contemporaries as Joseph to the Pharaoh Frederick, loyally putting the emperor's plans into effect, or even controlling Frederick's realms at the emperor's expense. It is possible that he was less incorruptible than the law-books expected the emperor's officers to be; Salimbene's hostile view was that della Vigna had accumulated vast wealth, and that the emperor was desperate to lay hands on it. And Frederick was by now prepared to use all expedients to raise money. Historians delude themselves if they imagine that the 'model bureaucracy' of the Sicilian state was able to operate without the engine oil of bribes, favours and perks. The ideal system proclaimed in the emperor's legislation depended for its operation not on natural processes of reason or routine, but on human beings able and often anxious to defraud the system they controlled. Such abuses became rife when a ruler was absent from the *regno*, or distracted by his wars and diplomacy from the kingdom's internal affairs; the career of a later king of Sicily, Charles of Anjou, culminating in the revolt of the Sicilian Vespers in 1282, is a good illustration of how fine intent on the ruler's part could turn into careless neglect. So probably della Vigna was vulnerable to charges that he had salted away in his own storehouses part of the treasure the emperor now urgently needed. It is no coincidence that the charges against della Vigna arose just when Frederick was most worried at the shortage of cash available to cover his war expenses. It is also likely that della Vigna's detractors seized the opportunity to condemn a rival at court whose long and un-trammelled exercise of power must have given rise to much jealousy. It was easier to accuse della Vigna once the second of Frederick's close advisers, Taddeo da Suessa, was no more. Frederick reacted to the complaints with the suspicion that tired and isolated despots often show towards their most ancient and loyal colleagues. It was early in 1249, at Cremona, that Piero della Vigna was suddenly arrested. It seems the Cremonesi, for all their affection towards the empire, reacted with glee to the news and would gladly have lynched him. But he was spirited away to Borgo San Donnino (now called Fidenza) and then to the imperial stronghold at San Miniato in Tuscany. He was tried and condemned for his peculation; he suffered blinding; but the imprisonment was too much to bear. He beat his brains out against a stone pillar to which he was shackled. His suicide is commemorated in Dante's pregnant words:

My soul, in its disdainful mood, thinking to escape disdain by death, made me, though just, unjust against myself.

For Dante it was the envy of his contemporaries that destroyed him; della Vigna's purity of approach to government only alienated those who were unable to share his high standards.

The probability that della Vigna's detractors sowed suspicion in the already over-wary mind of the emperor makes sense. On the other hand, there must have been a variety of ideas at court, about the best future procedure. Frederick's visit to Lyons had already been mooted. Some of his advisers (depending on their origin) would wish him to concentrate on the defence of southern Italy against a possible papal invasion; others, the Lombard allies for example, would prefer to see an imperial army active again against Milan, Parma and their friends. The hostility of the citizens of Cremona to Piero della Vigna is particularly suggestive. Here were long-time allies of the emperor who seem to have had enough of della Vigna's person or policies. It is quite possible that della Vigna wished Frederick to increase the financial and military load on the North Italian allies, even, perhaps, to make real the mainly mythical powers of the imperial vicar in Lombardy, either with a view to organizing a large loyalist army or with a view to creating a revived, centralized *regnum Italicum*: something Enzo had never, as imperial vicar, really tried to do. Matthew Paris, as usual, knew more than this. He links della Vigna with another assassination attempt against Frederick II. The emperor was unwell; the treatment advised was internal and external – medicine and a fumigated bath. Della Vigna and the emperor's doctor, supposedly acting at Innocent IV's behest, added poison to the medicine and to the bath salts. But the emperor had somehow discovered something was amiss. He invited the doctor to drink half the medicine with him. In terror, the doctor managed to spill much of the medicine. But enough remained to be tried out on some captives awaiting execution. It was seen to be a fast and deadly poison. There is little real reason to credit this story. It was embezzlement, disloyalty of a different sort, that Frederick publicly announced to be della Vigna's crime. And, had there been a papally inspired plot against his life, yet again, there is no doubt Frederick would have exploited the fact in his propaganda attacks on Innocent IV. Nor, indeed, did the unseating of Piero della Vigna greatly affect the imperial propaganda effort. The protonotary had trained a new generation of publicists of comparable skill to his own.

It was, rather, the loss of Enzo that had serious results. Modena was eventually captured by Bologna; other allies, such as Como, gave way to the Lombard League's threats and bribes. The Cisa pass could no longer be held. More serious was the arrival of Pietro Capoccio, cardinal deacon of San Giorgio in Velabro, who came to central Italy to continue Rainier of Viterbo's work. By September 1249 he had advanced with a papal army to the north-eastern border of the *regno*. This was not exactly the massive invasion that Innocent IV would have liked to see, but there were hopes that the border barons of the *regno* would link their fortunes to the invaders. Such hopes were dashed on 4 October 1249 when his troops were sent scuttling back northwards after an engagement with a Sicilian army. This did not deter Capoccio from trying to recruit yet more allies north and south of the border. Innocent and his cardinal remained optimistic about likely results. The main achievement lay, however, in central Italy where the presence of papal troops brought the submission of much of the march of Ancona.

In a sense these victories were ill-advised. They drew imperial armies into central Italy, concentrating the struggle further north than the cardinal had wished. He was made to fight for survival, and the chances of a renewed attack on the *regno* became remote. In early 1250 the Sicilian army entered the march of Ancona, achieving one victory after another. At Cingoli the papal store of arms was captured, and so, very nearly, was Capoccio. He disguised himself as a mendicant and escaped through the imperial lines. Papal power in the region crumbled, and at the end of the summer the majority of towns from Ravenna down to the frontier were in imperial hands, or deprived of real freedom of action. Pietro Capoccio was ignominiously recalled. Ottaviano degli Ubaldini was sent into the field instead, a choice that augured ill for papal success. The victories of imperial armies in central Italy were, moreover, capped by successes on other fronts. Uberto Pallavicini savaged the army of Parma at Victoria in August 1250; horrid torments are supposed to have been devised in order to dispatch the hundreds of captives. There was also a significant success in Germany, where Conrad of Hohenstaufen reasserted imperial authority in those Rhineland areas that had given support to the count of Holland. Count William was not destroyed, but his power was made to appear paper-thin. Thus in 1250 Frederick's armies were able to undo much of the temporary damage that had followed from the defeat at Parma two years earlier. Major defections stopped; the papacy had been shown to be incapable of sustaining the war against the emperor in Italy. It seemed quite possible that Frederick would resume his earlier plans to cross the Alps and present himself at Lyons; and Innocent remained convinced that the emperor would come with an army to coerce him. He stood by his convictions; if Lyons could not hold him, then he must find hospitable ground even further afield. He asked Henry III whether he might be allowed to move court to Bordeaux, in English Gascony.

Innocent's difficulties were compounded by the news from the Levant. In April 1250 the French crusaders were soundly defeated in the Nile delta; the king of France himself was carried into captivity, and there were massive demands from the rulers of Egypt for a ransom. It was clear that the French king's actions in Egypt were curtailed for good; though St Louis spent several months in the Holy Land once the ransom had been repaid, his attention began to turn again to western affairs. The pope had clearly hoped to crack Frederick's power in Italy while the king of France was away and unable seriously to interfere. Now the pope found himself besieged again with French demands for a negotiated settlement with the emperor. One of Louis IX's messengers to the pope was none other than Charles, count of Anjou, the king's brother and a future ruler of Sicily: on this occasion his brief was to defend the Hohenstaufen, not to destroy them. The strength of the French argument lay in the experience not merely of the pope but of St Louis. His disastrous crusade might have achieved better results had the papacy given it real priority over the crusade against the Hohenstaufen. The papacy stood accused of negligence, of imperilling the Holy Land, France and Christendom for the sake of a struggle that commanded less and less sympathy. The papacy did react to the calls for negotiations: it was made plain that discussion was always possible on existing conditions – Frederick's appearance without retainers to be judged by the pope, and his acceptance of papal terms for a settlement in Lombardy and central Italy. But Innocent as ever refused to negotiate without an assurance of his own success.

VI

Frederick II had been suffering from indifferent health for some months. The story that della Vigna tried to poison him alludes to an illness, though the entire tale may be fabrication, of course. It refers to the period around New Year, 1249. In late 1249 and 1250 the emperor was also feeling unwell. He did not campaign north of the border, leaving charge of his armies to capable generals instead. In any case there was disquiet in the area round Naples; Frederick may have felt that his presence in the *regno* would keep trouble off the boil. Such quiet conduct in a ruler who had spent several years rushing back and forth across Italy inspired hopes at the papal curia that he was in fact dead. The dissemination of rumours to this effect was an old propaganda ploy, tried by Gregory IX when Frederick was on crusade. Though very much alive, the emperor may well have been in declining health. In December 1250 he was at Castel Fiorentino in Apulia, when he was struck by a violent bout of dysentery. There is no real evidence that this was caused by another poisoning attempt. He realized that his strength was being drained away. He made his will on 7 December. It stands as clear testimony to his core policy: the maintenance of the Hohenstaufen inheritance from generation to generation. He named Conrad as his heir in Germany, Italy and Sicily, but if he died without heir, then Henry son of Isabella was to succeed. Henry himself was to receive either the throne of Arles or that of Jerusalem, depending on Conrad's wishes; 100,000 ounces of gold, no mean sum, was made available for the recovery of the Holy Land. This Henry seems to have been a much loved and favoured son of the emperor, but so too was Frederick's illegitimate son Manfred. Manfred was entrusted with the government of the *regno* during Conrad's absence in Germany (where, as has been seen, he was busy holding down what opposition there was). Frederick was also anxious to make restitution to those who had suffered at his hands. He ordered to be returned to the Church the lands and other rights that he had appropriated, unless by doing so the honour and dignity of the Roman empire would suffer: a conciliatory act that surely reveals his commitment to a negotiated peace with the Roman Church. An amnesty was to be declared for minor criminals. Certain taxes were to be remitted for all time: he was conscious of the heavy burdens imposed by the *collecta* and other war taxes. Passing to his own last needs, the emperor chose for his burial place the cathedral at Palermo where lay already his father Henry VI, his mother Constance, his grandfather Roger II, his first wife Constance. This wish was in time obeyed: nearly a century before, Roger II had willed that he be buried at Cefalù, and his body was temporarily placed in a plain porphyry sarcophagus pending transfer from Palermo to a more ornate tomb of the same material; but the transfer to Cefalù never took place, and Frederick took for himself the ornate empty tomb originally reserved for his grandfather. There, side by side, the rulers of Sicily now lie, entombed in the imperial marble of ancient Rome.

Surrounded by his councillors, the emperor began to sink. The archbishop of Palermo, Berardo, had always stood with Frederick against the papacy. He was among a large crowd present now. Since the pope refused absolution, it fell on him to shrive Frederick who, if Matthew Paris is to be believed, then had himself robed as a Cistercian monk. Once the most powerful ruler in Christendom, he now intended to leave the world in the humble station of a poor penitent, renouncing his earthly possessions. It was a signal to all around him and to God that he had never denied the fundamentals of his faith. On 13 December 1250, thirteen days short of his fifty-sixth birthday, the end came – abruptly, for the illness had seized upon him when he seemed likely to restore his fortunes in Italy and Germany. By his side was Manfred, his regent for Sicily, whose words, in a letter to King Conrad, express concisely the Hohenstaufen view of the emperor's achievements: 'The sun of justice has set, the maker of peace has passed away.' He had not achieved victory; but he had not after all suffered defeat. His greatest aim seemed within reach: that his sons would inherit his kingdoms and preserve or even restore the dynasty's good name.

CHAPTER THIRTEEN

THE GHOSTS OF THE HOHENSTAUFEN

I

New Year 1251, broke at Lyons with the news that the pope's greatest enemy was dead. 'Let heaven and earth rejoice,' proclaimed Innocent, at the death of the Church's sworn enemy, the tyrant Frederick. The pope's announcement of what he saw as God's victory is one of the less appetizing letters in the papal register. But Innocent also took care to warn his listeners of the continuing threat of the Hohenstaufen. The preaching of the crusade must now be turned against Conrad; the Sicilians must still be urged to throw off their Hohenstaufen masters and William of Holland must be set to work again in Germany. The events of the next two decades are understandably ignored in most histories of Frederick II's reign. The finale is dramatic enough: in optimistic accounts, the emperor seems to be on the point of recovering his political strength when his physical strength gives way; while, in pessimistic accounts, the imperial court is still reeling under the impact of events at Parma, and the doom of the dynasty now seems sealed. But later developments cannot be ignored: the disappearance of Frederick from the conflict was not in fact sufficient to end the conflict; Innocent IV remained at the Church's helm for nearly four more years, and his successors, many of whom represented a similar strand of curial thinking, worked hard to fulfil his ambition: the extirpation of the house of Hohenstaufen. The challenge these popes posed was aimed at the very heart of Frederick II's policy, the creation of a diverse but loyal dynastic empire, including both Sicily and Germany, as well as large areas of northern Italy, which could be passed down from generation to generation, in sections or as a whole, within the house of Hohenstaufen. Against this, the papacy sought to elevate to the thrones of Germany and of Sicily separate champions, neither of whom bore the blood of the Hohenstaufen, each of whom was believed to be loyal to papal commands.

The papacy tried first of all to take advantage of the sudden turn in its fortune by urging once again an invasion of southern Italy. The papal armies could gain comfort from unrest in Naples and the border regions, a slight distraction under Frederick that now threatened to go out of control. Conrad's absence in Germany certainly made it easier for rebels to show themselves in southern Italy, but they failed to recognize the energy of the regent Manfred. He proved an able commander in the field; indeed, his success in restoring order was such that Conrad felt able to contact the pope, suggesting that past differences be buried. He invited Innocent to recognize him as king of Sicily, which was a serious misunderstanding of the pope's outlook; Innocent simply would not contemplate a single Hohenstaufen succession in Germany and Sicily. The pope's mind turned in other directions: he was already, it seems, tempted by the idea of a papal champion who could lead the Church's armies to victory in southern Italy. Innocent resumed the search for a western prince who would act as his agent. Richard earl of Cornwall had already been on the list, but Innocent proved unable to win him over. The pope's eye settled on an English prince, Henry III's son and Richard's nephew, Edmund, a mere child. His advantage was that behind him must surely lie the resources of the vassal kingdom of England, whose ruler had been increasingly loyal to the papacy during the conflict with Frederick. More distinguished, certainly, was the brother of Louis IX, Charles of Anjou, who was interested in serving the papacy in Italy, but who met the stiff opposition of the French king, ever anxious to retain his studied neutrality in the conflict of pope and Hohenstaufen. A prince of Charles' standing might command widespread support, but the idea that young Edmund could lead a crusade into Sicily was laughed to scorn by the English barons. They were not interested in the dynastic glory that would accrue to Henry III if his son became Sicilian king; they realized instead that the winning of Sicily would have to be achieved with money raised in large part from themselves in the form of crusade taxes. The 'Sicilian business' in England rapidly ceased to have much to do with foreign affairs; it was the domestic implications that convulsed the English baronage, and even the papacy began to realize that the choice of a small child as king of Sicily had brought nothing but delays and controversy. Innocent's successors were glad to look elsewhere for the champion of Christ. In 1258 Edmund's title to Sicily was placed on ice, by agreement between the English king and the pope. Unfortunately for Henry, the political strife created by Edmund's nomination could not so easily be dispelled.

Conrad IV's career had come to a rapid end in 1254, with his untimely death. He had not come down to Sicily to claim his royal title. Henry FitzIsabella was also dead. It seemed as if the lapse of time had solved some of Pope Innocent's problems. Conrad had left in Germany a son of the same name, now aged two; he is generally known as Conradin, or 'little Conrad'. Conradin hardly posed a threat; the German princes were thrown into disorder by the virtual extinction of the ruling dynasty, and in Sicily the papacy only faced the regent Manfred, who was making no claims to rule in Lombardy, central Italy or Germany. Innocent became optimistic enough to negotiate with Manfred, Frederick's son though he was. He knew that Manfred was anxious to have the legitimacy of his rule in southern Italy confirmed, and here was a golden opportunity to exercise, at long last, the prerogatives of the pope as overlord of the kingdom of Sicily. Manfred was assured of his right to act as regent and was confirmed in the title prince of Taranto, an honour conferred on him by Frederick II. Delighting in his new power, the pope travelled south to Naples to supervise the reorganization of the *regno*: the creation at long last of free communes, and the dismantling or restructuring of the centralized Norman bureaucracy. Clearly offended by Innocent's assumption of full authority, Manfred did not even wait to quarrel with the pope. He withdrew suddenly from Naples to the Saracen stronghold at Lucera, defying papal anger and a papal army. He aimed now to win for himself the crown of Sicily. His origins placed no bar on this ambition. An earlier king of Sicily – Tancred – had also been a love-child; moreover, Manfred stood for the continuation of his father's method of government and his father's good name. A loyal son of Frederick, he even inherited the emperor's interest in falconry, producing a definitive edition of the emperor's book *De Arte venandi cum avibus*. He could not tolerate Innocent's methods, and may have suspected that the pope merely intended to use him as his agent until a non-Hohenstaufen prince could be nominated to the Sicilian throne.

The ascendancy of Manfred was confirmed with the death of Pope Innocent at the end of 1254. Like Frederick II, he had not lived to see the final act of the struggle to which he had committed so many of his energies. He was a firm believer in the power of the keys for whom the resistance of the Hohenstaufen was nothing less than blasphemy. But his unwillingness to compromise, and his ready use of the instrument of crusade against his foes, did much to tarnish the papacy's reputation at the European courts. He was not sensitive to such difficulties; and we may pay him grudging respect for his doggedness, his relative consistency and his sense of purpose. His understanding of canon law was second to none, and there was nothing cynical about his use of legal, theological or moral arguments in defence of his case. He saw compromise with his enemies merely as procrastination. The demonstration that papal authority extended not merely over the vassal kingdoms such as Sicily, but over all rulers in Christendom, could not be delayed. Whether the apocalyptic language of Rainier of Viterbo struck a chord in him it is harder to say. The papal curia had no difficulty concocting blood-curdling accounts of the errors and sins of Frederick II, enhanced by visionary language drawn from Daniel or Revelation. Whether or not Innocent himself felt moved by such language, he gave no ground on his sacred principles. 'A very papal pope', he has been called: the phrase captures well his consistent adherence to the maximalist view of papal authority in theory as in practice.

The replacement of Innocent IV by a like-minded pontiff (Alexander IV) barely bothered Manfred. Echoing once again the ascent to the throne of the bastard Tancred, Manfred of Hohenstaufen prevailed on the Sicilian barons to elect him king. As in 1190, the barons could argue that the prime interests of their kingdom demanded a ruler who was available on the spot and who was of age to govern. The assumption that it was the barons, with perhaps a sprinkling of leading townsmen, who elected the king obviously contradicted the papal view that the ruler of Sicily, as a papal vassal, must be confirmed in office or even chosen by the holy see. The use of a 'parliament' of barons to elect a king, repeating events in 1130 and 1190, and repeated again in 1282, was an effective way to by-pass the papal claim to overlordship: the method flattered the barons, and assured their loyalty in conflict with a papacy that would certainly deny them any such authority. Nor did an election necessarily detract from the power of the crown, if it took place when the nobility had become seriously concerned at the lack of a permanent leader.

And indeed Manfred moved fast to re-establish the methods of rule and policies of his father; the brief interference by Innocent IV had already done some damage. Within the kingdom, urban liberties were rapidly revoked. He recreated the brilliant court of his father. He continued to place trust in the Saracen bodyguard from Lucera. The port of Manfredonia, founded by him, was to remain an important centre of the grain trade of the Adriatic long after he died. Frederick II had cultivated contacts with the Greek rump states that survived the Latin conquest of Constantinople in 1204; Manfred took this further by negotiating a marriage alliance between his daughter Helena and Michael II, despot of Epiros: the island of Corfu, as well as Durazzo and the Albanian coast, came to the Hohenstaufen as dowry. Important also for the future was a marriage alliance with Aragon: the heir to Aragon-Catalonia, Peter, wedded Manfred's daughter Constance in 1260; she took with her to Barcelona her Sicilian taste-buds, introducing roast dove to the Spanish court. But she symbolized too the renewal of a bond that had brought pleasure and even some troops to Sicily in Frederick II's youth, when his own marriage to Constance of Aragon had taken place. Here was James I of Aragon, conqueror of Majorca, Valencia and other lands, vassal of the pope, a rising power in the west, consenting to a marriage with an enemy of his own technical overlord. Thus there were rulers in the Mediterranean who accepted Manfred's claim to the throne of Sicily, on the conspicuous evidence of his firm rule and of the backing of much of the baronage.

Manfred had, to all intents, immobilized the papacy. Without even an Edmund at Rome's beck and call, the popes made little progress towards the recovery of their claimed rights in southern Italy. Actually, Manfred was at first wary of intervention in central or northern Italy; he could not hope to settle the rivalries of the Lombard towns, nor, in the 1250s, was he trying to press any claims to territory in the north. However, he became increasingly anxious to sustain Ghibelline allies in central Italy, no doubt in the fear that their destruction would unleash a massive Guelf assault on his own territories. Thus he gave support to the Ghibellines of Siena in 1260, when at the battle of Montaperti they and their Tuscan allies defeated a league of Guelfs. But his policies seem very opportunistic: he had also opposed Siena several years before, and, unlike previous Hohenstaufen, he gave his patronage to the Genoese against the Pisans – long the most loyal allies of Frederick Barbarossa and his heirs. He even conferred a handsome trading privilege on the Genoese, whom his father had more usually shunned. The problem was that, as Manfred built ties to northern and central Italian cities, the papacy began to see an emergent threat to its influence in Lombardy and Tuscany. Particularly serious were Manfred's claims to lordship over one or two towns – by 1261 he claimed rights at Alessandria, in Piedmont, a city originally built as a symbol of Lombard resistance to the Hohenstaufen. The assertion of these rights in northern Italy stimulated the papacy to renew its search for a champion able to sweep Hohenstaufen power out of the peninsula.

II

Pope Urban IV (1261–4), a Frenchman, found a local champion in Obizzo d'Este, captain-general of a pro-papal league which included such important cities as Ferrara and Mantua. The Lombard troubles, which had never really disappeared, were given a new surge of life; but the problem was no longer an attempt by a Holy Roman Emperor to have his authority fully recognized in northern Italy. Manfred, rather, had become immersed in the faction-fighting of self-declared papal loyalists, or Guelfs, against self-declared adherents of a headless empire, or Ghibellines. The power of Ezzelino had already been cracked by a crusade launched against him at the end of Innocent IV's life. The Ghibellines therefore were in search of patrons, and Manfred's rise to power in the south came at a critical moment in their fortunes. Equally, Manfred's commitments to his northern allies were seen in Rome as an assurance that no peace could ever be achieved with the Hohenstaufen. Even without an imperial crown, the hated tribe seemed anxious to bring all Italy under its power. The problem was not simply, as Gregory IX had assumed, the union of empire and *regno*. Any Hohenstaufen king of Sicily was keen to extend his influence over Lombardy, and potentially central Italy, too. Thinking on these lines, Pope Urban revived the dormant hopes of choosing a papal general among the princes of Europe, an 'athlete of Christ' who would lead the crusade against the house of Frederick to final victory with the conquest of southern Italy and Sicily.

As early as 1252 the papacy had explored the possibility of securing the services of Charles of Anjou for such a task. Ten years later, after the fiasco of Prince Edmund, Charles was a still more appropriate and more susceptible candidate for the crown of Sicily. Since 1246 Charles had been count of Provence in right of his wife, Beatrice; as such he held lands which formed part of the Hohenstaufen empire (only in 1486 was Angevin Provence united to the kingdom of France). Provence was an ample source of wealth for a military commander who wished to launch what would undoubtedly be a costly Italian war: it was well administered and contained rich towns, above all the great port of Marseilles; it had earlier been ruled by a branch of the house of Aragon, and its acquisition by Charles aroused hostility at the court of Manfred's Aragonese allies. Charles' power was magnified by his vigorous destruction of sources of political opposition in Marseilles and other towns more used to communal autonomies than to the central government of an Angevin count. He also needed to gain the submission of powerful barons in the Provençal interior and to settle his relationship with the city of Genoa, whose territory abutted on that of Provence along the Mediterranean coast. Even the lords of western Piedmont, such as the count of Saluzzo, began to acknowledge Charles as over-lord. Not merely had he acquired, after fifteen years of intensive work, a wealthy Mediterranean domain; he had also begun to take careful notice of events inside Italy. Angevin and Hohen-staufen interests were in danger of colliding in north-west Italy: it has been seen that Manfred exercised claims of his own in Piedmont, and made friends with Genoa.

But Charles' other advantage to papal plans lay in his character. It is not easy to see beyond the image of an ambitious, self-righteous and opportunist man of war. Originally destined, as a cadet member of the house of Capet, for high office in the Church, he was early in his life granted instead the title to Maine and the lands of the central Loire valley, newly recovered from the English kings. Around 1254 he was also active in Flanders, aiming to acquire lands around Valenciennes. A Genoese poet remarked that he was 'greedy even when he was not a count; doubly so as king'. The thirteenth-century Italian sculptor, Arnolfo di Cambio, who carved a life-size statue of Charles for the commune of Rome, provided him with a stern, bleak ex-pression; it is perhaps intended to convey a sense of remote majesty, but it also suggests a remoteness of character, a grim determination. He did win praise from some troubadours, and was a generous patron of the arts; however, a poet's praise was much influenced by the possibility of winning a pension, and does not have to be taken at face value. French historians have done something to revise the traditional picture of Charles as an unfeeling brute; that he was guided in his actions, at least from 1264, by a sense of deep religious devotion cannot be denied. His vast ambitions in the Mediterranean were intended not merely for his own good, but for that of all Christendom. This did not make him a slave of the popes; he had his own, exaggerated, ideas of what must be done and pressed them further than most popes wished.

In 1262 and 1263 Charles was kept waiting, agonizingly, while the pope tried to decide on a possible pact with Manfred: the king of Sicily would give aid to the Latin emperor of Constan-tinople (newly dispossessed, in 1261, by the Greeks of Nicaea), and in return the pope would accept his title to the Sicilian throne. Finally, however, the pope decided this plan was moving nowhere — after all, Manfred posed a danger in northern Italy, and many of Urban's allies did not want to see peace made with the Hohenstaufen at any price. Terms were therefore agreed instead with Charles of Anjou. His brief was to conquer Sicily at the head of a large crusade, for which he promised considerable numbers of ships and men, paid for partly from his own resources and partly from the proceeds of a crusade tithe, of which more in a moment. Charles was expressly forbidden to lay any claim to the imperial lands or titles in Italy, or to the lands of the Church: the awful spectre of a king ruling northern, central and southern Italy, was to be banished for good. The pope would use his good offices to ensure that Conradin was blocked from receiving the crown of the Holy Roman Empire, and from thereby becoming a potential threat in Italy. Charles himself gained an assurance that the crusade would be preached on his behalf, and the right to take for his own use, for three years, ecclesiastical tithes levied in France, Provence and the old kingdom of Arles. In the longer term, the pope was promised the restoration of the annual *census*, or tribute, due from the king of Sicily to his overlord: at this stage a sum of 10,000 ounces of gold was agreed upon. Within a few months Charles revealed that his interpretation of the arrangements was a broad one. He received from the citizens of Rome the title of senator; it was a breach of his agreement with the papacy even to hold a position of honour in the city of the popes. Anti-Angevin cardinals in the curia were stimulated into action, to no effect. And Manfred responded with an exaggerated display of cheek: he petitioned the citizens of Rome for an imperial crown — flattery, indeed, since only the most radical elements in the city claimed the power to confer the crown of the empire. Such demands should not be taken too seriously; nor, at this stage, is Manfred likely to have felt very scared of Charles.

Yet Charles of Anjou was a good organizer. His military plans were well under way in 1265. He negotiated terms with Lombard towns and Italian lords through whose lands he proposed to take his anti-Hohenstaufen crusaders. He backed himself up, quite literally, by making agreements with the north Italian Guelfs, such as Obizzo d'Este, for he was rightly afraid that the pro-Hohenstaufen factions would agitate in his rear while he was hard at work conquering the south. He saw, as the new pope

(Clement IV) apparently did not, that his Sicilian campaign was conditional upon securing strong allies in northern Italy. It was one thing to be bound by an agreement not to take office in the imperial lands of northern Italy, but it was another to risk a strategy that left out of account Manfred's willing helpers in the north. The Tuscan Ghibellines were becoming particularly active. Charles' prime problem was of another character, however: finance. Louis IX was not willing to give Charles funds for his project, which the French king had only slowly been persuaded even to permit. The resources of Provence soon proved inadequate for the large-scale campaign Charles had in mind. Even the tithes granted to Charles failed to materialize on the scale that had been anticipated. The clergy of France was particularly lax in payments, though a vocal prelate, Simon of Brie, had been appointed to preach the crusade and ensure collection of funds. Charles for his part found allies among the Guelf bankers in Tuscany; but he was obliged to turn to the papacy for more money, and the pope mortgaged his interests to raise urgently needed cash. As Édouard Jordan remarked, 'the future king of Sicily had not even reached Sicily before the bottom of the papal coffers was exposed to view.' Nor does the hope that many volunteers would take the cross against Manfred, joining Charles' army at their own expense, seem to have been realized quite to the extent that the papacy had hoped. Nevertheless by winter 1265 there had gathered together in northern Italy a large, motley force of Frenchmen, Provençaux, Italians and even Germans, Englishmen and Spaniards, a potent mixture of crusaders, mercenaries, feudal vassals, adventurers. Some hoped for lands, offices and revenues in southern Italy; others were satisfied with the offer of remission of their sins, in return for their help in extirpating Frederick's heirs.

On 3 February 1266 Charles of Anjou's army crossed the frontier of the *regno* and marched south to an encounter at Benevento with the forces of Manfred of Hohenstaufen. He had already been crowned king by the pope before he invaded the *regno*: an event that symbolized the newly close dependence of the king of Sicily on his overlord. On 26 February Manfred's army was put to rout; Manfred himself fought with characteristic courage, refusing to flee from the field of battle. He was cut down. With him died, or were captured, many leading Sicilian loyalists and also Ghibelline allies from Tuscany who had remained faithful to Frederick's house. Since Manfred was under ban of excommunication, he was buried without ecclesiastical ceremonies but with the honour due to a defeated prince. Charles was a chivalrous man. And thus Charles found himself, rapidly and with ease, master of the kingdom. For once, papal plans against the Hohenstaufen had culminated in triumph. The victory that had eluded Gregory IX and Innocent IV had to all intents been achieved within a matter of weeks. Charles knew, moreover, that his victory was all the greater since the native opposition had lost not merely its elected king but very many of its lesser leaders. A few barons tried to hold out in the mountains; but he, for his part, showed mercy to past opponents. He did not yet try to displace the existing bureaucracy or nobility; indeed, he saw clearly that their help was essential if he were ever to gather the funds and resources owing to him from his new subjects. His own followers were sometimes disappointed at the new king's failure to grant them the great estates they had come south to win.

Charles did not, then, dismantle the system of government he found. The Angevin bureaucracy was not modelled on the Norman-Hohenstaufen bureaucracy; it *was* that bureaucracy, continued without a significant break. Thus it was under the Angevins that a fair copy was made of the Norman register of military service, the 'Catalogue of the Barons'; and the guiding hand seems to have been an official of Hohenstaufen days who transferred his loyalty to the new dynasty, one of that large band of Amalfitans and Salernitans who, having served Frederick with efficiency, now served a very different master without qualms. Certainly there were loyalists who refused to accept the new order: Giovanni da Procida, who had been with Frederick II in his last days, fled to the court of Aragon. More of him later. Nor, indeed, did Charles of Anjou discard the legislation of Frederick II that dated to the years before his formal deposition at Lyons. The *Constitutions of Melfi* were deliberately echoed when Charles, in 1267, called together an assembly of justiciars and financial officials, to examine complaints against them.

The battle of Benevento also brought Charles gains outside

the *regno*. He brazenly assumed rights over Corfu and Albania (taking the title of king of Albania), even though those lands had come to the Hohenstaufen family under a dowry agreement. More importantly, his prestige after Benevento assured Charles of a much-enlarged following in northern Italy. He had, it is true, to resign the senatorship of Rome under papal pressure; but he had his own observers at a conference of the Lombard League in Milan in 1266. Charles' seneschal in Piedmont and Provence was given a watching brief over Lombard affairs too. Charles realized that he had to take care, under his agreement with Rome, not to take any office of substance himself; but he accepted plenty of honorary offices, as *podestà* or *signore* of Guelf towns, such as Florence, and was able to draw extensive areas into an Angevin sphere of influence. The papacy was aware, as ever, that these developments could turn to its disadvantage. But the dominant groups in the curia were pro-Guelf, and there was a strong temptation to make use of Charles' political strength and military resources in settling scores in northern and central Italy also. Yet the aim of the papacy remained to confine Charles' activities to southern Italy and the Mediterranean. The 'athleta Christi' would turn his energies eastwards, it was hoped; the resources of the *regno* would be directed to a crusade for the recovery of Jerusalem and (some argued) of Constantinople as well, following that city's return to the hands of the schismatic Greeks. In northern Italy, and indeed Germany, an entirely distinct papal champion must be found, who would perpetuate the division of *regno* and empire.

III

The Ghibellines were, however, not without hope. That infant son of Conrad IV whom Manfred had displaced from the throne of Sicily emerged as a substitute patron. Fugitives from southern Italy, followed by Tuscan Ghibelline exiles, appealed to Prince Conradin in Germany to come to Italy and achieve for the Hohenstaufen cause what Charles had achieved on the pope's behalf. Charles' victory had already proved how easy victory might be, if only support were sufficient. Yet Conradin was only fourteen years old. His own enthusiasm was no compensation for his lack of military and diplomatic experience. Fortunately, there were many potential allies north and south of the *regno*'s borders. The appearance of the boy claimant in northern Italy in 1267 had a dramatic effect: just as the young Frederick had conjured much of Germany into obedience, so his grandson inspired the south Italian barons and towns to rise against the unwanted master from France. It seemed to the Ghibellines that past Hohenstaufen miracles were being repeated, and that future glories would yet be restored. Sicily rose in revolt, and a force of Berbers sent by the king of Tunis landed on the island. As a former vassal of the Hohenstaufen the ruler of Tunis may well have been seizing an excuse to detach himself from Sicilian overlordship. A swift blow against the Angevins might emancipate Tunis from its regular tribute payment to the Sicilian court. Chaos in Sicily, but no less serious developments on the mainland. Henry, prince of Castile, had supported Charles' invasion, and had expected lands and titles as his reward for helping conquer southern Italy. Receiving little, he turned on Charles and raised a small army which advanced on Rome. He was elected captain-general of the Ghibellines in Tuscany and seemed set to become one of Conradin's key generals.

A hearty welcome at Ghibelline Pisa encouraged Conradin to march southwards to claim his inheritance. He was in funds, and even some of the north Italian barons, such as the lords of Saluzzo, had decided to give him lukewarm support. They feared Charles' excessive influence in an area where they had expected a freer hand. Conradin was heartened, too, by the sight of Charles of Anjou hurrying south to attempt to quash at least some of the opposition before Conradin crossed the frontiers of the kingdom of Sicily. Charles saw a particular threat in the Saracen stronghold of Lucera, which opted to support Hohenstaufen masters. Despite the forceful condemnation of the Lucera Saracens in all the crusading bulls directed against Manfred, and indeed Frederick II, the colony of Muslims had survived under Charles, who even made use of the luxurious palace the hated emperor had built in Lucera. The colony was not suppressed until 1300. The nearest it came to extinction before then was, however, the siege of 1268.

Other events supervened. Conradin marched into the *regno*, backed by a substantial, modern army – Henry of Castile's men wore the heavy but newly fashionable plate armour. The Roman families of Orsini and Annibaldi (the latter of whom had furnished Pope Alexander IV, a recent foe of Manfred) now gave their support to the Hohenstaufen. The threat to Charles' authority was a critical one.

Charles abandoned the siege of Lucera, moving north-west to the border village of Tagliacozzo. There an extremely tough battle was fought. At first the Ghibellines gained the upper hand; it was only with a vigorous and desperate regrouping of Angevin troops that a final victory in Charles' favour was achieved. The slaughter on both sides was enormous. Conradin escaped, but was soon caught. There followed in southern Italy months of merciless repression of Charles' enemies, many of whom had clearly identified themselves in the 1267 revolt and 1268 invasion. It was now that many south Italian barons, previously loyal to Manfred and his father, were swept out of their fiefs, to be replaced by the new king's own men from Provence, France and northern Italy. Large numbers of French, Provençaux and Tuscans acquired high office in the central government at Naples and as justiciars or tax officials in the provinces. The Florentines won, over the years, especially large rewards as provisioners and bankers to a crown in whose success they had decided to invest before Tagliacozzo. It was an investment that paid off handsomely, with grants of tax exemption, minting rights and access to grain stocks that surpassed the opportunities available to the king's own subjects. This is not to say south Italians played no role henceforth in the government of the *regno*. The Amalfitan civil servants visible already under Frederick II did not disappear. The structure of government changed only very slightly. More documents were drawn up in French, for instance, since this was the language the king understood best; he could also maintain easier contact with his estates in Anjou and Maine if he had some French-speaking staff. But this hardly meant a revolution in government. Rather, there was a change in mood: the elaborate bureaucracy came to be seen as a machine for the milking of potentially disloyal subjects; heavy war taxes were imposed – the very *collecta* whose imposition had been so stridently criticized by the papacy in the days of Frederick. The wars they financed were in northern Italy, Africa, Albania, Greece and the Holy Land; so that, just as Frederick's subjects grew restive at taxes to pay for wars outside the *regno*, so too did Charles'.

After Tagliacozzo opposition elsewhere in southern Italy and Sicily crumbled. There were confiscations, hangings, occasional displays of mercy, to inspire awe or gratitude. One act, however, excited horror even at the time. Where contemporaries might have been content with the surreptitious murder of rivals for their power, Charles held a trial of Conradin and his closest companions. In one sense this speaks for Charles' desire to show that he was not a usurper, but a ruler who followed the due process of law. In another sense, as Émile Léonard said, such a trial could only be a 'façade': 'the disappearance of the last of the Hohenstaufen was a political necessity for the Angevin'. Conradin was condemned to be executed, along with his colleagues. Among them, the Hohenstaufen Frederick of Antioch: Charles did indeed intend to extirpate the Hohenstaufen, for they alone could claim the kingdom by right of inheritance, even if not by papal disposition; they alone, he thought, could inspire rebellion against the house of Anjou. The instructions of Innocent IV to his adherents twenty years earlier must be followed to the letter: the house of Frederick must be eliminated from power; if that meant its physical elimination, Charles was not one to shrink from such an act. So in October, 1268, the sixteen-year-old adventurer Conradin was led to the block: an act which inspired horror at the time and helped furnish a martyr to the Ghibelline cause. But for all his care, Charles had not met his last Hohenstaufen rival.

IV

=

There is no need here to examine in detail the effects of Tagliacozzo in the north: Charles' rise to ascendancy in northern Italy was now assured; and the papacy, though worried that the king of Sicily was so active in the north, could congratulate itself that Lombardy and Tuscany were now overwhelmingly Guelf.

A one-sided settlement on the lines of that which Innocent IV had aspired to achieve had at last been reached. Only the separation of Sicilian and Lombard affairs had not yet been effected. Charles was even able to reassert his authority as senator of Rome, although the city had fêted Conradin on his way south. None could stand in his way. In the 1270s it was precisely the strength of his power that generated a reaction: Pope Gregory X, anxious to reassert papal authority in the Romagna, sought a new champion who would concentrate on northern Italy, thereby assuring the separation of north and south at long last. His choice, Rudolf von Habsburg, king of the Romans, was never able to fulfil papal hopes, but his presence across the Alps served to remind Charles that the king of Sicily's rights in Lombardy and Piedmont could be seriously questioned. Both Pope Gregory X and Pope Nicholas III had further doubts about Charles. They worked hard to achieve a peaceful settlement of differences with the Byzantine empire. The recovery of Constantinople in 1261 by Michael VIII Palaiologos had reopened the two-hundred-year-old problem of open refusal by the Greek Church to acknowledge papal primacy, or to conform with western theology and practice. The papacy was aware that Michael VIII was beset by enemies and keen to hold at bay rival claimants to his throne, not least the deposed Latin emperor Baldwin de Courtenay. Michael was therefore disposed to come to terms with the papacy, as his ambassadors did at the Council of Lyons of 1274. But some western princes, led by Charles of Anjou, argued that the Greeks would never honour their obligations to St Peter; force alone was the way to bring them to heel. Charles argued persuasively for a crusade, to be led by himself, against Constantinople. The aim would be to place the Latin emperor on the throne again. But as lord of Albania and parts of Achaia, Charles undoubtedly had territorial interests of his own in mind, too. His overriding interest lay, however, still further east. He purchased the crown of Jerusalem in 1277 from Maria of Antioch, whose right to sell the crown was certainly dubious (the kings of Cyprus maintained a claim to the same throne); he sent provisions and men to the Holy Land. Mindful of the arguments that had justified his own crusade against Manfred, he sought to bring aid to a kingdom now under intolerable pressure from the Mamluks of Egypt. The resources of the kingdom of Sicily would be turned in this direction. He would show the world that an Angevin king of Sicily made a more effective crusader than a Hohenstaufen one. He probably saw his part in the recovery of Constantinople as an important strategic step on the way east.

Charles' plans to organize a crusade first against the Greeks, then to the Holy Land, came nearer resolution when Simon de Brie, who had collected tithes on his behalf in France during the preaching campaign against Manfred, was elected pope, under the name Martin IV, in 1281. An enthusiast for the Guelf cause, Martin also helped plan the military defeat of the Greek empire, excommunicating Michael VIII for his failure to enact the promised act of union with the Roman Church, and creating an alliance of western forces against Byzantium. Venice was to help the Angevins and the deposed Latins; the Venetians had been stalwart supporters of the Latin dynasty in Constantinople, which they had helped create after the capture of the city by the Fourth Crusade in 1204. Charles entered into a marriage alliance with the Courtenays, assuring him not of the crown of Constantinople – that was beyond his reach or real interests – but of the eventual succession of his daughter as empress. The Angevin lineage would be covered in glory: we see again, among the enemies of the Hohenstaufen, that same pride in the dynasty and its inheritance that had so powerfully motivated Frederick II.

In Spring 1282, the crusader fleet was under construction at Messina. But it never sailed. At the hour of Vespers on 30 March 1282 some Angevin soldiers insulted a young married Sicilian woman outside the church of Santo Spirito on the edge of Palermo. A struggle broke out, blood was drawn, and the cry went up: 'Maranu li francisi!' – 'Death to the French!' The Angevin garrison in Palermo was slaughtered and the revolt spread in a few weeks across the island of Sicily, until even the arsenal city of Messina was in rebel hands (28 April 1282). The Angevins had lost Sicily, suddenly and unexpectedly; and the Sicilian revolt only generated more uprisings, on the south Italian mainland. Who were the rebels and what did they want?

Both questions are surprisingly difficult to answer, in the light of subsequent events. At the height of the rebellion the repre-

sentatives of the Sicilian towns and nobility appealed to the pope
for protection: they wished to place Sicily under his direct authority, as a free community or group of communes – the towns
undoubtedly wished to acquire the sort of status Perugia or
Orvieto had in the papal states, as free communes nevertheless
under papal suzerainty. Messina in particular had long agitated
for communal privileges. But Martin IV was the last person, after
Charles himself, likely to heed such demands. He refused outright. Certainly, the rebels wished to drive out the Amalfitan,
French and Provençal administrators who had levied taxes with
such efficiency. But their system of government was, as has been
seen, essentially that of the Hohenstaufen, applied strictly, more
so perhaps than under Frederick. Even so the grievances of 1282
echo uncannily the grievances against Frederick II in the last
years of his reign: excessive taxes and other interference in economic life. It is possible that there was resentment in Sicily itself at
neglect of the island in favour of mainland southern Italy. Some
rebels, too, had suffered at Angevin hands when the revolt of
1267–8 was suppressed; the Greeks of Sicily, still considerable in
number, may have opposed Charles' policies towards Byzantium.
French historians have been understandably sensitive to the
accusation that Charles' government was any more repressive
than Frederick's, especially when the continuities in method are
taken into account. It is clear, because a later pope admitted the
point in 1285, that the regular meetings of justiciars, so they
could be examined for complaints against their conduct, did not
continue throughout Charles' reign. It is clear too that he spent
very little time in Sicily: only the Tunis crusade of 1270–71
brought him to the island. On the other hand it was not only the
island that rebelled. On balance, the first phase of the revolt of
the Sicilian Vespers must be seen as a revolt against misgovernment: the spark was tension between the Palermitans and
their foreign garrison, but there was plenty of fuel to be ignited
throughout the *regno*.

Other interests were, however, at work, seeking after more
than thirty years to redeem the claims of Frederick II's lineage to
rule in Sicily. It has been mentioned in passing that Manfred had
built a marriage tie to the court of Aragon. There, surrounded
by courtiers from the Hohenstaufen camp, Queen Constance,

wife of King Peter, retained her interest in her grandfather's and father's kingdom. Giovanni da Procida was an active member of her entourage. Her husband Peter was not likely to look with favour on Charles of Anjou for other reasons, too. The Aragonese kings had exercised influence in Provence, through dynastic links, before the Angevin acquisition of the county. The Aragonese, or rather the Catalan merchants of Barcelona, were keen to extend political and economic influence in north-west Africa, and saw Charles' overlordship at Tunis, confirmed by a brief crusade in 1270, as an obstacle to this policy. The clash of Anjou and Aragon did not begin in 1282; but events in Sicily brought to a head a long-brewed rivalry. A few weeks after the revolt of the Vespers, Peter of Aragon sailed with the Catalan navy from Barcelona eastwards, making it known that he wished to conduct a further 'crusade' against the ruler of Tunis – not that he had consulted Charles of Anjou, as that ruler's suzerain, before doing so. But in fact Tunis was no more than a reserve destination. His real target was Sicily. The Sicilian parliament met at Palermo and agreed to the suggestion of Aragonese envoys that Peter be summoned to Sicily to take the crown in right of his Hohenstaufen wife; and in August he landed at Trapani, travelling through western Sicily towards his coronation at Palermo in September, 1282. The pope's rejection of the Sicilian proposal for free communes had only pushed the Sicilians into the arms of the Aragonese king and his Hohenstaufen wife.

Peter's actions have been taken to reveal a grand conspiracy, uniting Aragon, Sicily and beleaguered Byzantium in an attempt to destroy the common Angevin enemy. Giovanni da Procida, undoubtedly a driving force behind the invasion of Sicily, has been cast in the role of arch-conspirator (most notably by Verdi). There is no doubt that there were contacts between Barcelona and Constantinople on the eve of the revolt of the Vespers, but the fact is that events moved faster than Peter had expected. Sicily rebelled spontaneously; this aided his invasion plans enormously, but it seems most likely that he had originally intended to invade only when the Angevin fleet was at sea on its way to Constantinople, and Sicily stood unprotected. The Sicilian fleet was much larger than his own, and he must have feared an engagement at sea. Anyway, Sicily fell into his lap. But this did not redeem all the claims of the Hohenstaufen. Aragonese armies pushed northwards into Calabria, having after all defeated Charles' fleet in the narrows between Sicily and the continent. Peter hoped for major successes in the Bay of Naples, and aimed to recover every inch of Frederick II's kingdom. He had the enthusiastic help of the Ghibellines in northern Italy, who provided convenient distraction by the eviction of papal and Angevin governors from the towns. Even papal Perugia renounced Martin IV. Charles' influence in northern Italy rapidly waned as the Pisans and other Ghibellines took heart. But the advance of the Aragonese was slow; Charles organized effective resistance in Apulia and seemed surprisingly resilient. The burden of cost on Peter was enormous; and further worries came to him from Spain, where the highland barons of Aragon had never been enthusiastic about his adventurism. A French crusade, blessed by the pope, was aimed at Aragon in 1285, and, though it was defeated, it won some support in Aragon and even in Barcelona. When, in 1285, both Charles I and Peter of Aragon died a stalemate had been achieved: the kingdom of Aragon was safe, Sicily was under Aragonese control, the heir of Charles I (Charles II) was even an Aragonese captive. But the mainland advance had been checked.

Seeing Sicily as a burden financially, militarily and diplomatically, King James II of Aragon, Peter's son, even declared himself ready to abandon the island in return for peace and the not insignificant surrender, in lieu, of Sardinia and Corsica by the papacy. His brother, however, Frederick, the regent of Sicily, staunchly opposed this policy, with ample support from a terrified Sicilian baronage. Frederick, indeed, defied his brother outright by accepting the crown of Sicily from a Sicilian parliament in December, 1297; thereafter, until peace came five years later, he found himself actually at war with Aragon as well as the Angevins of Naples, the papacy and other foes. This Frederick rapidly became the focus of Ghibelline loyalties; exiles from Guelf-dominated towns flocked to his court; the papacy condemned and excommunicated him; the radical Franciscans extolled him as a prince of peace come to cast down the Romish idols. North of the Alps he was acclaimed as the new Frederick, the returned emperor come to fulfil the promises of the

Hohenstaufen and to inaugurate the end of time. In reality, alas, he was a pragmatic figure who tried his best to perpetuate the old Norman system of government, in the face of erosion of royal power by mighty vassals. He was even prepared to help the papacy and the Angevins save face; in 1302 he agreed to style himself 'king of Trinacria' (the 'triangular place') and to arrange for the return of 'Trinacria' to the Angevins after his death (this was not in fact done); the Angevins continued to style themselves 'kings of Jerusalem and Sicily' though in reality they held no land in the one kingdom, entirely lost to the Mamluks in 1291, and only at best a niche (Milazzo) in the other after the revolt of the Vespers in 1282. In the Angevin kingdom too the Norman bureaucracy was gradually undermined by massive grants of rights and lands to north Italian merchants or feudal nobles. There were frequent, though individually insignificant, revolts on the countryside estates.

Peter of Aragon had, then, redeemed only a small part of Frederick II's inheritance. Germany did not enter into his calculations; his power in northern Italy was never as substantial as that of the Hohenstaufen in the past, nor of the Angevins in his own day, who had both sent their own armies into the region. Nor could Peter's career even convince his successors of the importance of holding Sicily: with the exception, of course, of Frederick II's namesake. A more powerful force in northern Italy than Aragonese armies or money was, however, the memory of Frederick II's name: a source of nostalgia to Ghibellines in the late thirteenth and early fourteenth centuries, and a reminder of tyranny to the dominant, Guelf, interest in Tuscany and Lombardy. It is necessary to look now at the impact of that name.

V

The importance of Frederick II lies, as has been suggested already, not merely in his own reign but in the dramatic aftermath: the power struggles in Sicily, culminating in the revolt of the Vespers in 1282. But other revolutionaries, of a very different character, sought inspiration in Frederick II, in Italy and, even more persistently, in Germany. Around the emperor's name gathered a bizarre but politically potent view of the events and meaning of his reign, bringing comfort to the opponents of a wealthy, hedonistic Church. The origins of this view can be found in Frederick's own first kingdom, in the Calabrian abbey where the prophet Joachim of Fiore (1145–1202) drew startling conclusions about the state of the world. His own writings were themselves a particularly influential contribution to a lively discussion, pursued even at the Norman Sicilian court, about the course of human history; Joachim was powerfully affected by an existing tradition among the Greek monks and hermits of Calabria, apocalyptic in tone, drawing not merely on biblical sources but on oracular texts preserved in Greek. These traditions were probably first stimulated into life when the Muslims conquered Sicily in the ninth century, prompting many Greek Christians to seek lonely refuge across the straits and to sit in gloomy contemplation of events that surely signalled the end of time. Among the most popular texts were the 'Sibylline oracles', not, of course, those of ancient Rome, but a Christianized, chiliastic fabrication compiled in the Byzantine empire on the basis of older oriental works. Eugenius, admiral of the Norman kings of Sicily, was interested enough to translate the Sibyl into Latin. What impact the oracles had on the Norman court it is hard to say; it is difficult, too, to be sure whether apparent points of contact between the oracles and Frederick's propaganda machine indicate direct influence, rather than a habit of drawing (for political purposes) from a common pool of ideas.

Joachim of Fiore worked out an elegant structure for human history. He identified three ages, to be followed by the Last Judgement and the end of time. In the first age, which reflected the first person of the Trinity, man was the bondsman of the law; man was tied to God by his fear of him. This 'Age of the Father' corresponded to the days of the Old Testament; it expresses the notion of the God of the Jews as an angry, merciless God – a common stereotype of Judaism in this (and subsequent) periods. The 'Age of the Son', on the other hand, was seen by Joachim as a time of faith and of humble acceptance of divine wishes, under the guidance of the Gospel. But it was nothing compared to the

'Age of the Spirit', when all mankind would enjoy a lasting sabbath in love of God and cognition of his goodness. It would be a period of mystical contemplation, of devotion to the praise of God. Joachim himself, needless to say, lived only in the second Age, but he could foresee the advent of the third. Elaborate calculations convinced him that the new order of mankind would finally be inaugurated in 1260, following the brief reign of the persecuting Antichrist: the persecutor, however, not simply of the good but of a Church given over to material interests, corrupted to the core. Such views were rapidly and widely disseminated; one of Joachim's first audiences was Richard Coeur-de-Lion, on his way to the crusade: an expedition on which other apocalyptic notions can also be identified among the followers of the German emperor, Frederick I. The impact of the Joachite movement was especially strong, in the half century after his death, on the newly licensed Franciscan order; its devotion to poverty and preaching, and the exemplary life of its founder, seemed to some of its more radical members to cast the order in the role of harbinger of the third Age. Although there were other considerations — such as internal struggles over the nature and extent of the order's renunciation of worldly wealth — the split between the 'conventual' and 'spiritual' Franciscans, the latter of whom espoused radical doctrines of Christ's absolute poverty, was undoubtedly fuelled by the apocalyptic ideas of the Joachites and similar prophets.

Nor could the dramatic struggle between pope and emperor in the first half of the thirteenth century escape the attention of these seers. Whereas St Francis had pointed forward to the third Age, Frederick and his papal foes were argued to signify the final days of the second Age. In the 1240s, the 'Commentary on Jeremiah' predicted to an Italian audience the chastisement and destruction of a worldly Church, culminating in the inauguration of the new order in 1260. The agent of this persecution was none other than Frederick II. All this produced rather an ambivalent view of the conqueror: on the one hand he was seen by the enthusiasts as the Antichrist, on the other as the scourge of a wicked and ungodly Church. Such ideas may also have gained force from other directions: the Tartar raids in eastern Europe at just this period contributed to the sense that human society was beginning to disintegrate. Moreover, the violent attacks in the papal letters, and in the friars' preaching campaigns, on Frederick as Antichrist seemed to sanction, from an unexpected quarter, the view that the last two decades of the Age of the Spirit were at hand. We should not look for great consistency: the millenarians were looking for signs of all descriptions, and they found them in every quarter. A striking example of the popular impact of these beliefs comes from Swabia, where in the 1240s there was widespread rejection of papal claims to authority; heretics argued for a Church of the poor and denied the validity of the clergy's power to administer the sacraments. In part this was a reaction to the interdict under which Germany now stood: pro-papal priests were refusing to offer the sacraments, *ergo* those who had once depended on them began to listen more carefully to critics who seriously questioned their very usefulness. Especially interesting is the claim of the Swabian heretics that the emperor and King Conrad were worthy to direct the new church of the poor; it was for them and not for the pope that one should pray. But the importance of the heresy as a social movement of the artisans should not be underestimated either. Local preachers such as Brother Arnold, himself actually a Dominican, encouraged the radical views; he placed the pope, not Frederick, on the throne of Antichrist and saw Frederick II as the patron of the poor. By 1260 the emperor would have dismantled the worldly Roman Church, and have redistributed its assets to the poor. Stress on the virtue of the poor was hardly new – it could be found in Jesus' own statements – but the conviction that this was where Frederick's political programme pointed was certainly novel. Criticism of the emperor for his lack of generosity to the Church in Sicily and elsewhere had strangely rebounded against the papacy; north of the Alps his 'crime' became a virtue.

Events in 1250 brought no comfort to the Joachites, however. As Norman Cohn remarks, 'his death was a catastrophic blow both to the German Joachites, whom it deprived of their saviour, and to the Italian Joachites, whom it deprived of their Antichrist'. The answer to the difficulty lay in a new prediction: the Age of the Spirit would indeed dawn in 1260 (or, once that year had passed, in the near future), with the help of Emperor Frederick. For the emperor would return. Either he had never died, but had gone into hiding, maybe as a secluded penitent; or he had died, but would be resurrected as a new Frederick, to continue the tasks he had left unfinished. For the Joachites of Sicily, his abode must surely be Mount Etna; indeed he had been seen at the volcano's mouth in December 1250, accompanied by his knights who rode ablaze down the slopes of the mountain, passing through the sea to join their master in the bowels of the earth. Not surprisingly, the volcano and its great lava flows had long been the subject of apocalyptic dreams. King Arthur, according to one tale, was supposed to lie underneath the mountain. The Sibylline oracles, still circulating in 1250, spoke of the mysterious return of him in whom man's hopes rested: 'he lives and he lives not'; a phrase that one modern historian of Frederick II, writing in the days of Weimar, unfortunately saw fit even to apply to the yet-to-be resurrected Germany of his own time.

The years after 1250 saw an endless succession of impostors or crazed enthusiasts who claimed to be the returned emperor. It was in Germany that the agitation was most acute. The image of Frederick II remained that of the scourge of the Church and friend of the poor: the impostors were themselves apparently of humble origin. In the 1280s, there emerged at Neuss a challenger to Rudolf von Habsburg, who did, it is true, offer to confer on the king of the Romans a crown, if Rudolf acknowledged the authority of the pseudo-Frederick. After securing a reasonably sized following in central Germany, this impostor was seized by King Rudolf and burned as a heretic. Nevertheless, his supporters refused to believe that he had died. He would return on the third day. It was rumoured that, after the execution, no human bones were found, only a bean, a symbol of regeneration. In 1284 a hermit from Worms proclaimed himself emperor Frederick. But, as time passed, the image of Frederick was also transformed. It was no longer the youthful, indeed 'ever-young', Frederick who would return – a figure recalling the image of the conquering boy of Apulia – nor even a Frederick gradually aged by years as hermit or pilgrim. The second Frederick's image merged with that of his grandfather Frederick Barbarossa, the old warrior who had gone east to Jerusalem to hang his shield on an olive tree and inaugurate a new era for mankind. The apocalyptic talk at Barbarossa's court, in which that emperor's uncle Otto bishop of Freising had freely indulged, had undoubtedly influenced Frederick I's crusading plans; here too was the emperor of the Last Days, but without the Joachite accretions. Barbarossa's sudden death by drowning had also been turned into a retirement from the world; the emperor sat in a cave under a German mountain, the Kyffhäuser, sleeping, but awaiting the moment when he must return to redeem Christendom. There were those who had seen him, with his beard growing right through the table on which he leaned. This Frederick and his grandson merged into a single figure in popular eschatology. The coming-together of these traditions merely intensified their impact. In the fourteenth century, when Frederick II would have passed the normal human span of life, it was still being broadcast in Germany that his return was imminent.

A powerful stimulus came, too, from mere accidentals: the appearance of rulers in western Europe who were named Frederick. It has been seen that Frederick of Aragon, king of Sicily, became the focus for the aspirations of Italian Joachites and Spiritual Franciscans in the fourteenth century. His very difficulties with the papacy reinforced the view that he had been sent to suppress the evils and errors of the contemporary Church. He tended to be seen as the heir to and fulfilment of the apocalyptic emperor rather than as Frederick II *redivivus*. It was really in Germany that the idea took root of a Frederick II who 'is still alive and will remain alive until the end of the world; there has been and shall be no proper emperor but he'. This is to cite a source from 1434, but it only refers to a resurgence of a belief apparent throughout the fourteenth century. The returned Frederick was seen as an ally of the poor, of course, a converter or persecutor of the Jews (who appear again and again in the guise of enemies of the poor), as also of the corrupt Church; but he is, too, the victorious crusader who leads the common people to Jerusalem, throwing open its gates and inaugurating either the new age, or at least a period of plenty and good government. The long reign of the fifteenth-century Emperor Frederick III attracted, at least in the early days, many such dreams. Enthusiasts projected him as the promised redeeming emperor, Frederick I, II and III rolled into one; alas, it was not a period in which the German monarchy achieved any of the high aims the poor seemed to demand.

Frederick III was all the more a disappointment in the light of the prophecies of a widely disseminated work known as the *Reformatio Sigismundi*, written in the 1430s and presented in part as the vision of the late Emperor Sigismund; this foretold the arrival of a new Emperor Frederick, who on this occasion seems to be none other than the book's author or a friend of the author, a radical priest named Friedrich von Lantnaw – no relation of the future Emperor Frederick III. The reformation of the Church, corrupted by pelf and avarice, is to be this emperor's aim. But he is also to protect the poor against the vagaries of price rises and of wage fixing. The book thus reflects the difficulties of the less well-off in the long economic crisis that succeeded the Black Death: for some, a period of new prosperity, but for others a time when their labour seemed undervalued and the profits of the rich appeared to be made at their expense. Nobody offered Friedrich von Lantnaw a crown, and Frederick III fulfilled none of these expectations. On the other hand, we find in fifteenth-century Germany several potent signs that the 'third Frederick' continued to exert influence. In the works of the humanist Celtis, far removed from the apocalyptic enthusiasm of the poor, there emerges a strong sense of German nationhood. It becomes the German-ness, not the *Romanitas*, of the empire that counts. The *Book of a Hundred Chapters* at the start of the sixteenth century presents the arguments of the humanists with an almost over-whelmingly apocalyptic flavour. A thousand-year Reich under the 'emperor from the Black Forest' is predicted; corrupt priests, Jews, Turks can expect no mercy. The Germans are presented as the true People of God. Even the Ten Commandments are rejected. In fact the new Frederick would bring Germany back to its ancestral religion, the worship of Jupiter. 'The Germans once held the entire world in their hands; they will do so again, and with more power than ever.' But the Black Forest emperor was not a Habsburg prince. He was humble in status and in ancestry. The name of Frederick, though used, is now no more than a code word, embodying the ideal of a restored, reunited Germany, under a new and radical social order in which the power of princes, landlords and wealthy merchants would be entirely smashed.

And this itself takes us back to 1250, for the Germany Frederick left behind was, and remained, a Germany of the princes. The long interregnum until 1273 (preceded in 1256 by the death of William of Holland); the ineffective rule of Rudolf von Habsburg's successors; the failed attempt of Emperor Henry VII to bring peace to Guelfs and Ghibellines in Dante's Italy; the final withdrawal of the emperors to a power base in Bohemia under Charles IV, in the mid-fourteenth century – all this removed from the German monarchy effective power of intervention either in Italy or even in large areas of Germany. The princes too, it must be admitted, had to struggle to hold their own estates together; the disintegration of royal power was paralleled by disintegration of princely power in some regions. There was, however, a distinct recovery of princely authority in the fifteenth century. The issue by Charles IV of the Golden Bull, in 1356, confirming and extending the rights of autonomy of the great princes, set the seal on the developments already visible under Frederick II. But the process of disintegration and dislocation had remarkable effects in the way it stimulated the poor and the dispossessed to dream of lost glories under Frederick II, and of a future restoration under a blessed emperor.

CONCLUSION

The subtitle of this book is intended (unlike other subtitles one could cite) to convey a meaning: the medieval emperor and king of Sicily in whom everyone has identified a *stupor mundi*, a wonder of the world, since the thirteenth century, was in fact a man of his time, and not the displaced Renaissance despot he is generally taken to have been. This statement involves an outright rejection of the views of (for example) Matthew Paris in the England of Henry III – a gossip, but a well-informed gossip when dealing with Frederick – or of Jacob Burckhardt in his magisterial study of the Renaissance *signori*, or of Ernst Kantorowicz in his epic biography of the emperor, and of Thomas Curtis van Cleve in his own very dreary foot-slog through the reign. Like contemporary rulers, Frederick had scientific interests, and he developed them to a higher level than other thirteenth-century monarchs; he was an able ornithologist. Still, a skill at bird-watching does not qualify a man for his crown; Frederick's abilities as a ruler must not be underestimated, but far from being an implacable foe of the papacy, as he is usually represented, he was sincere in his attempts at compromise, even appeasement, and was even a sincere devotee of the crusading movement all through his life. Of course, there were themes in his methods of government that marked him out from his neighbours in France or Spain: a more centralized bureaucracy in Sicily, though not of his creation; a very decentralized system of rule in Germany. In both cases he took what he found, restored it to pristine shape and acted the part of a thorough-going conservative: for that was what he was, and there is very little in his views that can be seen as truly radical.

What distinguishes his reign is the bitterness of the struggle between pope and emperor. Even here there were long periods of harmony. And when battle was joined it was not the popes but the Lombard cities who stood for a long time in the van. Yet to them the real issues concerned local politics, and Frederick's battles at Cortenuova or Parma were, in a sense, intrusions in a war that had been going on since the middle of the twelfth century between the Milanese and their allies and the Cremonesi and theirs – a war which popes and emperors certainly saw as a major threat to public peace in Europe, and which they hoped to settle by imposing their supreme authority as arbiter in Italian affairs. The popes also cared deeply about the union of Sicily and southern Italy with the Holy Roman Empire, under Frederick and his father; but here too the capacity for compromise of the emperor should not be ignored.

Frederick's policy was, in a word, dynastic. Like the king of France, Louis IX, or the king of Aragon, James the Conqueror, he aimed to hand down intact to his heirs the territories he had himself inherited and won; and like them he had to decide whether to divide these territories among his sons or to pass them as a whole to his eldest son. Two factors controlled his decision. One was that the pope wanted to decide the matter for him; this he could not accept. The other was that his eldest son, Henry, rebelled against him and had to be turned off the throne of Germany. Thus his dynastic policy emerged at the end of his reign in the form of a wish to secure a united inheritance for his second son Conrad; but earlier he had thought in terms much closer to the papal ideal of the division of Sicily from the empire.

Part of Frederick's attraction to historians and the wider public has always been that he was supposedly a rationalist, even a free-thinker, ahead of his time, nurtured in the tolerant setting of semi-Muslim Sicily, a friend of Jews and Saracens: the sort of ruler who, to be frank, does not really exist in the Christian Middle Ages, even in Sicily or Spain. Frederick, as generally interpreted, expresses the frustration of historians in dealing with a period when the world-outlook was remote from our own. Relatively speaking, yes, he was extraordinarily tolerant, but not according to modern canons of equal treatment before the law, and in the mind, of people of all religions; he was less overt in his piety than his devout contemporary Louis of France, but his links with the Cistercian order should not be ignored. He was a Christian, critical of the excesses of papal power that brought him much suffering; and contemporaries, including the monk Matthew Paris, found common ground with him on this.

He was a man of some intellectual ability and of reasonable political skills who was called on by his dual inheritance to grapple indecisively with the claims to higher authority of the Roman Church; and when the gauntlet was thrown down he made little serious attempt to challenge the claim of the pope to moral leadership in the Christian world. He sought to clear himself of specific charges, not to strike a blow against the man he still saw as the vicar of Christ. The idea of a Church of the virtuous poor was certainly known to members of his court, but was given only limited encouragement.

This book offers a reinterpretation of a reign that has, in reality, been interpreted all too consistently. And it would be quite wrong to assume that Frederick himself was consistent in the application of his political beliefs; they changed over time, but, like virtually all political leaders, he found it possible to pursue at a single moment aims that seem to a modern observer self-contradictory, or at least highly inconsistent. The fact that he attempted to revive the Norman autocracy in Sicily while confirming the power of the princes (and lack of power of the monarch) in Germany has surprised historians; if there did exist a common theme, it was the idea that the subjects over whom he ruled must be left with their age-old rights. Far too much has been made of his appointment of a justiciar in Germany or of a vicar-general in northern Italy. Again, it is a question of arch-conservatism, not of precocious enlightened despotism. Even so, Frederick could find himself in a great muddle when confronted by competing claims to authority within his many kingdoms: this was the case during his visit to Cyprus and the Holy Land. Such inconsistencies in outlook and behaviour do not always need to be resolved by historians. Frederick was not a political genius or visionary, and the attempts of his advisers, notably Piero della Vigna, to create a reasonably coherent theory of kingship only achieved a few concrete results, and then mainly in southern Italy. Nor should one confuse the enunciation of a programme of government with its enforcement; just as political manifestos of the twentieth century are rich in unfulfilled, even unrealistic, promises, the Capua Gate, the *augustalis* coins and the introduction to the law-book of 1231 could not make Roman autocracy a reality.

He lived less like an oriental prince than is easily assumed; this is not to say that his court, with its Muslim dancing-girls and trumpeters, appeared anything less than exotic to visitors from the north. But Frederick's cultural patronage was a pale shadow of that of his Norman ancestors. Partly this was the result of war, which distracted his attention and his funds towards Lombardy. And partly it was the result of a long, slow disengagement of Sicily from the Muslim world, culminating in the expulsion of the Saracens from Sicily and the refoundation of Lucera as a Muslim garrison town in Apulia. By the thirteenth century the coexistence of Christian, Muslim and Jew, committed to common cultural enterprises such as translation work, was a feature of the court of Castile rather than of that of Sicily. The reign of Frederick II marks the end, not the revival, of *convivencia* in his southern kingdom.

The interest of Frederick's reign lies in his adversaries as much as in himself, in popes who were more determined to destroy his power than he ever was to destroy theirs. It is in the fullest sense a tragic history, of a man forced by his opponents to act in his own defence, disappointed in his ideals, the victim of his dual dynastic inheritance. Yet among his great ideals was the preservation of that inheritance, not solely to achieve power for himself, but to pass on to his heirs, intact, the lands, titles and rights that he believed God had called him to possess. He was not a Sicilian, nor a Roman, nor a German, nor a *mélange* of Teuton and Latin, still less a semi-Muslim: he was a Hohenstaufen and a Hauteville.

BIBLIOGRAPHY AND NOTES

Abbreviations

====

AF   *Atti del convegno internazionale di studi federiciani, Palermo 1950* (Palermo, 1952)

HB   J. L. A. Huillard-Bréholles, *Historia diplomatica Friderici secundi*, 6 vols in 12 parts (Paris, 1852–61)

MGH   *Monumenta Germaniae Historica*
Ep. Sel. *Epistolae saeculi XIII e regestis Pontificum Romanorum Selectae*
Const. *Leges, Constitutiones Imperatorum*

PF   *Probleme um Friedrich II.*, ed. J. Fleckenstein (Vorträge und Forschungen, xvi, Sigmaringen, 1974)

SM¹   *Stupor Mundi: zur Geschichte Friedrichs II. von Hohenstaufen*, ed. G. Wolf, 1st ed. (Darmstadt, 1966)

SM²   *Stupor Mundi: zur Geschichte Friedrichs II. von Hohenstaufen*, ed. G. Wolf, 2nd ed. (Darmstadt, 1982)

This appendix is designed to indicate some of the most important primary sources and recent literature on Frederick II. A full bibliography would not merely be enormous; it would mix together items of very varied value; and good bibliographies exist already: the most important is that of C. A. Willemsen, *Bibliografia federiciana: fonti e letteratura storica su Federico II e gli ultimi svevi* (Società di storia patria per la Puglia, Bibliografie e fonti archivistiche, i, Bari, 1982), with a German edition published by

MGH (but quite a large number of items listed here do not appear even in Willemsen's bibliographies); and, for literature in Italian above all, a shorter critical listing in G. Pepe, *Lo stato ghibellino di Federico II* (2nd ed., Bari, 1951), repr. as *Carlo Magno e Federico II* (Florence, 1968). There is also a surprisingly dated survey of the literature in T. C. van Cleve, *The Emperor Frederick II of Hohenstaufen, Immutator Mundi* (Oxford, 1972).

(a) Biographies of Frederick II

Passing over older works such as T. L. Kington, *History of Frederick II, Emperor of the Romans, from chronicles and documents published within the last ten years*, 2 vols (Cambridge, 1862), the most important early studies are perhaps those of Eduard Winkelmann, *Philipp von Schwaben und Otto IV. von Braunschweig*, 2 vols (Leipzig, 1873–8), and *Kaiser Friedrich II.*, 2 vols (Leipzig, 1889–97), in the series *Jahrbücher des Deutschen Reiches*. The detailed chronological coverage is accompanied by lengthy citations from the original sources in the footnotes. But Winkelmann never completed his survey of the last twenty years of the reign; some clues to his approach can be gained from his short monograph 'Zur Geschichte Kaiser Friedrichs II. in den Jahren 1239 bis 1241', *Forschungen zur deutschen Geschichte*, xii (1872).

Sensational accounts of Frederick's reign abounded in the first half of the twentieth century, adorned by titles such as *The Infidel Emperor* (by P. Wiegler, London, 1930), or *The Boy from Apulia*, (by R. Oke, London, 1936), but one work combined scholarship about the past with prophecy about the future: E. Kantorowicz, *Kaiser Friedrich der Zweite* (Berlin, 1927) aroused a storm of debate when it was published. On the book's genesis see D. Abulafia, 'Kantorowicz and Frederick II', *History*, lxii (1977), 193–210, repr. in D. Abulafia, *Italy, Sicily and the Mediterranean, 1050–1400* (London, 1987). Much of the debate is collected in SM[1]. Kantorowicz himself is the focus of E. Grünewald, *Ernst Kantorowicz und Stefan George. Beiträge zur Biographie des Historikers bis zum Jahre 1938 und seinem Jugendwerk 'Kaiser Friedrich der Zweite'* (Wiesbaden, 1982), on which, however, see my critical comments 'The Elusive Emperor', *Theoretische Geschiedenis*, xii (1985), 204–208. In the same mental framework as Kantorowicz's book there is W. von den Steinen, '"Der Verwandler der Welt". Kaiser Friedrich der Zweite. Zum 700. Todestag', in W. von den Steinen, *Menschen im Mittelalter. Gesammelte Forschungen, Betrachtungen, Bilder*, ed. P. von Moos (Berne, 1967).

The first edition of Kantorowicz appeared without notes, but a supplement (*Ergänzungsband*) appeared in 1931, full of references and excursuses. Vol. i only was translated into English as E. Kantorowicz, *Frederick the Second, 1194–1250*, transl. E. O. Lorimer (London, 1931, and reprints). Kantorowicz's work exercised a powerful hold over later interpretations of Frederick as the Apulian wonder-child, a man at least partly out of his time, such as the engaging and spirited biography by Georgina Masson, an expert on Italian gardens, entitled *Frederick II of Hohenstaufen. A Life* (London, 1957). Bigger claims are made for the authority of T. C. van Cleve, *The Emperor Frederick II of Hohenstaufen, Immutator Mundi* (Oxford, 1972), but it is an unadventurous account, moving no great distance from Kantorowicz in organization and on points of interpretation, though it is much heavier in detail. Its assumptions about the nature of the continuities from Norman to Hohenstaufen Sicily are very questionable. It is also rather dated, failing to take into account much recent work on Sicily and northern Italy. A useful corrective is K. Leyser, 'Emperor Frederick II', in his *Medieval Germany and its Neighbours* (London, 1982) [originally printed in *The Listener*, xc, no. 2316, 16 August, 1973, 208–210], though perhaps it goes too far in the other direction.

Among shorter studies, easily the best is H. M. Schaller, *Friedrich der Zweite* in the series *Persönlichkeit und Geschichte*, vol. xxxiv (Frankfurt/Zürich, 1964; Italian transl., 1970), which, however, lays more emphasis on the rhetoric of imperial monarchy than I believe to be appropriate. Similarly, see A. de Stefano, *L'idea imperiale di Federico II* (Bologna, 1952) and the work by G. Pepe listed above in various editions. A popular life in German is E. Horst, *Friedrich der Staufer* (Düsseldorf, 1975). More recent is H. Fink, *Ich bin der Herr der Welt* (Munich, 1986), which looks at Frederick's role as a thirteenth-century 'tyrant' in spirited prose, but goes no great distance beyond Kantorowicz. And from the other Germany there is B. Gloger, *Kaiser, Gott und Teufel* (East Berlin, 1970), which has the advantage of dealing at length with Frederick's later medieval reputation.

Important collections of essays are A F, P F (see list of abbreviations). Two editions of G. Wolf, ed., *Stupor Mundi* (S M[1], S M[2]) have appeared, sharing about half their material; these volumes consist of reprints of key articles, nearly all of the highest quality, covering a wide variety of aspects of Frederick's reign – his chancery, his economic policy, his attitude to heretics, etc. The material in P F is, however, all new, and covers an equally wide range of topics.

(b) Themes throughout the reign
====

Frederick's attitude to the Church in Sicily has received close attention, first in a valuable article by H. J. Pybus, 'The Emperor Frederick II and the Sicilian Church', *Cambridge Historical Journal*, iii (1929/30), 134–63, later in some studies by James M. Powell, 'Frederick II and the Church in the Kingdom of Sicily, 1220–40', *Church History*, xxx (1961), 28–34, and 'Frederick II and the church: a revisionist view', *Catholic Historical Review*, xliv (1962/3), 487–97, and now in N. Kamp, *Kirche und Monarchie im staufischen Königreich Sizilien*, 4 vols so far (Münster, 1973 onwards), which consists of a prosopography, or Who's Who, of south Italian and Sicilian bishops from the late Norman to the early Angevin period.

On the Jews, and in particular their legal status and economic activities in Sicily, there is still no substitute for the elderly R. Straus, *Die Juden im Königreich Sizilien unter Normannen und Staufern* (Heidelberg, 1910). And on Frederick's relations with the Muslim world there is J. Hauziński, *Polityka orientalna Frideryka II* in the collection *Universytet Adama Mickiewicza w Posnaniu, Seria historica*, lxxix (Poznan, 1978), which contains a German summary.

(c) Primary sources
====

Any list must begin with the massive collection of charters and other material, J. L. A. Huillard-Bréholles, *Historia diplomatica Friderici secundi*, 6 vols in 12 parts, (Paris, 1852–61). But for the register of Frederick II originally preserved in the Archivio di Stato, Naples, see rather C. Carcani, ed., *Constitutiones regum regni utriusque Siciliae mandante Friderico II Imperatore per Petrum de Vinea Capuanum Praetorio Praefectum et Cancellarium . . . et Fragmentum quod superest Regesto eiusdem Imperatoris Ann. 1239 & 1240* (Naples, 1786). For the history of this document, see W. Hagemann, 'La nuova edizione del Regesto di Federico II', AF, 315–36.

Some important documents were recovered from the archives of Marseilles, Naples and elsewhere in E. Winkelmann, *Acta imperii inedita*, 2 vols (Innsbruck, 1880–5), where it is possible to identify material originally included in lost registers of Frederick II before 1239 and after 1240.

For the letters of Piero della Vigna, and his career as a whole, see J. L. A. Huillard-Bréholles, *Étude sur la vie, la correspondance et la rôle politique de Pierre de la Vigne* (Paris, 1865).

For papal correspondence, there are the volumes in the Monumenta

Germaniae Historica, *Epistolae Selectae*, series ed. C. Rodenberg (leaving very many gaps) and also the publications of the École Française de Rome: E. Berger, ed., *Les Registres d'Innocent IV (1243–54)*, 4 vols (Paris, 1884–1921), which, however, gives more emphasis to relations with France than to the empire, and provides many of the documents only in summary.

Honorius III received separate treatment from P. Pressutti, ed., *Regesta Honorii Papae III*, 2 vols (Rome, 1888–95). A new edition of Innocent III's letters, following the most exacting criteria, is being issued by the Austrian Institute in Rome; until it is complete, see the unreliable text in Migne, *Patrologia Latina*, vols 214–16.

The chronicle sources are too numerous to list here. Some, such as the *Annals of Cologne*, refer – though extensively – to Frederick in passing; those scholars who first pieced together the narrative of the reign had to work from a vast array of chronicles each of which provided only small fragments of evidence. Frederick II had no court chronicler, and, for all his impact on contemporaries, inspired few contemporary biographers. But the south Italian notary Richard of San Germano left an account of the reign from the perspective of the Regno, *Ryccardi de Sancto Germano, Chronica*, ed. C. A. Garufi, *Rerum italicarum scriptores*, 2nd series, vol. vii, pt 2 (Bologna 1936–8) (also in MGH, SS, xix). The English chronicler Matthew Paris was fascinated by Frederick: Matthew Paris, *Chronica majora*, 7 vols, ed. H. R. Luard (Rolls Series, 1872–83); also his *Historia minor*, 3 vols, ed. F. Madden (Rolls Series, 1865–9).

And Frederick was naturally the background figure in three important Lombard chronicles, the Guelf and Ghibelline annals of Piacenza and the annals (Guelf only) of Parma: *Annales placentini gibellini*, MGH, SS, xviii; *Annales placentini guelfi*, MGH, SS, xviii and MGH, *Scriptores in usum scholarum*, ed. O. Holder-Egger (Hanover–Leipzig, 1901); *Annales parmenses maiores*, MGH, SS, xviii; *Chronicon parmense*, *Rerum italicarum scriptores*, 2nd ed., vol. ix, pt 9.

The Franciscan Salimbene incorporated several dramatic tales of Frederick's career and conduct in his *Cronica*, ed. G. Scalia (Scrittori d'Italia, Bari, 1966; older ed. by F. Bernini, same series, Bari, 1942). A paraphrase into English of several sections was offered in G. C. Coulton, *From St Francis to Dante: translations from the chronicle of the Franciscan Salimbene (1221–1288)* (London, 1907; repr. Philadelphia, 1972); and there is also an edition in MGH, SS, xxxii.

The Genoese annalists, upholders of an ancient tradition of city chronicle-writing, also had much to say of great value: L. T. Belgrano and C. Imperiale di Sant'Angelo, eds, *Annali genovesi di Caffaro e de' suoi continuatori*, 4 vols (Fonti per la Storia d'Italia, Rome, 1890–1929). Other valuable

Italian sources include the *Carmina triumphalia tria de Victoria urbe eversa*, MGH, SS, xviii and (for Venice) the chronicle of Doge Andrea Dandolo, in *Rerum italicarum scriptores*, 2nd ed., vol. xii, pt 1.

Among German chronicles, all disappointing by comparison with those from Italy, see especially the *Chronica regia coloniensis* of Cologne, ed. G. Waitz, MGH *in usum scholarum* (Hanover, 1880). Among others, there are the *Annales Bremenses*, MGH, SS, xvii, *Annales Erphordenses*, MGH, SS, xvi and *Annales Wormatienses*, MGH, SS, xvii.

For the crusade there is nothing to compare with Philippe de Novare (Philip of Novara), *Mémoires*, ed. C. Kohler (Paris, 1913), also in English translation as *The Wars of Frederick II against the Ibelins in Syria and Cyprus*, transl. J. L. LaMonte with M. J. Hubert (New York, 1936). The Arabic chroniclers of the reign are available in not always reliable French translation in *Recueil des historiens des croisades, historiens orientaux*, vols i, ii, iv. But (with reference to Sicily only) see the Italian versions of M. Amari, *Biblioteca arabo-sicula, versione italiana*, 2 vols (Turin–Rome, 1880–81). Extracts in English – unfortunately translated from an Italian version of the Arabic – appear in F. Gabrieli, *Arab Historians of the Crusades* (London, 1969).

The Constitutions of Melfi have been edited many times, with a printing history of five centuries. For the beginning, see Sixtus Riessinger's Neapolitan edition of 1475, repr. as *Constitutiones regni Siciliae 'Liber Augustalis' Neapel 1475*, Faksimiledruck mit einer Einleitung von Hermann Dilcher (Glashütten/Taunus, 1973), though the reprinted text is small and makes for hard reading. As well as Carcani's edition (above, containing also the Register of 1239–40), there is the edition accompanied by the commentaries of Andreas of Isernia: *Constitutiones regni utriusque Siciliae, Glossis ordinariis, Commentariis excellentiss. I. U. D. Domini Andraeae de Isernia, ac Bartholomaei Capuani* (Lyons, 1568); but reference now needs to be made to the new German edition and studies, under the general editorship of Hermann Dilcher: *Die Konstitutionen Friedrichs II. für sein Königreich Sizilien*, ed. H. Conrad, T. von der Lieck-Buyken, W. Wagner; H. Dilcher, *Die sizilische Gesetzgebung Kaiser Friedrichs II. Quellen der Constitutionen von Melfi und ihrer Novellen*, in the series *Studien und Quellen zur Welt Kaiser Friedrichs II.* (Cologne and Sigmaringen, 1972–4). And for an English translation of the entire text see J. M. Powell, *The Liber Augustalis or Constitutions of Melfi promulgated by the Emperor Frederick II for the Kingdom of Sicily in 1231* (Syracuse, NY, 1971).

(d) Bibliography and notes to each chapter

==

CHAPTER 1

There is a lively narrative of the Norman conquest of Sicily and of the political history of the Norman kingdom in: J. J. Norwich, *The Normans in the South, 1013–1130* (London, 1967), and its sequel J. J. Norwich, *The Kingdom in the Sun, 1130–1194* (London, 1970). But greater accuracy will be found in the weighty standard work, F. Chalandon, *Histoire de la domination normande en Italie et en Sicile*, 2 vols. (Paris, 1907). On the economy, see I. Peri, *Uomini, città e campagne in Sicilia* (Bari, 1979) and D. Abulafia, *The Two Italies: economic relations between the Norman kingdom of Sicily and the northern communes* (Cambridge 1977), as well as D. Abulafia, 'The crown and the economy under Roger II and his successors', *Dumbarton Oaks Papers*, xxxvii (1983), 1–14, repr. in D. Abulafia, *Italy, Sicily and the Mediterranean, 1050–1400* (London, 1987). On methods of government, see in particular: E. Jamison, 'The Norman Administration of Apulia and Capua more especially under Roger II and William I', *Papers of the British School at Rome*, vi (1913); M. Caravale, *Il Regno normanno di Sicilia* (Milan, 1966); E. Mazzarese Fardella, *Aspetti dell'organizzazione amministrativa nello stato normanno-svevo* (Milan, 1966), and a study by H. Takayama, *Viator*, xvi (1985). L. R. Ménager, *Ammiratus – 'Αμηρᾶς. L'émirat et les origines de l'Amirauté* (Paris, 1960) is an extremely interesting account of the origins of the office of 'admiral', and of the derivation of the modern term by way of Sicily, Genoa and France. The question whether the Norman monarchy drew more on the west or on Byzantium for its ideas of rulership can be approached via the fundamental article of W. Ullmann, 'Rulership and the rule of law in the Middle Ages: the case of Norman Sicily', *Acta Juridica* (1978), but contrast L. R. Ménager, 'L'institution monarchique dans les états normands d'Italie', *Cahiers de civilisation médiévale*, ii (1959); repr. in L. R. Ménager, *Hommes et institutions de l'Italie normande* (London, 1981). Also important on this issue is J. Deér, *The Dynastic Porphyry Tombs of the Norman Period in Sicily* (Washington, DC, 1959).

On cultural life see E. Jamison, *Admiral Eugenius of Sicily. His Life and Work and the authorship of the 'Epistola ad Petrum' and the 'Historia Hugonis Falcandi Siculi'* (London, 1957) – with reservations; F. Giunta, *Bizantini e bizantinismo nella Sicilia normanna*, 2nd ed. (Palermo, 1974); C. H. Haskins, *Studies in the History of Medieval Science* (Cambridge, Mass., 1924) and on the fine arts: O. Demus, *Byzantine Art and the West* (London, 1970); O.

Demus, *The Mosaics of Norman Sicily* (London, 1949/50); E. Kitzinger, *The Art of Byzantium and the Medieval West: collected studies*, ed. W. E. Kleinbauer (Bloomington, Indiana, 1976).

On foreign policy, apart from Chalandon, there is P. Lamma, *Comneni e Staufer: Ricerche sui rapporti fra Bisanzio e l'Occidente nel secolo XII*, 2 vols. (Rome, 1955–7), for Byzantium, and, for Africa, D. Abulafia, 'The Norman Kingdom of Africa', in *Anglo-Norman Studies,* vii (1985), 26–49, repr. in D. Abulafia, *Italy, Sicily and the Mediterranean, 1050–1400* (London, 1987). One great work by a notable nineteenth-century Sicilian patriot ranges wider than its title suggests: M. Amari, *Storia dei musulmani di Sicilia*, 3 vols in 5 parts, 2nd ed. by C. A. Nallino (Catania, 1933–9). However, little trust can be placed in D. C. Douglas, *The Norman Fate* (London, 1976), or in A. Ahmad, *History of Islamic Sicily* (London, 1975).

CHAPTER 2

The literature on Barbarossa is no more satisfactory than that on Frederick II. One can begin, reliably, with H. Simonsfeld, *Friedrich I.* (Leipzig, 1908), in the *Jahrbücher*. Two biographies of recent date are P. Munz, *Frederick Barbarossa: a study in medieval politics* (London, 1969), and M. Pacaut, *Frederick Barbarossa* (London, 1969), translated from a French edition (Paris, 1967). But neither is entirely satisfactory. General accounts are given in: K. Hampe, *Germany under the Salian and Hohenstaufen Emperors*, transl. R. F. Bennett (Oxford, 1973); H. Fuhrmann, *Germany in the Central Middle Ages* (Cambridge, 1986); G. Barraclough, *The Origins of Modern Germany* (Oxford, 1946), which is wayward but very stimulating. An important and very sober work in German now available in English is K. Jordan, *Henry the Lion* (Oxford, 1987). See also the valuable collection of essays translated from German: G. Barraclough, ed., *Mediaeval Germany*, 2 vols (Oxford, 1938).

A varied and precious collection of essays is *Popolo e Stato in Italia nell'età di Federico Barbarossa. Alessandria e la Lega Lombarda. Relazioni al XXXIII congresso storico subalpino per la celebrazione dell'VIII centenario della fondazione di Alessandria, Alessandria, 1968* (Turin, 1970). There is important material on Barbarossa's motives in K. R. Brühl, *Fodrum, Gistum, Servitium Regis* (Cologne, 1968) and in K. Leyser, 'Frederick Barbarossa, Henry II and the Hand of St James', *Medieval Germany and its Neighbours* (London, 1982). The place to begin a study of his Italian policy is with the chronicle of the reign left by Frederick's uncle Otto of Freising and the continuator Rahewin; see MGH, SS, xx and, for a good translation, C. C. Mierow with R. W. Emery, transl., *The Deeds of Frederick Barbarossa* (New York, 1953).

But see also J. K. Hyde, *Society and Politics in Medieval Italy* (London, 1972) and D. Waley, *The Italian City-Republics* (London, 1969, third ed. 1988). E. F. Butler, *The Lombard Communes* (London, 1906; repr. Westport, Conn., 1969) still has much of value.

For Henry VI the *Jahrbücher* study by H. Toeche remains fundamental: *Heinrich VI.* (Leipzig, 1867); but see also J. Haller, *Heinrich VI. und die Römische Kirche* (Darmstadt, 1962), reprinting valuable studies of his relations with the papacy. C. M. Brand, *Byzantium Confronts the West, 1180–1204* (Cambridge, Mass., 1968), outlines Henry's relations with Constantinople very clearly. Henry's Sicilian policy has been studied by D. Clementi, 'Calendar of the Diplomas of the Hohenstaufen Emperor Henry VI concerning the Kingdom of Sicily', *Quellen und Forschungen aus italienischen Archiven und Bibliotheken*, xxxv (1955); see also D. Abulafia, *The Two Italies* (Cambridge, 1977) for the links between Henry and the Genoese, Pisans and Venetians at the time of the conquest of Sicily.

A massive and visually stunning exhibition catalogue, *Die Zeit der Staufer*, 5 vols (Stuttgart, 1977–9), concentrates rather heavily on Germany and on Frederick I, though it also has material on Italy and on later Hohenstaufen. There are important articles on the history as well as the art and architecture of the Hohenstaufen *Reich*.

CHAPTER 3

Preferable to his biography of Frederick is T. C. van Cleve's older *Markward von Anweiler and the Sicilian Regency* (Princeton, 1937). For the papal state in this period, see D. Waley's excellent *The Papal State in the Thirteenth Century* (London, 1961), and for Innocent III himself, H. Tillmann, *Papst Innocenz III.* (Bonn, 1954), with an English translation as *Pope Innocent III* (Amsterdam, 1980).

Peter of Eboli has been edited by G. B. Siragusa, *Carmen de rebus Siculis* (Fonti per la Storia d'Italia, Rome, 1905), with another edition, by E. Rota, in the series *Rerum italicarum scriptores*, 2nd ed., vol. xxxi, pt 1.

For Walter von der Vogelweide, see A. T. Hatto, 'Otto IV. und Walther von der Vogelweide', *Walther von der Vogelweide*, ed. S. Beyschlag (Darmstadt, 1971); and for Germany as a whole, E. Winkelmann, *Philipp von Schwaben und Otto von Braunschweig* (see above).

Markward and the 'political crusade' are the subject of E. Kennan, 'Innocent III and the first political crusade: a comment on the limitations of papal power', *Traditio*, xxvii (1971), on which see also N. Housley, *The Italian Crusades: the papal-Angevin alliance and the crusades against Christian lay powers, 1245–1343* (Oxford, 1982).

The Genoese freebooters are the subject of D. Abulafia, 'Henry Count of Malta and his Mediterranean Activities, 1203–1230', in *Medieval Malta: Studies on Malta before the Knights*, ed. A. T. Luttrell (London, 1975), repr. with a note on more recent literature in D. Abulafia, *Italy, Sicily and the Mediterranean, 1050–1400* (London, 1987). Cf. also L. R. Ménager, *Ammiratus – 'Αμηρᾶς* (Paris, 1960).

Van Cleve, *Frederick II* (above) settles decisively the issue of Frederick's education: contrast Kantorowicz here.

On Philip of Swabia's policies as far afield as Byzantium, see D. Queller, *The Fourth Crusade* (Leicester, 1978), and for the battle of Bouvines G. Duby, *Le dimanche de Bouvines, 27 juillet 1214* (Paris, 1973). Philip Augustus is the subject of J. Baldwin's majestic *The Government of Philip Augustus* (Baltimore, 1986).

On the Fifth Crusade, see now J. M. Powell, *Anatomy of a Crusade* (Philadelphia, 1986).

CHAPTER 4

Once again, E. F. Butler, *The Lombard Communes* (London, 1906) still makes very good sense. See also G. Fasoli, *Aspetti della politica italiana di Federico II* (Bologna, 1964).

Genoese relations with Frederick are studied to good effect in J. M. Powell, 'Genoese policy and the kingdom of Sicily, 1220–1240', *Mediaeval Studies*, xxviii (1966), 346–54.

The Assizes of Capua and the legislation at Messina can best be approached through Riccardo di San Germano's chronicle (see above). But see also the important comments of H. J. Pybus, 'The Emperor Frederick II and the Sicilian Church', *Cambridge Historical Journal*, iii (1929/30), stressing the effects of the recovery of royal demesne on the Church in the *regno*. On the Jews, see R. Straus (above) and on the Saracens M. Amari (above). Lucera was studied in depth by P. Egidi, *La colonia saracena di Lucera e la sua distruzione* (Lucera, 1915; and in the *Archivio storico per le provincie napoletane*, xxxvi–xxxix, 1911–14), as well as his *Codice diplomatico dei Saraceni di Lucera* (Naples, 1917), but the impressive documentation mainly concerns the destruction of the settlement by Charles II around 1300. Cf. E. Pontieri, 'Lucera svevo-angioina', *Atti dell'Accademia Pontiniana*, n.s., xvii (1966), 5–26. For the excavations there, see D. Whitehouse, 'Ceramici e vetri medioevali provenienti dal Castello di Lucera', *Bollettino d'Arte* (1966), 171–8.

For the crusade, see bibliography to Chapter 5.

CHAPTER 5

The best account of the crusade is in J. Prawer, *Histoire du royaume latin de Jérusalem*, vol. ii (Paris, 1970). There is also T. C. van Cleve, 'The crusade of Frederick II' in K. Setton, ed., *A History of the Crusades*, vol. ii, *The Later Crusades* (Philadelphia, 1962). For the key text of Philip of Novara's memoirs, see section (c) above. The French edition by C. Kohler, of 1913, outlines the complex textual history of this work. For convenience, ibn Wasil is cited from the Gabrieli translation (section (c), above).

Frederick's problems in the Latin East are discussed by G. F. Hill, *A History of Cyprus*, 4 vols (Cambridge, 1940–52) vol. iii, which now needs replacement; constitutional issues are the subject of a lively debate, dominated by J. Prawer, 'Estates, Communities and the Constitution of the Latin Kingdom of Jerusalem', in *Proceedings of the Israel Academy of Sciences and Humanities*, ii (1966), and by J. Riley-Smith, *The Feudal Nobility and the Kingdom of Jerusalem, 1099–1277* (London, 1973), which is particularly worthwhile on the period of Frederick II.

For events in the Church of the Holy Sepulchre, see H. E. Mayer, 'Das Pontifikale von Tyrus', *Dumbarton Oaks Papers*, xxi (1967).

The early history of the Teutonic Knights is the subject of M. L. Favreau, *Studien zur Frühgeschichte des Deutschen Ordens* (Kiel, n.d.), to which should be added, for eastern Europe, the spirited book of E. Christiansen, *The Northern Crusades* (London, 1980).

For artistic developments such as the Riccardiana Psalter, see H. Buchthal, *Miniature Painting in the Latin Kingdom of Jerusalem* (Oxford, 1957). On the architectural side, M. Benvenisti, *The Crusaders in the Holy Land* (Jerusalem, 1970) is the best starting-point, with, on Starkenberg, much amusement to be derived from the American excavation report, ed. M. Benvenisti, *The Crusaders' Fortress of Montfort* (Jerusalem, 1983), repr. (with additional material) from the *Bulletin of the Metropolitan Museum of Art, New York* (1927).

The 'war of the keys' of Gregory IX must be approached via Gregory's letters (e.g., in the MGH Ep. Sel. collection) and via Roger of Wendover, *Chronica sive Flores Historiarum*, 4 vols, ed. H. O. Coxe (London, 1831–44). See also W. Koster, *Der Kreuzablaß im Kampfe der Kurie mit Friedrich II.* (Münster, 1913).

CHAPTER 6

A vast literature here, culminating in the new German edition of the *Constitutions* under the direction of H. Dilcher (see above).

Especially important is earlier work by T. Buyken, *Das römische Recht in den Constitutionen von Melfi* (Wissenschaftl. Abh. d. Arbeitsgemeinschaft für Forschung des Landes Nordrhein-Westfalen, xvii, Cologne, 1960), and *Die Constitutionen von Melfi und das Jus Francorum* (Abh. der Rheinisch-Westfälischen Akad. der Wissenschaften, li, Opladen, 1973). Cf. too the Polish historian I. Malinowska-Kwiatkowska, *Prawo prywatne w ustawodawstwie Królestwa Sycylii (1140–1231)* (Polish Academy of Sciences, Warsaw, Wroclaw, etc., 1973).

The English translation by J. M. Powell, *The Liber Augustalis or Constitutions of Melfi* (Syracuse, N Y, 1971), contains a short introduction to the document and the period by a specialist in the reign.

On *jus* and *justitia* see W. Ullmann, *The Growth of Papal Government* (3rd ed., London, 1970) and E. Kantorowicz, *The King's Two Bodies* (Princeton, 1957). The theme of purgatory is discussed to disconcertingly good effect by J. Le Goff, *The Birth of Purgatory*, Eng. transl. (London, 1985).

Frederick's economic policies have received close attention in two important studies: J. M. Powell, 'Medieval monarchy and trade: the economic policy of Frederick II in the Kingdom of Sicily', *Studi medievali*, ser. 3, iii (1966), 420–524, a massive article making good use of the laws of 1231; but E. Maschke, 'Die Wirtschaftspolitik Friedrichs II. im Königreich Sizilien', *Vierteljahrschrift für Sozial- und Wirtschaftsgeschichte*, lv (1966), 289–328, repr. in S M², is often at odds with Powell. My own interpretation steers a middle course. There are some further ideas in F. M. De Robertis, 'La politica economica di Federico II di Svevia', *Atti delle seconde giornate federiciane, Oria, 16/17 ottobre 1971* (Società di storia patria per la Puglia, Convegni, iv, Bari, 1974), 27–40.

On links between Sicily and northern Italy under Frederick II, see H. Chone, *Die Handelsbeziehungen Kaiser Friedrichs II. zu den Seestädten Venedig, Pisa, Genua* (Berlin, 1902, repr. Liechtenstein, 1965); J. M. Powell, *Mediaeval Studies*, xxxviii (1966).

On the *augustales*, there are valuable insights in R. Lopez, 'Back to Gold, 1252', *Economic History Review*, ser. 2, ix (1956/7); for a fuller discussion, see D. Abulafia, 'Maometto e Carlomagno: le due aree monetarie dell'Italia medievale, dell'oro e dell'argento', *Annali della Storia d'Italia Einaudi*, vi, ed. U. Tucci and R. Romano (Turin, 1983), repr. in D. Abulafia, *Italy, Sicily and the Mediterranean, 1050–1400* (London, 1987).

On monopolies, D. Abulafia, 'The crown and the economy under Roger II and his successors', *Dumbarton Oaks Papers*, xxvii (1983), 1–14, attempts to place Frederick's regulations in a wider context.

CHAPTER 7

For the course of events, see van Cleve, *Frederick II*; cf. G. Blondel, *Études sur la politique de l'empereur Frédéric II en Allemagne et sur les transformations de la constitution allemande dans la première moitié du XIIIe siècle* (Paris, 1892). Important is the study by E. Klingelhöfer, *Die Reichsgesetze von 1220, 1231–2 und 1235, ihr Werden und ihre Wirkung im deutschen Staat Friedrichs II.*, in Quellen und Studien zur Verfassungsgeschichte des Deutschen Reiches in Mittelalter und Neuzeit, viii, Heft 2 (Weimar, 1955), repr. (though with omissions) in S M¹, S M². See also Z S.

For relations with Denmark, see J. Danstrup and H. Koch, eds, *Danmarks Historie*, vols iii, *Kongemagt og Kirke, 1060–1241*, by H. Koch (Copenhagen, 1963), and iv, *Borgerkrig og Kalmarunion, 1241–1448*, by E. Kjersgaard (Copenhagen, 1963).

The privileges to the German princes are printed in M G H, Const ii, as is the *Mainzer Landfriede*.

On the Jews of Germany, G. Kisch, *The Jews of Medieval Germany* (2nd ed., New York, 1970) is fundamental.

CHAPTER 8

The best starting-point is the collection of essays by C. H. Haskins reprinted in his *Studies in the History of Medieval Science* (Cambridge, Mass., 1924) and in *Studies in Medieval Culture* (Oxford, 1929), where Greek and Latin letters, falconry and other subjects are discussed. But for the Jews see C. Sirat, *A History of Jewish Philosophy in the Middle Ages* (Cambridge, 1985). On Michael Scot, as well as Haskins see L. Thorndike, *Michael Scot* (London, 1965). There is useful material too in P F, S M¹, S M².

On Greek learning, see M. B. Wellas, *Griechisches aus dem Umkreis Kaiser Friedrichs II.* (Münchener Beiträge zur Mediävistik und Renaissance-Forschung, xxxiii, Munich, 1983); cf. the short article by J. M. Powell, 'Frederick II's knowledge of Greek', *Speculum*, xxxviii (1963), 481–2.

For falconry, see the facsimile of Vatican M S Palatine Latin 1071 ed. C. A. Willemsen (Graz, 1969); a further study and edition by this expert (Leipzig, 1942), and the excellent English translation and discussion by C. A. Wood and F. M. Fyfe, *The Art of Falconry, being the 'De Arte Venandi cum Avibus' of Frederick II of Hohenstaufen* (Stanford, 1943). Also, Haskins, *Medieval Science*, has good points to make.

On the *scuola siciliana* there is a particularly large literature. A combination of comments, texts and translations can be found in the worthwhile study of F. Jensen, *The Poets of the Scuola Siciliana* (Garland Library, New York, 1986). For the poets themselves, M. Catalano, *La scuola poetica siciliana* (Messina, 1948) is a good but often neglected survey. R. Baehr, 'Die sizilianische Dichterschule und Friedrich II.', PF, is more up to date.

There are selections with a German translation by C. A. Willemsen in *Kaiser Friedrich II. und sein Dichterkreis*, 2nd ed. (Wiesbaden, 1977). But the full edition of this material is by B. Panvini, *La scuola poetica siciliana*, 2 vols (Florence, 1955–8), vol. i containing the material from Frederick's court. On Giacomo da Lentini there is a study and edition by E. F. Langley, *The Poetry of Giacomo da Lentino, Sicilian poet of the thirteenth century* (Cambridge, Mass., 1915). The early history of the European love lyric is covered, controversially, in P. Dronke, *Medieval Latin Literature and the Rise of the Love Lyric*, 2 vols (2nd ed., Oxford, 1968), and in less revolutionary an approach by L. T. Topsfield, *Troubadours and Love* (Cambridge, 1975).

On Frederick's buildings, the main authority, delighting in the presence of a son of Germany and of the Northmen in southern Italy, is C. A. Willemsen, especially *Kaiser Friedrichs II. Triumphator zu Capua* (Wiesbaden, 1953); also *Castel del Monte: das vollendste Baudenkmal Kaiser Friedrichs des Zweiten* (Frankfurt, 1982); but more general surveys by the same author include *Apulien: Kathedralen und Kastellen* (DuMont Reiseführer, 2nd ed., Cologne, 1973) and the well-illustrated *Apulia: Imperial Splendour in Southern Italy* (with D. Odenthal) (London, 1959). A survey first published in Z S, vol. iii, has been republished separately in Italian: C. A. Willemsen, *I castelli di Federico II nell'Italia meridionale* (Naples, 1978).

For the castle at Prato, see A F. For Frederick's German castles see W. Holtz, *Pfalzen und Burgen der Stauferzeit* (Darmstadt, 1981).

There is still much of value in C. Shearer, *The Renaissance of Architecture in Southern Italy. A Study of Frederick II of Hohenstaufen and the Capua Triumphtor Archway and Towers* (Cambridge, 1935). On Gothic tendencies, see also F. Bologna, *I pittori alla corte angioina di Napoli, 1266–1414, e un riesame dell'arte nell'età federiciana* (Rome, 1969).

E. Kantorowicz, *The King's Two Bodies* (Princeton, 1957), has important ideas about the Capua gate and the concept of *justitia*.

For more extensive discussion of the arts under Frederick II see Z S, vols iii and v, in particular the study of Roman-style cameos attributed to the emperor's court (R. Kahnsitz, 'Staufische Kameen', vol. v, 477–520). But some authorities prefer to date much of the material analysed there to the Medicean period in Florence.

CHAPTER 9

On the Italian tyrants, the best discussion is J. Larner, *Italy in the Age of Dante and Petrarch, 1216–1380* (London, 1980); cf. his *Lords of the Romagna* (London, 1965). A general survey of value is D. M. Bueno de Mesquita, 'The place of despotism in Italian politics', in J. Hale, R. Highfield, B. Smalley, eds, *Europe in the late Middle Ages* (London, 1965), 301–31. For Frederick and the tyrants, see G. Fasoli, *Aspetti della politica italiana di Federico II* (Bologna, 1964).

Frederick's troubles with the Genoese are discussed in Chone, *Handelsbeziehungen* (above), but the Sardinian question has a large literature of its own, e.g., A. Boscolo, *La Sardegna dei Giudicati* (Cagliari, 1969), and F. Artizzu, *La Sardegna pisana e genovese* (Sassari, 1985), for the basic narrative. See also C. Imperiale di Sant'Angelo, *Genova e le sue relazioni con Federico II* (Venice, 1923).

For the conflict with the popes, see Huillard-Bréholles, *Pierre de la Vigne*; MGH Ep.; and – for central Italy – Waley, *Papal State*.

CHAPTER 10

This chapter is based on a close reading of Frederick II's register, in Carcani's edition of 1786 and from the photographs preserved in Naples. See also HB, vol. v, for the register, and HB, Introduction, pp. cdxx–cdxxii, for the bank loans.

A coy account of the events of 1943 appears in W. Hagemann, 'La nuova edizione del Regesto di Federico II', AF; cf. D. Abulafia, 'Kantorowicz and Frederick II'.

For the grain exports, Maschke, 'Wirtschaftspolitik', is especially valuable. Cf. also Peri, *Città e campagna*, and Powell, 'Medieval Monarchy and Trade'.

On officials, N. Kamp, 'Von Kämmerer zum Sekreten: Wirtschaftsreformen und Finanzverwaltung im staufischen Königreich Sizilien', PF, is of capital importance. See also W. E. Hempel, *Der sizilische Großhof unter Kaiser Friedrich II.* (Leipzig, 1940).

On the Jews, Straus, *Die Juden*, contains a register of documents in summary.

CHAPTER 11

The letter to the archbishop of Messina is from the register of 1239–40 – see above.

Gregory IX's calling of a crusade against Frederick II is the subject of study in W. Koster, *Der Kreuzablaß im Kampfe der Kurie mit Friedrich II.* (Münster, 1913). Compare N. Housley, *The Italian Crusades* (Oxford, 1982), F. H. Russell, *The Just War in the Middle Ages* (Cambridge, 1975). Important sources here are Matthew Paris and the Genoese Annals, as well as the papal letters.

Richard, earl of Cornwall, is studied by N. Denholm-Young, *Richard of Cornwall* (Oxford, 1947). For events in Rome, see, e.g., P. Partner, *The Lands of St Peter* (London, 1972).

Innocent IV is discussed well by C. Rodenberg, *Innocenz IV. und das Königreich Sizilien, 1245–1254* (Halle, 1892). See also W. Ullmann, 'Reflections on the conflict between Frederick II and the papacy', *Archivio storico pugliese*, xiii (1960), 16–39, repr. in W. Ullmann, *Scholarship and Politics in the Middle Ages* (London, 1978); and the same author's 'Frederick II's opponent Innocent IV as Melchisedek', in A F.

CHAPTER 12

As well as summarizing the papal registers of Innocent IV in the four-volume series of the École française de Rome, E. Berger analysed the role of the French king in international politics in his *Saint Louis et Innocent IV* (Paris, 1893).

The plot against Frederick was discussed by K. Hampe, *Papst Innocenz IV. und die sizilische Verschwörung von 1246*, Sonderband der Heidelbergischen Akademie, phil.-hist. Kl., viii, (Heidelberg, 1923).

For the siege of Parma and its antecedents, see especially the study in A F.

For the fall of Piero della Vigna, Huillard-Bréholles, *Pierre de la Vigne.*

For the tomb of Frederick II (and Roger II) see J. Deér, *The Dynastic Porphyry Tombs of the Norman Period in Sicily* (Washington DC, 1959).

The main source for this chapter is Vat. Reg. 21 in the Secret Archive of the Vatican.

CHAPTER 13

A highly readable account of events after 1250 is provided by Sir Steven

Runciman, *The Sicilian Vespers: a history of the Mediterranean world in the later thirteenth century* (Cambridge, 1958), though his view of Frederick II is rather different from my own. See also E. Léonard, *Les Angevins de Naples* (Paris, 1954; Italian ed. as *Gli Angioni di Napoli*, dall'Oglio, 1967); David Abulafia, 'Charles of Anjou and the Sicilian Vespers', *History Today*, xxxii (May, 1982); H. Wieruszowski, *Politics and Culture in Medieval Spain and Italy* (collected studies) (Rome, 1970); and, for the important continuities in methods of government, L. Cadier, *Essai sur l'administration du royaume de Sicile sous Charles Ier et Charles II d'Anjou* (Paris, 1891; Italian ed. as *L'amministrazione della Sicilia angioina*, Palermo, 1974). N. Housley, *The Italian Crusades* (Oxford, 1982) has much of value to say on Manfred – even if the book's flavour is in many ways neo-Guelf. H. Bresc, *Un monde méditerranéen: Économie et Société en Sicile, 1300–1450*, 2 vols (Rome/Palermo, 1986) looks further back in time and has intriguing ideas about thirteenth-century Sicilian concepts of 'nationhood'.

For the rise of Aragon, see J. Hillgarth, *The Problem of a Catalan Mediterranean Empire* (English Historical Review supplement no. 8, London, 1975), and T. N. Bisson, *The Medieval Crown of Aragon: a short history* (Oxford, 1986).

On Germany after Frederick, the literature disappoints. A recent German work, H. Thomas, *Deutsche Geschichte im Spätmittelalter, 1250–1500* (1983) has the texture and weight of a German dumpling. The best account perhaps remains G. Barraclough, *The Origins of Modern Germany* (Oxford, 1946), rather than F. R. H. du Boulay, *Germany in the Later Middle Ages* (London, 1983).

For Frederick's reputation in the fourteenth and fifteenth century, see N. Cohn, *The Pursuit of the Millennium*, 2nd ed. (London, 1970); B. Gloger, *Kaiser, Gott und Teufel* (East Berlin, 1970); and A. G. Dickens, *Martin Luther and the German Nation* (London, 1967). There is also some material in *Die Zeit der Staufer*, vols iii and v (see above). His reputation in the twentieth century is the subject, in part, of my article 'Kantorowicz and Frederick II' (see above), and deserves further study. A recent article by M. Burleigh on Albert Brackmann's historical career (*History Today*, xxxvii, March 1987) reveals that there is a subterranean history of scholarship awaiting exposure. Much of the work conducted on the Hohenstaufen in the late 1930s and early 1940s was at least indirectly financed by the German regime, and several scholars sullied their reputation by enthusiastic studies of such themes as the racial purity of the German dynasty. Brackmann's involvement is doubly surprising since it was he who had berated Kantorowicz with the words 'one can write history neither as a pupil of George nor as a Catholic nor as a Protestant nor as a Marxist, but only as an individual in search of truth'. And, in any case, this has often meant excessive attention to the very small details and too little attention to the general problems of interpretation: a fanaticism for minute details, which is also in its way harmful to the understanding of the past.

INDEX

Note: certain constantly recurrent names and places are not listed, e.g., Frederick II, Italy, Sicily.